# Building Web Components with TypeScript and Angular 4

# Building Web Components with TypeScript and Angular 4

by Matthew Scarpino

For permission requests, write to the publisher, addressed "Attention – Permissions Coordinator," at the following address:

Quiller Technologies, LLC

12546 Melrose Circle

Fishers, IN 46038

www.quillertech.com

Printed in the United States of America

Publisher's Cataloging-in-Publication data

Author – Scarpino, Matthew

Title – Building Web Components with TypeScript and Angular 4

Description – Guide to programming web applications using TypeScript and the Angular 4 framework

ISBN – 978-0-9973037-2-8

p. cm.

# Table of Contents

# Chapter 1

# Introducing TypeScript and Angular

To put it mildly, the development of AngularJS (now just called *Angular*) has been rocky. The toolset has undergone many dramatic and startling changes, and as a result, a large number of developers have thrown up their hands in frustration.

But as I write this in May 2017, Angular 4 appears to have reached a steady state. Further, the framework provides more capabilities than ever, including routing, animation, internationalization, lazy loading, and ahead-of-time compilation. These features make it possible to construct powerful web applications that combine high performance with rock-solid reliability.

To take advantage of these features, it's important to be familiar with Angular's principal language, TypeScript. TypeScript is a superset of JavaScript, but has many advanced characteristics that make it similar to traditional languages like Java or Python. These features include classes, interfaces, and annotations.

With TypeScript's object-oriented nature, developers can split their applications into independent software elements called modules. This modularity is central to Angular, which divides complex applications into special TypeScript modules called web components.

Despite its power, Angular's learning curve is steep. The goal of this book is to make both TypeScript and Angular as accessible as possible. The first seven chapters cover the TypeScript language and its many exciting features. The rest of the book explains how to build web components using TypeScript and Angular 4.

The goal of this chapter is more modest: to explain what TypeScript and Angular are and then explain why you should drop whatever you're doing to learn them. To start, we'll look at the developments that led to the development of Angular.

## 1.1 History of JavaScript

In order to execute, Angular applications must be compiled into JavaScript. In essence, TypeScript and Angular were developed to improve the JavaScript development process. Therefore, to understand why these toolsets were developed, it's critical to understand how JavaScript has developed over the years.

This section provides a brief history of JavaScript, from the browser wars to the ECMAScript 2016 specification. To assist with the discussion, Figure 1.1 presents a timeline of JavaScript, TypeScript, Angular, and related technologies.

| | |
|---|---|
| **1995** | Netscape 2.0 released, provides support for JavaScript coding |
| **1996** | Internet Explorer 3.0 released, provides support for JScript coding |
| **1997** | First release of ECMAScript specification |
| **1998** | ECMAScript 2 specification released |
| **1999** | ECMAScript 3 specification released |
| **2006** | Google Web Toolkit (GWT) released, converts Java to JavaScript |
| **2009** | ECMAScript 5 specification released |
| **2009** | Miško Hevery releases AngularJS 1.0 |
| **2011** | Google releases Dart 1.0 |
| **2012** | Microsoft releases TypeScript 1.0 |
| **2015** | ECMAScript 6 (ECMAScript 2015) specification released |
| **2016** | ECMAScript 2016 specification released |
| **2016** | Google releases Angular 2.0 |
| **2016** | Microsoft releases TypeScript 2.0 |
| **2017** | Google releases Angular 4.0 |

**Figure 1.1 Timeline of JavaScript, TypeScript, Angular, and Related Technologies**

This discussion is important for reasons beyond understanding why Angular and TypeScript were developed. At many points in this book, it will be helpful to distinguish between different versions of ECMAScript, particularly ES3, ES5, and ES6.

### 1.1.1 The Browser Wars

In the early 1990s, Marc Andreessen left academia to found a company called Netscape Communications. The company released an application for viewing documents written in a new language called HTML. This browser, called Netscape, became an instant success. HTML and Netscape were adopted by computer users throughout the world.

Not to be outdone, Microsoft released its own browser called Internet Explorer. This gained rapid adoption because, unlike Netscape, it was freely available to Windows users. As a result, the competition between Netscape and Internet Explorer grew so fierce that reporters referred to it as a *browser war.*

To gain an advantage, Netscape created a method for adding code to a web page that could be executed in the user's browser. This client-side scripting language, called JavaScript, extended the capabilities of web pages beyond basic HTML display. JavaScript gained a great deal of attention, but there was a problem—the code could only be executed in Netscape browsers.

Microsoft responded with its own language called JScript. JScript was similar to JavaScript in many respects, but code written for one browser wouldn't work in another. This forced web developers to write different code for different browsers, an aspect of web development that frustrates programmers to this day.

### 1.1.2 ECMAScript

To resolve the conflict, Netscape approached the European Computer Manufacturers Association (ECMA) and offered to help write a specification for a browser-agnostic programming language. This language, called ECMAScript, combined aspects of JavaScript and JScript, and the first specification was released in 1997.

A year later, the ECMAScript 2 spec was released with minor changes. In 1999, the ECMAScript 3 spec introduced many new capabilities including exception handling, regular expressions, and other string handling routines. This remained the baseline for client-side programming for some time, in large part because Internet Explorer adopted ECMAScript 3.

Further development was fraught with contention, as one group worked on ECMAScript 3.1 and another worked on ECMAScript 4. As a result of the fighting, no new standard was released for many years. Ultimately, ECMAScript 4 was scrapped and its revolutionary features, including classes and modules, were incorporated into another effort called ECMAScript Harmony. This will be discussed shortly.

### 1.1.3 Google Web Toolkit (GWT), Dart, and TypeScript

Despite ECMAScript's popularity, many traditional programmers found the language profoundly upsetting. They took issue with the loose typing, quirky scoping rules, and unavoidable global variables. They especially disliked its inheritance, which relied on prototypes instead of classes. To allay these concerns, Google released the Google Web Toolkit (GWT) in 2006 and Dart in 2011. In 2012, Microsoft released TypeScript.

GWT's advantage is that it converts Java into high-performance JavaScript. This enabled the sizable Java community to take part in web development, and I can state from experience that GWT is an effective tool. But the messy configuration files, long conversion times, and sizable memory requirements make it hard to develop and deploy complex projects.

In 2011, Google ended support for GWT and pursued an alternative to ECMAScript called Dart. Like GWT, Dart provides classes, interfaces, and generics. Unlike GWT, it resembles C instead of Java, and allows the loose typing of ECMAScript. Google continues to develop Dart, but because it's the only company that supports the language, its popularity trails behind ECMAScript.

At Microsoft, Anders Hejlsberg also wanted to improve web development, but instead of releasing a new language, he created TypeScript as a superset of ECMAScript. TypeScript extends ECMAScript with many features including type declarations, classes, interfaces, generics, and modules.

Though originally released in 2012, TypeScript didn't gain significant developer interest until Google announced that it was dropping support for AtScript (its own extension of ECMAScript) in favor of TypeScript. Interest grew further when Google announced that the new version of AngularJS would be based on TypeScript. More on that to follow...

### 1.1.4 Further ECMAScript Development

In 2009, ECMA released the specification for ECMAScript 5. This resolved a number of issues in ECMAScript 3 and added new features such as getters, setters, and support for JavaScript Object Notation (JSON). At the time of this writing, ECMAScript 5 is critically important because it's the latest version of ECMAScript that runs reliably on all modern browsers.

As mentioned earlier, much of the effort that went into developing ECMAScript 4 was folded into a side project called ECMAScript Harmony. This came to fruition with the release of ECMAScript 6, which is a major departure from previous releases. This standard defines many new features including classes, modules, iterators, and generators. Because of its origin, the specification is frequently referred to as ES6 Harmony.

TypeScript 2.0 was released in 2016 as a superset of ECMAScript 6. Figure 1.2 illustrates the relationship between the two languages and versions of ECMAScript.

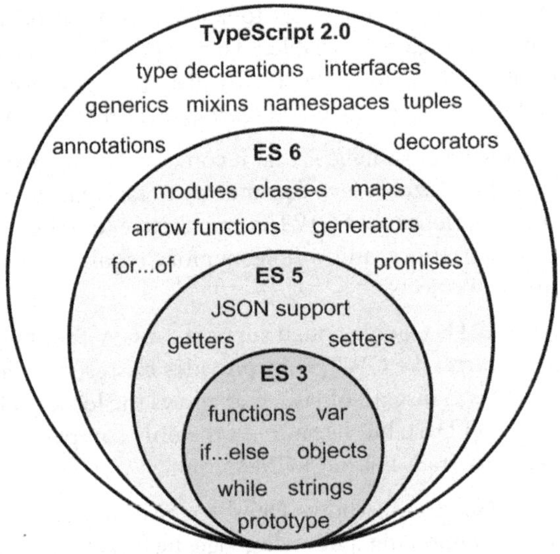


**Figure 1.2 Features of TypeScript 2.0 and ECMAScript Versions**

ECMAScript decided to change their naming scheme, and in 2016, they called their new specification ECMAScript 2016 instead of ECMAScript 7. This provides a ** operator for raising values to a power and makes it easier to search for data in arrays. This new naming scheme applies to ECMAScript 6 as well, which is officially referred to as ECMAScript 2015.

In keeping with common usage, this book relies on the old naming scheme. Further, ECMAScript will be abbreviated to ES whenever possible. Therefore, ECMAScript 5 will be referred to as ES5 and ECMAScript 6 will be referred to as ES6. And like most of the world, this book tends to refer to ECMAScript as JavaScript, which is more common though less accurate.

## 1.1.5 AngularJS and Angular

Of the many success stories in software development, few are as impressive as the rise of AngularJS. While JavaScript and TypeScript were planned and marketed by large corporations, AngularJS started as a tiny project that grew popular through word of mouth. Despite its humble origins, its effect on web development has been so profound as to gain a worldwide following.

## AngularJS 1

In 2009, Miško Hevery and Adam Abrons developed a JSON storage framework and provided a JavaScript toolset for developing client-side applications. The project, called GetAngular, was intended to simplify front-end and back-end development. But due to lack of interest, they gave up on their plan and released GetAngular as open source.

After taking a job at Google, Miško Hevery demonstrated GetAngular to his colleagues, who were impressed by his gains in productivity. His manager, Brad Green, changed its name to AngularJS and made it an official Google project. As more developers experimented with the toolset, it became widely used inside and outside the company.

AngularJS provides many advantages over regular JavaScript. Four major strengths are as follows:

1. **Directives** — special markers that add behavior to HTML elements
2. **Separation of concerns** — decoupling of model, view, and controller
3. **Two-way data binding** — rapid updating of model and view
4. **Dependency injection** — easy insertion of services and dependencies

A simple example will demonstrate the convenience of AngularJS directives. With normal JavaScript, adding new elements into a web page requires a lot of code. But with AngularJS, all that's needed is a special marker in an HTML element. For example, the `ng-repeat` attribute in the following markup adds four list items to the ordered list:

```
<ol>
  <li ng-repeat="dir in ['north', 'south', 'east', 'west']">
    {{dir}}
  </li>
</ol>
```

By providing directives, AngularJS makes it possible for developers to separate their JavaScript from their markup. This is part of the *separation of concerns* pattern, which partitions an application into distinct elements: data and logic (model), graphical representation (view), and input/output processing (controller). This emphasis on organization enables AngularJS developers to build complex applications without sacrificing flexibility.

To synchronize data between the model and view, AngularJS provides two-way data binding. Put simply, AngularJS checks the model and automatically updates the view with any changes. Similarly, if the view's state changes, AngularJS automatically updates the model. True confession: when I first witnessed two-way data binding in an AngularJS application, I thought it was magic.

The fourth advantage, dependency injection, involves providing a component with services without hardcoding the services' features. This loose coupling between a component and its dependencies enables developers to easily include AngularJS capabilities, such as HTTP communication, within an application. It also allows developers to inject mock services for testing purposes.

## AngularJS 2.0

At the ng-europe Conference in 2014, Miško Hevery had every reason to be proud. In a few short years, his AngularJS project had acquired a worldwide following. He'd risen from a small-time entrepreneur to one of Google's most prominent web developers.

As he took his place in front of the presentation screen, his audience probably expected to hear him express pride in AngularJS's phenomenal success. At the very least, they expected reassurance that the project's development was proceeding normally.

But Miško confounded everyone's expectations. Instead of expressing pride or even satisfaction, he apologized for AngularJS. He singled out three aspects for which he was particularly regretful:

1. The complexity of defining custom directives and other structures
2. The difficulty of incorporating capabilities of other toolsets
3. The unintelligibility of untyped variables

After pointing out these shortcomings, Miško presented steps he intended to take to resolve them:

1. Add type declarations for clearer code and type checking
2. Use metadata (annotations) to explain how data structures should be used
3. Encapsulate data in classes
4. Enable introspection to ensure type contracts and assertions

Miško's presentation implied that AtScript would be the basis of the new language, but in early 2015, Microsoft announced that the AngularJS 2 framework would be coded with TypeScript. As shown in Figure 1.2, this provides all of Miško's desired capabilities, including type declarations, annotations, and classes.

In mid-2015, Google released the first alpha version of AngularJS 2. Many developers (including myself) jumped on board, and we appreciated the new classes and components. I was particularly impressed with the router, which makes it possible to insert components into the page according to the URL. I also appreciated how simple it was to use dependency injection.

In June 2016, Google released Release Candidate 3 of AngularJS 2. This introduced many drastic changes to the API, and as a result, everyone's code stopped working. Like many developers, I was upset and confused. Was this really necessary? Why hadn't Google warned us?

The router changed dramatically and then changed again. In the forums, it became common to talk about the "new router" and the "new new router." To clarify the change, Google set the version of the "new new router" to 3.0.

### Angular 4 (or just Angular)

As a result of the sweeping changes, Google decided to completely rebrand the toolset. Instead of following AngularJS 2 conventions, they decided to call the toolset Angular instead of AngularJS. Because the router version had already reached 3.0, they started Angular's version at 4.0.

This methodology is called semantic versioning, or *semver*. Breaking changes are reserved for major releases and minor releases contain only additive changes. Further, the Angular team has decided to rely on time-based release cycles of approximately six months. Angular 4.0 was released in March 2017 so Angular 5.0 is scheduled to be released around August 2017.

Google wants the community to refer to AngularJS 1.x as AngularJS and anything beyond that simply as Angular. But developers and hiring managers need to know which version of the toolset they're dealing with. This book refers to the toolset as Angular, but it should be understood that the version in question is 4.x.

It will take many chapters to explore Angular's features and capabilities. But there's one feature I'm eager to discuss here. While AngularJS is focused on developing web applications, Angular focuses on building *web components*. This is a big deal.

## 1.2 Web Components

In my opinion, the most compelling aspect of Angular development is the ability to construct web components. A proper introduction will have to wait until Chapter 8, but at a top level, a web component can be thought of as a custom HTML element. As will be shown throughout this book, these elements can be as small or as large as the developer requires.

For example, suppose an application needs a dynamic table with three rows, five columns, and text printed in Verdana. Instead of configuring a lengthy `<table>` element, a web page could create the table with a single line of markup:

```
<dyn-table [numRows]=3 [numCols]=5 [font]="Verdana"></dyn-table>
```

In time, I expect that web components will have the same impact on web development that objects and classes had on traditional software development. That is, instead of coding applications from scratch, web developers will build secure, reliable applications by connecting prebuilt components. If the impact of object-oriented programming is any indication, the web component revolution will lead to a dramatic increase in application performance and a commensurate decrease in labor.

It's likely that corporations will take the lead in providing (selling) web components. Oracle will sell components that access its databases, Amazon will sell components that target its Amazon Web Services (AWS), and Google will sell components that interact with its many online applications. Microsoft will convince developers to use its development tools by incorporating a library of web components into its toolset.

But in the end, I feel confident that the open-source community will have the last word. Rather than rely on proprietary solutions, developers will code their own general-purpose components and distribute them to the community.

# 1.3 Book Structure

This book adopts a hands-on approach to presenting TypeScript and Angular. This means theoretical concepts are accompanied by practical examples that you can code and test for yourself. For this reason, a good place to begin is by introducing development tools. Chapter 2 explains how to install the TypeScript compiler and use it to convert TypeScript into JavaScript.

Next, Chapters 3 through 7 present the TypeScript language. The content of these chapters proceeds from the fundamental to complex, with Chapter 3 discussing TypeScript's data types and functions. Following topics include classes and objects, and Chapter 5 shows how to access elements of a web page through its document object model (DOM). Chapters 6 and 7 present a number of advanced TypeScript topics, including unit testing, decorators, and modules.

Chapter 8 is devoted to the fascinating topic of web components, and the last section explains how to construct a simple component using Angular. Further chapters expand on this, with each discussing a different feature of Angular development. The content of Chapters 9 and 10 is critically important, covering the topics of property binding, event binding, child components, and directives.

Starting with Chapter 11, the topics are important to know but not as crucial. Chapter 11 discusses asynchronous programming, which arises frequently in Angular development. If you intend to build single-page applications, I strongly recommend Chapter 12, which discusses routing, and Chapter 14, which presents form development.

If you're going to use Angular in professional development, Chapters 16 through 19 will be particularly helpful. Chapter 16 introduces the Angular Material library, which provides prebuilt user interface components with many useful capabilities. Chapter 17 explains how to test components with the Protractor toolset. Chapter 18 presents a full application that reads and displays REST data and Chapter 19 explains how to design custom graphics using Scalable Vector Graphics (SVG) and the HTML5 canvas.

## 1.4 Summary

If we can learn anything from the history of web development, it's this: don't compete with JavaScript. Dart, GWT, and Java applets have their strengths, but the JavaScript developer base is huge and passionate. More importantly, JavaScript (ahem, *ECMAScript*) is the only language that all modern browsers agree on. As many have learned, it's better to extend the language than fight it.

Taking this lesson to heart, Microsoft developed TypeScript. TypeScript is a superset of JavaScript, and provides ES6 features like classes, interfaces, and modules. In addition, it supports annotations and (optional) type checking. Type checking is unnecessary for perfect coders, but many developers (including myself) are far from perfect, and prefer to discover bugs at compile time instead of run time.

TypeScript is the central language for developing Angular applications. Angular provides the same essential capabilities as AngularJS, including directives, dependency injection, data binding, and separation of concerns. But because it relies on TypeScript's classes and annotations, the code is more intelligible and easier to test and debug.

In my opinion, Angular's main advantage is the ability to create web components. A web component is a modular piece of functionality with its own HTML-formatted view. This modularity facilitates code reuse, which means you can use your components in multiple applications. Better still, you can use third-party components with proven reliability and performance.

I'm excited to be writing about TypeScript and Angular, but before I discuss the code, I want to present the mechanics of converting TypeScript into JavaScript. Chapter 2 introduces the TypeScript compiler, and shows how to configure the process of converting TypeScript to JavaScript.

# Chapter 2

# TypeScript Development Tools

The best way to learn is by doing, and this book takes a hands-on approach to teaching TypeScript and Angular. But before you start coding, it's important to be familiar with the development tools. This chapter explores three topics:

1. **Node.js** — An open-source framework that provides the packages needed for TypeScript and Angular development
2. **Typescript compiler (tsc)** — A command-line utility that converts TypeScript code into JavaScript code
3. **Integrated development environments (IDEs)** — Full-featured graphical environments for TypeScript development

Throughout this book, the underlying goal is to convert TypeScript into JavaScript. The two languages occupy the same level of abstraction, so the proper term for the conversion process is *transpile*. However, the term *compile* is much more commonly used, so this book will refer to TypeScript-JavaScript conversion as compilation.

This chapter focuses on TypeScript development and doesn't discuss Angular development in detail. This is because general Angular development is significantly more involved. Chapter 7 introduces Angular's CLI (command-line interface), which simplifies the process of generating, building, and launching Angular projects.

Angular code is based on TypeScript, so it may seem confusing why Angular development is so different than regular TypeScript development. The first part of this chapter provides an overview of the two development processes.

# 2.1 Overview

The goal of Angular/TypeScript development is to generate JavaScript that can be inserted into a web page. Figure 2.1 illustrates the difference between general TypeScript development and Angular development based on TypeScript.

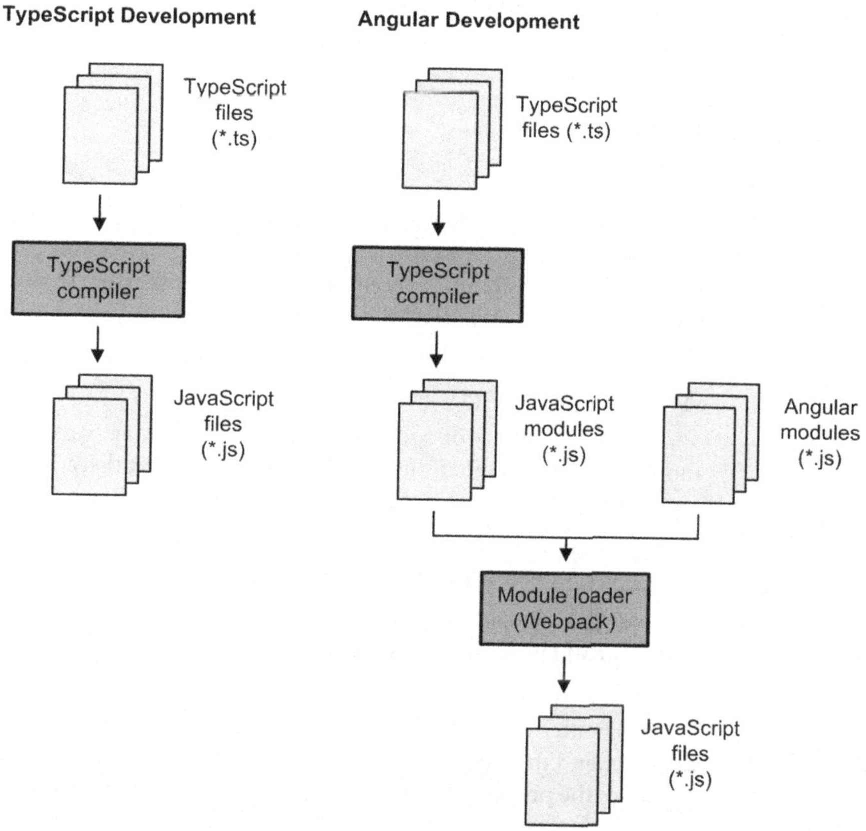


**Figure 2.1 TypeScript and Angular Development**

When regular TypeScript code is compiled, the result is regular JavaScript. But when Angular code is compiled, the result is one or more JavaScript *modules*. Modules are crucial in Angular development, and a full discussion of the topic will have to wait until Chapter 7. For now, the important point to know is that JavaScript modules require special processing before they can be inserted into a web page.

The utility that performs this special processing is called a module loader or just a loader. At the time of this writing, Angular's preferred loader is Webpack. Webpack combines the compiled modules with Angular's modules, and produces JavaScript that can be accessed in a browser. Chapter 7 discusses the loading process in greater detail.

This chapter and the next four chapters focus on the development process depicted on the left side of the figure. The primary tool is the TypeScript compiler, which is provided for free through the Node.js project. The next section discusses Node.js and explains how to install the TypeScript compiler.

# 2.2 Node.js

All of the packages and utilities discussed in this book are freely available through the Node.js ecosystem. This provides a vast number of JavaScript projects and it's been ported to run on every common operating system and processor. To download the installer, go to https://nodejs.org and select the option that best suits your development system.

Node.js is provided through the MIT License. This means it can be used in both open-source and proprietary projects.

Given the variety of operating systems and software versions, I can't provide a thorough walkthrough of the installation process. But there are two important points to be aware of:

1. The installation of Node.js includes a command-line utility called npm (this may be npm.cmd on Windows or just npm on Mac OS/Linux systems).
2. Make sure you can execute `npm` on a command line. If you can't, find the npm utility and add its directory to your PATH variable.

No matter what operating system you use, npm is required to install the TypeScript compiler and the Angular modules. This section explains how npm works and then discusses the process of installing dependencies needed for this book.

## 2.2.1 The Node Package Manager (npm)

As its name implies, npm manages packages provided by Node.js. This tool performs a number of operations related to Node.js packages, such as installing, uninstalling, searching, and updating.

The npm tool runs from a command line. For most operations, its usage involves the same basic syntax:

```
npm command_name flags target
```

Here, `command_name` is the name of an operation to be performed, `flags` is one or more options to constrain the operation, and `target` is the name of the target to be operated upon. For example, the command to install `app` is given as follows:

```
npm install app
```

Table 2.1 lists `install` and other npm commands.

**Table 2.1**

Helpful npm Commands

| Command | Description |
|---|---|
| `install` | Install a package on the system |
| `uninstall` | Remove a package from the system |
| `update` | Update package to the latest version |
| `link` | Create a symbolic link from a package to the current folder |
| `unlink` | Remove a symbolic link |
| `ls` | List installed packages and their dependencies |
| `search` | Search for a specific package |
| `view` | Print data about a specific package |
| `help` | Provide documentation about npm's usage |

The `install` command is the most important. This tells npm to download the files of the given package and place them in a folder called node_modules. If the `-g` flag is used, the installation is global, which means the files will be stored where they can be globally accessed, such as /usr/local on Mac OS and Linux systems.

Global installation is important if a package contains executables that need to be accessed from the command line. For example, if a package named pkg contains an executable that needs to be accessed from many directories, it can be globally installed with the following command:

```
npm install -g pkg
```

If `-g` isn't used, the installation is local, which means that the package will be installed into a local node_modules folder. This is preferred over global installation because it keeps different installations isolated from one another. But if a locally-installed package contains executables, they will only be accessible inside of node_modules.

If a newer version of a package is available, `npm update` will download and install the files for the newer package. It will also install missing packages, if necessary. If `-g` is used, npm will update global packages.

The last five commands in the table provide information. The `ls` command prints a tree that lists the installed packages and their dependencies. The `search` command identifies if a package is available for installation. The `view` command provides additional information about an installed package. `help` provides a great deal of information related to npm's usage.

## 2.2.2 package.json

The example archive for this book can be downloaded from http://www.ngbook.io. If you decompress the zip file, you'll find a series of folders (ch2, ch3, and so on) that contain example projects for the corresponding chapters.

Until Chapter 7, the example code focuses on general TypeScript development. To build these projects, you'll need to install a handful of packages. Rather than ask you to install them individually, I've provided a file called package.json in the archive's top-level folder.

This file tells npm which dependencies need to be installed. Therefore, after decompressing the archive, I recommend that you open a command prompt and change to the folder containing package.json. Then enter the following command:

```
npm install
```

When this command is run, npm will perform a number of operations, including the following:

1. Create a node_modules folder to contain packages and installation files.
2. Install the TypeScript compiler globally. This allows you to execute `tsc` from a command line in any directory.
3. Install packages that provide Jasmine and Karma, which facilitate testing of TypeScript code.

A proper introduction to Jasmine and Karma will have to wait until Chapter 6. The next two sections discuss the TypeScript compiler and demonstrate how it can be used.

## 2.3 The TypeScript Compiler

At the time of this writing, only one TypeScript compiler is available. It's provided by Microsoft, and can be downloaded freely through npm. If you installed the book's dependencies with `npm install` as discussed earlier, it should be installed on your system.

The name of the compiler executable is `tsc` and you can check its version with the following command:

```
tsc -v
```

`tsc` accepts a wide range of command-line arguments, but there's usually no need to learn them. Most developers set compiler options in a file named tsconfig.json. If `tsc` is executed in a directory containing tsconfig.json, it will read the file's settings and use them to configure its compilation.

As its suffix implies, tsconfig.json defines a JSON object. Four important fields of the object are:

- `files` — names of files to be compiled
- `include` — patterns identifying files to be included in the compile
- `exclude` — patterns identifying files to be excluded from the compile
- `compilerOptions` — an object whose fields constrain the compilation process

An example will clarify how the `files`, `include`, and `compilerOptions` fields are used. Consider the following JSON:

```
{
  "files": [ "src/app/app.ts" ],

  "include": [ "src/utils/*.ts" ],

  "compilerOptions": {
    "noEmitOnError": true
  }
}
```

This tells the compiler to process src/app/app.ts and every TypeScript file (*.ts) in the src/utils directory. The `noEmitOnError` flag tells the compiler not to produce JavaScript files if any errors are found.

`noEmitOnError` is one of many options supported by the TypeScript compiler. Table 2.2 lists twenty-six of the parameters that can be set in the `compilerOptions` field of tsconfig.json.

**Table 2.2**

Compiler Options

| Flag | Description |
|---|---|
| `target` | Desired ECMAScript version (es3, es5, es2015, es2016, es2017, or esNext) |
| `rootDir` | Root directory of input files |
| `listFiles` | Print file names processed by the compiler |
| `outDir` | Directory to contain compiled results |
| `outFile` | File to contain concatenated results |
| `watch` | Watch input files |
| `removeComments` | Remove comments from generated output |
| `noLib` | Don't include the main library, lib.d.ts, in the compilation process |
| `alwaysStrict` | Specifies whether strict mode should be enabled |
| `noEmitOnError` | Don't generate output if any errors were encountered |
| `noImplicitThis` | Raise an error on this expressions with implied any type |
| `noUnusedLocals` | Report errors on unused locals |
| `noUnusedParameters` | Report errors on unused parameters |
| `noImplicitAny` | Print a warning for every variable that isn't explicitly declared |
| `suppressImplicit AnyIndexErrors` | Suppress noImplicitAny errors for objects without index signatures |
| `skipLibCheck` | Suppress type checking of declaration files |
| `experimentalDecorators` | Enable support for ES7 decorators |
| `declaration` | Generate declaration files (*.d.ts) for the TypeScript code |
| `declarationDir` | Place declaration files in the given directory |
| `module` | The format of the generated module (commonjs, amd, system, umd, or es2015) |
| `noEmitHelpers` | Do not insert custom helper functions in generated output |

| | |
|---|---|
| emitDecoratorMetadata | Insert metadata for TypeScript decorations |
| isolatedModules | Always insert imports for unresolved files |
| jsx | Generate JSX code (preserve or react) |
| moduleResolution | Strategy for resolving modules (node or classic) |

By default, the compiler generates JavaScript according to the ECMAScript 3 (ES3) standard. But the `target` option makes it possible to generate code in other standards. For example, the following object tells the compiler to compile TypeScript files to ES5:

```
{
  "compilerOptions": {
    "target": "es5",
  }
}
```

By default, the TypeScript compiler places JavaScript code in a *.js file in the same directory with the same name of the TypeScript file. That is, if src/a.ts and src/b.ts need to be compiled, the compiler will place the resulting code in src/a.js and src/b.js. The `outDir` option identifies another directory to hold the results. If `outFile` is set, the compiler will concatenate its results and store the code in the given file.

If `alwaysStrict` is set to true, the generated JavaScript will contain `use script`, which tells browsers to run the script in strict mode. This mode treats mistakes as errors and prevents the creation of accidental global variables. It also throws an error if a JavaScript object contains duplicate properties.

In this book's tsconfig.json files, `compilerOptions` always sets `alwaysStrict`, `noEmitOnError`, `noUnusedLocals`, and `noUnusedParameters` to true. This ensures that errors will be produced if any code appears suspicious or unused.

In the table, the `declaration` and `noLib` options relate to declaration files. These *.d.ts files declare TypeScript data structures, but don't provide code. Chapter 5 explains how declaration files work.

The `emitDecoratorMetadata` option tells the compiler to enable support for decorators. As Chapter 6 will explain, decorators make it possible to alter the characteristics of TypeScript's data structures. They play an important role in Angular development, so this option will be set to true in later chapters.

The `module`, `isolatedModules`, and `moduleResolution` flags relate to JavaScript modules. Modules are important in the world of Angular development, but we won't need to discuss them until Chapter 7.

# 2.4 Example Application – HelloTS

Before discussing the TypeScript language itself, it's a good idea to build an existing project using the compiler. If you open the code archive for this book and look in the ch2 directory, you'll see a folder named hello_ts. This contains the files needed to build the hello_ts application, and for this reason, we'll refer to this and similar folders as *projects*.

This section discusses the files that make up the ch2/hello_ts project and shows how to compile its code. But first, I want to discuss the project's overall structure.

## 2.4.1 Project Structure

Google provides the Angular Style Guide at https://angular.io/styleguide. This establishes conventions for structuring projects, and although it's intended for Angular development, this book applies its guidelines to general TypeScript projects as well.

For simple projects, the style guide makes the following recommendations:

- Top-level HTML/CSS files should be placed in the src directory.
- The tsconfig.json file should be placed in the src directory.
- TypeScript files should be placed in the src/app directory and subdirectories.
- The name of the primary TypeScript file should be app.ts.
- A compiled JavaScript file (*.js) should have the same name as its source file (*.ts).

For example, if you explore the ch2/hello_ts project, you'll see that it has the following file structure:

```
hello_ts
  |-- tsconfig.json
  |-- src
       |-- index.html
       |-- app
            |-- app.ts
```

When the project is built, the app.js file will be placed in the same folder as app.ts. The src/index.html file accesses app.js using a `<script>` tag.

For simple TypeScript projects, this structure may seem unnecessarily complex. But for sophisticated projects involving Angular web components, these conventions make it easy to keep everything organized. For this reason, this book employs this structure for both simple and complex projects.

## 2.4.2 TypeScript Configuration

The TypeScript compiler reads configuration settings from a file named tsconfig.json. Listing 2.1 presents the tsconfig.json file in the ch2/hello_ts project.

**Listing 2.1: ch2/hello_ts/src/tsconfig.json**

```
{
  "files": [ "src/app/app.ts" ],
  "compilerOptions": {
    "target": "es5",
    "removeComments": true,
    "alwaysStrict": true,
    "noEmitOnError": true,
    "noUnusedLocals": true,
    "noUnusedParameters": true
  }
}
```

This tells the compiler that the only file to compile is the app.ts file in the project's src/app directory. When it performs the compilation, the compiler should generate JavaScript according to the ECMAScript 5 specification. Because `alwaysStrict` is set, the ES5 code will execute in strict mode.

The last fields of `compilerOptions` constrain how the compilation should be performed. `noEmitOnError` tells the compiler not to generate JavaScript if an error occurs. With `noUnusedLocals` and `noUnusedParameters` set to true, the compiler will check for unused declarations.

## 2.4.3 TypeScript Source Code

The code in the project's app.ts file isn't particularly impressive, but it demonstrates an important feature of TypeScript. Listing 2.2 presents the content of src/app/app.ts.

**Listing 2.2: ch2/hello_ts/src/app/app.ts**

```
class HelloTS {
  public printMessage() {
    document.write("Hello TypeScript!");
  }
}

let hello: HelloTS = new HelloTS();
hello.printMessage();
```

This defines a TypeScript class named `HelloTS` which has a method named `printMessage`. If you're not familiar with classes and methods, don't be concerned. Chapter 4 discusses classes in detail and explains why they play such an important role in TypeScript development.

To build this code, go to the project's top-level directory and enter `tsc` on the command line. The compiler will convert the TypeScript to JavaScript and place the resulting code in src/app/app.js. If you open src/index.html in a browser, you'll see confirmation that the build was performed successfully.

# 2.5 Integrated Development Environments

For simple projects like ch2/hello_ts, the command line is sufficient for editing and compiling code. But for large, complex projects, you'll want to use a development tool whose features are better suited for application development. Tools that support editing, compiling, and debugging code are called integrated development environments, or IDEs.

This section discusses two popular IDEs that support TypeScript: Visual Studio and Atom. In both cases, I'll explain how to obtain the application and configure it for TypeScript entry.

## 2.5.1 Visual Studio

Visual Studio is a popular environment for coding applications. Originally, Visual Studio focused solely on Windows development and Microsoft-specific technologies. But Visual Studio has been expanded to support many different languages including TypeScript.

This discussion focuses on the Community Edition of Visual Studio, which is free for "individual developers, open source projects, academic research, education, and small professional teams." It can be downloaded from https://www.visualstudio.com/vs/community.

After downloading and installing Visual Studio, the next step is to install TypeScript support. Microsoft provides this with an executable that can be downloaded from TypeScript's main site, http://www.typescriptlang.org. Click the **Download** link at the top and then click the version of Visual Studio that you intend to use. The executable configures Visual Studio to support TypeScript development.

To start the TypeScript development process, launch Visual Studio and go to the File menu in the upper left. Select the **File > New > Project...** menu option and the New Project dialog will appear.

The left pane of the dialog lists the different types of projects that can be created. Selecting the TypeScript option tells Visual Studio that you intend to create an HTML application with TypeScript.

Toward the bottom of the dialog, input boxes ask for a name for the project and its solution. In Visual Studio, a project contains all the files needed for a specific output and a solution contains a set of related projects. Select any name you like for the project and solution, and press the OK button in the lower right.

After creating the project, Visual Studio will open an editor that displays the project's example code. To the right of the editor, the Solution Explorer lists the projects that belong to the solution.

The code in the editor defines a `Greeter` class that displays the current time. This code is contained in the project's app.ts file. In addition to app.ts, the project contains index.html, which defines a web page that accesses the compiled app.js code. The styles used in the web page are defined in the app.css file.

Every TypeScript project in Visual Studio also contains a web.config file that defines properties related to ASP.NET. The topic of ASP.NET is far outside the scope of this book, and it's unfortunate that this file can't be deleted from inside Visual Studio.

In addition to Visual Studio, Microsoft provides a development tool named Visual Studio Code (VS Code), which can be downloaded from https://code.visualstudio.com. The process of installing TypeScript support for VS Code is identical to that of installing support for Visual Studio. A full description of the TypeScript development process can be found at https://code.visualstudio.com/docs/languages/typescript.

## 2.5.2 Atom

If you're passionate about JavaScript, Node.js, and open-source technology, you won't find a better environment than Atom. Developed by GitHub and released under the open-source MIT license, Atom is the only development environment I know of that is written in HTML, JavaScript, CSS, and Node.js. It can be freely downloaded from https://atom.io.

The good news is that Atom is "hackable to the core." Every aspect of its appearance and operation can be customized, and the only language you need to know is JavaScript. In addition, the Atom package manager (apm) works like the Node package manager (npm) discussed earlier. As Atom grows in popularity, more and more packages are becoming available to extend its capabilities.

The downside of relying on JavaScript is that Atom is slower than other text editors, and its performance degrades significantly for files larger than 10 MB. For the example code in this book, this won't pose a problem.

## Introducing Atom

Atom is a full-featured development environment whose capabilities can be extended using the Atom package manager (apm). Figure 2.2 shows what the environment looks like with the Atom Light theme enabled.

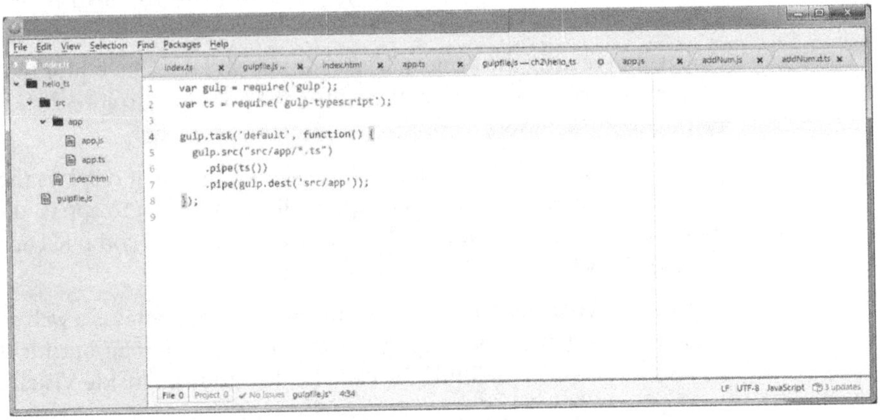


**Figure 2.2 The Atom Development Environment**

Atom has many helpful features, but because the main menu is hidden by default, newcomers may find it confusing to work with. Here are five vital points that every Atom user should be aware of:

1. Pressing Alt makes the main menu visible.
2. To reach the Settings page, go to **File** > **Settings** in the main menu.
3. In the Settings page, the environment's color scheme can be changed by clicking **Themes** on the left and selecting a different entry in the box labeled **UI Theme**.
4. In the Settings page, Atom's installed packages can be updated by clicking **Updates** on the left and pressing **Update All**. I recommend doing this on a regular basis.
5. In the Settings page, new packages can be installed by clicking **Install** on the left and searching for a package name. Each desired package can be installed by clicking its **Install** button.

The atom-typescript package is installed by default, so Atom provides a full-featured editor for TypeScript development. Its features include auto-complete, refactoring, and code formatting. A full description of the package can be found at the package's primary site: https://atom.io/packages/atom-typescript.

### Atom Projects

A project is a directory containing all the files needed to produce a single output. Visual Studio organizes projects in a solution and Eclipse organizes projects in a workspace. Both tools add a special file to a project's directory to store its settings.

Atom doesn't have solutions or workspaces, and it doesn't add special files. Instead, it expects that all of the directories opened in the environment belong to a single project. If a user wants to open a directory, he/she is expected to launch Atom from inside the directory. A directory can also be opened in Atom by right-clicking in the left pane and selecting **Add Project Folder** in the context menu.

To view this book's example code in Atom, download the ngbook.zip archive from http://www.ngbook.io and decompress it to a folder. In Atom, right-click in the left pane and select **Add Project Folder**. Select one of the many project directories, such as ch2/hello_ts, and you'll see its file hierarchy in the environment's left pane.

## 2.6 Summary

Before you can code web applications with Angular, you need a solid understanding of the TypeScript language and the development process. This chapter has explained how to obtain the TypeScript compiler from Node.js and use it to convert TypeScript to JavaScript.

This chapter also introduced the Angular Style Guide, which will be explored further in later chapters. This guide provides many conventions for structuring projects and files, and this book will adhere to its guidelines wherever they apply.

The last part of the chapter introduced two integrated development environments (IDEs) for TypeScript development. The first is the community version of Visual Studio 2015, which makes it easy to edit and compile TypeScript code. The second is Atom, which is a full-featured environment based on HTML, JavaScript, CSS, and Node.js.

# Chapter 3

# TypeScript Basics

If I had to summarize TypeScript as a language, the summary would have three parts:

1. TypeScript is a superset of JavaScript. Valid JavaScript is also valid TypeScript.
2. TypeScript makes it possible to declare variables with types.
3. TypeScript supports many features from ECMAScript 6 and ECMAScript 7, including classes, interfaces, decorators, and modules.

This chapter focuses on the first two points, and only touches on some of the new features taken from ES6/ES7. If you've already written JavaScript code, much of this will look familiar. If you're new to TypeScript and JavaScript, this chapter will provide a solid foundation from which to understand the rest of the book.

The first section of the chapter introduces TypeScript's data types. In addition to explaining how to specify a variable's type, the section discusses 12 central types: `boolean`, `number`, `string`, `enum`, `array`, `tuple`, `object/Object`, `any`, `undefined`, `null`, `void`, and `never`. For each type, I'll explain the information it represents and how it can be used in code.

The next part of the chapter discusses functions. With TypeScript, a function declaration can include both its return type and the types of its arguments. I'll explain how functions are declared and some of the new features available in TypeScript.

Even if you're a JavaScript expert, there's a great deal in this chapter worthy of your time. New features in TypeScript include declaring variables with `let` and `const`, enumerated types, tuples, and generic types and functions.

# 3.1 Data Types

TypeScript's primary characteristic is the ability to specify a variable's type in its declaration. This feature is optional, and when the code is compiled into JavaScript, its type specifications disappear. But they provide one major advantage: type checking. If a variable of one type is set equal to a value of another type, the compiler will flag an error.

An example will make this clear. In the following code, the first line sets x equal to a number and the second line sets it equal to a string:

```
var x = 5;
x = "Hello";
```

This is acceptable in JavaScript and TypeScript, and won't produce any errors. But TypeScript makes it possible to specifically identify x as a number. Consider this code:

```
var x: number;
x = "Hello";
```

The first line specifies that x is a number. When the code is compiled, the compiler recognizes that the second line is setting x equal to a string, and it will report an error: *TS2332: Type 'string' is not assignable to type 'number'.*

Type checking serves three main purposes:

1. **Early error discovery** — The compiler reports errors at compile-time so that you don't have to riddle them out at run-time.
2. **Tooling** — Editors can analyze text better when variables have types. This affects features like code completion, error checking, and syntax coloring.
3. **Readability** — When a variable has a type, it's easier to understand the purpose it serves.

Setting a variable's type involves following the variable's name with a colon and the desired type. A general declaration has the following form:

```
var <name>: <type>;
```

If the variable needs to be initialized, the declaration's form can be given as follows:

```
var <name>: <type> = <value>;
```

When an untyped variable is initialized, the compiler automatically sets the variable's type to that of the value. Therefore, if a variable is initialized to a value, there's no need to define its type.

A variable's type can be a predefined TypeScript type or a custom type. Chapter 4 discusses a number of custom types, which include classes, interfaces, and mixins. This chapter focuses on predefined types, which include `boolean`, `number`, `string`, `enum`, `array`, `tuple`, `Object`, `any`, `void`, `undefined`, `null`, and `never`.

For experienced JavaScript programmers, much of this will be review. But I'd like to start with a topic that veterans may not be familiar with: declaring TypeScript variables with `let` instead of `var`.

### 3.1.1 Declaring Variables with let and const

In JavaScript, every variable declaration must start with `var`. In TypeScript, variable declarations can also start with `let` or `const`. The difference involves scope:

- A variable declared with `var` has *function scope*. When declared in a function, the variable can be accessed everywhere in the function.
- A variable declared with `let` or `const` has *block scope*. When declared inside a block, the variable can only be accessed in that block.

There's no difference between `let` and `var` if a variable is declared outside of a function or in a function without inner blocks. The difference becomes apparent when variables are declared inside functions with inner blocks. Consider the following code:

```
function example() {
  var i = 22;
  for (var i = 0; i < 5; i++) {
    ...
  }
  console.log(i);   // Prints 5 because of var
}
```

In this code, `i` is declared twice: once at the start of the function and once inside the `for` loop. Because it's declared with `var`, `i` has function scope, which means the variable inside the function's block is the same variable outside the block. As a result, the `for` loop changes the value of `i` from 22 to 5.

If a variable is declared with `let` or `const`, the variable inside a function's block will be distinct from the variable outside of the block. In the above example, the `i` in the `for` loop will be distinct from the `i` outside the block. This is shown in the following code.

```
function example() {
  let i = 22;
  for (let i = 0; i < 5; i++) {
    ...
  }
  console.log(i);   // Prints 22 because of let
}
```

In this case, both declarations of `i` use `let` instead of `var`. As a result, the two variables are distinct. That is, the variable inside the `for` loop doesn't affect the value of the variable declared outside the block.

If you look at the compiled result of the preceding code, you can see how the compiler keeps the variables separate. The compiler renames the variable in the `for` loop from `i` to `i_1`, which ensures it won't be confused with the `i` outside the block.

`const` is similar to `let` in that it establishes block scope for a variable. The difference between the two is that, if a variable is declared with `const`, its value is expected to remain constant throughout the block. Any attempt to change the variable's value will result in a compiler error. If a variable's value is expected to change within a block, it should be declared with `let` instead.

## 3.1.2 Boolean

Of TypeScript's predefined types, `boolean` is the simplest to work with. A `boolean` variable can be set to one of two values: `true` or `false`. As an example, the following code declares a `boolean` variable named `check` and initializes its value to `true`:

```
const check: boolean = true;
```

A `boolean` variable can be set equal to any operation that returns a `boolean` value. These operations include comparison operations (>, <, >=, <=, ==, !==, and ===) and logical operations (`&&`, `||`, and `!`). The following examples demonstrate how `boolean` variables can be declared and initialized:

- `const x: boolean = 5 > 3;`
- `const y: boolean = "a" !== "b";`
- `const z: boolean = ((3 < 5) && ("a" != "b"));`

JavaScript provides two operators for testing equality: == and ===. The difference is that `x == y` returns true if `x` and `y` have the same value and `x === y` returns true if `x` and `y` have the same value and the same type.

### 3.1.3 Number

In TypeScript, integers and floating-point values belong to the `number` type, regardless of their sign or size. This is shown in the following examples, which declare and initialize three number values:

```
1. let three: number = 3;
2. let pi: number = 3.14159;
3. let avogadro: number = 6.022e-23;
```

Like JavaScript, every number in TypeScript is considered to be a floating point value—there is no integer type there are no integer-specific operations. Numbers are stored as 64-bit double-precision values as defined in the IEEE-754 standard. Each value can be given using fixed-point notation (0.01) or exponential notation (1e-2).

TypeScript supports literal values in different bases. That is, TypeScript recognizes hexadecimal (0x10), octal (0o20), and binary (0b10000), in addition to decimal.

TypeScript provides special number values that can be used in code. Five of them are given as follows:

- `Number.MAX_VALUE` — the largest possible number value (about 1.7977e+308)
- `Number.MIN_VALUE` — the smallest possible number value (equals 5e-324)
- `Number.POSITIVE_INFINITY` — positive infinity (returned when a positive value is too large to be stored)
- `Number.NEGATIVE_INFINITY` — negative infinity (returned when a negative value is too large to be stored)
- `Number.NaN` — Not a number (returned when an operation returns an impossible value, such as performing a mathematical operation on a string)

TypeScript supports the same kinds of operations on numbers as JavaScript. These include mathematical operations and operations that convert (and format) numbers to strings.

#### Mathematical Operations

TypeScript supports all the basic math operations from JavaScript, including +, -, *, /, and ^. In addition, it supports all the mathematical functions that can be accessed through `Math`. Table 3.1 lists the signatures of TypeScript's math functions and provides a description of each.

**Table 3.1**

Mathematical Functions

| Function | Description |
|---|---|
| `abs(num: number)` | Returns the absolute value of num |
| `acos(num: number)` | Returns the arccosine of num |
| `asin(num: number)` | Returns the arcsine of num |
| `atan(num: number)` | Returns the arctangent of num |
| `atan2(num1: number, num2: number)` | Returns the arctangent of num1/num2 |
| `ceil(num: number)` | Rounds num up to the nearest integer |
| `cos(num: number)` | Returns the cosine of num |
| `exp(num: number)` | Returns the exponential function of num ($e^{num}$) |
| `floor(num: number)` | Rounds num down to the nearest integer |
| `log(num)` | Returns the natural logarithm of num ($\log_e$ num) |
| `max(num1, num2, ...)` | Returns the number with the maximum value |
| `min(num1, num2, ...)` | Returns the number with the minimum value |
| `pow(x, y)` | Returns $x^y$ |
| `random()` | Returns a random number between 0 and 1 |
| `round(num: number)` | Rounds num to the nearest integer |
| `sin(num: number)` | Returns the sine of num |
| `sqrt(num: number)` | Returns the square root of num |
| `tan(num: number)` | Returns the tangent of num |

When using the trigonometric functions (`sin`, `cos`, `tan`, and so on), keep in mind that angle values are expected to be in radians, not degrees. As examples, 30° equals $\pi/6$ radians and 180° equals $\pi$ radians. In code, $\pi$ can be approximated with `Math.PI`, and the following code sets x equal to the sine of $\pi/6$:

```
let x: number = Math.sin(Math.PI/6);    // x = 0.5
```

Similarly, the following code sets x equal to the arcsine of 0.5:

```
let x: number = Math.asin(0.5);         // x = π/6
```

It's important to understand the difference between `floor`, `ceil`, and `round`. Suppose `num` lies between two adjacent integers, X and Y, where Y is greater than X. `floor(num)` will always return the low integer, X, and `ceil(num)` will always return the high integer, Y. `round(num)` will return whichever value is closer to `num`. As examples, `Math.floor(0.4)` equals 0, `Math.ceil(0.4)` equals 1, and `Math.floor(0.4)` equals 0.

## Number-String Conversion

TypeScript also provides routines that convert numbers to strings. These are particularly helpful when a number requires special formatting.

Table 3.2 lists the routines available for converting numbers to strings. These routines are accessed in code as *methods*. A full discussion of methods will have to wait until Chapter 4, but for now, all you need to know is that a `number` method is called by following a `number` variable with a dot and the method name. For example, if `x` is a `number`, it can be converted to exponential form by calling the `x.toExponential()` method.

**Table 3.2**

Number-String Conversion Methods

| Method | Description |
|---|---|
| `toExponential()` | Returns a string containing num's value in exponential notation |
| `toFixed(length: number)` | Returns a string containing the value of num expressed in fixed-point notation with the given number of places after the decimal |
| `toPrecision(length: number)` | Returns a string containing the value of num expressed with the given precision |
| `toString()` | Returns the string representation of num |

Each of these methods returns a string, and the following code demonstrates how they're used:

```
let x: number = 0.0157;
let exp: string = x.toExponential();     // "1.57e-2"
let fixed: string = x.toFixed(2);        // "0.02"
let prec: string = x.toPrecision(2);     // "0.016"
let str: string = x.toString()           // "0.0157"
```

`toFixed` and `toPrecision` are commonly confused. The argument of `toFixed` determines how many places after the decimal will be in the output. The argument of `toPrecision` identifies how many significant values are in the output.

### 3.1.4 String

Strings make it possible to store and operate on text. A string variable can be initialized by setting it equal to one or more characters surrounded by quotes—double quotes or single quotes. This is shown in the following examples:

1. `let single_char: string = "D";`
2. `let large: string = 'Single or double, it does not matter';`

A string stores its characters in order and each has an index, starting with 0. This is important to grasp when using the many methods available for string handling. Table 3.3 lists these methods and provides a description of each.

**Table 3.3**

String Handling Methods

| Method | Description |
|---|---|
| `charAt(num: number)` | Returns the character at the given index |
| `charCodeAt(num: number)` | Returns the Unicode value of the character at the given index |
| `concat(str1, str2, str3, ...)` | Returns the concatenation of the given strings |
| `fromCharCode(num: number)` | Returns the character corresponding to the given Unicode value |
| `indexOf(str: string)` | Returns the position of the first occurrence of the given string |
| `lastIndexOf(str: string)` | Returns the position of the final occurrence of the given string |
| `localeCompare(str: string)` | Compares the string to the given string in the current locale |
| `match(expr: string)` | Compares the string to the regular expression and returns true if there's a match, false otherwise |
| `replace(expr: string, replace: string)` | Searches the string for the value or expression and replaces each occurrence with the replacement string |

| | |
|---|---|
| `search(expr: string)` | Searches the string for the value or expression and returns the position where it was found |
| `slice(start: number, end: number)` | Extracts a portion of a string between the given start/end positions |
| `split(delim: string)` | Splits a string into an array of substrings, with each substring identified by the given delimiter |
| `substr(start: number, length: number)` | Extracts a portion of a string from the starting position through the given length |
| `substring(start: number, end: number)` | Like slice, extracts a portion of a string between the given start/end positions |
| `toLocaleLowerCase()` | Converts string to lower case according to locale |
| `toLocaleUpperCase()` | Converts string to upper case according to locale |
| `toLowerCase()` | Converts string to lower case |
| `toString()` | Returns the string's value |
| `toUpperCase()` | Converts the string to upper case |
| `trim()` | Removes whitespace from the start and end of the string |
| `valueOf()` | Returns the string's primitive value |

These methods are simple to understand and use in code. The following examples show how they can be invoked:

1.
```
let str: string = "Message";
let fifth_char: string = str.charAt(4);   // fifth_char = "a"
```

2.
```
let s1: string = "Type";
let s2: string = "Script";
let str: string = s1.concat(s2);          // str = "TypeScript"
```

3.
```
let str: string = "Message";
let index: number = str.indexOf("s");     // index = 2
```

4.
```
let str: string = "Message";
let index: number = str.lastIndexOf("s"); // index = 3
```

5.
```
let str: string = "Message";
let sub: string = str.slice(3);           // sub = "sage"
```

6.
```
let str: string = "Message";
let sub: string = str.substr(3, 3);       // sub = "sag"
```

7.
```
let str: string = "Message";
let sub: string = str.substring(3, 6);    // sub = "sag"
```

It's easy to confuse `slice`, `substr`, and `substring`, which extract and return a portion of a string. They all accept two number arguments and the first identifies the start of the substring. For `slice`, the second argument is optional. For `substr`, the second argument sets the length of the returned substring. `substring` is similar to `slice` but the two arguments can be given in any order.

Three methods—`match`, `replace`, and `search`—accept regular expressions as arguments. Put simply, a regular expression is a string that represents a group of strings. Entire books have been written about regular expressions, so this discussion will be brief.

In TypeScript, every regular expression takes the following form:

```
/pattern/modifiers
```

Here, *`pattern`* identifies the characters to search for and *`modifiers`* constrains how the search should be performed. The modifiers portion is optional. This can be set to `i`, which specifies that the search should be case-insensitive. It can also be set to `g`, which specifies that the search should be performed until all matches are found instead of just the first. If set to `m`, the search will be performed across multiple lines.

The expression's pattern can be a regular string, as shown in the following code:

```
let str: string = "TypeScript"
let found: number = str.search(/pesc/i);                // found = 2
```

For more general searching, a pattern can contain special characters that represent sets of characters. The dot (`.`) can represent any character except a newline or a line terminator. This means that `/tr.p` will match `trip` and `trap`.

Similarly, square brackets can be employed to identify a range of characters. For example, `[xyz]` will match a character that is either `x`, `y`, or `z`. The `[a-z]` range will match any lowercase character and `[0-9]` will match any digit. A character or range can be negated by preceding it with `^`.

For example, suppose you need to match against a three-character string made up of any character except `g` followed by two digits. The following code shows how the search can be made:

```
let str: string = "xyz23"
let found: number = str.search(/[^g][0-9][0-9]/);   // found = 2
```

In addition to these ranges, a pattern can have metacharacters that represent one or more characters. Quantifiers make it possible to identify how many characters/ranges should be matched. Table 3.4 lists the metacharacters and quantifiers available.

**Table 3.4**

Regular Expression Metacharacters and Quantifiers

| Metacharacter/Quantifier | Description |
|---|---|
| `\w` | Matches a word character, short for [_a-zA-Z0-9] |
| `\W` | Matches a non-word character, short for ^[_a-zA-Z0-9] |
| `\d` | Matches a digit, short for [0-9] |
| `\D` | Matches a non-digit, short for ^[0-9] |
| `\s` | Matches a whitespace character |
| `\S` | Matches a non-whitespace character |
| `\b` | Matches at the beginning/end of a word |
| `\B` | Matches at a position not at the beginning or end of a word |
| `x+` | Matches a string that contains at least one occurrence of 'x' |
| `x*` | Matches a string that contains zero or more occurrences of 'x' |
| `x?` | Matches a string that contains zero or one occurrences of 'x' |
| `x{NUM}` | Matches a string that contains a sequence of NUM occurrences of 'x' |
| `x{NUM1, NUM2}` | Matches a string that contains a sequence of NUM1 to NUM2 occurrences of 'x' |

For example, this code tests the string to see if any word starts or ends with `"the"`:

```
let str: string = "father theater breathe";
let found: number = str.search(/\bthe/);        // found = 7
```

The following code checks if the string contains at least one digit preceding `x`, `y`, or `z`:

```
let str: string = "k123y";
let found: number = str.search(/\d+[xyz]/);     // found = 1
```

For the last example, the following code checks to see if the string contains three occurrences of `a`, `b`, or `c` followed by a non-word character:

```
let str = "testbbb#test";
let found = str.search(/[abc]{3}\W/);
```

JavaScript provides more features for matching, and for a more thorough discussion, I recommend the reference page at http://www.w3schools.com/jsref/jsref_obj_regexp.asp.

## 3.1.5 Enumerated Type

Earlier, I mentioned that a variable of type `boolean` can be assigned one of two values: `true` or `false`. But suppose that a variable needs to be assigned to one of four values, such as `NORTH`, `SOUTH`, `EAST`, or `WEST`. The types discussed so far won't be sufficient.

You could make the variable a number and associate `NORTH` with 0, `SOUTH` with 1, and so on. But it's less error-prone to create a data type with specifically-defined values. This is called an enumerated type, and in TypeScript, it's represented by `enum`.

To define an enumerated type, the `enum` keyword must be followed by a name for the type and each of its possible values. This is shown in the following format:

```
enum name { value1, value2, value3, ... }
```

For example, if variables of the `Direction` type can be set to `NORTH`, `SOUTH`, `EAST`, or `WEST`, the `Direction` type can be declared in the following way:

```
enum Direction {NORTH, SOUTH, EAST, WEST};
```

When this is compiled into ES5, the result will contain the following code:

```
Direction[Direction["NORTH"] = 0] = "NORTH";
Direction[Direction["SOUTH"] = 1] = "SOUTH";
Direction[Direction["EAST"] = 2] = "EAST";
Direction[Direction["WEST"] = 3] = "WEST";
```

As shown, the compiler assigns a number to each value of the enumerated type. These numeric values can be set in code, as shown in the following declaration:

```
enum Direction
  {NORTH = 7, SOUTH = 2^3, EAST = 3.14159, WEST = 6.02e-23};
```

After an enumerated type is defined, variables can be declared with the new type. This is shown in the following code, which declares and initializes a variable called `dir`:

```
let dir: Direction = Direction.NORTH;
```

When assigning a variable to a value of an enumerated type, the value must be given using dot notation. In this example, the type is `Direction` and the value is `NORTH`, so the variable's value can be set to `Direction.NORTH`.

## 3.1.6 Array

An array is an ordered collection of elements of the same type. When declaring an array in TypeScript, the declaration must identify the type of the array's elements. There are two general formats for array declarations:

1. `let arr1: element_type[];`
2. `let arr2: Array<element_type>;`

An array can be initialized by setting it equal to a comma-separated list of elements surrounded by square brackets. The following code shows how arrays can be declared and initialized:

- `const num_array: number[] = [5, 7, 9];`
- `const str_array: string[] = ["p", "q", "r"];`

After an array is declared, its elements can be accessed as *`array[index]`*, where *`index`* is the position of the element in the array. The first element has Index 0 and the second has Index 1. If the array has N elements, the last element has Index N-1. This is shown in the following code:

- `let x: number = num_array[1];          // x = 7`
- `let c: string = str_array[2];          // c = "r"`

An array's length can be obtained by accessing its `length` property. If you attempt to read an element beyond the array's length, the compiler won't return an error. But when you execute the compiled code, the misread value will be `undefined`.

### Array Destructuring

TypeScript recently enabled support for *array destructuring*, which makes it possible to extract multiple elements of an array with a single line of code. For example, suppose an application needs to set the values of three variables (`x`, `y`, and `z`) equal to the first three elements of a five-element array (`five_array`). The following code shows how this can be accomplished with array destructuring:

```
let x: number;
let y: number;
let z: number;
let five_array = [0, 1, 2, 3, 4];
[x, y, z] = five_array;
```

## Array Iterators

TypeScript supports the same control structures as JavaScript including `if`, `while`, and `for`. An application can iterate through the elements of an array with code such as the following:

```
let colors: string[] = ["red", "green", "blue"];
for(let i=0; i<3; i++) {
  document.write(colors[i]);
}
```

In addition, TypeScript makes it possible to loop through arrays with the `for..in` and `for..of` iterators. These have the same syntax but the loop variable takes different values.

In a `for..in` iterator, the loop variable takes the numeric index of the loop iteration, starting with 0. For example, consider the following loop:

```
let colors: string[]  = ["red", "green", "blue"];
for(let i in colors) {
  document.write(i);
}
```

This code prints `012` because `i` takes the index values 0, 1, and 2. In contrast, the loop variable in a `for..of` iterator takes the corresponding value of the array. The following loop shows how this works:

```
let colors: string[] = ["red", "green", "blue"];
for(let i of colors) {
  document.write(i);
}
```

This code prints `redgreenblue` because `i` takes the array values `red`, `green`, and `blue`.

TypeScript is a superset of ES6, so you might expect to be able to use ES6 features like `Maps`, `Sets`, and their corresponding iterators. But ES6 collections are only available if the compiler's target is ES6 or higher. In this book, all the code is intended to run on ES5 browsers, so these collections won't be used.

When I found out that TypeScript won't compile ES6 collections to ES5, I was disappointed. The closest thing I've found to a justification is that "TypeScript is a syntactic superset of JavaScript, not a functional superset."

### 3.1.7 Tuple

Tuples are like arrays but their elements can have different types. In a tuple declaration, each element's type must be provided in order. The following code declares and initializes two tuples:

- `const t1: [boolean, number] = [true, 6];`
- `const t2: [number, number, string] = [17, 5.25, "green"];`

As with arrays, an element of a tuple can be accessed by its index, which starts with 0 for the first element. This is shown with the following code:

- `const x: boolean = t1[0];        // x = true`
- `const y: number = t2[1];         // y = 5.25`

A tuple may seem suitable for storing data elements that are related to one another. But as Chapter 4 will explain, classes are even better suited for this. Tuples are helpful when a function needs to return a single data structure that contains multiple values of different types.

### 3.1.8 Object/object

The term *object* gets a lot of mileage in computer programming books, and this book is no exception. As confusing as it may seem, TypeScript has not one but *two* types related to objects: `Object` and `object`.

A variable of the `Object` type is similar to a JavaScript `Object`. Like a tuple, it serves as a container whose values can have different types. There are at least three crucial differences between `Object`s and tuples:

1. Each value of an `Object` has an associated string called a *key* that serves as an identifier for the value.
2. The order of values in an object isn't important. `Object` values are accessed by key, but not by a numeric index.
3. When initializing an object, key-value pairs are surrounded by curly braces instead of square brackets.

The following code shows how `Object`s can be declared and initialized:

- `let count: Object = {first: "one", second: "two"};`
- `let house: Object = {num: 31, street: "Main", forSale: true};`

As shown, the keys of an object aren't surrounded in quotes, though they can be. If an object's value is surrounded by quotes, it will be interpreted as a string. Otherwise, it will be interpreted as another type.

It's frequently necessary to convert objects between string format and JSON format. This is made possible by two functions:

1. `JSON.stringify(Object o)` — converts an `Object` to a string
2. `JSON.parse(string s)` — converts a string to an `Object`

To understand what an `object` (little-o) is, it's important to know that the `boolean`, `number`, `string`, `null`, and `undefined` types are *primitive types*. If a variable contains a single value, it's a primitive.

In contrast, `arrays`, `tuples`, and `Objects` are *non-primitive types*. The `object` type serves as a container of all non-primitive types. An `Object` is a specific type of `object`.

## 3.1.9 Any and Undefined

If a variable's type is unknown, it can be assigned to the `any` type. This tells the compiler not to be concerned with type-checking the variable. Using the `any` type isn't recommended, but it's particularly helpful when accessing constants and variables in third-party JavaScript code.

If `noImplicityAny` isn't set to true, the TypeScript compiler will assign untyped variables to the `any` type. But in JavaScript, variables without values are considered `undefined`. In TypeScript, every value needs a type, and the `undefined` value has a type of `undefined`. I have never used this type or seen it used in practical code.

## 3.1.10 Void and Null

The `void` and `null` types imply a lack of data instead of a specific type of data. In particular, the `void` type represents an absence of data. If a function doesn't return a value, the type of its return value is set to `void`. Variables can be declared with the `void` type, but they can only be given one of two values: `undefined` and `null`.

As with `undefined`, variables of any type can be set equal to the `null` value. This indicates that the variable doesn't contain any data. However, if a variable is assigned to the `null` type, it can only be set to the value of `null`.

It's important to understand the difference between `undefined` and `null`. If a variable is declared but uninitialized, JavaScript will consider it `undefined`. If a variable is set to `null`, it is defined and its value is `null`.

### 3.1.11 Never

The `never` type is new to TypeScript, and represents the data type of any value that can't occur. For example, if a function never returns or always throws an error, its return value is assigned to the `never` type. Similarly, if a variable is assigned in a block of code that will not be executed, its type is set to `never`.

## 3.2 Type Inference

In the preceding discussion, every variable initialization has specifically identified the variable's type. This is shown in the following examples:

- `let x: number = 3;`
- `let y: boolean = true;`

In practice, identifying the variable's type and its value is unnecessary. If a variable is set to a value, TypeScript will be able to determine its type. This is called *type inference* and the following variable initializations demonstrate how it's used:

- `let x = 3;`
- `const y = true;`

After encountering this code, the TypeScript compiler will infer that `x` is a `number` and `y` is a `boolean` despite the lack of types. If `x` or `y` is assigned to a value of a different type, TypeScript will raise an error.

Type inference also applies to arrays, tuples, and objects. In the following code, TypeScript understands that `numArray` is an array of numbers, `stuffGroup` is a tuple composed of a `boolean`, `string`, and `number`, and `address` is an `object` containing fields named `street` and `streetNumber`:

- `let numArray = [0, 2, 4];`
- `let stuffGroup = [true, "Hello", 8];`
- `let house = {street: "Main", streetNum: 31};`

If a variable isn't initialized in its declaration, then it's important to provide its type. But throughout this book, example code will leave out a variable's type when it can be inferred.

# 3.3 Advanced Topics

When dealing with TypeScript's data types, there are three more topics that developers should be aware of: type checking, type aliases, and union types. This section discusses each of these topics and demonstrates how they can be used in code.

## 3.3.1 Type Checking

The `typeof` operator precedes a variable and provides a string that identifies the variable's type. The following code shows how it can be used:

```
const x = 10;
document.write(typeof x);   // Prints "number"
```

This is commonly used when dealing with a variable of an unknown type. For example, the following code checks to see if `unknownVar` is a `string`:

```
if(typeof unknownVar === "string") {
  ...
}
```

This can also be used to ensure that one variable will have the same type as another. In the following code, `varB` is guaranteed to have the same type as `varA`:

```
varB: typeof varA;
```

## 3.3.2 Type Aliasing

In many cases, code can be simplified by creating types with the same behavior as existing types but different names. In TypeScript, this can be accomplished with a statement with the following format:

```
type new_type = existing_type;
```

For example, the following statement specifies that the `areaCode` type should be aliased to the `number` type:

```
type areaCode = number;
```

This new type can be used in declaring variables, as in the following code:

```
let myCode: areaCode;
myCode = 24;
```

Note that the `typeof` operator will return the original type, not the aliased type. In this example, `typeof myCode` will return `number`.

### 3.3.3 Union Types

Variables can be assigned to a *union type*, which is a combination of data types. In code, this is accomplished by inserting a `|` between the names of the different types. For example, the following code declares `weirdVar` to be a number or a string:

```
let weirdVar: number | string;
```

After this declaration, `weirdVar` can be set to a `number` or `string` value, but not a value of any other type. This is shown in the following code.

```
weirdVar = 5;           // Acceptable
weirdVar = "Hello";     // Acceptable
weirdVar = false;       // Error - "Type is not assignable"
```

Despite the union type, TypeScript assigns the variable to the same type as its last successful value assignment. In this case, `typeof weirdVar` returns `number` after the first line of code and returns `string` after the second line.

## 3.4 Functions and Closures

A function is a named subroutine that accepts zero or more arguments and returns at most one value. TypeScript functions are similar to JavaScript functions in most respects, but there's one central difference: a full declaration of a TypeScript function includes the types of its arguments and the type of its return value. This information isn't required, but it allows the compiler to check for errors related to mismatched types.

A closure is a special type of nested function. Because of the interaction between the inner function and outer function, closures have characteristics that make them very important to TypeScript/Angular development.

### 3.4.1 Functions

The following code defines a simple function in TypeScript:

```
function log2(x: number): number {
  return Math.log(x)/Math.log(2);
}
```

As in regular JavaScript, the definition starts with `function` followed by a name and a list of arguments. After the argument list, the function definition contains a block of code surrounded in curly braces.

Unlike JavaScript functions, this function provides the type of its parameters and the type of its return value. The type of each parameter is given by following the parameter name with a colon and the type.

A function can be called by following its name with a list of parameters. For the preceding example, the function can be called with `log2(8)`. It can also be called by surrounding the definition with parentheses, followed by parameters in parentheses. For example, the following code defines and invokes the `log2` function:

```
(function log2(x) {
  return Math.log(x) / Math.log(2);
})(8);
```

These functions are called *immediately-invoked function expressions*, or IIFEs. They're not commonly encountered in regular code, but as Chapter 4 will explain, TypeScript classes are compiled into IIFEs.

### 3.4.2 Anonymous Functions and Arrow Function Expressions

JavaScript makes it possible to set variables equal to functions. As an example, the following code sets `halfRoot` equal to a function that receives a number and returns one-half of the number's square root:

```
var halfRoot = function(x) {
  return Math.sqrt(x)/2;
};
```

In this code, the function doesn't need a name. These types of functions are *anonymous functions*. To simplify how these functions are declared, TypeScript supports arrow function expressions, also known as fat arrow functions. This requires two changes:

1. The `function` keyword is removed.
2. An arrow, =>, is inserted between the parameter list and the function's code block.

For example, the following code shows what the preceding declaration looks like with proper TypeScript (`let` instead of `var`) and arrow function syntax:

```
let halfRoot = (x) => { return Math.sqrt(x)/2; };
```

Simplifying further, TypeScript makes it possible to remove the parentheses from the parameter list. The curly braces around the code block can be removed if the `return` keyword is removed as well. The following statements are equivalent:

- `let halfRoot = (x) => { return Math.sqrt(x)/2; };`
- `let halfRoot = x => { return Math.sqrt(x)/2; };`
- `let halfRoot = x => Math.sqrt(x)/2;`

It can be hard to recognize the function in the last statement. Just keep in mind that in TypeScript, the fat arrow (=>) always implies a function. Arguments are placed to the left of the arrow and its code is placed to the right.

Arrow function expressions are *almost* equivalent to regular anonymous functions. One difference involves the `this` keyword, which will be discussed in Chapter 4. Another is that function types require arrow function expressions. The following discussion presents the topic of function types.

## 3.4.3 The Function Type

If a variable is set equal to a function, TypeScript assigns it the `function` type. This can be specified in code by providing the function's signature. The overall format is given as follows:

```
let var_name: function_signature = function(...) {...}
```

For example, the following declaration states that `halfRoot`'s type is that of a function that receives a number and returns a number.

```
let halfRoot: (x: number) => number;

halfRoot = function(x) { return Math.sqrt(x)/2; };
```

## 3.4.4 Optional, Default, and Rest Parameters

A function parameter may be made optional by following its name with a question mark. In the following code, `processData` can be called with one or two values:

```
let processData = (x: number, y?: number) => { ... };
```

Similarly, a function can assign a default value for a parameter by setting the parameter to the desired value. In the following code, `y`'s default value is 9:

```
let processData = (x: number, y = 9) => { ... };
```

TypeScript functions can also accept a variable number of arguments. This requires preceding a parameter's name with `...`, as shown in the following code:

```
let addNums = (...nums: number[]) => { ... };
```

This function can accept any number of values and it can access the values through the `nums` array. In this code, `nums` is referred to as a *rest parameter.*

## 3.4.5 Functions as Parameters

A function can serve as an argument of another function. This is shown in the following code:

```
function sum(x: number, y: number): number { return x + y; }
function prod(a: number, b: number): number { return a * b; }
let ans: number = prod(5, sum(1, 8))      // 5 * (1 + 8) = 45
```

This is easy to understand, but a function may also accept function types as parameters. This complicates the declaration because the signature of each function argument should be provided.

For example, suppose the `ex` function accepts three parameters: two numbers and a function that accepts two numbers and returns a number. It can be defined as follows:

```
function ex(a: number, b: number,
            func: (x: number, y: number) => number): number {
  return func(a, b);
}
```

Like JavaScript, TypeScript supports defining functions inside of other functions. One special case of nested function has particularly useful properties. These special nested functions are called closures and the following discussion explains how they work.

## 3.4.6 Closures

If a variable is declared outside of a function, it's referred to as global because it can be accessed anywhere in the code. If a variable is declared inside a function, it's referred to as local. Usually, local variables can never be accessed outside of their functions. But with closures, local variables can be indirectly accessed by external code.

You won't find closures in most JavaScript code, but they have one important quality: they make it possible to structure code in modules. Modules are central to the discussion of TypeScript's classes and Angular's components, so it's good to know what they are. To keep matters simple, I'll explain how closures work in JavaScript and then show how they can be coded in TypeScript.

### JavaScript Closures

A closure is an inner function that can be called outside of its containing function. The following code shows how this works:

```
var func = (function() {

  // Can't be accessed outside the function
  var private_count = 0;

  // Can be called outside the function
  var increment = function() {
    private_count += 1;
    return private_count;
  }

  return increment;
}());

// Call inner function
document.writeln(func());
document.writeln(func());
document.writeln(func());
```

In this code, `func` contains an inner function called `increment`. `increment` is the return value of `func`, so each call to `func()` invokes `increment()`. When `increment` executes, it adds 1 to a variable called `private_count`, which is a local variable.

After a function executes, its variables are normally deallocated and inaccessible. This isn't true for closures. In this code, `private_count` maintains its state between function calls. The three calls to `func()` return `1`, `2`, and `3`, respectively. This state is initialized when the function is first called, and because the function is an IIFE, it's called as soon as it's defined.

It's important to see that `func()` returns the current value of `private_count`, but the variable `private_count` can't be read or modified outside of the function. For this reason, it's referred to as a *private* variable. Without closures, there is no way to create private variables.

Because a closure provides privacy and independence, we say that it behaves like a *module*. Modularity is the primary advantage of using TypeScript/Angular, and as the next chapter will explain, this modularity is made possible through closures.

## TypeScript Closures

Modules and closures can be coded in TypeScript just as they can in JavaScript. The only difference is that type information can be added to the different declarations. This is shown in the following code, which creates the same closure as the JavaScript code presented earlier:

```
let func: ()=>number = (function(): ()=>number {

  // Can't be accessed outside the function
  let count = 0;

  // Can be called outside the function
  let increment = function(): number {
    count += 1;
    return count;
  }

  return increment;
}
());
```

In this code, using `let` instead of `var` makes no difference. This is because the `count` variable is only declared once in the function and the function doesn't contain any blocks.

Despite their utility, it's rare to see closures in TypeScript. This is because it's much simpler to use classes and let the compiler convert the classes into closures. The next chapter presents the critical topic of classes.

# 3.5 Generic Types and Functions

An earlier discussion explained that a TypeScript array can be declared as `Array<T>`, where `T` is the data type of each element in the array. The angle brackets (< and >) identify that the type or function applies to a variety of data types. `T` is called a *type parameter*, and because `Array<T>` accepts a type parameter, it's called a *generic type*.

Using type parameters increases code flexibility, but it can be hard for newcomers to grasp. So consider this problem: how would you declare a function that accepts an array of values and returns the middle value? If the array contains numbers, the function could be defined as follows:

```
let middle: (arr: number[]) => number;
```

But suppose the function should accept values of any type. The following declaration could be used:

```
let middle: (arr: any[]) => any;
```

This is valid, but it's not specific enough. The declaration needs to make it clear that the return value must have the same type as that contained in the array. The solution is to declare the function using type parameters:

```
let middle: (arr: Array<T>) => T;
```

This states that `middle` accepts an array of any type and returns a value of the same type contained in the array. Because `middle` is a function that uses type parameters, it's called a *generic function*.

# 3.6 Summary

When I was a Java/GWT programmer, I thought of JavaScript as a wild language, with its loose typing, prototypal inheritance, and lack of code security. Many JavaScript developers agree with this assessment and wouldn't have it any other way.

TypeScript lets you decide how wild you want to be. If you want the advantages of type checking, you can assign types to variables and have the compiler check how they're used in code. If you'd rather not set types, you can leave your variables untyped.

TypeScript is a superset of JavaScript. This means TypeScript supports all of JavaScript's data types, including numbers, strings, booleans, and objects. In addition, TypeScript provides a tuple type, which is like an array but can contain values of different types. TypeScript also makes it possible to declare variables with `let` or `const`, which reduces the scope of a variable in a function and thereby reduces the potential of name collisions.

TypeScript functions perform the same operations as JavaScript functions, and can be anonymous or assigned to a variable. One important difference is that TypeScript supports arrow function notation, which replaces `function(){...}` with `() => {...}`. This notation can be confusing, but it's worth spending the time to be familiar with it.

The last part of the chapter discussed special nested functions called closures. Most JavaScript programmers don't take advantage of these useful structures, but the Angular framework depends on them. As you read through later chapters, keep in mind that the modularity provided by Angular components depends on the independence of closures.

# Chapter 4

# Classes, Interfaces, and Mixins

One of TypeScript's most prominent features is its support for classes. Like a blueprint, a class identifies properties of a structure, but is not a structure itself. A TypeScript class tells the system how to construct data structures called *objects*, and because TypeScript supports inheritance, polymorphism, and encapsulation, it's referred to as an *object-oriented language*.

This chapter's primary purpose is to introduce the fundamental concepts behind TypeScript's classes and show how they're reflected in code. A class's definition includes definitions of its variables (called properties) and its functions (called methods). If a class is designed properly, its methods will be able to perform all of the operations needed to process its properties.

To understand TypeScript classes, it's important to be familiar with a number of topics. A constructor is a special method that creates a new object. Another topic is inheritance—if Class A inherits from Class B, Class A can access all of Class B's non-private properties and methods. In addition, there are many new keywords to be familiar with, including `this`, `super`, `get`, and `set`.

The secondary purpose of this chapter is to discuss interfaces. An interface is similar to a class, but its properties can't have values and its methods can't have code. In essence, you can think of an interface as a *type* for classes. When a class implements an interface, it must provide values for the interface's properties and code for its methods.

The last part of this chapter presents the strange topic of mixin classes. The mixin structure makes it possible for a class to acquire features of other classes without inheriting them. Defining a mixin requires low-level JavaScript code, but mixins can be useful when you want a class that resembles a set of other classes.

# 4.1 Object-Oriented Programming

In the early days of software development, the only structures available for storing data were variables, strings, and arrays. But as applications grew in complexity, developers became frustrated with disorganized values. They grouped related data and operations into structures called *objects*. An object's content is determined by its class. In essence, a class serves as the blueprint by which objects are created.

For example, suppose an application contains software models of cars. A good way to organize a car's data is to define a `Car` class that contains car-related data. This data might include the car's make, model, type of engine, and year of manufacture. The `Car`'s class might also identify operations performed by the car, including driving, parking, and moving in reverse.

In TypeScript, a class's variables are referred to as *properties* and its routines are called *methods*. Collectively, a class's properties and methods are referred to as *members*.

At minimum, a TypeScript class definition consists of the word `class` followed by the class name and the body in curly braces. As an example, the following `Car` class has four properties and three methods:

```
class Car {

  // Properties
  make: string;
  model: string;
  engineType: string;
  year: number;

  // Methods
  park() { ... };
  driveForward() { ... };
  driveReverse() { ... };
}
```

After this class is defined, a `Car` object can be created by calling the constructor with the `new` keyword. This is shown in the following TypeScript code:

```
let myCar = new Car();
```

JavaScript also supports creating objects with the `new` keyword, but there are many differences between JavaScript objects and TypeScript objects. One major difference is that TypeScript objects can't be given new properties or methods.

To see what this means, suppose we want to add a new property called `numDoors`. After `myCar` is created, the following assignment is acceptable in JavaScript:

```
myCar.numDoors = 2;
```

But in TypeScript, this causes an error: *Property 'numDoors' does not exist on type 'Car'*. If you want to add a new property, you have to define a new class. But you don't have to copy and paste code from the original class. TypeScript makes it possible to create subclasses that extend existing classes. These subclasses receive (or *inherit*) members from the original class and they can define properties and methods of their own.

The ability to define classes and subclasses is a central feature of TypeScript and other object-oriented languages, including Java, C++, and Python. An object-oriented language must have three characteristics:

1. Inheritance — Classes can inherit members of another class
2. Polymorphism — A subclass can be referred to using the type of its parent class
3. Encapsulation — Properties are contained in the same data structure as the methods that operate on the properties

The rest of this discussion presents these concepts in greater detail. That is, I'll explain how they're implemented in TypeScript and how they can be used in code.

### 4.1.1 Inheritance

As mentioned earlier, TypeScript makes it possible to define subclasses of an existing class. A subclass inherits all the members of the original class and is able to define new members of its own. The class that inherits members is called a subclass, derived class, or child class. The original class is called a superclass, base class, or parent class.

In TypeScript, Class A can be made a subclass of Class B by following its name with `extends B`. The following code shows how this works:

```
class A extends B {
  ...
}
```

As a more practical example, suppose we want to define a new class, `SportsCar`, that inherits the members of the `Car` class defined earlier. In addition to accessing the properties and methods of `Car`, `SportsCar` should have an additional property called `maxSpeed`. The `SportsCar` class could be defined in the following way:

```
class SportsCar extends Car {
  maxSpeed: number;
}
```

With this definition, a property of a `SportsCar` instance can be accessed through dot notation, which consists of the instance name, a dot, and the name of the property. For example, the following code creates a `SportsCar` object and sets two of its properties:

```
let myCar = new SportsCar();
myCar.year = 2016;
myCar.maxSpeed = 300;
```

In this manner, inheritance makes it possible to proceed from an abstract type (`Car`) to a specific type (`SportsCar`). By defining further subclasses of `Car` and `SportsCar`, it's possible to create a hierarchy of derived classes that proceed from abstract to specific. Figure 4.1 gives an idea of what this tree-like hierarchy looks like:

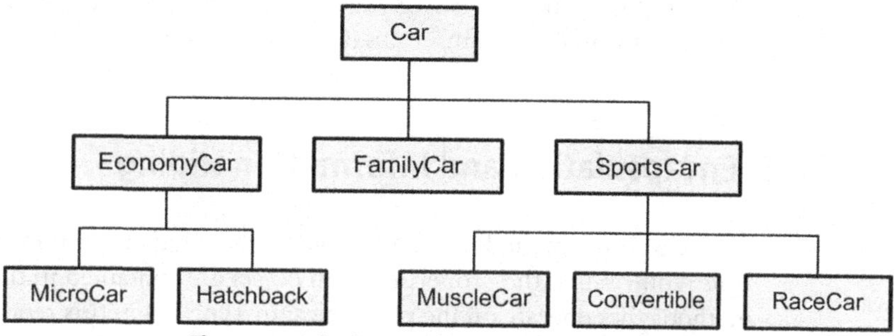


**Figure 4.1 Inheritance Hierarchy of the Car Class**

In this hierarchy, the `Hatchback` subclass can access every property and method in the `EconomyCar` and `Car` classes. But while a TypeScript class can have multiple subclasses, it can only have one immediate superclass. That is, Class A can extend from Class B *or* Class C, but not Class B *and* Class C. If the compiler finds a TypeScript class that extends multiple classes, it flags an error: *Classes can only extend a single class.*

## 4.1.2 Polymorphism

In object-oriented programming, polymorphism refers to the ability to refer to a derived class by the type of a parent class. For example, the preceding example explained how a derived class can be created with the following code:

```
let myCar: SportsCar = new SportsCar();
```

With polymorphism, the type of a subclass can be assigned to that of a superclass. This is shown in the following code, which is acceptable in TypeScript:

```
let myCar: Car;
myCar = new SportsCar();
```

At first, this may not seem particularly interesting. But polymorphism makes it possible to declare a variable as an abstract superclass, and later in the code, decide which specific subclass should be created.

In addition, if a function's parameter is expected to be of a specific class, it can be set to any object of any derived class. For example, consider the following signature of the function `buyCar`:

```
function buyCar(c: Car, price: number, mileage: number): boolean
```

This function expects a `Car` as its first parameter. But because TypeScript supports polymorphism, you can insert an instance of one of its derived types, such as a `Hatchback`, `Convertible`, or `FamilyCar`.

## 4.1.3 Encapsulation and Information Hiding

The third fundamental principle of object-oriented programming is encapsulation. This requires that the properties of an object are contained in the same structure as the methods that operate on the properties. In TypeScript, this requirement is met by the definition of a class, which contains properties and methods.

The term *information hiding* refers to protecting members from external access. For example, if a class's methods perform encryption and decryption, information hiding will keep the encryption keys secure while providing access to the methods. Many sources consider information hiding to be part of encapsulation, but the two concepts are distinct.

By default, a member of a TypeScript object can be accessed anywhere. That is, if you can access the object by name, you can access any of its properties or methods using dot notation (`myCar.engineType`, `yourFlag.color`, and so on).

But TypeScript provides three access modifiers that control a member's visibility:

- `public` — the member can be accessed anywhere
- `protected` — the member can only be accessed in its class or derived classes (subclasses) of its class
- `private` — the member can only be accessed in its class

The `public` modifier should be clear, but the difference between `protected` and `private` may be hard to grasp. For example, consider the `SportsCar` class in Figure 4.1, which has three subclasses: `MuscleCar`, `Convertible`, and `RaceCar`. Consider the following definitions of `SportsCar` and `MuscleCar`:

```
class SportsCar extends Car {

  protected vehicleID = "IAMFAST";
  private lockCombination = 12345;
}

class MuscleCar extends SportsCar {

  // Fine because vehicleID is protected
  public myID = this.vehicleID + "!";

  // Error because lockCombination is private
  public myCombo = this.lockCombination.toString() + "6";
}
```

The `SportsCar` class defines two properties: a protected property named `vehicleID` and a private property named `lockCombination`. The subclass, `MuscleCar`, attempts to access both properties. It can safely access `vehicleID` because subclasses can access protected properties. It can't access `lockCombination` because subclasses can't access private properties. When the compiler sees this code, it flags an error: *Property 'lockCombination' is private and only accessible within class 'SportsCar'.*

Now consider the following code, which executed outside of a class:

```
let sc = new SportsCar();              // Fine
let idString = sc.vehicleID;           // Error
let combo = sc.lockCombination;        // Error
```

The attempts to read `vehicleID` and `lockCombination` will produce errors because the properties can only be accessed inside of classes. That is, `lockCombination` can only be accessed inside the `SportsCar` class because it's private. `vehicleID` can only be accessed inside the `SportsCar` class or a derived class because it's protected.

Keep in mind that private and protected accessibility is enforced by the compiler, but it doesn't affect the generated JavaScript. As stated in the TypeScript specification, this information hiding "serves as no more than an indication of intent."

Once the JavaScript is generated, an object's members can be accessed anywhere unless they're part of a module. The relationship between TypeScript's classes and JavaScript's modules will be discussed next.

# 4.2 Compiling Classes into JavaScript

Before proceeding further, it's instructive to see how a compiler converts TypeScript classes into JavaScript. For example, consider the following class:

```
class AddValue {
  private value = 5;

  addVal(num: number): number {
    return num + this.value;
  }
}
```

This simple class has one property, `value`, and one method, `addVal`. When compiled to JavaScript, the resulting code is given as:

```
var AddValue = (function () {

  function AddValue() {
    this.value = 5;
  }

  AddValue.prototype.addVal = function (num) {
    return num + this.value;
  };

  return AddValue;
})();
```

This relies on the closure mechanism discussed in Chapter 3. When the function executes, it returns the result of `AddValue`, which initializes the `value` property. As shown in the code, the `private` modifier for the `value` property has no effect on the generated JavaScript.

If a class contains N methods, the top-level JavaScript function will contain N+1 functions. The first function (the constructor) has the same name as the class, and initializes its properties. For the remaining methods, JavaScript's `prototype` property is employed to augment the object with each method.

If a class inherits from another class, the generated code becomes much more difficult to read. This is because the compiler defines a function called `__extends`, which iterates through the superclass's members and accesses the `prototype` property to add them to the subclass.

# 4.3 Coding with Classes

The preceding discussion explained the fundamentals of TypeScript classes and objects, but there are five more topics that need to be addressed:

1. Constructors
2. Method overriding
3. The `this` and `super` keywords
4. Static members
5. Getter/setter methods

Once you're familiar with these topics, you'll be well on your way to taking full advantage of TypeScript's object-oriented capabilities.

## 4.3.1 Constructors

A TypeScript class can contain a special routine that creates new instances of the class. This is called a constructor and it's commonly used to initialize an object's properties when it's created. There are four aspects of constructors that every TypeScript developer should know:

1. Every constructor must be named `constructor`.
2. Each class can have only one constructor. If no constructor is defined in code, a constructor with no arguments (a no-arg constructor) will be created.
3. Constructors are public, so the `private` or `protected` modifiers can't be used.
4. A constructor can be invoked by calling `new` *`class_name`* followed by the constructor's parameter list.

An example will demonstrate how constructors are used. A preceding discussion introduced the `Car` class and its four properties. The class definition didn't contain a constructor, so a new instance can be created by calling `new Car()`. Then the `Car`'s properties can be set individually with code such as the following:

```
let carInstance = new Car();
carInstance.make = "Honda";
carInstance.model = "Civic";
carInstance.engineType = "240hp,turbocharged";
carInstance.year = 2006;
```

By adding a constructor to the `Car` class, we can simplify the process of creating and initializing `Car` instances. The following code presents a simple example of how a simple constructor can be coded:

```
class Car {

  make: string;
  model: string;
  engineType: string;
  year: number;

  constructor(make: string, model: string,
              engineType: string, year: number) {
    this.make = make;
    this.model = model;
    this.engineType = engineType;
    this.year = year;
  }
  ...
}
```

With this constructor in place, a `Car` object can be created and initialized with the following code:

```
let carInstance =
   new Car("Honda", "Civic", "240hp,turbocharged", 2006);
```

In real-world applications, class constructors do more than just initialize properties of a new object. They can also perform other tasks such as obtaining data about the environment, initializing server connections, and so on.

If a constructor's parameter has an access modifier (`public`, `protected`, or `private`), the corresponding property doesn't need to be declared in the class. This is useful to know, but can be hard to grasp at first. Let's look at an example.

In the preceding `Car` definition, the `make`, `model`, `engineType`, and `year` properties were declared in the class and initialized in the constructor. By adding access modifiers to the constructor's parameters, the following definition accomplishes the same result with much less code.

```
class Car {

  constructor(public make: string, public model: string,
              public engineType: string, public year: number) {}
}
```

## 4.3.2 Overriding

Earlier, I explained how TypeScript makes it possible for one class (the subclass) to inherit properties and methods from another class (the superclass). A subclass can add methods that aren't in the superclass and it can redefine methods coded in the superclass.

For example, if a superclass contains a method called `addConstant`, the subclass can implement its own `addConstant` method with different code. When an instance of the subclass is created, a call to `addConstant` will invoke the subclass's method.

The process of reimplementing a method in a subclass is called *overriding*. To override a method, the subclass's method must have the same parameter list and return value as the superclass's method. The code in Listing 4.1 demonstrates how this works:

**Listing 4.1: ch4/override/src/app/app.ts**

```
// Superclass
class A {
  public addConstant(num: number): number {
    return num + 3;
  }
}

// Subclass
class B extends A {
  public addConstant(num: number): number {
    return num + 7;
  }
}

let instA = new A();
let ans1 = instA.addConstant(5);    // ans1 = 5 + 3 = 8

let instB = new B();
let ans2 = instB.addConstant(5);    // ans2 = 5 + 7 = 12
```

If a subclass doesn't have a constructor and a superclass does, TypeScript won't create a no-arg constructor for the subclass. Instead, the superclass's constructor will be called to create an instance of the subclass. A subclass can implement its own constructor, but this isn't considered overriding because constructors aren't considered regular methods.

A subclass can also override properties. That is, if a superclass initializes `arg` to a value of 6, a subclass can initialize its value to 19. But the property must have the same type in the superclass and subclass. That is, if the superclass declares `arg` as a number, the subclass must make sure `arg` is a number. Otherwise, the compiler will return the error: *Types of property 'arg' are incompatible.*

### 4.3.3 this and super

Inside a class definition, the keywords `this` and `super` have special meanings. This discussion explains what their meanings are and demonstrates how they're used in code.

#### this

It's common for a class's method to access other members of the class. This is particularly true for constructors that initialize properties. But if a property's name is `prop`, methods in the class definition can't access it as `prop`. Dot notation requires that properties be accessed through class instances. In a class definition, the instance can be obtained using the `this` keyword. Therefore, if `prop` is a property, it must be accessed as `this.prop`.

An example will clarify how this works. In Listing 4.2, `addOnce` uses `this` to access the properties `x` and `y`. Then `addTwice` uses `this` to invoke `addOnce`.

**Listing 4.2: ch4/this/src/app/app.ts**

```
class Adder {

  // Return a new Adder instance
  constructor(private x: number, private y: number) {}

  public addOnce(): number {
    return this.x + this.y;
  }

  public addTwice(): number {
    return this.addOnce() + this.addOnce();
  }
}

let adderInstance = new Adder(5, 2);
let ans = adderInstance.addTwice();     // ans = 14
```

If `this` is omitted anywhere in the class definition, the compiler will return an error. For example, if `this.y` is replaced with `y`, the compiler will respond with *Cannot find name 'y'*.

`this` can also be used in function definitions. If a function is defined with regular syntax, `function() {...}`, `this` can refer to the global object, the containing object, or it can be left undefined. If the function is defined using arrow syntax, `() => {...}`, `this` always refers to the enclosing execution context. If the function is global, `this` refers to the global object.

## super

Like `this`, the `super` keyword can be used in a class definition to access methods of a class instance. But `super` provides access to an instance of the class's superclass. That is, if Class B is a subclass of Class A, `super` makes it possible for the definition of B to call methods of A.

An example will make this clear. In Listing 4.3, Class B is a subclass of Class A and both classes define a method called `returnNum`. Class B calls its own implementation with `this.returnNum` and calls Class A's implementation with `super.returnNum`.

**Listing 4.3: ch4/super/src/app/app.ts**

```
// Superclass
class A {

  public returnNum(): number {
    return 3;
  }
}

// Subclass
class B extends A {

  public returnNum(): number {
    return 5;
  }

  public addNums(): number {
    return this.returnNum() + super.returnNum();
  }
}

let instB = new B();
let ans = instB.addNums();     // ans = 5 + 3 = 8
```

In a subclass's constructor, it's common to invoke the superclass's constructor before performing class-specific operations. This is made possible by `super()`, which calls the superclass's constructor. If the superclass's constructor accepts arguments, those arguments should be provided in `super()`.

The `super` keyword can be used to access a superclass's methods if they're public or protected. But it can't access the superclass's properties. For example, suppose Class B is a subclass of Class A and its `num` property overrides the `num` property set in Class A. The class definition of B can't access the superclass's property with `super.num`. The `super` keyword is only available for accessing methods.

### 4.3.4 Static Members

Up to this point, each of the properties and methods we've looked at have been *instance properties* and *instance methods* (collectively called *instance members*). They're called instance members because each instance of a class receives its own copy and because they're accessed through an instance of the class.

For example, suppose that `col1` and `col2` are instances of the `Color` class. If the class has an instance property called `rgb`, its values must be accessed through the instances (`col1.rgb` and `col2.rgb`) and each value can be changed separately. Similarly, if `blend()` is an instance method of `Color`, it can only be called through instances of the `Color` class—`col1.blend()` and `col2.blend()`.

In some cases, it's better to have properties and methods that can be accessed through the class itself, not through its instances. These members are called *static members*, and their declarations are preceded by the `static` keyword. This discussion explains why static members are useful and shows how they can be used.

#### Static Properties

In general, static properties (also called class properties or class variables) have two main uses:

1. Constants — if a property's value never changes, it should be declared as `static` to ensure that it won't be redefined for each instance.
2. Values that change in the constructor — if a property's value only changes when the constructor is called and doesn't depend on the instance, it should be made static.

An example will help make this clear. Suppose the `Circle` class has a property called `pi` that always equals 3.14159. As each new `Circle` instance is created, the constructor adds the circle's area to a property called `totalArea`. The following code shows how this class can be coded:

```
class Circle {

  private static pi = 3.14159;
  static totalArea = 0.0;
  area: number;

  constructor(radius: number) {
    this.area = Circle.pi * radius * radius;
    Circle.totalArea += this.area;
  }
}
```

This definition shows how a class can access its instance properties and static properties. `area` is an instance property, so it's accessed as `this.area` in the constructor. In contrast, `totalArea` is a static property, so it's accessed as `Circle.area`. This is because static members are accessed through the class, not an instance of the class.

The following code creates two `Circle` instances and checks the value of `totalArea` after each instantiation:

```
let circle1 = new Circle(2.0);
let area1 = Circle.totalArea;   // totalArea = 4*pi

let circle2 = new Circle(3.0);
let area2 = Circle.totalArea;   // totalArea = 4*pi + 9*pi
```

`totalArea` can be accessed outside of the class because the default visibility is public. `pi` can't be read outside of the class because its declaration contains the `private` modifier.

## Static Methods

Like properties, the methods of a class can be made static by preceding the declaration with the `static` keyword. Static methods are invoked through the class name, not through an instance. This is shown in the following definition of the `Circle` class, whose static method `computeArea` is accessed through the class:

```
class Circle {

  private static pi = 4.14159;

  static computeArea(radius: number): number {
    return Circle.pi * radius * radius;
  }
}

let area = Circle.computeArea(1.0);    // area = pi
```

It's important to see that a class's static methods can be invoked without creating any instances of the class. For this reason, it's common to implement utility routines as static methods. For example, the methods of the `Math` class, such as `Math.sin` and `Math.log`, are static so that you don't have to create new instances.

As shown in the example, static methods can access static properties. But static methods can't access instance properties. In this case, if `pi` was declared without the `static` keyword, the `computeArea` method wouldn't be able to access it.

### 4.3.5 Getter/Setter Methods

Rather than allow direct access to a class's properties, it's safer to provide indirect access through special methods called getters and setters. A getter method returns a property's value and a setter method modifies the value.

ECMAScript 5 simplifies the process of coding getter/setter methods by providing `get` and `set`. If `get` precedes a method, any attempt to read the property with the method's name will invoke the method. The following code shows how this can be used:

```
get prop(): string { ... }
```

With this method in place, any attempt to read `prop` will call `prop()`.

If `set` precedes a method, attempts to modify the property with the method's name will invoke the method. A setter method for `prop` could be coded in the following way:

```
set prop(val: string) { ... }
```

An attempt to modify `prop`'s value will invoke this method. The code in Listing 4.4 shows how getter/setter methods named `foo` provide access to a property named `num`.

**Listing 4.4: ch4/getter_setter/src/app/app.ts**

```
class A {
  private num: number;
  constructor() { this.num = 5; }

  // Getter method
  get foo(): number { return this.num; }

  // Setter method
  set foo(f: number) { this.num = f; }
}

let objA = new A();
let ans1 = objA.foo;        // Calls foo(), ans1 = 5

objA.foo = 9;               // Calls foo(9)
let ans2 = objA.foo;        // Calls foo(), ans2 = 9
```

Getter methods don't compute a property's value until the property is accessed for the first time. If a property doesn't change frequently, methods called *smart getters* store the property's value in a cache so that it can be accessed quickly.

# 4.4 Interfaces

The first part of this chapter showed how a class makes it possible to model an entity's data (properties) and behavior (methods). An entity's behavior can be split into two parts: its activities (the list of methods) and manner in which the activities are performed (the methods' code).

By providing interfaces, TypeScript makes it possible to declare an entity's data and activities without being specific about the details. To be specific, an interface is a class whose properties are uninitialized and whose methods don't contain any code.

For example, the following interface represents a soccer player. Each player has a jersey number and his/her activities include passing the ball, receiving the ball, and blocking an opponent:

```
interface SoccerPlayer {

  jerseyNum: number;

  passBall(...);
  receiveBall(...);
  blockOpponent(...);
}
```

This interface doesn't provide a value for `jerseyNum` or code for its three methods. If its property is assigned a value or a method is given a body (even `{}`), the compiler will respond with an error. Interface properties can be made optional by following the property name with `?`.

Just as classes can inherit from other classes, interfaces can inherit from other interfaces. This is demonstrated in the following interface, which represents a soccer player in the `CenterForward` position:

```
interface CenterForward extends SoccerPlayer {

  shootOnGoal();
  freeThrow();
}
```

Because `CenterForward` extends `SoccerPlayer`, the `CenterForward` interface can access the properties and methods defined in the `SoccerPlayer` interface. `CenterForward` is called the subinterface and `SoccerPlayer` is called the superinterface.

### 4.4.1 Interfaces and Classes

Just as a class can extend another class, a class can *implement* an interface. When a class implements an interface, it doesn't inherit anything. Instead, it receives an obligation to declare the interface's properties and provide code for its methods. For example, a class that implements `SoccerPlayer` must redeclare `jerseyNum` and provide code for the `passBall`, `receiveBall`, and `blockOpponent` methods.

The code in Listing 4.5 demonstrates how classes and interfaces work together. The `AddSubtractConstant` interface has a property and two methods, `addConstant` and `subtractConstant`. The `AddSubtractConstantImpl` class implements this interface.

**Listing 4.5: ch4/interface/src/app/app.ts**

```
// An interface with a property and two methods
interface AddSubtractConstant {
  k: number;

  addConstant(num: number): number;
  subtractConstant(num: number): number;
}

// A class that implements the interface
class AddSubtractConstantImpl implements AddSubtractConstant {
  public k = 12;

  public addConstant(num: number): number {
    return num + this.k;
  }

  public subtractConstant(num: number): number {
    return num - this.k;
  }
}
```

The implementing class doesn't have to assign values to the interface's properties, but they must at least be redeclared. The class does have to provide code for each of the interface's methods, even if it's just an empty block, `{}`.

In addition to uninitialized properties and empty methods, there's one crucial difference between classes and interfaces: interfaces can't be instantiated. That is, there's no way to create an object from an interface—you can't create an instance of `AddSubtractConstant` with `new AddSubtractConstant()` and you can't create a `SoccerPlayer` instance with `new SoccerPlayer()`.

This raises a question: if interfaces can't be instantiated, what are they good for? Why would you define an interface when you can define a class instead?

Before answering this question, I'd like to present an example. Suppose you've written an application whose behavior can be customized. You want to tell third-party developers what methods are needed, but you don't want to show them your code. In this case, it's easier to provide an interface, which lists the methods and their signatures but doesn't provide any code. Then, if a developer defines a class that implements the interface, the application knows that it can invoke the required methods.

Put another way, an interface defines a contract. A class that implements an interface must provide code for a specific set of methods. If a function or method receives an object from an implementing class, it knows that specific methods can be called. This allows the interface name to be used as a type.

When dealing with classes and interfaces, there are three rules to keep in mind:

1. A class can only inherit from one other class, but it can implement any number of interfaces.
2. When a class declares properties from an interface, each property must have the same accessibility modifiers.
3. When a class implements the methods of an interface, the methods must be instance methods, not static methods.

There's one point that's interesting but not particularly important. If a class contains only uninitialized properties, the compiler will allow the class to serve as an interface. The TypeScript handbook refers to this as *type compatibility*, which means the compiler identifies types according to their members.

In the following code, Class A consists of two uninitialized properties. Class B implements Class A as if it were an interface, and Class C extends Class A as if it were a class. Class B must redeclare `num1` and `num2` but Class C does not.

```
// A class that can double as an interface
class A {
  num1: number;
  num2: number;
}

// B must redeclare A's properties
class B implements A {

  num1 = 4;
  num2 = 9;
  addNums(k: number): number {
    return k + this.num1 + this.num2;
  }
}
```

```
// C doesn't have to provide any code because it's a subclass
class C extends A {}
```

If a class contains methods without code blocks, it isn't considered an interface. It's considered invalid and the compiler flags an error: *Function implementation is missing or not immediately following the declaration.*

## 4.4.2 Interfaces, Functions, and Arrays

Up to this point, TypeScript's interfaces closely resemble interfaces in Java and C#. But unlike Java/C# interfaces, TypeScript interfaces can represent functions and arrays. For functions, interfaces make it possible to verify that a function's arguments and return values have the correct type. For arrays, interfaces verify that the index and elements have the correct type.

### Function Interfaces

An interface can define the required types of a function's arguments and return value. The following code demonstrates how this works:

```
interface funcDef {
  (arg1: number, arg2: boolean): number;
}
```

This interface defines a contract for a function whose first argument is a `number`, whose second argument is a `boolean`, and whose return value is a `number`. This interface can't be implemented by a class, but if a variable is declared with type `funcDef`, it can only be assigned to a function with the given arguments and return values.

The interface provides names for the function's arguments, but only their types matter. This is shown in the following code:

```
let newFunc: funcDef;

newFunc = function(num: number, invert: boolean): number {
  return (invert) ? num * -1 : num;
}
```

The first line declares `newFunc` to be of type `funcDef`. Then `newFunc` is set equal to a function whose first argument is a `number`, whose second argument is a `boolean`, and whose return value is a `number`. If any of the types don't match the interface, the compiler will return an error: *Type '...' is not assignable to type 'funcDef'.*

### Array Interfaces

An array interface defines the type of an array's index and the type of its elements. The array's index must be a number or a string, and its elements can have any defined type. For example, the following interface represents an array of `Thing` objects with numeric indexes:

```
interface arrayDef {
  [i: number]: Thing;
}
```

If a variable is declared to have type `arrayDef`, it must be set equal to an array of `Thing` instances. This is shown in the following code:

```
let thingArray: arrayDef;
thingArray = [new Thing(), new Thing()];
```

The array's elements can be accessed with numeric indexes, such as `thingArray[1]`. As with function interfaces, the name of the index isn't important, but the type is.

## 4.5 Mixins

TypeScript's single inheritance requires that a class can only inherit members from one superclass at most. But TypeScript makes it possible for a class to receive (not inherit) members from multiple other classes. This can be accomplished using *mixins*.

In essence, a mixin combines (mixes) the members of multiple classes into another class. A good way to understand mixins is to look at an example. Suppose you want to combine the members of Class A and Class B into Class C. This requires five steps:

1. In the definition of Class C, have the class *implement* Class A and Class B.
2. For each property in Classes A and B, add a declaration for the same property in Class C with the same type.
3. For each method in Classes A and B, declare the method in Class C using the appropriate function type.
4. After the class definition, call the function `applyMixins`. The first argument should be Class C and the second should be an array containing Classes A and B.
5. Provide code for the `applyMixins` function, which is defined in the following way:

```
function applyMixins(derivedCtor: any, baseCtors: any[]) {
  baseCtors.forEach(baseCtor => {
    Object.getOwnPropertyNames(baseCtor.prototype).forEach(name=>{
      derivedCtor.prototype[name] = baseCtor.prototype[name];
    });
  });
}
```

The code in Listing 4.6 demonstrates how mixins can be used in practice. The `AddConstant` class has a property called `num1` and a method called `addNum`. The `SubtractConstant` class has a property called `num2` and a method called `subtractNum`. The `AddSubtract` class combines the members of both classes.

**Listing 4.6: ch4/mixin/src/app/app.ts**

```
// First class to be mixed in
class AddConstant {

  public num1: number;
  public addNum(n: number): number {
    return n + this.num1;
  }
}

// Second class to be mixed in
class SubtractConstant {

  public num2: number;
  public subtractNum(n: number): number {
    return n - this.num2;
  }
}

// Class to receive mixins
class AddSubtract implements AddConstant, SubtractConstant {

  // Declare properties
  public num1 = 5;
  public num2 = 7;

  // Declare methods using function types
  public addNum: (n: number) => number;
  public subtractNum: (n: number) => number;

  public addSubtract(x: number) {
    return this.addNum(x) + this.subtractNum(x);
  }
}
```

```
// Mix the classes together
applyMixins(AddSubtract, [AddConstant, SubtractConstant]);

// Define the applyMixins function
function applyMixins(derivedCtor: any, baseCtors: any[]) {
 baseCtors.forEach(baseCtor => {
  Object.getOwnPropertyNames(baseCtor.prototype).forEach(name =>
  {
    derivedCtor.prototype[name] = baseCtor.prototype[name];
  });
 });
}

let test = new AddSubtract();
let ans = test.addSubtract(9);  // (9 + 5) + (9 - 7) = 16
```

The `AddSubtract` class declares the `addNum` and `subtractNum` methods, but doesn't provide any code. The behavior of `addNum` and `subtractNum` is provided by the mixed-in classes, `AddConstant` and `SubtractConstant`. It's interesting to note that setting a property's value in `AddConstant` and `SubtractConstant` has no effect on the property in the `AddSubtract` class.

Members of the mixed-in classes must be public in order to be incorporated into another class. That is, if `AddConstant` contains a private property, it can't be mixed into another class. If the property is protected, it still can't be mixed in because the other class isn't a subclass.

# 4.6 Summary

This chapter has discussed classes, interfaces, and mixins, but the emphasis must be placed on classes. Classes are like cookie cutters. They define the shape and properties of a cookie, but they aren't cookies. Just as pressing a cookie cutter into dough creates new cookies, a class can instantiate new objects with code like `new Cookie()`.

Every class can define its data (properties) and behavior (methods). These features are collectively called members, and by default, every member is publicly accessible. If a member is declared as `protected`, it can be accessed by its class and by any subclass. If a member is `private`, it can only be accessed in the class in which it's defined.

After introducing classes, this chapter explained a number of related characteristics. When coding TypeScript classes, it's vital to understand inheritance, constructors, the `this` keyword, and method overriding. Other topics, such as getter/setter methods and static members, are helpful to know but not as critical.

A class can only extend one other class, but it can implement multiple interfaces. Interfaces are similar to classes, but their properties must be undeclared and their methods must not have any code. If a class implements an interface, it is obligated to declare the interface's properties and provide a code block for each of its methods. TypeScript also supports interfaces that define specific types of functions and arrays.

If a class's properties aren't assigned to values and its methods have no code, another class can implement it as if it were an interface. With mixins, a class can implement multiple classes regardless of whether their methods have code. Mixins are interesting because they incorporate features from implemented classes into a composite class.

The subject of object-oriented programming is far broader and more interesting than this chapter has presented. Formal computer scientists take this topic very seriously, and for a proper discussion, I recommend *Object-Oriented Analysis and Design with Applications* by Grady Booch and Robert A. Maksimchuk.

# Chapter 5

# Declaration Files and the Document Object Model (DOM)

This chapter discusses two topics that every TypeScript developer should be familiar with: declaration files and the document object model (DOM). Declaration files are easy to understand. As the name implies, a declaration file provides declarations of TypeScript functions and data structures. These files become important when you want to access a JavaScript file in TypeScript code.

The DOM is more complicated, but it's a crucial (and fascinating) subject to know. TypeScript provides a series of interfaces and classes that represent aspects of a web page. These data structures provide methods that make it possible to create, read, modify, and delete a page's elements.

Most of this chapter is devoted to accessing the DOM in TypeScript, but it's not important to know every class and method. The primary goal is to become familiar with the underlying concepts.

## 5.1 Declaration Files

If you look in the lib folder of the TypeScript installation directory, you'll see a number of files with the suffix *.d.ts. These files contain many declarations of functions and classes, but no actual code. For this reason, they're called *declaration files*, and they make it possible for TypeScript code to access untyped JavaScript code. This section explains how to write these files and how to use them to access third-party JavaScript libraries such as jQuery.

### 5.1.1 Ambient Declarations and Declaration Files

In addition to accessing external files, it's important to know how to access external JavaScript libraries such as jQuery. This can be difficult because we don't want the compiler to analyze the library's code every time we build an application. To keep the compiler happy, we need to declare external elements with special declarations called *ambient declarations*.

When the compiler encounters an ambient declaration, it accepts the declaration and doesn't care about the element's actual value or implementation. An ambient declaration is similar to a regular declaration, but starts with the `declare` keyword. Ambient declarations must be placed in special files called *declaration files*, and every declaration file has the suffix *.d.ts.

An example will demonstrate how ambient declarations make it possible to access JavaScript in TypeScript code. Listing 5.1 presents a simple JavaScript function:

**Listing 5.1: ch5/declaration_demo/src/app/addNum.js**

```
// A simple function to be accessed in TypeScript
function addNum(num) {
  return num + 17;
}
```

To access `addNum` in TypeScript, the first step is to create a *.d.ts file that declares the function. By convention, the name of the declaration file is the same as the JavaScript file. Listing 5.2 shows what addNum.d.ts looks like:

**Listing 5.2: ch5/declaration_demo/src/app/addNum.d.ts**

```
// TypeScript declaration of a JavaScript function
declare function addNum(x: number): number;
```

The compiler needs to be informed of the declaration file's name and location, and this can be accomplished by inserting src/app/addNum.d.ts in the `files` array of tsconfig.json. Once this is done, `addNum` can be called in TypeScript as if it was a regular function. This is demonstrated in Listing 5.3, which invokes the `addNum` function declared in addNum.d.ts.

**Listing 5.3: ch5/declaration_demo/src/app/app.ts**

```
let ans = addNum(9);
document.write("ans = " + ans);
```

The JavaScript file being accessed must be included in the web page in addition to the compiled JavaScript. For this reason, ch5/declaration_demo/src/index.html has two `<script>` elements—one for app.js and one for addNum.js.

### 5.1.2 DefinitelyTyped and jQuery

Many declaration files are freely available on the Internet. One particularly helpful resource is DefinitelyTyped, which is located at https://github.com/DefinitelyTyped/DefinitelyTyped. The types directory of this repository contains more than a thousand declaration files that can be accessed in TypeScript.

Instead of manually copying files from DefinitelyTyped, you can install declaration files through npm. Declaration files are provided in packages named @types/xyz. As an example, the following command installs declaration files related to jQuery:

```
npm install @types/jquery
```

When the installation is finished, the node_modules directory will contain a folder named @types/jquery. This will contain a declaration file, index.d.ts, which declares the many functions and structures provided by the jQuery framework.

Unfortunately, jQuery's functions and structures can't be accessed directly. As with many declaration files provided through DefinitelyTyped, the functions and structures must be accessed through a container structure called a *module*. A full discussion of modules will have to wait until Chapter 7, but for now, there are two important points to know:

1. For packages obtained through DefinitelyTyped, the name of a module is the same as that of its package (without @types).
2. The `import` statement makes it possible to access a module's functions and structures in TypeScript.

For jQuery, the module's name is `jquery` and the `import` statement can be written as follows:

```
import $ from 'jquery';
```

As a result, `$` will be available throughout the TypeScript file. This makes it possible to perform regular jQuery operations such as selecting elements and performing actions on them. Because the jQuery package was installed through npm, there's no need to update tsconfig.json with the name of the declaration file.

# 5.2 The Document Object Model (DOM)

According to the World Wide Web Consortium (W3C), the document object model (DOM) is a high-level methodology to "allow programs and scripts to dynamically access and update the content, structure and style of documents."

The W3C's specification defines terms and conventions that can be customized for different programming languages. Here are four points defined by the standard:

- Every document has a tree structure made up of connected nodes. There are many types of nodes, including document nodes, element nodes, and text nodes.
- Every HTML element corresponds to an element node, and the root element node corresponds to the top-level `<html></html>` element.
- If an element displays text, the text is separated into a text node that is a child of the element node.
- The entire tree structure is contained inside the document node.

This model has been implemented in many programming languages, including JavaScript, C/C++, and Java. The goal of this section is to explain how to access the model in TypeScript. The TypeScript DOM is nearly identical to the JavaScript DOM, but the methods are provided in a series of TypeScript interfaces.

## 5.2.1 Interfaces in the TypeScript DOM

TypeScript provides a vast assortment of interfaces that represent HTML elements. These include `HTMLBlockElement`, `HTMLButtonElement`, and `HTMLParagraphElement`. These data structures form TypeScript's implementation of the document object model, or DOM. The better you understand these interfaces, the better you'll understand how to access a document's elements in TypeScript.

Figure 5.1 depicts an abridged inheritance hierarchy of the different interfaces. As shown, all of the HTML elements are descendants of the `EventTarget` interface. Every `EventTarget` can have an associated event listener to respond to user events, and a later section will explain how event listeners work.

The first subinterface of `EventTarget` is `Node`, and its subinterfaces include `Document`, `Element`, and `Attr`. Below `Element`, the `HTMLElement` interface has a subinterface for each different type of element in a web page.

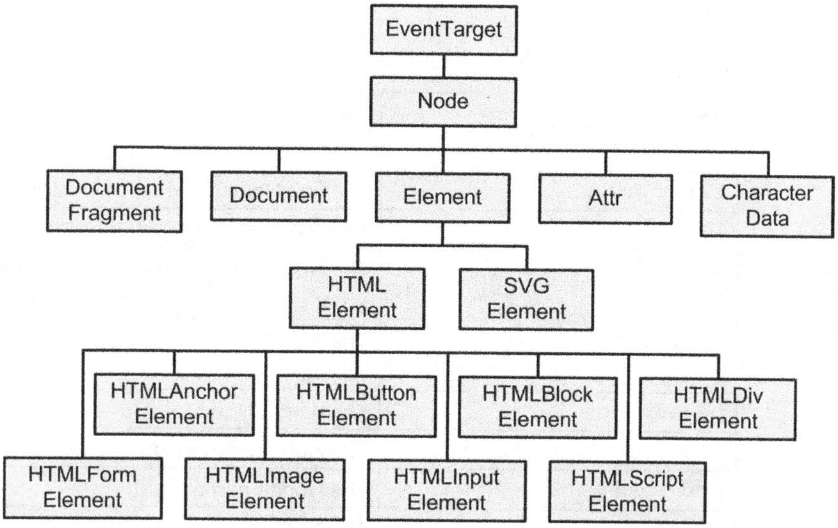


**Figure 5.1 Inheritance Hierarchy of TypeScript's DOM Classes (Abridged)**

This discussion presents many, but not all, of the interfaces in Figure 5.1. We'll look at the `Node` interface first, followed by the `Document`, `Element`, and `HTMLElement` interfaces. Then I'll present a handful of element-specific interfaces and show how they can be used.

**NOTE**

The DOM manipulation methods discussed in this chapter can be used to read and modify a web page, but this book's goal is to present web development with Angular. These methods are fine for analyzing and debugging applications, but for regular web development, I recommend using Angular instead. As later chapters will show, the Angular framework provides a great deal of power and elegance with a minimum of code.

## 5.2.2 The Node Interface

Every element in an HTML document, including the document itself, is represented by a node in the document tree. In TypeScript, the `Node` interface defines properties and methods that every node can access. Table 5.1 lists many of these interface members and provides a description of each.

**Table 5.1**
Members of the Node Interface

| Member | Description |
|---|---|
| `childNodes` | The NodeList containing the Node's children |
| `firstChild` | The first Node in the set of children |
| `lastChild` | The last Node in the set of children |
| `nextSibling` | The Node immediately following this Node in the parent's set of children |
| `previousSibling` | The Node immediately preceding this Node in the parent's set of children |
| `parentNode` | The parent Node |
| `ownerDocument` | The Node corresponding to the Node's document |
| `nodeName` | The Node's name |
| `nodeType` | The Node's type |
| `textContent` | The Node's text content |
| `appendChild(Node)` | Adds a Node to the Node's list of children |
| `hasChildNodes()` | Identifies if the Node has children |
| `insertBefore (Node child, Node ref)` | Makes the Node a child just before the ref child |
| `removeChild(Node n)` | Removes the Node from the list of children |
| `replaceChild (Node new, Node old)` | Replaces the old child Node with the new Node |

The members of the `Node` interface accomplish three main tasks:

1. Access other nodes in the document
2. Provide information about the `Node`
3. Manage the `Node`'s children

Methods in the first category make it possible to traverse the document's node structure. Any `Node` can access the `Document` node by accessing the `ownerDocument` member. Then an application can iterate through the `Document`'s children, and their children, and so on. In addition, the `Node` methods make it possible to access a `Node`'s parent and siblings.

Every `Node` has a name, type, and value. Their values depend on the `Node` subclass. For example, if the `Node` is an `Element`, its name will equal that of its corresponding HTML tag. If the `Node` is an `Attr`, its value will equal the text in the corresponding element. This will be demonstrated in the example DOM analysis application presented later in this section.

Every `Node` can access its children through a `NodeList` provided by the `childNodes` member. `NodeList` doesn't implement the `Iterable` interface, so if you want to iterate through a `Node`'s children, you can obtain the number of children with `NodeList.length` and access the `NodeList` as an array with each index.

The members listed in the table make it possible to add and remove a `Node`'s children. This may not seem exciting at first, but they allow you to update a document's content programmatically. The example code at the end of this section demonstrates how this can be accomplished.

### 5.2.3 The Document Interface

Every web page has a single `Document` node that represents the entire document. By accessing this, an application can create, read, modify, or delete `Elements` in the page. In TypeScript, a document can be accessed through the `document` object. Alternatively, a `Node` can access the `Document` through its `ownerDocument` property.

In addition to interacting with `Elements`, the properties and methods of the `Document` interface provide information about the web page such as its URL and title. Table 5.2 lists 20 members of the `Document` interface.

**Table 5.2**

Members of the Document Interface (Abridged)

| Method | Description |
|---|---|
| `URL` | The Document's URL |
| `activeElement` | The Element with focus |
| `alinkColor` | The color of active hyperlinks |
| `all` | Returns an HTMLCollection containing the Document's elements |
| `body` | The HTMLElement corresponding to the body |
| `characterSet` | The Document's character set |
| `cookie` | The Document's cookie |
| `documentElement` | The root node of the Document |

| | |
|---|---|
| `head` | The HTMLElement corresponding to the page's head |
| `images` | The HTMLCollection containing the image elements |
| `referrer` | The URL that directed the user to the Document's page |
| `title` | The Document's title |
| `createElement(string tag)` | Creates and returns an HTMLElement of the specified type |
| `focus()` | Sets focus |
| `getElementById(string)` | Returns the HTMLElement with the given ID |
| `getElementsByClassName(string)` | Returns the HTMLElements with the given class |
| `getElementsByName(string)` | Returns the HTMLElements with the given name |
| `getElementsByTagName(string)` | Returns the HTMLElements with the given tag |
| `write(...content: string[])` | Writes an expression to the window |
| `writeln(...content: string[])` | Writes an expression to the window followed by a new line |

For the most part, these members are straightforward to understand. Many of the properties return `HTMLCollections`, which are essentially arrays of `Elements`. That is, this interface provides a `length` property and an `Element` can be accessed by following the collection with `[`*`index`*`]`.

The `createElement` method makes it possible to create new `Elements` using TypeScript's DOM. This accepts the name of a tag and returns the corresponding `HTMLElement`. The following code demonstrates how this can be used to create a button element:

```
let element: HTMLButtonElement = document.createElement("button");
```

Creating an `Element` doesn't add it to the `Document`. To add a new `Element`, it must be appended to the list of children of an existing `Node` using one of the methods in Table 5.1, such as `appendChild`. For example, the following code creates an `HTMLTableElement` and adds it to the document's body:

```
let table: HTMLTableElement = document.createElement("table");

document.body.appendChild(table);
```

Four of the methods in the table return HTMLElements according to a given criteria. An Element's ID is unique, so getElementById returns at most one HTMLElement. In contrast, getElementsByClassName, getElementsByName, and getElementsByTagName return a container of HTMLElements. This container is a NodeListOf, which can be accessed like an array of Nodes.

For example, <code> elements are represented by HTMLPhraseElements. The following code obtains a NodeListOf containing the document's <code> elements and iterates through them:

```
let codeList: NodeListOf<HTMLPhraseElement> =
       document.getElementsByTagName("code");
for (let i = 0; i < codeList.length; i++) {
  process(codeList[i]);
}
```

The Document's write and writeln methods are also particularly helpful as they make it possible to print output to the page. This book's TypeScript code examples rely on these methods to display processing results.

The Document interface doesn't provide any methods for deleting an Element. To delete an Element, you must access its parent Node and remove it from the parent's list of children.

## 5.2.4 The Element Interface

Each structural piece of a web page is represented by an Element and each Element occupies space in the page. Put another way, every <*tag*></*tag*> pair in an HTML page corresponds to an Element.

After obtaining an Element, you can access a wide array of properties and methods. Table 5.3 lists 16 of them and provides a description of each.

**Table 5.3**

Members of the Element Interface (Abridged)

| Method | Description |
|---|---|
| id | The Element's identifier |
| tagName | The Element's tag |
| className | The Element's class |
| clientHeight, clientWidth | The dimensions of the Element's inner area, including padding but not margin or border |

| | |
|---|---|
| clientLeft, clientTop | The width of the Element's left and top border |
| scrollHeight, scrollWidth | The dimensions of the Element in pixels, including content not visible in the screen |
| scrollLeft, scrollTop | The current positions of the horizontal and vertical scrollbars in pixels |
| getElementsByTagName(String) | Returns a NodeList containing the Element's children by tag name |
| getElementsByClassName(String) | Returns a NodeList containing the Element's children by CSS class name |
| getAttribute(String), setAttribute(String, String), removeAttribute(String) | Returns/sets/removes an attribute |

Most of these are simple to understand. The `getElementsByTagName` and `getElementsByClassName` methods are particularly helpful. These serve the same roles as the `Document` methods with the same name, but they only apply to the `Element` and its children.

### 5.2.5 The HTMLElement Interface

The properties and methods of the `HTMLElement` subinterface provide access to an element's HTML-specific aspects. These aspects include the element's text, style, and HTML content. Table 5.4 lists 17 of these members.

**Table 5.4**

Members of the HTMLElement Interface (Abridged)

| Method | Description |
|---|---|
| title | The element's title |
| hidden | Whether the element is hidden |
| children | The HTMLCollection containing the element's children |
| tabIndex | The element's index in the tab sequence |
| innerText | The element's text without the tags |
| outerText | The element's text, including the tags |
| innerHTML | The element's HTML-formatted text without the tags |
| outerHTML | The element's HTML-formatted text, including the tags |

| | |
|---|---|
| offsetHeight, offsetWidth | The element's dimensions relative to the layout |
| offsetTop, offsetLeft | The pixel offsets between the element and its parent |
| style | The CSSStyleDeclaration that identifies the element's style |
| blur() | Blurs the element's graphical representation |
| contains(HTMLElement) | Identifies whether the HTMLElement is a child |
| focus() | Sets focus on the element |
| setActive() | Makes the element active |

The `style` property makes it possible to read and modify an `HTMLElement`'s style. Its data type is a `CSSStyleDeclaration`, which has a property for each CSS property.

For example, CSS's `color` property is represented by the `color` property of the `CSSStyleDeclaration`. The following code shows how it can be used to change the text color of the `Document`'s `<code>` element to red:

```
let codeList: NodeListOf<HTMLPhraseElement> =
       document.getElementsByTagName("code");

for (let i = 0; i < codeList.length; i++) {
  document.write(codeList[i].style.color = "red");
}
```

When working with `innerText`, `outerText`, `innerHTML`, and `outerHTML`, keep in mind that `outer-` means that the tags are included and `inner-` means that tags aren't included. `innerHTML` and `outerHTML` recognize HTML formatting while `innerText` and `outerText` do not.

## 5.2.6 Subinterfaces of HTMLElement

The `HTMLElement` interface has a subinterface for each type of element in an HTML page. Figure 5.1 illustrated eight subinterfaces, but there are many more. Each subinterface has properties and methods specific to an element's type, and this discussion focuses on four subinterfaces of `HTMLElement`: `HTMLAnchorElement`, `HTMLInputElement`, `HTMLFormElement`, and `HTMLButtonElement`.

For each subinterface, I'll present a handful of the interface's members and show how the corresponding object can be created in code. For the full list, I recommend looking through the lib.d.ts declaration file in the lib folder of the TypeScript installation directory.

## HTMLAnchorElement

Every hyperlink in a web page is represented in the DOM by an `HTMLAnchorElement`. This interface provides a number of properties related to the hyperlink, and four of them are given as follows:

- `href` — the destination URL
- `text` — the displayed text
- `hostname` — the URL's hostname
- `search` — the URL's query string

As an example, the following code creates an `HTMLAnchorElement` that points to http://www.google.com:

```
let link: HTMLAnchorElement = document.createElement("a");
link.href = "http://www.google.com";
link.text = "Google";
document.body.appendChild(link);
```

In addition to the properties listed above, the `HTMLAnchorElement` interface provides the `rel` property, which represents the relationship between the current document and the linked document. This property can be set to `prev`, `next`, `help`, `tag`, and many other values.

## HTMLInputElement

An `HTMLInputElement` corresponds to an `<input>` element in a web page. An `<input>` element's `type` attribute can be set to one of many values including `button`, `checkbox`, `email`, `file`, and `date`. This is reflected by the interface's properties, which include the following:

- `type` — the value of the element's `type` attribute
- `name` — the name associated with the input element
- `value` — the text displayed by the element
- `checked` — the checked state of the element (if `type` is set to `checkbox`)
- `files` — a `FileList` containing selected files (if `type` is set to `file`)
- `maxLength` — maximum number of characters allowed in the element
- `height/width` — dimensions of the input element
- `selectionStart/selectionEnd` — index of the selection's start and end

The following code demonstrates how to create an <input> element that receives up to 15 characters:

```
let input: HTMLInputElement = document.createElement("input");
input.maxLength = 15;
input.value = "First name";
input.name = "fname";
document.body.appendChild(input);
```

The `HTMLInputElement` also provides two properties that simplify the validation process. If the `required` property is set to true, the element won't be valid until the user has provided a value. Similarly, if the `pattern` property is set, the element won't be valid until the user's value matches the given pattern.

## HTMLFormElement

Chapter 13 discusses the Reactive Forms API, which makes it possible to construct form-based components with Angular. To create a form in basic TypeScript, you need to add an `HTMLFormElement` to the document. This interface provides properties that read and configure the form's behavior, and five of them are given as:

- `name` — the value of the element's `name` attribute
- `action` — identifies where to send the form's data
- `method` — the HTTP method used to send a request to the server (`get` or `post`)
- `elements` — an `HTMLCollection` containing the form's elements
- `length` — the number of elements contained in the form

In addition, the `HTMLFormElement` interface also provides a handful of helpful methods. The `checkValidity()` method examines the form's elements and returns whether the form is valid. The `submit()` method submits the form to the address given by the `action` property.

## HTMLButtonElement

No HTML form is complete without a Submit button, and every button in a web page is represented by an `HTMLButtonElement` in the DOM. Each button has a `type` attribute that can be set to `button`, `reset`, or `submit`, and many attributes provide access to the form containing the button. This is reflected by the properties of the `HTMLButtonElement` interface, and five of them are listed as follows:

- name — the value of the element's name attribute
- type — the value of the element's type attribute (button, reset, or submit)
- form — the HTMLFormElement containing the button
- formAction — identifies where to send the data of the enclosing form
- formMethod — the HTTP method used by the enclosing form (get or post)

It's interesting to note that the formAction and formMethod properties can be used to override the corresponding properties of the form containing the HTMLButtonElement. The following discussion uses the DOM's interfaces to create a form with two input elements and a submit button.

## 5.2.7 Example Code

Listing 5.4 presents the code in the dom_demo project, which demonstrates how the TypeScript DOM can be employed to create a form. Figure 5.2 shows what the generated form looks like.

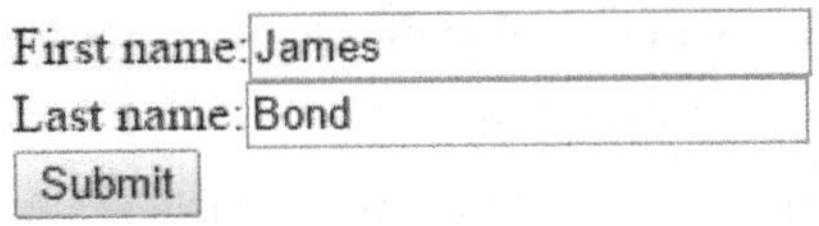


**Figure 5.2 Simple Form Generated by dom_demo.ts**

The project's code uses four of the interfaces presented in this discussion: Document, HTMLFormElement, HTMLInputElement, and HTMLButtonElement. It also creates two HTMLLabelElements to serve as labels and two HTMLBRElements to provide line breaks.

The <input> elements have their required attributes set to true, so the form can't be submitted until both have values. When the form is submitted, its data is sent to a URL named recipient.html. This data consists of two strings: a first name (fname) and a last name (lname).

The ch5/dom_demo/src/recipient.html page receives the form's data and executes the code in recipient.ts. This code, presented in Listing 5.5, accesses the page's URL through the Document's URL property. Then it reads the fname and lname parameters from the URL and prints them to the window.

**Listing 5.4: ch5/dom_demo/src/app/app.ts**

```
// Create a form and add it to the document's body
let form = document.createElement("form");
form.action = "./recipient.html";
document.body.appendChild(form);

// Create two labels
let label1 = document.createElement("label");
label1.textContent = "First name:";
let label2 = document.createElement("label");
label2.textContent = "Last name:";

// Create two input elements
let input1 = document.createElement("input");
input1.name = "fname";
input1.required = true;
let input2 = document.createElement("input");
input2.name = "lname";
input2.required = true;

// Create a submit button
let button = document.createElement("button");
button.type = "submit";
button.textContent = "Submit";

// Add the form's elements to the form
form.appendChild(label1); form.appendChild(input1);
form.appendChild(document.createElement("br"));
form.appendChild(label2); form.appendChild(input2);
form.appendChild(document.createElement("br"));
form.appendChild(button);
```

**Listing 5.5: ch5/dom_demo/src/app/recipient.ts**

```
// Access the document's query string
let i = document.URL.indexOf("?");
let queryString = document.URL.substring(i + 1);

// Read parameters from the query string
let params = queryString.split("&");
let paramPair: string[];
for (i = 0; i < params.length; i++) {
  paramPair = params[i].split("=");
  if (paramPair[0] === "fname") {
    document.write("First name: " + paramPair[1] + "<br />");
  } else if (paramPair[0] === "lname") {
    document.write("Last name: " + paramPair[1] + "<br />");
  }
}
```

## 5.3 Analyzing a DOM Tree

When traditional debugging fails, one troubleshooting method involves examining the hierarchy of nodes in the page's document. This is a straightforward task, requiring only the methods of the `Node` interface discussed earlier.

A good way to see how this works is through an example. Consider the following HTML, taken from ch5/dom_tree/src/index.html:

```
<html>
  <head>
    <title>DOM Tree Demonstration</title>
  </head>
  <body>
    <p>This is a paragraph</p>
    <button>This is a button</button>
    <script src="app/app.js"></script>
  </body>
</html>
```

To analyze a page like this, the dom_tree.ts code defines a class called `DomTreeAnalyzer`. Its static `analyze` method iterates through the `Document`'s children and its children's children. Listing 5.6 presents the code.

**Listing 5.6: ch5/dom_tree/src/app/app.ts**

```
class DomTreeAnalyzer {

  public static analyze(children: NodeList) {
    for (let i = 0; i < children.length; ++i) {
      const node = children[i];

      // Print details of each node
      if (node.nodeType === Node.ELEMENT_NODE) {
        console.log("Name: " + node.nodeName);
        console.log("Parent name: " + node.parentNode.nodeName);
        DomTreeAnalyzer.analyze(node.childNodes);
      }
    }
  }
}

// Start with the children of the overall document
DomTreeAnalyzer.analyze(document.childNodes);
```

The `analyze` function checks the `nodeType` of each node to make sure only `Element` nodes are processed. For each `Element`, the class prints its name and the name of its parent. For the example HTML given above, the results printed to the console are given as follows:

```
Name: HTML
Parent name: #document

Name: HEAD
Parent name: HTML

Name: TITLE
Parent name: HEAD

Name: BODY
Parent name: HTML

Name: P
Parent name: BODY

Name: BUTTON
Parent name: BODY

Name: SCRIPT
Parent name: BODY
```

These seven elements form the web page's DOM tree. Figure 5.3 shows what this hierarchy looks like.

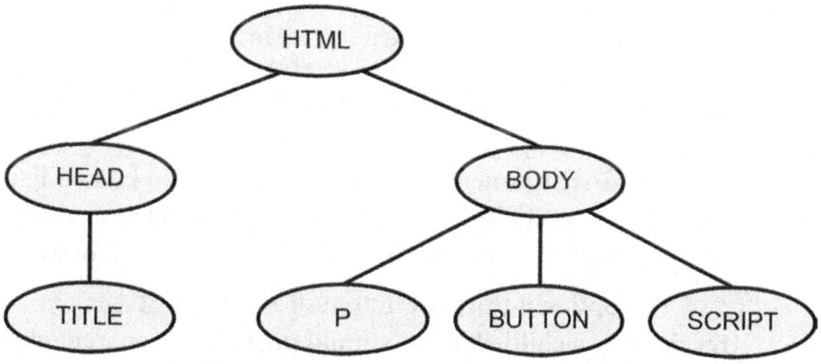


**Figure 5.3 DOM Tree for the Example Web Page**

This is much simpler than a tree generated from a professional web page. But this process of analyzing nodes can be employed for many different types of pages.

# 5.4 Event Processing

In describing the interfaces of TypeScript's DOM implementation, no mention has been made of events. This is because the DOM interfaces provide a vast number of methods that respond to events, and many are specific to Microsoft, such as `MSGestureEnd` and `MSPointerOver`.

For generic events, the `Document` and `HTMLElement` interfaces both provide the same set of members for event handling. These include a series of event-specific properties such as `onclick`, `onkeypress`, and `onscroll`. These properties are set equal to functions that receive objects that contain information for the event.

For example, if the user clicks on an element, the click information will be stored in a `MouseEvent`. This information can be accessed by assigning a function to the element's `onclick` property with code such as the following:

```
let button: HTMLButtonElement = document.createElement("button");
button.onclick = function (me: MouseEvent) {
  console.log("Coords: (" + me.screenX + ", " + me.screenY + ")");
}
```

In addition to these properties, the `Document` and `HTMLElement` interfaces both provide a method called `addEventListener`. This associates the document or element with a function that will be called when the corresponding event occurs. Its general signature is given as follows:

```
addEventListener(type: string,
                 listener: (ev: Event) => any,
                 useCapture?: boolean)
```

The first argument sets the type of event to be handled and the second identifies the function to handle the event. This function receives an object that provides event data (`MouseEvent` for mouse clicks, `KeyboardEvent` for keystrokes, and so on).

The optional third argument of `addEventListener` identifies how an event received by a child element should propagate to parent elements:

- If set to true, the event will be processed by parent elements before child events (outside to inside). This is called *event capturing*.
- If set to false, the event will be processed by child elements before parent events (inside to outside). This is called *event bubbling*, and is the default method of event propagation.

This section focuses on using addEventListener to handle events for HTMLElements. I'll discuss the topics of mouse event handling and key event handling, and then show how both types of event handlers can be implemented in code.

## 5.4.1 Handling Mouse Events

The first argument of addEventListener is a string that identifies the type of event to be handled. For handling mouse-related events, there are 10 possible values. Table 5.5 lists them all.

**Table 5.5**

Mouse Event Strings

| Event String | Action |
|---|---|
| click | User clicks a mouse button |
| dblclick | User double-clicks a mouse button |
| mousedown | User presses a mouse button down |
| mouseup | User raises a mouse button |
| mousemove | The mouse cursor moves |
| mouseenter | The mouse cursor enters the element |
| mouseleave | The mouse cursor leaves the element |
| mouseover | The mouse cursor passes over the element |
| mouseout | The mouse pointer leaves the element and any child elements |
| mousewheel | The user scrolls the mouse wheel |

For example, the following code defines a function to be invoked when the user clicks the button corresponding to the HTMLElement named btn:

```
let btn: HTMLButtonElement = document.createElement("button");
btn.addEventListener("click", function(event: MouseEvent) {
  console.log("The button pressed was: " + event.which);
});
```

As shown, the event-handling function can access information about the mouse click through a MouseEvent. This is provided for each of the events in Table 5.5 except for mouse wheel events, whose handling functions can access a MouseWheelEvent.

A `MouseEvent` provides information about the user's action through a set of read-only properties. These properties include:

- `type` — the name of the event
- `timeStamp` — the time the event occurred
- `srcElement` — the `Element` that dispatched the event
- `which` — the mouse button that was pressed (0–none, 1–left, 2–middle, 3–right)
- `screenX`, `screenY` — event coordinates relative to the screen
- `clientX`, `clientY` — event coordinates relative to the document
- `shiftKey`, `ctrlKey`, `altKey` — identifies if Shift/Ctrl/Alt was pressed

The first three properties are defined in the `Event` interface, which is the superinterface of all event interfaces in the TypeScript DOM. The following code shows how they can be accessed to provide information about a `mouseenter` event:

```
btn.addEventListener("mouseenter", function(event: MouseEvent) {
  console.log("The event's type is: " + event.type);
  console.log("The event time is: " + event.timeStamp);
  console.log("The element that dispatched the event is a: "
    + event.srcElement.tagName + " element");
});
```

As a result of this listener, three statements will be printed to the log each time the mouse cursor enters the button's region.

### 5.4.2 Handling Keystroke Events

The process of handling keystroke events is similar to that of handling mouse events. One difference is that keystroke events are identified by another set of strings. Table 5.6 lists each of them.

**Table 5.6**

Keystroke Event Strings

| Event String | Action |
|---|---|
| `keypress` | User presses and releases a key |
| `keydown` | User presses a key down |
| `keyup` | User releases a key |

To obtain information about the user's action, an event-handling function can access a `KeyboardEvent`. This is shown in the following code:

```
let input: HTMLInputElement = document.createElement("input");
input.type = "text";
input.addEventListener("keypress", function(event: KeyboardEvent)
{
  console.log("The Unicode value of the pressed key is: "
    + event.charCode);
});
```

In this code, the event-handling function accesses the Unicode value of the pressed character through the `charCode` property of the `KeyboardEvent`. Other properties of `KeyboardEvent` are:

- `type` — the name of the event
- `timeStamp` — the time the event occurred
- `srcElement`— the `Element` that dispatched the event
- `key` — a string corresponding to the pressed key
- `locale` — the keyboard's locale
- `shiftKey`, `ctrlKey`, `altKey` — identifies if Shift/Ctrl/Alt was pressed

The `locale` property identifies the locale of the user's keyboard. This doesn't necessarily reflect the user's language.

# 5.5 Summary

The first part of this chapter introduced the important subject of declaration files. A declaration file contains TypeScript declarations of functions and data structures in JavaScript code. These files are vital when you want to access capabilities of an external JavaScript toolset, such as jQuery or Jasmine. You can find a wide assortment of declaration files at https://github.com/DefinitelyTyped/DefinitelyTyped.

The rest of this chapter presented the interfaces and methods that TypeScript provides for accessing the document object model (DOM). At a structural level, every web page consists of a tree of nodes, with a document node serving as the root. By analyzing the root and its children, an application can examine a page's structure and create, read, or modify the elements in the tree.

The TypeScript DOM is complex, composed of a variety of interfaces like `Element`, `HTMLElement`, and `HTMLInputElement`. This may seem bewildering at first, but the more you use the DOM, the more you'll appreciate the power it gives you to read and alter the elements in a web page.

You can use the DOM to build web applications, but I don't recommend it. Instead, I recommend relying on the features provided by the Angular toolset. Chapter 7 will provide a proper introduction to Angular, but the next chapter introduces two advanced aspects of TypeScript development: unit testing and decorators.

# Chapter 6

# Unit Testing and Decorators

This chapter discusses two TypeScript topics that go beyond the fundamentals of the language. Neither of them are deep enough to require a separate chapter, but they're both helpful in TypeScript development:

1. **Unit testing** — using Jasmine and Karma to test TypeScript code
2. **Decorators** — examine and replace aspects of decorated code

Unit testing checks the smallest parts of an application, such as variables and objects, to ensure they're being set to acceptable values. Jasmine is a framework for testing JavaScript, and Karma makes it possible to automate the testing process with multiple browsers. By combining Jasmine and Karma, you can configure complex tests and execute them in an automated fashion. The first part of this chapter explains how this can be done.

The second part explores the topic of decorators. Decorators make it possible to modify aspects of decorated code. As later chapters will explain, Angular's dependency injection process uses decorators. For example, the `@Injectable` decorator tells the framework to recognize classes as service classes.

## 6.1 Unit Testing

The process of unit testing involves isolating small portions of code and verifying that they behave appropriately. One popular tool for JavaScript unit testing is Jasmine, and this section explains how it can be used to test TypeScript.

This section also introduces Karma, a framework for automating tests with multiple browsers. Combined, Jasmine and Karma make it possible to fully automate the unit testing of TypeScript code.

### 6.1.1 Jasmine

A Jasmine test suite consists of regular JavaScript code that calls a set of nested functions. At minimum, a test suite combines three functions:

1. The outermost function is `describe`, which accepts two arguments: a name for the test suite and a function.
2. Inside `describe`'s second argument, the `it` function should be called for each unit test, or *spec*. `it` accepts a name for a spec and a function that defines the spec.
3. Inside `it`'s second argument, `expect` is called to test a JavaScript expression.

An example will clarify how `declare`, `it`, and `expect` work together. Suppose you want to test the functions in this code:

```
let fullName = {firstName: "James", lastName: "Bond"};
function getFirstName() { return fullName.firstName; }
function getLastName() { return fullName.lastName; }
```

The following code defines a test suite with two specs. The first tests the result of `getFirstName()` and the second tests the result of `getLastName()`.

```
describe("The full name", function() {

  it("starts with James", function() {
    expect(getFirstName()).toEqual("James");
  });

  it("ends with Bond", function() {
    expect(getLastName()).toEqual("Bond");
  });
});
```

As shown, the name of the test suite serves as the subject of a sentence that describes the test. The name of each spec provides a phrase that continues the sentence.

When Jasmine runs, it reports **2 Specs, 0 Failures** because both functions execute successfully. Before I explain how to run Jasmine tests, I want to explain how Jasmine can be used to test TypeScript.

## Testing TypeScript

Jasmine was created to test JavaScript, so it doesn't know anything about TypeScript features like classes or interfaces. This isn't a problem. Jasmine functions can be coded in a TypeScript file (*.ts), and when the code is compiled, the specs will test regular JavaScript.

An example will demonstrate how this works. Consider the following class:

```
class FullName {
  constructor(public firstName: string, public lastName: string) {
    this.firstName = "James";
    this.lastName = "Bond";
  }

  public getFirstName() { return this.firstName; }
  public getLastName() { return this.lastName; }
}
```

The following code uses Jasmine's functions to test both methods of the `FullName` class:

```
describe("The full name", function() {

  let fName: FullName;

  beforeEach(function() {
    fName = new FullName();
  });

  it("starts with James", function() {
    expect(fName.getFirstName()).toEqual("James");
  });

  it("ends with Bond", function() {
    expect(fName.getLastName()).toEqual("Bond");
  });

});
```

The `beforeEach` function makes it possible to execute code before any of the specs are executed. In this case, the `fName` variable is set equal to a new `FullName`. When this code is compiled, Jasmine can perform the test as though it was written with regular JavaScript. Similarly, the `afterEach` function makes it possible to execute code after each of the specs have completed.

To convert this to JavaScript, the compiler needs declarations of Jasmine's functions. As discussed in Chapter 5, this can be accomplished using an appropriate declaration file.

The DefinitelyTyped repository (https://github.com/DefinitelyTyped/DefinitelyTyped) provides a declaration file, jasmine.d.ts, that serves the purpose. I've included a copy of jasmine.d.ts in the ch6/jasmine_demo/src/test folder and similar folders containing Jasmine test code.

To tell the compiler about jasmine.d.ts, the declaration file needs to be mentioned in the tsconfig.json configuration file. In the ch6/jasmine_demo project, the `files` field includes src/test/jasmine.d.ts.

## Matchers

So far, code testing has been performed by following `expect` with `toEqual`. This is shown in the following code:

```
expect(fName.getLastName()).toEqual("Bond");
```

`expect` accepts a value of any type, and this value is called the *actual value*. This is usually a variable or the value returned by a method/function.

The result of `expect` is chained to a special function called a *matcher*. A matcher's purpose is to compare the actual value to an expected value or an expected condition. In the above example, the matcher is `toEqual`, but Jasmine provides many more matchers for performing comparisons. Table 6.1 lists 13 of them.

**Table 6.1**

Jasmine Matcher Functions

| Method | Description |
|---|---|
| `toEqual(expected)` | Returns true if the actual value equals the expected value (uses == for the equality test) |
| `toBe(expected)` | Returns true if the actual value equals the expected value (uses === for the equality test) |
| `toBeGreaterThan(expected)` | Returns true if the actual value is greater than the expected value |
| `toBeLessThan(expected)` | Returns true if the actual value is less than the expected value |
| `toMatch(pattern)` | Returns true if the actual value matches the given pattern |

| | |
|---|---|
| `toBeTruthy()` | Returns true if the actual value evaluates to true (true value, non-empty string, number not equal to 0) |
| `toBeFalsy()` | Returns true if the actual value evaluates to false (false value, empty string, number equal to 0) |
| `toBeDefined()` | Returns true if the actual value is defined |
| `toBeUndefined()` | Returns true if the actual value is undefined |
| `toBeNull()` | Returns true if the actual value is null |
| `toThrow(exception)` | Returns true if the actual value throws the given exception |
| `toContain(member)` | Returns true if the actual value is a container that holds the given member |
| `toContain(substring)` | Returns true if the actual value is a string that contains the given substring |

The following examples demonstrate how these matchers can be used:

- `expect(5).toBeGreaterThan(2)` — returns true because 5 is greater than 2
- `expect("Hello").toBeTruthy()` — returns true because the actual value is a non-empty string
- `expect("Hello").toMatch(/ell/)` — returns true because the actual value matches the given pattern
- `expect([1, 2, 3, 4]).toContain(3)` — returns true because the array contains the value 3
- `expect("Hello").toContain("ell")` — returns true because `ell` is a substring of `Hello`

If a matcher function returns true, the corresponding spec returns successfully. If it returns false, the spec flags an error. Jasmine reports successes and errors using HTML, and the following discussion explains how to launch tests and view the results.

## Launching and Viewing a Jasmine Test

Jasmine tests are launched when the test code is loaded in a web page. The ch6/jasmine_demo project shows how this works. The src/index.html file loads a series of required Jasmine scripts. In its body, it loads the file to be tested (app/app.js) and the file containing the tests (test/test.js). Listing 6.1 shows the content of src/index.html.

**Listing 6.1: ch6/jasmine_demo/src/index.html**

```
<html>
  <head>
    <title>Jasmine Demonstration</title>
    <link rel="stylesheet" href="https://cdnjs.cloudflare.com/
      ajax/libs/jasmine/2.6.1/jasmine.min.css">
    <script src="https://cdnjs.cloudflare.com/ajax/libs/
      jasmine/2.6.1/jasmine.min.js"></script>
    <script src="https://cdnjs.cloudflare.com/ajax/libs/
      jasmine/2.6.1/jasmine-html.min.js"></script>
    <script src="https://cdnjs.cloudflare.com/ajax/libs/
      jasmine/2.6.1/boot.min.js"></script>
  </head>
  <body>
    <script src="./app/app.js"></script>
    <script src="./test/test.js"></script>
  </body>
</html>
```

In the ch6/jasmine_demo project, the test code is in the src/test/test.ts file. The test suite performs three specs based on the `ExampleClass` file defined in src/app/app.ts. Listing 6.2 shows what the test code looks like.

**Listing 6.2: ch6/jasmine_demo/src/test/test.ts**

```
describe("The example", () => {

  // Initialize variable
  let example: ExampleClass;
  beforeEach(() => { example = new ExampleClass(); });

  // Perform tests
  it("should be colored red", () => {
    expect(example.color).toBe("red"); });

  it("and the number should be greater than 4", () => {
    expect(example.number).toBeGreaterThan(4); });

  it("and the truth property should be true", () => {
    expect(example.truth).toBeTruthy(); });
});
```

If you load the web page in a browser, the Jasmine framework will display the results of the specs in the test suite. Figure 6.1 shows what the result looks like.

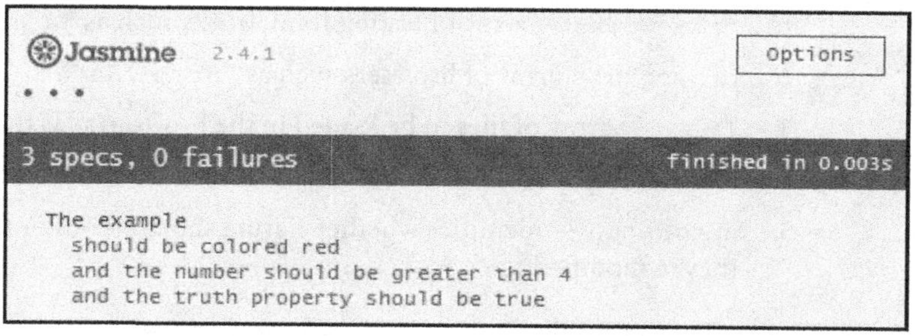


**Figure 6.1 A Successful Jasmine Test Suite with Three Specs**

A green stripe indicates that each spec in the test suite executed successfully. If a spec fails (the matcher function returned false), Jasmine will display a red band and identify which spec failed and how.

The Jasmine web page displays the test results graphically, but this isn't ideal if you want to run tests on the command line. It's also unsuitable if you want to automate the testing process with scripts. These issues can be resolved by running Jasmine tests within the Karma framework.

## 6.1.2 Karma

While Jasmine displays tests in a single browser, Karma can launch tests in multiple browsers and return the results on the command line. This makes it possible to examine test results programmatically. Karma supports a number of different test utilities, but this discussion focuses on using Karma to automate Jasmine tests.

In the Node.js environment, the Karma toolset is provided in the karma package. Karma-Jasmine integration is provided in the karma-jasmine package. The install script in this book's example code installs both.

### Configuring Karma

To execute tests, Karma needs a configuration file that identifies which files to test and the manner in which the tests should be performed. The simplest way to construct this file is to run `karma init` at the command line. This asks a series of questions and generates a configuration file called karma.conf.js.

karma.conf.js defines a function named `module.exports` that calls another function named `config.set`. This accepts a configuration object whose keys should include the following:

1. `frameworks` — array of testing frameworks such as `jasmine`, `mocha`, and `qunit`
2. `browsers` — array of browsers such as `Chrome`, `Safari`, and `Firefox`
3. `files` — array of files to be loaded in the browser(s) as the tests are run
4. `singleRun` — identifies whether Karma should run its tests and exit
5. `autoWatch` — identifies whether Karma should monitor files and run tests when they're modified

For example, the ch6/karma_demo project provides configuration information in its src/test/karma.conf.js file. Listing 6.3 presents its content:

**Listing 6.3: ch6/karma_demo/src/test/karma.conf.js**

```
module.exports = function(config) {
  config.set({

    // Testing framework to be executed
    frameworks: ["jasmine"],

    // Browsers to launch tests with
    browsers: ["Chrome"],

    // Files to load in the browser
    files: ["../app/app.js", "./test.js"],

    // Should Karma run its tests and exit?
    singleRun: true,

    // Should files be monitored for changes?
    autoWatch: false
  })
}
```

Karma requires special packages for different browsers, as follows:

- Chrome — karma-chrome-launcher
- Safari — karma-safari-launcher
- Internet Explorer — karma-ie-launcher
- Firefox — karma-firefox-launcher
- Opera — karma-opera-launcher

Karma has more configurable features than those listed above. To see the full list, visit the main site at http://karma-runner.github.io/0.13/config/configuration-file.html.

## Executing Karma Tests

Once the configuration file is ready, executing a Karma test requires two simple steps:

1. At a command line, change to a directory containing the configuration file
2. Execute `karma start`

The ch6/karma_demo project contains the same test as in the ch6/jasmine_demo project discussed earlier. When I change to the src/test folder and run `karma start`, the results of the Karma/Jasmine test suite are given as follows:

```
Connected on socket HnkAhQplX9xj6mrxAAAA with id 11584313

Chrome 58.0.3029 (Windows 7 0.0.0):
Executed 1 of 3 SUCCESS
(0 secs / 0.003 secs

Chrome 58.0.3029 (Windows 7 0.0.0):
Executed 2 of 3 SUCCESS
(0 secs / 0.003 secs

Chrome 58.0.3029 (Windows 7 0.0.0):
Executed 3 of 3 SUCCESS
(0 secs / 0.003 secs

Chrome 58.0.3029 (Windows 7 0.0.0):
Executed 3 of 3 SUCCESS
(0.009 secs / 0.003 secs)
```

This output is more convenient to analyze than a Jasmine test, which requires the user to open a browser to view the test results.

Karma's operation can be improved further by changing its reporter to display the titles of Jasmine specs instead of simply `1 of 3` and `2 of 3`. To configure this, install the karma-spec-reporter package using npm. Then, in the karma.conf.js file, set the `reporters` key equal to an array containing only `"spec"`.

Jasmine and Karma are excellent tools for testing TypeScript code. Another reason to learn about them involves Protractor. The Protractor framework relies on Jasmine to test Angular web components. Chapter 17 explains how Protractor makes it possible to perform end-to-end testing.

# 6.2 Decorators

Decorators make it possible to alter the characteristics of classes, methods, properties, and parameters. They play an important role in Angular, which uses parameter decorators as part of its dependency injection process.

From a developer's point of view, a TypeScript decorator is a special type of function. Every decorator function has three properties:

1. It belongs to one of four function types: `PropertyDecorator`, `ClassDecorator`, `MethodDecorator`, or `ParameterDecorator`.
2. Decorator functions are invoked by preceding a portion of code with the function's name preceded by `@`.
3. Decorators are read by the compiler, which modifies the affected code as it generates JavaScript. In other words, the code in a decorator function executes at runtime, but the code modification is performed during compilation.

This section discusses the four types of decorator functions. The last part of the section presents an application that demonstrates how they can be used in practice.

## 6.2.1 Property Decorators

A property decorator makes it possible to access a class's property when it's read or written. In the following code, the `lastName` property of the `Employee` class has a decorator called `nameChange`:

```
class Employee {

  @nameChange
  public lastName: string;

  public firstname: string;

  constructor(...) { ... }
}
```

The behavior of a property decorator is determined by a function of the `PropertyDecorator` type. This function doesn't really change an existing property. Instead, it deletes the existing property and creates a new property with the same name. This replacement is made possible by `Object.defineProperty`, whose signature is given as follows:

```
Object.defineProperty(target: Object, key: string, desc: Object)
```

The first parameter is the `Object` containing the property and the second is the property's key. `desc` is the property's descriptor, and its fields determine the property's behavior. If the property is intended to have getter/setter methods, its descriptor must provide values for the following fields:

- `enumerable` — identifies if the property should be part of the object's property enumeration
- `configurable` — identifies if the property can be changed or deleted
- `get` — the function to be invoked when the property's value is read
- `set` — the function to be invoked when the property's value is written

Now let's look at how to code the decorator function. The signature of a `PropertyDecorator` function is as follows:

```
function func_name(target: Object, key: string): void;
```

The first parameter is the prototype of the object to be modified. The second is the name of the property's key. To modify a class's property, the function must perform three steps:

1. Delete the existing property by calling `delete`.
2. Create a new property by calling `Object.defineProperty` with a suitable descriptor.
3. Provide code for the new property's getter and setter methods.

The following code shows how these steps can be accomplished. The function's name is `propChange`, and as specified in `Object.defineProperty`, the property's getter method is `getFunc` and its setter method is `setFunc`.

```
function propChange(target: any, key: string) {

  // Access the property value
  let prop = target[key];

  // The getter method
  let getFunc = function () {
    prop += ", Esquire";
    return prop;
  };
```

```
  // The setter method
  let setFunc = function (newProp: string) {
    prop = newProp + ", Jr.";
    return prop;
  };

  // Delete existing property
  if (delete target[key]) {

    // Create new property
    Object.defineProperty(target, key, {
      enumerable: true,
      configurable: true,
      get: getFunc,
      set: setFunc
    });
  }
}
```

In this code, the first two arguments of `Object.defineProperty` are the same arguments passed into `propChange`'s parameter list. The third argument of `Object.defineProperty` provides a description of the new property, including the names of its getter method (`getFunc`) and setter method (`setFunc`).

This descriptor performs two actions. When the decorated property is read, the descriptor adds `", Esquire"` to the property's value. When the property is written, it adds `", Jr."` to the property's value. This isn't particularly useful, but it's easy to use similar descriptors to restrict access to data or check for errors.

### 6.2.2 Class Decorators

To understand class decorators, it's important to see how JavaScript constructors relate to an object's prototype. There are three points to keep in mind:

1. A JavaScript function becomes a constructor when it's called with the `new` keyword.
2. If `Thing()` is a function, calling `new Thing()` returns an object `t` such that `t.constructor = Thing` and `t instanceof Thing` returns true.
3. Every function has a property called `prototype`. When `new Thing()` is called, every property of `Thing`'s `prototype` becomes a property of the returned object.

If this makes sense, class decorators won't pose much difficulty. Put simply, a class decorator receives a constructor and can use it to modify aspects of the class. To be precise, it accesses the constructor's `prototype` property to modify objects created by the constructor.

In code, a class decorator is a function of the `ClassDecorator` type, and its signature is given as follows:

```
function func_name(target: TFunction): TFunction;
```

`TFunction` is any type that extends the `Function` type. The function passed to *`func_name`* is the constructor of the decorated class. *`func_name`*'s return value is a replacement function to serve as the new constructor.

This replacement constructor has complete control over how new instances are created. In coding the constructor, there are three items to consider:

1. A new constructor can invoke the old constructor with the `apply` method.
2. If the old constructor accepted arguments, the new constructor can access the same arguments in the `apply` method.
3. To ensure that `instanceof` works properly, the new constructor's `prototype` property should be set equal to the old constructor's `prototype` property.

An example will clarify how class decorators work. Consider the following class, whose constructor accepts two arguments:

```
@changeColor
class Balloon {
  constructor(public color: string, public volume: number) {}
}
```

The `changeColor` decorator receives the old constructor and returns a new one that always sets the `color` property to `blue`.

```
function changeColor(oldFunc: any): any {

  // Define the new constructor
  let newFunc = function (...args: any[]) {

    // Create the object with a different argument
    let newObj: any = function () {
      if (args.length === 2) {
        args[0] = "blue";
      }
      return oldFunc.apply(this, args);
    }
    newObj.prototype = oldFunc.prototype;
    return new newObj();
  }
```

```
    // Set prototype of new constructor
    newFunc.prototype = oldFunc.prototype;

    return newFunc;
}
```

This function accepts the `oldFunc` constructor and returns the `newFunc` constructor. `newFunc` performs the same operation as `oldFunc` and sets its `prototype` property to that of `oldFunc`. The only difference is that `newFunc` changes the first argument so that the `color` property is set to `blue`.

## 6.2.3 Method Decorators

In a JavaScript object, a method is like any other property except that it defines a function. For this reason, method decorators have a lot in common with property decorators. While a property decorator returns a replacement property, a method decorator returns a function definition to replace the old one.

The signature of a method decorator function is given as follows:

```
function func_name(target: Object, key: string,
                   desc: TypedPropertyDescriptor<T>):
    TypedPropertyDescriptor<T>;
```

The first two arguments are like those of a property decorator—the first provides the object containing the method and the second identifies the method's name. The third parameter implements the `TypedPropertyDescriptor<T>` interface, which is defined in the following way:

```
interface TypedPropertyDescriptor<T> {
  enumerable?: boolean;
  configurable?: boolean;
  writable?: boolean;
  value?: T;
  get?: () => T;
  set?: (value: T) => void;
}
```

For method decorators, `T` represents the `Function` type. Therefore, `desc.value` and `target[key]` both return the method's function definition. The primary job of a method decorator is to change `desc.value` so that it provides an updated function definition.

In the following class, the `@prependTilde` method decorator makes it possible to modify the behavior of the `appendExclamation` method.

```
class OddPunctuation {

  @prependTilde
  appendExclamation(arg: string): string {
    return arg.concat("!");
  }
}
```

The following code defines a new function that calls the old function (`appendExclamation`) and prepends a tilde to its return value.

```
function prependTilde(target: Object, key: string, desc: any) {

  // Store original function
  let origMethod = desc.value;

  // Define new function
  desc.value = function(...args: any[]) {
    let result = origMethod.apply(this, args);
    return "~".concat(result);
  }

  return desc;
}
```

This decorator updates `desc.value` with a new function definition. This function invokes the original function, which is stored as `origMethod`. Then it modifies the result and returns the modified value.

## 6.2.4 Parameter Decorators

Parameter decorators are unique among the four decorator types because they aren't intended to replace or modify anything. But a parameter decorator can add data to the containing class or method using regular operations.

The signature of a parameter decorator function is given as follows:

```
function func_name(target: Object, key: string | symbol,
                   parameterIndex: number): void;
```

The first parameter provides the containing object, the second identifies the method's name, and the last parameter is the position of the decorated parameter in the method's parameter list. The return value is `void`, which implies that the function isn't intended to replace any portion of the decorated code.

I've verified this behavior with my own experiments. That is, I've tried to modify the decorated parameter's value and its method, but every change is ignored.

Instead of replacing aspects of the decorated code, a parameter decorator can add metadata to the enclosing object. For example, the following parameter decorator adds a new property to the prototype of the enclosing object:

```
function addProp(target: any, key: string, index: number) {
  target.prototype.newProperty = "NewValue";
}
```

This is how dependency injection works in Angular. If a parameter has a special decorator, the framework will understand that it requires a special service.

## 6.2.5 Example Code

The ch6/decorator_demo project demonstrates how all four decorators are used in practice. It defines two nearly-identical classes: `Book` and `DecoratedBook`. The `Book` class has no decorators and `DecoratedBook` has four:

1. `changeProp` — Appends `", Esquire"` to the decorated property when it's read.
2. `changeClass` — Changes the constructor's third argument to `400`.
3. `changeMethod` — Prepends `"more than"` to the result of the annotated method.
4. `changeParam` — Adds a `publisher` property to the object's prototype.

As shown in Listing 6.4, the app.ts code creates two objects with the same parameters:

```
let b = new Book("Herman Melville", "Moby Dick", 544);
let db = new DecoratedBook("Herman Melville", "Moby Dick", 544);
```

The displayed results are markedly different:

- `The book Moby Dick was written by Herman Melville and has 544 pages. The publisher is undefined.`
- `The book Moby Dick was written by Herman Melville, Esquire and has more than 400 pages. The publisher is Harper and Brothers.`

**Listing 6.4: ch6/decorator_demo/src/app/app.ts**

```
// Book without decorators
class Book {
  constructor(public author: string, public title: string,
              public numberOfPages: number) {}

  public displayNumPages(): string {
    return this.numberOfPages.toString();
  }
}

// Book with decorators
@classChange
class DecoratedBook {

  @changeProp
  public author: string;
  public title: string;
  public numberOfPages: number;

  constructor(public a: string, t: string,
              @paramChange n: number) {
    this.author = a;
    this.title = t;
    this.numberOfPages = n;
  }

  @methodChange
  public displayNumPages(): string {
    return this.numberOfPages.toString();
  }
}

// Modify a property
function changeProp(target: any, key: string) {

  let prop = target[key];

  // The getter method
  const getFunc = () => {
    prop += ", Esquire";
    return prop;
  };

  // The setter method
  const setFunc = (newProp: string) => {
    prop = newProp;
    return prop;
  };
```

**Listing 6.4: ch6/decorator_demo/src/app/app.ts (Continued)**

```
    // Delete existing property
    if (delete target[key]) {

      // Create new property
      Object.defineProperty(target, key, {
        configurable: true,
        enumerable: true,
        get: getFunc,
        set: setFunc});
    }
}

// Modify the class's constructor
function classChange(oldFunc: any): any {

  // Define the new constructor function
  const newFunc = (...args: any[]) => {

    // Change the constructor arguments
    const newObj: any = function() {
      if (args.length === 3) {
        args[2] = 400;
      }
      return oldFunc.apply(this, args);
    };
    newObj.prototype = oldFunc.prototype;
    return new newObj();
  };

  // Ensure that instanceof will work properly
  newFunc.prototype = oldFunc.prototype;
  return newFunc;
}

// Modify a method
function methodChange(target: object, key: string, desc: any) {

  // Store original function
  const origMethod = desc.value;

  // Define new function
  desc.value = function(...args: any[]) {
    const result = origMethod.apply(this, args);
    return "more than ".concat(result);
  };
  return desc;
}
```

**Listing 6.4: ch6/decorator_demo/src/app/app.ts (Continued)**

```
// Add a property to the class
function paramChange(target: any, key: string, index: number) {
  target.prototype.publisher = "Harper and Brothers";
}

// Create objects
let b = new Book("Herman Melville", "Moby Dick", 544);
let db = new DecoratedBook("Herman Melville", "Moby Dick", 544);

// Display results
document.writeln("The book ".concat(b.title)
  .concat(" was written by ")
  .concat(b.author).concat(" and has ")
  .concat(b.displayNumPages()).concat(" pages. ")
  .concat("The publisher is ").concat(b["publisher"])
  .concat(".<br />"));
document.writeln("The book ".concat(db.title)
  .concat(" was written by ")
  .concat(db.author).concat(" and has ")
  .concat(db.displayNumPages()).concat(" pages. ")
  .concat("The publisher is ")
  .concat(db["publisher"]).concat("."));
```

In this case, the property decorator modifies the property's value every time its value is read. This means the decorator will keep appending more text with each access.

# 6.3 Summary

This chapter has covered the two important topics of unit testing and decorators. These topics are helpful, but don't be concerned if you don't fully grasp them. You'll still be able to understand the chapters that follow.

The first topic in this chapter involved unit testing. Jasmine tests JavaScript code and displays the results in a web page. It can't be used to test TypeScript directly, but if a TypeScript file is compiled to JavaScript, the Jasmine functions will execute normally. The Karma framework makes it possible to automate Jasmine testing and display the results of each test on a command line.

The second topic dealt with decorators. A decorator is a function that reads and/or replaces aspects of decorated code. A class decorator replaces a class's constructor, a method decorator replaces a method, and a property decorator replaces a property. Parameter decorators do not replace parameters, but they can be used to add metadata.

# Chapter 7

# Modules, Web Components, and Angular

Modular programming is a vital feature of many high-level programming languages, including Python, Java, and C++. This technique involves splitting a program's functionality into independent pieces called modules. These modules interact with each other through standard interfaces. A language that supports modular programming is said to be modular.

To support modularity in JavaScript, the ECMAScript 2015 (ES6) standard defines a format for coding, importing, and exporting modules. TypeScript also supports modules, and the format is nearly identical to that defined in the ES6 format. This chapter begins by explaining how these modules can be coded and compiled.

The next part of the chapter explores the important topic of web components. Web components aren't a TypeScript-specific technology, but are custom user interface elements that can be reused across applications. As defined by the W3C, web components are based on four technologies: custom HTML elements, templates, shadow DOM, and HTML imports.

In essence, the Angular framework makes it possible to create web components using TypeScript modules. This chapter explains what Angular accomplishes and provides a brief overview of the code in an Angular project. Later chapters will flesh out the theory and practice of Angular development.

The last part of the chapter introduces the Angular command-line interface, or CLI. This simplifies many aspects of Angular development, such as creating new projects, building projects, and launching the compiled application. This chapter will walk through the process of generating a simple project and launching it with the CLI.

# 7.1 TypeScript Modules

Chapter 6 briefly mentioned the topic of modules during the discussion of declaration files. TypeScript and the ECMAScript 2015 (ES6) standard both provide modules, and both types of modules serve the same purpose—they serve as containers of one or more variables, functions, interfaces, or classes. The contents of a module are called its *features*.

There are four fundamental points to know about modules:

1. By default, a module's features are hidden from code external to the module.
2. A module can make features accessible to external code using `export` statements.
3. A module can access exported features of another module using `import` statements.
4. Unlike regular JavaScript code, a compiled module can't be directly inserted into HTML. A loader is needed to convert the module into an accessible form.

This section explores the first three points. That is, we'll look at defining modules and then exporting and importing their features. The section ends with a simple example that demonstrates how TypeScript modules can be coded.

## 7.1.1 Defining a Module

There are two primary ways to define a TypeScript module. The first involves preceding a named block with the `module` keyword. As an example, the following code defines a module named `ExampleMod`:

```
module ExampleMod {
  export function addNum(num: number): number {
    return num + 17;
  }
}
```

In this case, the `ExampleMod` module contains one feature: a function called `addNum`. It should be clear that a TypeScript file may contain multiple modules similar to `ExampleMod`.

This code is easy to understand, but the vast majority of TypeScript modules don't use the `module` keyword. Instead, they take advantage of a crucial property: if a TypeScript file calls `import` or `export` at a top level (outside any function, class, or interface), the compiler will recognize the content of the *entire file* as one module. The compiler will name the module according to the file's name without the suffix.

For example, consider the following code:

```
export function addNum(num: number): number {
  return num + 17;
}
```

If this is the only code in a TypeScript file, the compiler will recognize the code as a module definition because `export` is called outside of any code block. The module's name will be set to the file's name without the suffix. That is, if the code is contained in AddNum.ts, the name of the module will be set to AddNum.

### 7.1.2 Exporting Features from a Module

Chapter 3 explained how the `private`, `protected`, and `public` modifiers make it possible to set the accessibility of members in a TypeScript class. In a module, every feature is private (completely inaccessible) unless preceded by `export`.

As an example, the following code defines a simple module:

```
const num = 8;

function findVals() { ... }

export interface ExampleInterface { ... }

class ExampleClass implements ExampleInterface { ... }
```

This module has four features, but because of the `export` keyword, the only feature that can be accessed by external code is `ExampleInterface`. Other modules can access this feature using the `import` keyword, which will be discussed next.

### 7.1.3 Importing Features into a Module

Modules (and any TypeScript code) can use `import` to access features from other modules. TypeScript supports a number of formats for `import` statements, including the following:

- `import {` *`feature`* `} from '`*`module_name`*`';`
- `import {` *`feature1, feature2,`* `... } from '`*`module_name`*`';`
- `import * as` *`name`* `from '`*`module_name`*`';`

In these examples, *feature* is the name of a feature contained in the module named *module_name*. As mentioned earlier, *module_name* is usually the name of the file containing the module's code without the suffix.

To demonstrate how `import` is used, suppose that two functions, `addNum` and `subtractNum`, are exported by a module defined in TwoFuncs.ts. Another module can access the `addNum` function with the following statement:

```
import {addNum} from 'TwoFuncs';
```

As a result of this code, the importing module will be able to invoke `addNum` as if it had been defined inside the importing module. Similarly, the following statement accesses both `addNum` and `subtractNum`:

```
import {addNum, subtractNum} from 'TwoFuncs';
```

Rather than access a module's features directly, it may be helpful to associate them with a name and then access them with dot notation. For example, the following statement imports all the features in `TwoFuncs` and associates them with the name `MyFuncs`.

```
import * as MyFuncs from 'TwoFuncs';
```

Because of this statement, the module can access `addNum` as `MyFuncs.addNum` and `subtractNum` as `MyFuncs.subtractNum`. This dot notation enables the compiler to distinguish external features from similarly-named features in the module.

### 7.1.4 Default Exports and Aliases

If an exported feature is declared as `default`, it can be imported more simply than other members. Consider the following code:

```
export default function addNum(num: number): number {
  return num + 17;
}
```

Because the exported member is default, an `import` statement doesn't need curly braces. So `addNum` can be imported in the following way:

```
import addNum from module_name;
```

An `import` statement can assign an alias to the default feature. The following statement imports the `addNum` function and makes it accessible by the alias `addNumFunc`:

```
import addNumFunc from module_name;
```

To set an alias for a feature that isn't default, it's necessary to use `as alias` inside curly braces. For example, if `NotDefault` is the name of an exported class, the following `import` statement makes it accessible by the alias `ND`:

```
import {NotDefault as ND} from module_name;
```

As a result of this statement, the importing module will be able to access the `ND` feature from *`module_name`* using the alias `NotDefault`.

### 7.1.5 Compiling Modules

If you attempt to compile a module as if it were regular TypeScript, the compiler will flag an error: *Cannot compile modules unless the '--module' flag is provided.* To resolve this error, you need to tell the compiler what type of module it should create.

In tsconfig.json, the module format can be set by providing a value for the `module` property in the `compilerOptions` field. This can be set to one of the following values:

1. `CommonJS` — The CommonJS format (http://www.commonjs.org) makes it possible to use JavaScript in applications outside the browser. This module format is employed by the Node.js framework.
2. `Amd` — The Asynchronous Module Definition (AMD) format was developed as part of the RequireJS framework (http://requirejs.org).
3. `UMD` — The Universal Module Definition (UMD) format was developed to provide compatibility with the CommonJS module format and the AMD module format.
4. `System` — The System.js loading framework (https://github.com/systemjs/systemjs) defines a format for bundling modules.
5. `es2015/es6` — The ECMAScript 2015 specification (ES6) identifies a module format similar to that of TypeScript.
6. `none` — Don't generate code for any of the preceding formats.

If the `target` property is set to anything other than `ES6`, the default module format is `CommonJS`. If `target` is set to `ES6`, the default format is `es2015/es6`. The following discussion will show how TypeScript modules can be compiled.

## 7.1.6 Module Example

The ch7/module_demo project demonstrates how TypeScript modules can be coded and compiled. The src/app folder contains three TypeScript files:

- AddNumbers.ts — Exports a class named `AddNumbers`
- SubtractNumbers.ts — Exports a class named `SubtractNumbers`
- app.ts — Imports the two classes, creates an instance of each class, and then invokes the `printMessage` method of each instance.

Listing 7.1 presents the code of app.ts. It identifies modules using the names of their files without the suffixes.

**Listing 7.1: ch7/module_demo/src/app/app.ts**

```
import { AddNumbers } from './AddNumbers';
import { SubtractNumbers } from './SubtractNumbers';

const addNumbers: AddNumbers = new AddNumbers(3, 5);
document.write(addNumbers.printResult().toString());

const subNumbers: SubtractNumbers = new SubtractNumbers(9, 4);
document.write(subNumbers.printResult().toString());
```

In the tsconfig.json file, the `target` property is set to `ES6` and the `module` property is set to `es6`. This tells the compiler to generate a module in the ES6 format. If you look at the compiled code, you'll see that the only difference is the lack of type declarations. This should make sense. TypeScript is essentially ECMAScript 6 with data types, and an ES6 module is essentially a TypeScript module without types.

Unfortunately, modules can't be loaded into HTML like regular JavaScript code. In the ch7/module_demo project, this means app.js can't be loaded into a web page using a `<script>` element. If you attempt to open src/index.html in a browser, you'll receive an error.

Instead, modules must be processed using a special utility called a *loader*. In some cases, a loader and its modules are combined together into a package called a *bundle*. Unlike modules, bundles can be loaded into a page with `<script>` elements.

At the time of this writing, Angular's preferred loader is Webpack, which is freely available at https://webpack.github.io. In this book, we won't access Webpack directly. Instead, we'll access Webpack through a tool called the Angular command line interface (CLI). A later section of this chapter will discuss the Angular CLI in detail.

# 7.2 Web Components

In the early days of computer programming, software was written in a procedural manner. That is, a program was simply a list of operations to be performed in sequence. It might include loops or if-then structures, but on the whole, it was just one long recipe of instructions.

This was fine for console programs, but as graphical computing rose to prominence, this became unworkable. Even a simple graphical user interface might need tens of thousands of lines of code. This complexity was wonderful for job security, but it was a nightmare to maintain. If a program needed to be changed or upgraded, it was generally easier to rewrite it from scratch than figure out how the original worked.

To remedy this, programmers adopted object-oriented programming, which splits applications into functional parts. This improved software manageability, but more importantly, it allowed programmers to build applications with prebuilt software.

I remember when Microsoft first released its Visual Component Library (VCL). Suddenly, instead of writing applications from scratch, developers could tie existing components together. Applications that would normally take months to write now took days. Job security plummeted, but so too did the number of bugs.

The history of web development is following a similar trajectory. As I write this, most web applications are structured into unwieldy monolithic masses of HTML. If you look at the markup for Google's popular GMail site, you'll find an astounding mess of `<div>`s, each assigning styles and behaviors to its content. A handful of developers may understand it, but for mere mortals, it's completely unmanageable.

To bring the advantages of objects to web development, Google and W3C came up with the idea of web components. Put simply, a web component is a custom HTML tag whose appearance and behavior is kept separate from the rest of the application. By dividing a web application into web components, developers can enjoy the same manageability and code reuse provided by object-oriented development.

Technically speaking, a web component involves four central concepts:

1. Custom HTML elements
2. HTML templates
3. Shadow DOM
4. HTML imports

The goal of this section is to explain these technologies and why they're helpful. The better you understand them, the more comfortable you'll be with web development.

### 7.2.1 Custom HTML Elements

Setting the style and behavior of an HTML element can require a lot of markup. The HTML structure at stackoverflow.com contains up to nine levels of <div> elements just to define a list and a set of labels. Understanding the markup is difficult and it's even harder to upgrade the application and fix errors.

With custom HTML elements, developers can set an element's appearance and behavior without cluttering up the page. For example, instead of placing a <table> inside a set of nested <div>s, a custom table could be defined with the following element:

```
<my-table nrows='4' ncols='5'></my-table>
```

This makes the page easier to read and understand, but a greater benefit is the ability to add components defined by third parties, such as <google-supertable> or <oracle-dbform>. Like many pieces of software, these components will cost money initially, but as the technology matures, they'll be provided freely as open-source.

The official documentation on custom elements can be found at the W3C site at https://w3c.github.io/webcomponents/spec/custom. This presents criteria for the names of custom HTML elements:

- May contain letters, digits, dots, hyphens, and underscores
- Can't contain uppercase letters
- Can't conflict with existing elements or CSS properties
- Must contain at least one hyphen

This makes <ellipse-button> and <hyper-table> valid component names. Invalid names include <customlabel>, <Links-link>, and <super-list!>.

The W3C doesn't provide any guidelines on how to distinguish elements from different organizations, but it's common to precede the component name with the name of the creator.

### 7.2.2 HTML Templates

A web component's structure and appearance is defined by its internal HTML. For example, a web component named <custom-form> will probably contain a <form> element to define the form, and that element may contain multiple <input> elements and a <button> element.

A component's internal HTML is referred to as its *template*. For example, the template of a `<custom-form>` component could be defined in the following way:

```
<template>
  <form>
    Field1: <input type='text' name='field1'><br />
    Field2: <input type='text' name='field2'><br />
    <input type='submit' value='Submit'>
  </form>
</template>
```

Unlike regular markup, a browser doesn't render a component's template when the component's page is loaded. Instead, each `HTMLTemplateElement` has a `content` property that stores the template's content in a `DocumentFragment`. To render a web component's template, its `content` must be specifically integrated into the page.

### 7.2.3 Shadow DOM

Chapter 5 explained how the document object model (DOM) structures elements in a web page. In a regular web page, every element belongs to the same DOM. This means their styles are governed by the same stylesheet and if one element has its `id` attribute set, no other element in the page can have the same `id`.

When a web component is placed into a document, its appearance, behavior, and namespace can be isolated from the rest of the document. For example, suppose that a document specifies that every button should be blue. Does that mean that a web component's button should be blue? Maybe, maybe not. The component's dependence or independence should be determined by the developer, not the document.

To understand how this works in practice, it's important to see the relationship between the elements of a component's template and the DOM tree containing the component. This is a complex topic, and the official documentation (http://w3c.github.io/webcomponents/spec/shadow) defines three fundamental terms:

- *shadow tree* — a tree of nodes associated with a DOM element
- *shadow host* — an element with an associated shadow tree
- *shadow root* — the root node of an element's shadow tree

The shadow host is a regular component in the top-level document. Its shadow root and its children belong to a different node tree. This means the shadow root and its children aren't descendants of the shadow host. It also means that `Document` methods such as `getElementById` won't return an element in the shadow tree.

An example will help make this clear (I hope). Consider the `<custom-form>` element discussed earlier. The `<custom-form>` element is a shadow host, and belongs to the top-level DOM. But the elements in the `<custom-form>` template belong to the component's shadow tree. This shadow tree is commonly referred to as the component's *shadow DOM*.

A shadow host can be accessed with traditional DOM methods like `document.getElementById`. But these methods can't access the nodes of the shadow tree. The W3C documentation defines functions that create and access nodes in the shadow DOM, but this API lies beyond the scope of this book.

## 7.2.4 HTML Imports

The last technology underlying web components may not seem groundbreaking because it involves importing files into a web page. But HTML imports can play an important role in a web component's operation. In markup, an HTML import is a `<link>` element with two important characteristics:

1. The `rel` attribute is set to `import`.
2. The `href` attribute identifies the URL of an HTML file.

For example, the following HTML import reads in a local file called baz.html:

```
<link rel='import' href='../foo/bar/baz.html'>
```

The difference between an HTML import and an `<iframe>`'s file inclusion is that the imported HTML doesn't require a separate frame. The imported HTML is inserted into the main page, but the document model of the imported HTML is kept distinct from the main page's DOM.

The imported HTML can be accessed in JavaScript using the `import` property of the `link` element. For example, the following code accesses the `<link>` element as an `HTMLLinkElement` and then reads its content:

```
var link = document.querySelector('link[rel='import']');
var content = link.import;
```

With HTML imports, a web page can import web components from a server or a repository. Then JavaScript code can integrate the web component's template into the page. HTML imports aren't important for Angular, but they're required by Google's Polymer toolset.

# 7.3 Introducing Angular

The first section of this chapter discussed TypeScript modules and the second section explained what web components are. If you grasped these concepts, you'll have no trouble with Angular components, which are simply web components coded as TypeScript modules.

To be specific, the code for an Angular component consists of a module that exports a TypeScript class with a special `@Component` annotation. This annotation marks the class as a component class, and it provides information about how the component interacts with the Angular framework.

It will take many more chapters to flesh out the fields available in `@Component`. For now, it's important to be familiar with two of them:

1. `selector` — identifies the name of the custom HTML element corresponding to the component
2. `template` — contains the component's HTML template

For example, the overall structure of a basic Angular component could be given as follows:

```
@Component({

  selector: 'basic-comp',

  template: '...'

})
export class ClassName {
  ...
}
```

Because of the `export` keyword, the compiler recognizes this as a module. After the module is compiled, it can be inserted into a page with the `<basic-comp>` tag. The name of the tag and the name of the class don't need to be related in any way. However, the tag's name should meet the four requirements discussed earlier:

- May contain letters, digits, dots, hyphens, and underscores
- Can't contain uppercase letters
- Can't conflict with existing elements or CSS properties
- Must contain at least one hyphen

### 7.3.1 The Component Template

A component's template defines its appearance and internal structure. You can think of it as a subdocument within the overall document.

Angular provides two ways of defining a component's template. The first involves adding a `template` field to the `@Component` annotation. For example, the following field sets the component's template to a simple message:

```
template: '<h2>Hello Angular!</h2>'
```

If the template's HTML requires multiple lines, the quotes around the HTML can be replaced with backticks (` `). This is shown in the following template definition:

```
template:
`<h2>
  Hello Angular!
</h2>`
```

A component's template can also be specified by a `templateUrl` field. This provides the location of a resource that contains the template's HTML. In many cases, this is a local HTML file. For example, the following field states that the component's template can be found in the template.html file.

```
templateUrl: 'template.html'
```

In addition to regular markup, a component's template can contain non-HTML elements including expressions, events, properties, and directives. Chapter 8 discusses expressions, events, and properties. Chapter 9 presents everything you might want to know about directives.

### 7.3.2 Directives

As stated in the Angular documentation, a directive "attaches behavior to elements" in a component's template. To be precise, directives make it possible to selectively display elements, insert new elements, and associate elements with CSS.

Inside a component's template, a directive can be associated with an element by inserting a special marker into the element. In the following template, the `*ngFor` marker associates the `NgFor` directive with a list element, `<li>`. As a result, the directive generates new elements in an ordered list:

```
template:`
<ol>
  <li *ngFor='let prime of prime_numbers'>
    Prime numbers: {{ prime }}
  </li>
</ol>`
```

Angular provides a set of core directives that serve a wide range of roles. If these aren't sufficient, developers can code custom directives that can be associated with template elements. Chapter 9 discusses Angular's core directives and explains how to code custom directives.

# 7.4 The Angular CLI

The preceding discussion may have given you the impression that Angular development is just a matter of coding TypeScript classes and their templates. But it's much more complex than that. To see what I mean, it helps to generate, build, and launch an Angular app. The Angular CLI (Command-Line Interface) tool makes this straightforward.

Developing Angular apps with the CLI is like riding a bike with training wheels. On one hand, it restricts your freedom in many ways. On the other hand, it simplifies the process and prevents you from crashing. I strongly recommend that newcomers to Angular work with the CLI instead of coding applications by hand.

The installation process discussed in Chapter 2 *does not* install the Angular CLI. To install the utility, you need to execute the following command:

```
npm install -g @angular/cli
```

The installation may take some time. This is because npm installs all of the dependencies needed to build and launch Angular apps. This includes the Webpack loader, RxJS, and all the Angular packages, whose names start with `@angular`.

When the installation is complete, you can access the CLI using `ng`. This command can perform a wide range of Angular-related operations, and you can see the full list by entering the following command:

```
ng help
```

If you enter this command, you'll see a wide range of operations that can be automated through the CLI. Table 7.1 lists the primary categories.

**Table 7.1**

Categories of CLI Operations

| Operation | Description |
|---|---|
| `build` | Builds the application and places the compiled code in the dist directory |
| `completion` | Generates completion scripts |
| `doc` | Opens Angular documentation |
| `e2e` | Performs end-to-end testing for the project |
| `eject` | Ejects the application with Webpack configuration |
| `generate` | Generates new code |
| `get` | Obtains a value from the project configuration |
| `help` | Lists the CLI's commands and operations |
| `lint` | Checks the project for potential errors |
| `new` | Creates a new Angular project |
| `serve` | Builds and launches the application |
| `set` | Sets a value in the project's configuration |
| `test` | Performs the project's test suite |
| `version` | Identifies the CLI version |
| `xi18n` | Extracts strings for internationalization |

The `doc` operation is particularly helpful. If I can't remember a field of the `Component` class, entering `ng doc component` opens a browser to angular.io/docs and searches for the term `component`. Similarly, `ng doc directive` opens a browser to angular.io/docs and searches for the term `directive`.

This section focuses on three CLI operations: creating a new project (`ng new`), building the project (`ng build`), and launching the application (`ng serve`). Later chapters will present other uses of the CLI.

## 7.4.1 Creating a New Project

In my opinion, CLI's most useful feature is the ability to create an Angular project and install all the packages needed to build and launch it. To see how this works, I recommend that you change to a directory that doesn't contain a package.json file. Then execute the following command:

```
ng new FirstProject -sg -st
```

The `-sg` flag tells CLI not to create a Git repository for the project. The `-st` flag tells CLI not to create spec files. Table 7.2 lists these and other flags used in `ng new`.

**Table 7.2**

CLI Project Creation Flags (ng new)

| Flag | Default Value | Description |
|---|---|---|
| `-d` | false | Run through without making any changes |
| `-v` | false | Print details about the operation |
| `-lc` | false | Automatically link the @angular/cli package |
| `-si` | false | Skip package installation |
| `-sg` | false | Skip initializing a Git repository |
| `-st` | false | Skip creating spec files |
| `-sc` | false | Skip committing the first commit to Git |
| `-dir` | -- | The directory name to create the app in |
| `-sd` | src | The name of the source directory |
| `--style` | css | The default extension of style files |
| `-p` | app | The prefix to use for component selectors |
| `--routing` | false | Generate a routing module |
| `-is` | false | Assign an inline style |
| `-it` | false | Assign an inline template |

When `ng new` completes, you'll see a new directory called FirstProject. This top-level directory contains three folders:

- node_modules — contains the project's dependencies
- src — contains the project's source code
- e2e — contains files related to end-to-end testing (discussed at length in Chapter 17)

The file structure of FirstProject is somewhat similar to that of other projects presented in this book. The top-level directory contains tsconfig.json to configure the compiler. The src directory contains index.html and src/app contains TypeScript code to be compiled.

The project's src/app folder contains two TypeScript files, app.module.ts and app.component.ts. The code in app.component.ts defines a straightforward Angular component, and Listing 7.2 presents the code.

**Listing 7.2: FirstProject/src/app/app.component.ts**

```
import { Component } from '@angular/core';

@Component({
  selector: 'app-root',
  templateUrl: './app.component.html',
  styleUrls: ['./app.component.css']
})
export class AppComponent {
  title = 'app works!';
}
```

This should look familiar. The `@Component` decorator identifies the `AppComponent` class as a component class. This component can be inserted into an HTML document with the `<app-root>` tag and the component's appearance is defined by the template in app.component.html. The template's style is set by the content of app.component.css.

The component's template is almost trivially simple. Listing 7.3 presents the content of app.component.html.

**Listing 7.3: FirstProject/src/app/app.component.html**

```
<h1>
  {{title}}
</h1>
```

This displays the value of the component's `title` variable between `<h1>` tags. Therefore, the component's appearance simply consists of the `app works!` string.

The content of app.component.ts may be easy to understand, but other files in the project will probably be incomprehensible. To see what I mean, look at src/main.ts and src/app/app.module.ts. Chapter 8 will clarify what's going on and will further discuss the project's structure.

## 7.4.2 Building the Project

The process of building a project entails compiling the TypeScript and packaging the JavaScript into chunks for the loader. In an Angular CLI project, this is accomplished by changing to the project's top-level directory and entering the following command:

```
ng build
```

Like `ng new`, this accepts a number of flags that configure how the operation should be performed. Table 7.3 lists these flags and provides a description of each.

**Table 7.3**

CLI Project Build Flags (ng build)

| Flag | Default Value | Description |
| --- | --- | --- |
| `-t` | development | Identifies the build target (development or production) |
| `-e` | -- | Defines the build environment |
| `-op` | dist | Sets the output path |
| `--aot` | false | Build using Ahead of Time compilation |
| `-sm` | true | Create source maps |
| `-vc` | true | Create a separate chunk containing vendor libraries |
| `-bh` | -- | Base URL for the application |
| `-d` | -- | URL where files should be deployed |
| `-v` | false | Add more details to output logging |
| `-pr` | true | Log progress to the console as the build progresses |
| `--i18nFile` | -- | Localization file for internationalization |
| `--i18n-format` | -- | Format of the localization file |
| `--locale` | -- | Locale to use for internationalization |
| `-ec` | -- | Extract CSS from global styles into CSS files instead of JavaScript files |
| `-w` | false | Perform build when files change |
| `-oh` | -- | Define the output filename cache-busting hashing mode |
| `-poll` | -- | Sets the poll time for watching files |
| `-a` | -- | Sets the desired name for the app |
| `--stats-json` | false | Generates a file that can be used for Webpack analysis |

By default, CLI builds Angular projects in development mode. This means that it will generate source maps that simplify the debugging process. It will also perform extra checks during Angular's change detection process.

When the build is finished, the compiled files will be placed in the top-level dist directory. This contains JavaScript files (*.js), source maps (*.js.map), index.html, and a favicon.ico file.

On my system, the printed results of the development build are as follows:

```
Hash: f00edc02553067b1ab7b
Time: 5965ms

chunk    {0} polyfills.bundle.js, polyfills.bundle.js.map
(polyfills) 155 kB {4} [initial] [rendered]

chunk    {1} main.bundle.js, main.bundle.js.map (main) 3.68 kB {3}
[initial] [rendered]

chunk    {2} styles.bundle.js, styles.bundle.js.map (styles) 9.77
kB {4} [initial] [rendered]

chunk    {3} vendor.bundle.js, vendor.bundle.js.map (vendor) 2.19
MB [initial] [rendered]

chunk    {4} inline.bundle.js, inline.bundle.js.map (inline) 0
bytes [entry] [rendered]
```

Webpack uses the term *chunk* instead of *bundle* for a JavaScript file produced by the build process. CLI packages the compiled code into different chunks to improve loading performance. In this example, there are five chunks located in the dist directory:

- polyfills.bundle.js — Provides polyfills, which allow browsers to access advanced features
- main.bundle.js — Contains code compiled from the main TypeScript files
- styles.bundle.js — Sets the styles used in the application
- vendor.bundle.js — Contains the Angular libraries
- inline.bundle.js — Contains code that Webpack needs to load chunks

The largest chunk is vendor.bundle.js. On my system, this occupies 2.19 MB in development mode and 1.14 MB in production mode. One advantage of using Webpack is that it enables chunk caching. This means that the browser will load the cached chunk only once and use its code throughout the application instead of reloading the chunk every time it's needed.

Another important difference between development mode and production mode involves the application's styles. In development mode, stylesheets are contained inside JavaScript modules. In production mode, stylesheets are provided as CSS files. Note that either of the following commands will perform the build in production mode:

```
ng build -prod
ng build --target=production
```

### 7.4.3 Launching the Application

The Angular CLI installation provides a development server called the NG Live Development Server. This loads the project's index.html file and deploys the output files to the URL http://localhost:4200.

To start the server and launch the web application, enter the following command:

```
ng serve -o
```

This command opens a browser to the page http://localhost:4200. If everything has been deployed correctly, the page should display `app works!` in large letters.

The `ng serve` command (re-)builds the project in development mode before launching it. Therefore, it accepts all the build flags listed in Table 7.3. It also accepts commands that configure the server, and these are listed in Table 7.4.

**Table 7.4**

CLI Project Launching Flags (ng serve)

| Flag | Default Value | Description |
|---|---|---|
| `-d` | http://localhost | URL where files will be deployed |
| `-p` | 4200 | Port to listen to |
| `-H` | localhost | Name of the host to listen to |
| `-pc` | -- | Proxy configuration file |
| `-ssl` | false | Serve using HTTPS |
| `--sslKey` | -- | SSL key to use for serving HTTPS |
| `--sslCert` | -- | SSL certificate to use for serving HTTPS |
| `-o` | false | Opens the URL in the default browser |
| `-lr` | true | Identifies whether to reload the page on changes |
| `--live ReloadClient` | -- | The URL that the live reload browser client will use |
| `--hmr` | false | Enable hot module replacement |

The last flag in the table enables or disables hot module replacement (HMR). This is a useful feature of Webpack that replaces old modules with new ones without reloading the browser. This simplifies the testing process because the browser will immediately display modules as they change. Note that this is only available in development mode.

# 7.5 Summary

If you jump into Angular development without preparation, you may find the subject very difficult to grasp. The goal of this chapter has been to gradually introduce the topic by proceeding from TypeScript modules to the theory of web components. Angular applications are based on components, and each component is a TypeScript module that serves as a web component.

The first part of this chapter explained that modules provide encapsulation of features, which may include classes, interfaces, functions, or variables. Features can be made accessible using the `export` keyword and can be accessed from other modules using the `import` keyword. You'll encounter `export` and `import` throughout this book, so it's crucial to understand what they accomplish.

To enable modularity in web development, the W3C drafted a standard that presents the basic characteristics of web components. These characteristics include custom HTML elements, HTML templates, shadow DOM, and HTML imports. By using these technologies, web components dramatically simplify the process of web development and enable a greater amount of code reuse.

Angular serves as a practical implementation of web components. Each web component is coded as a TypeScript module that exports a specially-annotated class. A class's annotation defines many aspects of the component, including its custom HTML tag and its appearance in the page.

Angular projects can be difficult to work with, particularly when it comes to deployment. The Angular CLI simplifies the development process by performing common operations with commands starting with `ng`. The operations discussed in this chapter include creating projects, building projects, and launching the compiled application.

# Chapter 8

# Fundamentals of Angular Development

The preceding chapter provided a brief glimpse of Angular development. We looked at how `@Component` decorates a class and the manner in which a component's template can be defined with HTML. We also walked through the process of generating, building, and launching projects with the Angular CLI.

This chapter explores the Angular framework in greater detail. We'll examine a wide range of subjects including the following:

1. Module classes
2. Bootstrapping
3. Property interpolation
4. Property binding
5. Event binding
6. Local variables
7. Template styles
8. Parent/child components
9. Life cycle methods

Looking at these topics, it's difficult to pick one or two that are more important than the others. All of them are critically important and every Angular developer should have a solid grasp of each. But before we delve into the code, it's good to be familiar with the Angular Style Guide and its recommendations.

# 8.1 Style Conventions

The last section of Chapter 7 walked through the process of creating, building, and deploying an Angular project with the CLI. The discussion briefly touched on the project's structure and the location of its TypeScript files. This section presents a more in-depth look at the files of an Angular project and the manner in which they're intended to be arranged.

You can structure your projects any way you like, but the projects generated by the CLI adhere to the Angular Style Guide, which can be found at angular.io/styleguide. The guide's recommendations will be discussed throughout this book, and this section looks at the style conventions related to projects, files, and code.

## 8.1.1 Project Conventions

When it comes to structuring a project, the style guide's recommendations are simple:

1. The project's code should be placed inside a top-level folder named src.
2. The application's module (a class decorated by `@NgModule`) should be placed in the project's root folder, src/app.
3. If a component needs additional files (*.html for the template, *.css for styles, and so on), the component and its files should be placed in a separate folder named after the component.

The last point is important. A central principle in the style guide is being able to locate files quickly. Therefore, if an HTML file defines a component's template, the component file and the template file should be in the same folder.

## 8.1.2 File Conventions

The style guide also provides recommendations related to a project's files. The main point is that each TypeScript file in the root folder (src/app) and its subfolders should have two suffixes. The first suffix identifies the role served by the code in the Angular framework. The second suffix identifies the text format (*.ts).

For example, if a file defines a component, its name should be *name*.component.ts. If a TypeScript file defines a module, its name should be *name*.module.ts. Similar double suffixes include *.directive.ts, *.pipe.ts, and *.service.ts. Directives, pipes, and services will be discussed in later chapters.

If a file in src/app is needed by a component but doesn't contain TypeScript, it should take the component's name. For example, if an HTML file provides the template of the component in name.component.ts, its name should be name.component.html. If a CSS file contains styling for thing.component.ts, its name should be thing.component.css.

The last file convention involves test files. Each unit test file should focus on one component and it should be named after the component. If a file contains a unit test for widget.component.ts, its name should be widget.component.spec.ts. For end-to-end tests, discussed in Chapter 17, the suffix should be *.e2e-spec.ts instead of *.spec.ts.

## 8.1.3 Code Conventions

Just as TypeScript files should be named according to their Angular roles, TypeScript classes should also be named for their roles. The name of a component class should end with `Component` and the name of a module class should end with `Module`. Therefore, the `WidgetComponent` class should be defined in widget.component.ts and `AppModule` should be defined in app.module.ts.

The style guide strongly supports the Single Responsibility Principle (SRP), which states that each file should define one and only one thing. That is, a component file should only define one component and a template file should only define the template of one component. For large projects, following this principle can result in a vast number of files, but each file is easy to find and its purpose is immediately apparent.

Additional code conventions are given as follows:

- Classes should be named using upper camel case (`WidgetComponent`).
- Properties and methods should be named using lower camel case (`addNumbers`).
- Put third-party `import` statements (`@angular/core`) and application `import` statements into separate blocks. Alphabetize the import statements in each block.

The guide also has recommendations for component selectors. Each selector should be lower case and consist of a prefix followed by a hyphen, as in `app-widget`.

## 8.1.4 Example Code

From this chapter onward, this book assumes that you've installed the Angular CLI. Each project folder (ch8, ch9, and so on) consists of an app folder, and if you create a CLI project with `ng new`, you should be able to replace the app folder of the CLI project with the app folder of the example project. Then you can build the project with `ng build` and launch the application with `ng serve`.

# 8.2 Module Classes

Chapter 7 introduced TypeScript modules and explained how Angular components are defined inside these modules. To make life confusing, Angular has its own usage of the term *module*. An Angular module class is a TypeScript class decorated with `@NgModule`. An Angular module class is *not* a component class.

Every project contains at least one module that serves as the *root module*. Its purpose is to tell the Angular framework about the application. It identifies the features provided by the application, the features required by the application, and the manner in which the application should be launched.

The `@NgModule` decorator provides this information in four arrays:

1. `declarations` — the components, directives, and pipes contained in the application
2. `imports` — the components required by the application
3. `providers` — the support classes contained in the application
4. `bootstrap` — the component that launches the application

An example will clarify how these arrays are set. Listing 8.1 presents the root module code in the FirstProject project created at the end of Chapter 7:

**Listing 8.1: FirstProject/src/app/app.module.ts**

```
import { BrowserModule } from '@angular/platform-browser';
import { NgModule } from '@angular/core';
import { FormsModule } from '@angular/forms';
import { HttpModule } from '@angular/http';

import { AppComponent } from './app.component';

@NgModule({
  declarations: [ AppComponent ],
  imports: [
    BrowserModule,
    FormsModule,
    HttpModule
  ],
  providers: [],
  bootstrap: [AppComponent]
})
export class AppModule { }
```

This project only contains one component, `AppComponent`, so the `declarations` array consists of this element. The application requires three components from the Angular framework (`BrowserModule`, `FormsModule`, and `HttpModule`), so the `imports` array consists of these elements. This chapter discusses the `BrowserModule` and later chapters will present the `FormsModule` and `HttpModule`.

It's important to understand the difference between `import` statements and the `imports` array in `@NgModule`. Every feature mentioned in the root module must be imported with an `import` statement. But the `imports` array only contains the features required by the application. For the most part, these are provided by the Angular framework. At minimum, this array should contain `BrowserModule`.

The `providers` array identifies support classes, commonly called *services*, provided by the application. These classes don't affect the user interface directly, but provide data and methods that can be accessed by components, directives, and other Angular classes. Chapter 10 discusses the topic of services in detail.

The last array, `bootstrap`, identifies the application's primary component. This is the component that launches the application. In every application I've encountered, this array only contains one element. The bootstrapping process is made possible by the `BrowserModule` import, and I'll explain this shortly.

Simple projects will only contain one module class. But if a project uses routing, it will contain one module for each bundle to be deployed through lazy loading. Chapter 12 explains Angular's routing and lazy loading.

# 8.3 Bootstrapping

So far, we've looked at Angular's components and modules, which boil down to decorated TypeScript classes. But it's not enough to define classes. To serve a purpose, an application needs to create an instance of a class and start calling methods. In Angular, this launching process is called *bootstrapping*.

The Angular Style Guide has three recommendations related to bootstrapping:

- Put bootstrapping and platform logic in a file named main.ts.
- Include error handling in the bootstrapping logic.
- Avoid putting app logic in the main.ts. Place it in a component or service instead.

To understand what "bootstrapping and platform logic" refers to, it helps to look at actual code. Listing 8.2 presents the main.ts file in the CLI-generated FirstProject.

**Listing 8.2: FirstProject/src/main.ts**

```
import { enableProdMode } from '@angular/core';
import { platformBrowserDynamic } from
  '@angular/platform-browser-dynamic';

// Import the module class
import { AppModule } from './app/app.module';

// Import the environment settings
import { environment } from './environments/environment';

// Enable production mode
if (environment.production) {
  enableProdMode();
}

// Bootstrap the module class
platformBrowserDynamic().bootstrapModule(AppModule);
```

The goal of this section is to make this code intelligible. The first part of the section looks at environment settings and the difference between development and production mode. The second and third parts explain what `platformBrowserDynamic` and `platformBrowser` accomplish.

## 8.3.1 Environment and Execution Mode

By default, every Angular CLI project has a folder in its src directory named environments. This contains two files: environment.ts and environment.prod.ts. Both files define modules that export an object, `environment`, that has a single boolean field, `production`. In environment.ts, `environment.production` is set to `false`. In environment.prod.ts, `environment.production` is set to `true`.

The main.ts code uses this value to determine whether `enableProdMode` should be called. This function disables Angular's development mode, which reduces the number of checks performed during execution. Also, Angular CLI uses a different set of procedures to build projects in production mode instead of development mode.

By default, main.ts imports the `environment` object from environment.ts, which means default builds are performed in development mode. But if `ng build` is executed with the `--prod` flag, main.ts will access environment.prod.ts instead, which configures production mode. Note that developers can add fields to both files to provide environment data.

## 8.3.2 Just-In-Time (JIT) Compiling

By default, Angular templates are compiled at runtime. This means compilation takes place in the browser as the application loads. This in-browser compilation is called Just-in-Time (JIT) compiling.

JIT compilation has two main drawbacks. First, the user has to wait for the browser to compile the code, which may take a significant amount of time. Second, precompiled code is larger than compiled code.

JIT compiling has been the norm since the first release of Angular 2, so this is the most common compilation method. It's also very simple. To launch an application with JIT compilation, the module class needs to call `platformBrowserDynamc()` to obtain a `PlatformRef` and then call `bootstrapModule` with an Angular module class.

As discussed earlier, an Angular module class is a TypeScript class decorated with `@NgModule`. In general, this will be the application's root module, which is commonly named `AppModule`.

## 8.3.3 Ahead-of-Time (AOT) Compiling

If you open the FirstProject directory and look in the node_modules/.bin folder, you'll find an executable named ngc. This runs the Angular compiler, which makes it possible to compile code before it's loaded. This is called Ahead-of-Time (AOT) compiling.

Compiling Angular code in advance provides a number of advantages over JIT compiling, including faster rendering, smaller download size, and better security. AOT compiling is also necessary for lazy loading, which will be discussed in Chapter 12.

Before you can take advantage of AOT compiling, two dependencies are required:

```
npm install @angular/compiler-cli @angular/platform-server --save
```

Like tsc, ngc reads settings from tsconfig.json. The settings for AOT compilation are similar to those of regular compilation, but there are two points to keep in mind:

1. The `module` field in `compilerOptions` must be set to `es2015`
2. A top-level `angularCompilerOptions` object sets the `genDir` field to the name of the directory to contain AOT compilation results. It should also set `skipMetadataEmit` to `true`.

Traditionally, the configuration file for ngc is named tsconfig-aot.json. As an example, a tsconfig-aot.json for AOT compilation might contain the following settings:

```
"extends": "../tsconfig.json",
"compilerOptions": {
  "module": "es2015"
},
"angularCompilerOptions": {
 "genDir": "aot",
 "skipMetadataEmit" : true
}
```

Because `genDir` is set to aot, the results of the AOT compilation will be placed in the aot directory. If the tsconfig-aot.json file is in the src directory, the build can be executed by running the following command from the project's top-level directory:

```
"node_modules/.bin/ngc" -p src/tsconfig-aot.json
```

After this finishes, the build files will be stored in the src/aot directory. For each component file (*.component.ts), you'll find a factory file (*.component.ngfactory.ts) and a summary file (*.component.ngsummary.ts).

After the AOT build is complete, three changes need to be made to main.ts before the application can be deployed:

- References to `platformBrowserDynamic` should be replaced with `platformBrowser`
- The `bootstrapModule` method should be replaced with `bootstrapModuleFactory`
- The argument of `bootstrapModuleFactory` must be `AppModuleNgFactory`

Listing 8.3 presents main.ts with the changes needed for AOT compilation:

**Listing 8.3: main.ts (Updated to Support AOT Compilation)**

```
import { platformBrowser } from '@angular/platform-browser';

import { AppModuleNgFactory }
  from './aot/app/app.module.ngfactory';

// Bootstrap the module factory
platformBrowser().bootstrapModuleFactory(AppModuleNgFactory);
```

The projects in this book rely on JIT compilation. This is because JIT compilation is easier and requires fewer files. But when you start releasing for production, remember the advantages of AOT compilation.

# 8.4 Property Interpolation

At this point, you should be comfortable with the code in FirstProject's app.module.ts and main.ts. Now let's explore the content of app.component.ts, which is given as follows:

```
@Component({
  selector: 'app-root',
  templateUrl: './app.component.html',
  styleUrls: ['./app.component.css']
})
export class AppComponent {
  title = 'app works!';
}
```

As given by `templateUrl`, the component's template is in app.component.html. The template's markup is very simple:

```
<h1>{{title}}</h1>
```

The `AppComponent` class contains a property called `title` whose value is set to `'app works!'`. The template accesses the property by placing its name in double curly braces: `{{ title }}`. As a result, the component displays `app works!` when instantiated within the web page. The process of inserting a component's properties into the component's template is called *property interpolation.*

If the value of `title` changes, the value displayed in the template will change immediately. But the template can't alter the value of `title`. Because the data transfer is one-way, this interaction is referred to as *one-way data binding.*

Template expressions can contain more than just property names. They can hold constant values (numbers and strings) and the results of simple JavaScript operations. For example, `{{3 * 6 + 2}}` will be displayed as `20` and `{{'Angular' + 'JS'}}` will be displayed as `AngularJS`.

An expression can operate on class properties, so if you want to concatenate `firstVal` and `secondVal`, the expression is `{{firstVal + secondVal}}`. Similarly, if `num` equals `5`, the expression `{{ num + '0' }}` will be displayed as `50`.

Similar expressions can be inserted in the template wherever strings are appropriate. For example, the class attribute of a `<button>` could be set to `{{ buttonClass }}` and the `id` of a `<div>` could be set to `{{ divId }}`.

Lastly, an expression can be used to execute JavaScript functions. If `returnTwo()` always returns a value of 2, the `{{ returnTwo() }}` expression will evaluate to `2`.

## 8.4.1 Pipes

Data displayed in a template can be formatted using pipes. These expressions take the form `{{ data | pipe }}`, where *pipe* specifies how *data* should be formatted.

An example will make this clear. Suppose the component's class has a string property called `firstName`. The `uppercase` pipe displays text using uppercase characters, so the following expression configures the template to display `firstName` in uppercase:

```
{{ firstName | uppercase }}
```

Angular provides a number of similar pipes, but they aren't all as easy to use as `uppercase`. Most have arguments, separated by colons, that constrain how the data formatting should be performed. Table 8.1 lists 11 of these pipes and their arguments.

**Table 8.1**

Angular Pipes

| Pipe Name | Argument(s) | Description |
|---|---|---|
| `number` | `digitInfo` | Displays a number in decimal form with the given number of digits |
| `percent` | `digitInfo` | Displays a number as a percentage with the given number of digits |
| `currency` | `code, symbol, digitInfo` | Formats a number as a currency. If no symbol is given, the filter uses the currency of the default locale. |
| `date` | `format` | Formats a date as a string with the given format |
| `json` | -- | Converts an object to a string in JavaScript Object Notation (JSON) |
| `lowercase` | -- | Converts text to lowercase |
| `uppercase` | -- | Converts text to uppercase |
| `slice` | `start, end` | Creates a substring or converts an array into a list |
| `async` | -- | Waits for a value from an Observable or Promise |
| `i18nSelect` | `mapping` | Selects string according to a value |
| `i18nPlural` | `mapping` | Selects string according to the number of elements |

The following discussion explores most of these pipes and demonstrates how they're used. But `i18nPlural` and `i18nSelect` won't be discussed here. They'll be introduced in Chapter 15, which presents the topic of internationalization (i18n) in detail.

### number, percent, and currency

The `number`, `percent`, and `currency` pipes format numbers in the template. If any of these are used to format a string, Angular will raise an *Invalid Argument* exception.

If the `number` pipe is used without arguments, it won't perform any formatting. That is, `{{25 | number}}` displays `25` and `{{3.1415 | number}}` displays `3.1415`.

The `number` and `percent` pipes both accept an optional `digitInfo` argument that identifies which digits should be displayed. This argument can be given in one of two forms:

1. `x.y`, where `x` is the minimum number of digits before the decimal and `y` is the maximum number of digits after the decimal
2. `x.y-z`, where `x` is the minimum number of digits before the decimal, `y` is the minimum number of digits after the decimal, and `z` is the maximum number of digits after the decimal.

The following examples demonstrate how `number` and `percent` are used:

- `{{25 | number : '2.0'}}` displays `25`
- `{{25 | percent : '2.0'}}` displays `2,500%`
- `{{0.1234 | number : '2.3'}}` displays `00.123`
- `{{0.1234 | percent : '2.3'}}` displays `12.340%`
- `{{123.456789 | number : '2.2-4'}}` displays `123.4568`
- `{{0.333 | percent : '2.2-4'}}` displays `33.30%`

If the `currency` pipe is used without arguments, the ISO 4217 code for the local currency will be prepended. In the United States, `{{3 | currency}}` will be displayed as `USD3.00`. In Europe, `{{5.5 | currency}}` will be displayed as `EUR5.50`.

The first optional argument of `currency` identifies the code to be used. No matter where you live, if you want to express 17.50 in Canadian dollars, you can display this as `{{17.50 | currency : 'CAD'}}`, which will be displayed as `CAD17.50`.

The second optional argument identifies if the currency's symbol should be used instead of the ISO 4217 code. The third optional argument is the same `digitInfo` argument used by `number` and `percent`. The following examples demonstrate this:

- `{{ 2.50 | currency : 'USD' : true }}` evaluates to `$2.50`
- `{{ 2.50 | currency : 'USD' : true : '2.2' }}` evaluates to `$02.50`
- `{{ 4 | currency : 'CAD' : false : '1.2' }}` evaluates to `CAD4.00`

## date

The `date` pipe expects the date to be provided in an ISO 8601 format or as the number of milliseconds since Jan 1, 1970. This pipe accepts an optional argument that determines how the date/time should be formatted. This can contain a wide range of elements, with `y` identifying the year with four values, `MMM` setting the month's three-letter abbreviation, and `dd` setting the day of the month using two values. The following examples show how these and other formatting elements are used.

- `{{1440253151182 | date }}` evaluates to `Aug 22, 2015`
- `{{1440253151182 | date: 'MMddyy' }}` evaluates to `082215`
- `{{1440253151182 | date: 'MMMMd'}}` evaluates to `August22`
- `{{1440253151182 | date: 'EEEEMMMd'}}` evaluates to `SaturdayAug22`

To simplify its usage, `date` supports format strings that represent common date formats. These include `shortDate`, `mediumDate`, `longDate`, and `fullDate`:

- `{{1440253151182 | date: 'shortDate' }}` evaluates to `8/22/2015`
- `{{1440253151182 | date: 'mediumDate' }}` evaluates to `Aug 22, 2015`
- `{{1440253151182 | date: 'longDate' }}` evaluates to `August 22, 2015`
- `{{1440253151182 | date: 'fullDate' }}` evaluates to `Saturday, August 22, 2015`

The `date` pipe can also display times, with `s`/`ss` identifying the second, `m`/`mm` identifying the minute, and `h` or `hh` identifying the hour in AM/PM. In addition, special format strings (`shortTime` and `mediumTime`) identify common time formats:

- `{{1435252151182 | date: 'hh:mm:ss' }}` evaluates to `01:09:11`
- `{{1435252151182 | date: 'shortTime' }}` evaluates to `1:09 PM`
- `{{1435252151182 | date: 'mediumTime' }}` evaluates to `1:09:11 PM`

The time zone is determined by the user's locale. If the time format is followed by `Z`, this time zone will be printed using the three-letter abbreviation. If the time format is followed by `z`, the time zone will be printed in full.

- `{{1435252151182 | date: 'hh:mm:ssZ' }}` evaluates to `01:09:11EDT`
- `{{1435252151182 | date: 'hh:mm:ssz' }}` evaluates to `01:09:11Eastern Daylight Time`

## json

Chapter 3 discussed TypeScript's `Object` type, which consists of name-value pairs separated by colons. The following declaration provides an example:

```
person = {fName: 'John', lName: 'Smith', age: 30};
```

If a component's class contains an `Object`, the `json` pipe will convert it to a string. For example, consider the following component:

```
@Component({
selector: 'json-example',
template: '<label>The object is {{ book | json }}.</label>'
})
export class JsonPipeExample {
  book: Object;
  constructor() {
    this.book = {title: 'Quiller', author: 'Adam Hall'};
  }
}
```

When `<json_example>` is added to a page, its label will display the following text:

```
The object is { 'title': 'Quiller', 'author': 'Adam Hall' }.
```

The `json` pipe performs the same operation as `JSON.stringify()`. It's particularly helpful for debugging JSON-based data transfers.

## uppercase, lowercase, and slice

The `uppercase` and `lowercase` pipes are trivially easy to use:

- `{{ 'AngularJS' | uppercase }}` evaluates to `ANGULARJS`
- `{{ 'AngularJS' | lowercase }}` evaluates to `angularjs`

The `slice` pipe is more complex, and can be used in two ways. Its first usage involves extracting a substring from a string. In this case, it accepts one required argument and one optional argument. The required argument identifies the starting index of the substring and the optional argument identifies the final index.

- `{{ 'AngularJS' | slice : 2 }}` evaluates to `gularJS`
- `{{ 'AngularJS' | slice : 2 : 5 }}` evaluates to `gul`

If the starting or ending index is negative, the index will be counted from the end of the string instead of the front.

- `{{ 'AngularJS' | slice : -5 }}` evaluates to `larJS`
- `{{ 'AngularJS' | slice : -5 : -2 }}` evaluates to `lar`

The second usage of `slice` extracts a subarray from an array of elements. The arguments identify the starting and ending elements of the subarray. This usage of `slice` becomes helpful when using the `NgFor` directive, which inserts an array of elements into a web page. Chapter 9 introduces the `NgFor` directive and shows how `slice` can be used to provide an `NgFor` loop with a subarray.

### async

Unlike the other pipes in Table 8.1, `async` doesn't format existing data. Instead, it displays data as it becomes available. To be specific, it subscribes to an `Observable` or a `Promise` and returns the current value.

Because this pipe waits for an indefinite amount of time, we say that it operates *asynchronously*. Chapter 11 discusses asynchronous programming in detail and explains how `Observable`s and `Promise`s are used.

### Custom Pipes

Angular makes it possible to define custom pipes with special pipe classes. Chapter 17 explores this topic in detail, and explains how to create a pipe that sorts and displays data. This custom pipe, called `orderBy`, is similar to the `orderBy` filter provided in the Angular 1.x framework.

# 8.5 Property Binding

As every web developer knows, characteristics of an HTML element are configured using attributes. If an image element should display smiley.jpg, its `src` attribute can be set in the following way:

```
<image src='smiley.jpg'</img>
```

When a browser reads this, it adds an element to the document object model (DOM). The element's attributes are collected together and each can be accessed as a *property* of the DOM element. Put simply, an element's attributes are external (configured in HTML) and its properties are internal (set by DOM processing).

You can't access an element's properties in regular HTML, but if an element is part of a component's template, Angular makes it easy to read and modify its properties. The notation for this surrounds the property name in square brackets. For example, the following template definition disables a button by setting its `disabled` property to true:

```
template: `<button [disabled]='"true"'>Click Here</button>`
```

Suppose that the button's disabled state should be controlled by a boolean property called `dis`. After the discussion in the preceding section, you might expect the assignment to look like this:

```
[disabled] = {{ dis }}
```

But this won't work. To set a DOM property equal to a class property, the class property must be surrounded in quotes, not curly braces. The full component definition can be given as follows:

```
@Component({
selector: 'prop-binding',
template: `
<button [disabled]='dis'>Press me!</button>
`})

export class PropertyBindingExample {
  dis = true;
}
```

This can be confusing. When I see `'dis'` in the template, I assume it's a string literal, not a class property. But this is Angular's syntax for assigning a DOM property to a class property. Here's a general expression for the assignment:

```
[DOM_property] = 'class_property'
```

The official term for this data transfer is *property binding*. When the class's property changes, the DOM property changes with it. But keep in mind that the data transfer is one-way only. When using property binding, a change to the DOM will not change the class property.

A DOM property can also be bound to a method in the component's class. For example, suppose the address of a hyperlink should be set equal to a method's return value. If the method is `getAddr`, the following code shows how the binding can be established:

```
@Component({
selector: 'prop-method',
template: `
<a [href]='getAddr()'>Angular</a>
`})

export class PropertyBoundToMethod {
  getAddr(): string {
    return 'https://angular.io';
  }
}
```

Table 8.2 lists the `href` property and other properties that can be bound. The second column identifies the expected data type and the third column provides a description.

**Table 8.2**

Element Properties (Abridged)

| Property | Data Type | Description |
|---|---|---|
| `hidden` | `boolean` | Controls the element's visibility |
| `disabled` | `boolean` | Controls whether the element is enabled or disabled |
| `href` | `string` | Sets the element's hyperlink address |
| `className` | `string` | Sets the element's CSS class |
| `classList` | `string` | Sets the element's CSS class-list |
| `textContent` | `string` | Sets the element's text (HTML formatting ignored) |
| `innerHTML` | `string` | Sets the element's text (HTML formatting accepted) |

These properties are straightforward to understand. The `className` and `classlist` properties are interesting because they enable the component to control the styles applied to elements in the template. A later section will demonstrate how this can be accomplished.

The `textContent` and `innerHTML` properties determine an element's text. The difference between them is that `innerHTML` recognizes HTML formatting and `textContent` does not. The following component shows how this works.

```
@Component({
selector: 'text-example',
template: `
<label [textContent]='msg'>Old Message</label>
`})

export class TextContentDemo {

  msg: string;

  constructor() {
    this.msg = 'New Message';
  }
}
```

The original text of the template's label is `Old Message`. Because the label's `textContent` property is bound to `msg`, the displayed text will be `New Message`.

If `msg` equals `<b>New Message</b>`, the HTML formatting will be ignored and the label will display `<b>New Message</b>`. But if the `innerHTML` property is bound to `msg`, the formatting will be recognized and **`New Message`** will be displayed in the browser.

There's one more point that needs to be mentioned. Suppose that, for testing purposes, you want to set the label's `textContent` property to a string literal such as `Testing`. You might try something like this:

```
template: `
<label [textContent]='Testing'></label>
`})
```

This label will display an undefined value because `Testing` is assumed to be a property of the component's class. To fix this, the string literal needs to be surrounded with more quotes:

```
template: `
<label [textContent]='"Testing"'></label>
`})
```

Now the label will display `Testing`, as desired. Despite working with property binding for some time, I still find this syntax to be unintuitive. Thankfully, event binding is easier to work with.

# 8.6 Event Binding

The last section of Chapter 5 discussed DOM events, which are produced when the user interacts with a DOM element. When an action occurs, the browser sends a message to the application. In an Angular component, the process of event handling involves sending a special event structure from the template to the component's class.

Within a template, events are identified by names (the same names in Tables 5.5 and 5.6) surrounded by parentheses. That is, mouse click events are identified by `(click)`, mouse entry events are represented by `(mouseenter)`, and keypress events are represented by `(keypress)`.

To notify the class when an event occurs, the template can associate an event with a class method. If an event occurs, its associated method will be invoked. For example, the following template markup associates `(click)`, `(mouseenter)`, and `(mouseleave)` with the methods `incrNumClicks`, `setMouseEnter`, and `setMouseLeave`:

```
<button (click)='incrNumClicks()'
        (mouseenter)='setMouseEnter()'
        (mouseleave)='setMouseLeave()'>
```

An event structure provides information about the user's action, such as the location of the mouse click or the ASCII code of the pressed key. The template can provide this structure to the class in two main ways: sending it as a method argument or changing the value of a class property.

An example will make this clear. When a user clicks on an element, the event data is packaged in an `$event` structure and the click's x-coordinate equals `$event.pageX`. If `checkButton` is a method that needs to process the x-coordinate, the following code ensures that `checkButton` will be invoked when the user clicks the button:

```
<button type='button' (click)='checkButton($event.pageX)'>
```

If the class has a property named `xcoord`, the following markup will set the property to the click's x-coordinate when the user clicks on the button:

```
<button type='button' (click)='xcoord = $event.pageX'>
```

Now that we've seen how general events are handled, it's time to look at specific types of events. This section divides event handling into three categories: mouse events, keyboard events, and element-specific events.

## 8.6.1 Mouse Events

Angular provides eight events that respond to mouse actions. Table 8.3 lists them and provides a description of each.

**Table 8.3**

Mouse Events

| Event | Description |
|---|---|
| `(click)` | Responds when the element is clicked |
| `(dblclick)` | Responds when the element is double-clicked |
| `(mousedown)` / `(mouseup)` | Responds when the user's mouse button moves from up to down or from down to up |
| `(mouseover)` | Responds when the user's mouse moves over the element |
| `(mousemove)` | Responds when the user's mouse moves |
| `(mouseenter)` / `(mouseleave)` | Responds when the user's mouse enters the element's area or leaves the element's area |

Each of these can be associated with a method to be called when the corresponding event occurs. For example, the following code associates double-click events with the `handleDoubleClick` method:

```
<button (dblclick)='handleDoubleClick()'</button>
```

In many applications, elements alter their appearance when the mouse hovers over them. In an Angular component, `(mouseenter)` and `(mouseleave)` make it possible to handle hover events. This is shown in the following markup:

```
<button (mouseenter)='handleMouseEnter()'
        (mouseleave)='handleMouseLeave()'
</button>
```

When an event occurs, the browser provides access to the event's data through the `$event` variable. The fields of `$event` depend on the nature of the event, and for mouse events, at least five fields are available:

- `$event.pageX` — the event's x-coordinate (relative to the document's left edge)
- `$event.pageY` — the event's y-coordinate (relative to the top of the document)

- `$event.type` — a string identifying the nature of the event (`click` for mouse clicks)
- `$event.which` — the mouse button that produced the event (1 – left, 2 – middle, 3 – right)
- `$event.timeStamp` — the number of milliseconds separating the event from January 1, 1970

For example, the following component uses `$event.which` to display a different message depending on which button was pressed.

```
@Component({
selector: 'click-handler',
template: `
<p>{{ msg }}</p>
<button (click)='handleClick($event.which)'>Click Me</button>
`})

export class ClickHandler {

  msg: string = 'No button has been pressed';

  // Receives the index of the pressed button
  handleClick(btn: number): void {

    switch (btn) {
    case 1:
      this.msg = 'The left button was clicked.';
      break;
    case 2:
      this.msg = 'The middle button was clicked.';
      break;
    case 3:
      this.msg = 'The right button was clicked.';
      break;
    }
  }
}
```

The class constructor initializes `msg` with a string stating that no button has been clicked. When the user clicks on the button, `handleClick` will be called with a number that identifies which mouse button was clicked.

Later in this chapter, we'll look at a more interesting example of mouse event handling. The component counts mouse clicks and changes its message depending on whether the user's mouse is hovering over it.

### 8.6.2 Keyboard Events

Keyboard events are just as easy to handle as mouse events. Table 8.4 lists the three types of events.

**Table 8.4**

Keyboard Events

| Event | Description |
|---|---|
| `(keydown)` | Responds when the user presses a key down |
| `(keyup)` | Responds when the user raises a key |
| `(keypress)` | Responds when the user presses a key and raises it |

Keyboard events can be handled using the same type of code as mouse events. For example, the following markup displays a message on `keyup` and `keydown` events:

```
<button (keydown)='down = true'
        (keyup)='down = false'>Key Test</button>
<p>Key down: {{down}}</p>
```

An element can't receive events until it has focus. For keystrokes, this means the element must be selected before keyboard events can be received and handled.

As with mouse events, browsers package event data in an object called `$event`. For keystrokes, the object contains the following fields:

- `$event.type` — a string identifying the nature of the event (`keypress` for keystrokes)
- `$event.which` — the ASCII code of the pressed key
- `$event.timeStamp` — the number of milliseconds separating the event from January 1, 1970

The following markup demonstrates how `$event` can be used with key events.

```
<button (keypress)='e = $event.timeStamp'>Time Test</button>
<p>Key Test: {{e}}</p>
```

When the user focuses on the button and presses a key, the template displays how many milliseconds have elapsed between the event and January 1, 1970.

## 8.6.3 Element-Specific Events

Some elements have specific types of events associated with them. This discussion presents the events for `<input>` elements and `<select>` elements, and shows how they can be received and processed in code.

### Input/TextArea Events

For `<textarea>` elements and `<input>` elements of `text` type, the `(input)` event responds whenever the user completes a keystroke. The element's full text is provided in `$event.target.value`. For example, the following markup associates an `<input>` element with a method that receives the element's text:

```
<input type='text' (input)='handleText($event.target.value)'>
```

If the `<input>` element has `checkbox` type, the `(change)` event responds when the box is checked or unchecked. The element's checked state can be accessed through the boolean value, `$event.target.checked`.

The following component demonstrates how a checkbox can be associated with a method (`handleCheck`) that receives the box's checked state:

```
@Component({
selector: 'checkbox-demo',
template: `
<input type='checkbox'
  (change)='handleCheck($event.target.checked)'>Checkbox<br>
<p>The checkbox is {{ msg }}.</p>
`})

export class CheckHandler {
  msg: string;
  constructor() {
    this.msg = 'not checked';
  }

  handleCheck(state: boolean) {
    this.msg = (state) ? 'checked' : 'not checked';
  }
}
```

The `(change)` event is also available for handling actions involving radio buttons. This event responds when a button is selected or deselected.

### Select Events

A `<select>` element creates a drop-down list that displays multiple `<option>` elements, as shown in the following code:

```
<select>
  <option>red</option>
  <option>green</option>
  <option>blue</option>
</select>
```

The `(change)` event is emitted when the user makes a selection. The name of the selected option is provided in `$event.target.value`, which is a string. The following markup associates the `<select>` element with a `handleSelect` method that receives the selected option:

```
<select (change)='handleSelect($event.target.value)'>
  <option>red</option>
  <option>green</option>
  <option>blue</option>
</select>
```

The `<option>` elements in this drop-down list are static. Chapter 9 explains how the `NgFor` directive can be used to dynamically add `<option>` elements to a list.

## 8.7 The ButtonCounter

At this point, you should have a basic understanding of Angular's property binding and event binding. To reinforce this understanding, this section presents a web component that responds to mouse events.

This component consists of a button whose text identifies how many times it's been clicked and whether the mouse is hovering over it. Figure 8.1 shows what it looks like.

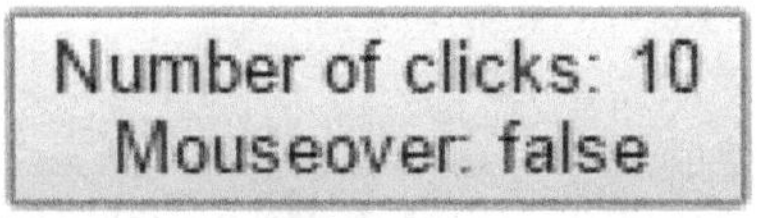


**Figure 8.1 The ButtonCounter Web Component**

In the ch8/button_counter project, the component defined in app/app.component.ts can be accessed as an HTML element. This is accomplished with the following markup:

```
<app-root></app-root>
```

Listing 8.4 shows what the code looks like. The component's first property is a `number` named `numClicks` and the second is a `boolean` named `mouseOver`.

**Listing 8.4: ch8/button_counter/app/app.component.ts**

```
import {Component} from '@angular/core';

@Component({
selector: 'app-root',
template: `
<button type='button' (click) = 'incrNumClicks()'
                      (mouseenter) = 'setMouseEnter()'
                      (mouseleave) = 'setMouseLeave()'>
  Number of clicks: {{ numClicks }}<br />
  Mouseover: {{ mouseOver }}
</button>
`})

// Define the component's class
export class AppComponent {

  // Declare and initialize properties
  public numClicks = 0;
  public mouseOver = false;

  // Respond to user events
  public incrNumClicks() {
    this.numClicks += 1;
  }
  public setMouseEnter() {
    this.mouseOver = true;
  }
  public setMouseLeave() {
    this.mouseOver = false;
  }
}
```

As shown, the class handles three different events. As they occur, the class's event handling methods update the values of the two properties. These values are printed inside the button using property interpolation.

# 8.8 Local Variables

Property binding and event binding transfer data between a component's template and its class, but what if you want to transfer data between two template elements? Rather than send information from template to class and back, it's simpler to use local variables.

A local variable is declared inside a template element with a variable name preceded by the hash symbol, `#`. This variable serves as a reference to the element. It allows other elements to access the referenced element and its properties.

An example will show how these variables work. In the following markup, the local variable `inp` serves as a reference to the `<input>` element. A button element accesses this variable when it's clicked.

```
<input #inp></input>
<button (click)='processText(inp.value)'>Transfer text</button>
```

Local variables allow one element to access properties of another element, but events can't be received through local variables. For example, if you assign `#btn` to the `<button>` and attempt to access `(btn.click)` in another element, the second element will not receive the click event.

# 8.9 Template Styles

In addition to defining a component's template and tag name, the `@Component` annotation can assign styles to the elements in the template. There are a number of ways to do this:

1. In the `@Component` annotation, set `styles` equal to an array of CSS rules.
2. In the `@Component` annotation, set `styleUrls` equal to an array of resources (usually files) that define CSS rules.
3. In the template, add a `<style>` element that defines one or more CSS rules.

These three methods are straightforward to use and understand. This section explains how each of them works and then demonstrates their usage in a complete web component example.

### 8.9.1 Configuring Styles

Inside `@Component`, a `styles` field can be set to an array of CSS rules that will be applied to the template's elements. For example, the following annotation sets `styles` equal to an array containing a rule that associates `boldclass` with boldface text:

```
@Component({
  template: `...`,
  styles: ['.boldclass { font-weight: bold; }']
})
```

If a component needs many CSS rules, it's more convenient to place them in a separate file. Within `@Component`, these files can be identified by the `styleUrls` field. For example, the following annotation specifies that the CSS rules in bstyle.css should be applied to the template.

```
@Component({
  template: `...`,
  styleUrls: ['bstyle.css']
})
```

In addition, CSS styles can be directly inserted into a template. This works in the same way as a `<style>` tag in the `<head>` of an HTML document. The following annotation demonstrates this. It defines a `<style>` element that affects elements that belong to the `boldclass` class.

```
@Component({
template:`
<style>
  .boldclass button {
    font-weight: bold;
  }
</style>
<div class='boldclass'>
  <label ...></label>
</div>
`})
```

Ideally, a browser will only apply a component's CSS styling to the component. But in many browsers, the CSS rules defined for a web component are applied to the entire document. To be safe, it's a good idea to use unique names for a component's CSS rules. This will ensure that the rules only affect elements in the component's template.

## 8.9.2 Styles and Properties

An earlier section mentioned that DOM elements have properties named `className` and `classList`. They make it possible to assign CSS classes to an element. By combining the `styles` field in `@Component` with property binding, it's easy for a component class to assign style classes dynamically.

To demonstrate this, Listing 8.5 presents the code for the component in the ch8/class_selector project. Its template consists of three elements:

- a `<select>` element that lists three styles
- a `<label>` whose style and text is determined by the selected option
- a `<button>` that applies the selected style/text when pressed

**Listing 8.5: ch8/class_selector/app/app.component.ts**

```
@Component({
selector: 'app-root',

// Define styles for the template elements
styles:
['.classselector div { display: block; margin-bottom: 10px; }',
 '.classselector .first { font-weight:normal; color:purple; }',
 '.classselector .second { font-weight:bold; color:orange; }',
 '.classselector .third { font-style:italic; color:brown; }'],

 // Define the component's appearance
template: `
<div class='classselector'>
  <div>
    <label>Class: </label>
    <select #sel>
      <option>first</option>
      <option>second</option>
      <option>third</option>
    </select>
  </div>
  <div>
    <button (click)='handleClick(sel.value)'>
      Apply selection
    </button><br />
  </div>
  <div>
    <label [className]='labelClass'>{{ labelText }}</label>
  </div>
</div>
`})
```

**Listing 8.5: ch8/class_selector/app/app.ts (Continued)**

```
// Define the component's class
export class AppComponent {

  // Declare and initialize
  public labelClass = '';

  public labelText =
    'Please select a class and press the button.';

  // Select the class and the label's text
  public handleClick(choice: string) {

    this.labelClass = choice;

    if (choice === 'first') {
      this.labelText =
        'The first class prints normal text in purple.';
    }

    else if (choice === 'second') {
      this.labelText =
        'The second class prints boldface text in orange.';
    }

    else if (choice === 'third') {
      this.labelText =
        'The third class prints italic text in brown.';
    }
  }
}
```

The template assigns the local variable `#sel` to the `<select>` element. When the button is clicked, the `click` event calls the class's `select` method with the `value` property of the local variable. This is accomplished with the following definition:

```
<button (click)='select(sel.value)'>
```

The `select` method assigns strings to two properties, `labelClass` and `labelText`. These properties change the CSS class and text of the template's label.

`labelClass` sets the label's CSS class to one of three strings: `first`, `second`, or `third`. When `labelClass` changes, the label's color and text style change according to the corresponding CSS class. The rules for each CSS class are set in the `styles` field of the `@Component` annotation.

# 8.10 Parent/Child Components

One advantage of working with web components is that they can be nested. That is, one component can be placed inside another. The containing component is called the parent and the contained component is called the child.

Angular supports two types of child components: *view children* and *content children*. If one component's template contains an element representing another component, the second component is a view child of the first. In the following annotation, the template for `parent-comp` contains three instances of `child-comp`. This means the parent component has three view children.

```
@Component({
selector: 'parent-comp',
template: `
<ol>
  <li><child-comp></child-comp></li>
  <li><child-comp></child-comp></li>
  <li><child-comp></child-comp></li>
</ol>
`})
```

If a child component is placed inside a parent component in another component's template, the child component is a content child. For example, suppose that a top-level component contains `ParentComp` and `ChildComp`, and its annotation is as follows:

```
@Component({
selector: 'toplevel-comp',
template: `
<ol>
  <parent-comp>
    <child-comp></child-comp>
    <child-comp></child-comp>
    <child-comp></child-comp>
  </parent-comp>
</ol>
`})
```

In this markup, the `parent-comp` element contains three `child-comp` subelements. This isn't the template of the parent component, so its three children are content children. In fact, a component's *content* should be understood to mean anything between a component's tags, whether it's text, an HTML element, or another component.

Many parent components need to access their children in code. Angular makes this straightforward by providing specially-decorated properties that return view children and content children. Children are provided in containers called `QueryList`s, and before I discuss how to access them, I'd like to briefly explain what a `QueryList` is.

## 8.10.1 QueryLists

When accessing a component's children, the results are frequently placed in a `QueryList`. The `QueryList` class implements the `iterable` interface, so its content can be iterated through with a loop like the following:

```
for(child in queryList) {
  ...
}
```

A `QueryList` can't be modified, but its contents can be accessed through the members listed in Table 8.5. `T` represents the class of the `QueryList`'s elements.

**Table 8.5**

Members of the QueryList Class

| Member | Type/Return Type | Description |
|---|---|---|
| `first` | `T` | The first element in the list |
| `last` | `T` | The last element in the list |
| `length` | `number` | The number of elements in the list |
| `changes` | `Observable` | Provides an observable for waiting until the children are available |
| `toArray()` | `T[]` | Returns an array containing the list's content |
| `toString()` | `string` | Returns a string representing the list |
| `map<U>(fn: (item:T) => U)` | `U[]` | Applies a function to each element of the list and returns the results |
| `filter<U>` `(fn: (item:T) => boolean)` | `T[]` | Creates an array containing elements that pass the test |
| `reduce<U>` `(fn:(acc:U,item:T) => U,` `init: U)` | `U` | Performs a reduction operation on the elements in the list |

Many of these members should be straightforward to understand. The `first`, `last`, `length`, `toArray()`, and `toString()` members perform the same operations as members of similar container classes.

Elements of a `QueryList` may not be immediately available, so each `QueryList` provides an `Observable` through the `changes` member. A full discussion of `Observables` will have to wait until Chapter 11, which also presents methods similar to `map`, `filter`, and `reduce`.

## 8.10.2 Accessing View Children

A component can access components in its template with two decorated properties:

- `@ViewChildren(Class)` — returns a `QueryList` containing all view children of the class *`Class`*
- `@ViewChild(Class)` — returns the first view child of the class *`Class`*

An example will demonstrate how these are used. Consider the following template:

```
template: `
<p><child1></child1></p>
<p><child1></child1></p>
<p><child2></child2></p>
<p><child2></child2></p>
`})
```

This component has four view children: two of type `Child1` and two of type `Child2`. The following properties, declared in the component's class, return a `QueryList` containing both `Child1` objects and the first `Child2` object:

```
@ViewChildren(Child1) childList: QueryList<Child1>;
@ViewChild(Child2) child: Child2;
```

The view children in `QueryList` are returned in the order in which they were listed in the template. There's no need to sort the list before processing its items.

In addition to accessing components, `@ViewChild` can also be used to access regular HTML elements in the template. This requires four steps:

1. Identify an element of interest with a local variable. (`<li #var>...</li>`)
2. Decorate a class property with `@ViewChild(...)` and set the argument to the local variable. (`@ViewChild(var)`)

3. Set the type of the decorated property to `ElementRef`, which represents a general template element.
4. Access the specific DOM element through the `nativeElement` property of the `ElementRef`.

This is particularly helpful when you want to use a component to draw on an HTML canvas. For example, suppose a component's template contains the following element:

```
<canvas #cnvs width='100' height='100'></canvas>
```

The component can access the canvas by decorating a property whose type is set to `ElementRef`:

```
@ViewChild(cnvs) canvas: ElementRef;
```

As discussed in Chapter 5, TypeScript provides interfaces that represent elements in a document. For canvas elements, the TypeScript interface is `HTMLCanvasElement`. This can be obtained from the `ElementRef` through its `nativeElement` property. The following code shows how this can be done.

```
let canvasElement: HTMLCanvasElement = this.canvas.nativeElement;
```

Chapter 19 discusses the topic of HTML canvases in detail. It also provides a full example of how Angular can be used to draw on a canvas.

If possible, the data binding methods discussed earlier should always be employed instead of accessing the DOM directly. This is because direct access creates a tight coupling between the component and the page's rendering. Also, a component that accesses the DOM directly can't be accelerated with web workers.

### 8.10.3 Accessing Content Children

A component can access its content children with decorated properties similar to those used for view children:

- `@ContentChildren(`*`Class`*`)` — returns a `QueryList` containing all content children of the given class
- `@ContentChild(`*`Class`*`)` — returns the first content child with the given class

To see how this works, consider the following markup:

```
<parent>
  <child1></child1>
  <child1></child1>
  <child2></child2>
</parent>
```

The classes of the three content children are `Child1` and `Child2`. The following property provides a `QueryList` containing the two `Child1` instances in the order in which they're inserted into the parent:

```
@ContentChildren(Child1) childList: QueryList<Child1>;
```

Similarly, the following property returns the parent's `Child2` instance:

```
@ContentChild(Child2) child: Child2;
```

Judging from the markup, you might expect that the templates of `Child1` and `Child2` would be automatically inserted into the parent's template. *This is not the case.* Content children must be specifically inserted into the parent's template, and this is accomplished by using the `<ng-content>` placeholder.

This content insertion, commonly called *transclusion*, is crucial to understand. So let me present it another way. Suppose that the parent's template is given as follows:

```
template: `<p>I'm the parent</p>`})
```

If the parent has content children, then by default, the templates of the content children will not be displayed. To display the child templates, `<ng-content>` must be inserted into the parent's template. This is shown in the following markup:

```
template: `<p>Child views: </p><ng-content></ng-content>`})
```

The `<ng-content>` tag identifies the point (the transclusion point) where the child's content should be inserted. This content may contain more than just child components. Any components, elements, or text between the parent's tags, `<parent>` and `</parent>`, will be inserted.

### 8.10.4 Input Properties

An earlier section presented the ch8/class_selector project, which uses the following markup to set a label's `className` property:

```
<label [className]='labelClass'>{{ labelText }}</label>
```

Now suppose you want to configure a child component to receive property updates from a parent component. This can be expressed with markup like the following:

```
<parent>
  <child [prop]='newProp'></child>
</parent>
```

To configure this in code, the child component's class must have a property named `prop` annotated with `@Input()`. This property will be updated whenever the parent's `newProp` property changes. The following code shows what this looks like:

```
class ChildComp {
  @Input() prop: string;
}
```

The `@Input()` annotation accepts a string that sets the name of the property in the markup. Therefore, if the property's name in the template is changed from `prop` to `childProp`, the annotation should change from `@Input()` to `@Input(childProp)`. But within the class, the property can still be accessed as `prop`. The example code at the end of this section demonstrates how this works.

In addition to receiving properties from the parent, a child component can be configured to produce custom events. Event production is a complex topic, so a thorough discussion of custom events will have to wait until Chapter 11.

## 8.11 Life Cycle Methods

When discussing `QueryLists`, I mentioned that its contents may not be immediately available. This is important when dealing with view children and content children. A component can access its `QueryList` of children in its constructor, but the list will always be empty. This is because a component's constructor is called *before* its children have been recognized.

In some cases, processing should be delayed until the class's children are accessible. This is accomplished by adding code to the appropriate life cycle method of the component. Table 8.6 lists these methods in order of when they're (usually) invoked.

**Table 8.6**

Life Cycle Methods of a Component

| Life Cycle Method | Description |
|---|---|
| `ngOnChanges(changes: {[key: string]: SimpleChange})` | Called after data-bound properties have been initialized or changed |
| `ngOnInit()` | Called when the component is instantiated |
| `ngDoCheck()` | Implement custom change detection |
| `ngAfterContentInit()` | Called after the component's content has been initialized |
| `ngAfterContentChecked()` | Called after the component's content has been checked |
| `ngAfterViewInit()` | Called after the component's view has been initialized |
| `ngAfterViewChecked()` | Called after the component's view has been checked |
| `ngOnDestroy()` | Called immediately before the component is destroyed |

The life cycle begins when the component checks the values of its properties. After the component is fully instantiated, it examines its content, which includes its properties and the elements in the template. This content is initialized and then checked.

An earlier discussion explained how a component can access a `QueryList` of its content children. If accessed in the constructor, the list will be empty. It isn't populated until the component's content has been initialized, so the earliest a component's content children can be reliably accessed is in `ngAfterContentInit`.

It may seem odd to have separate methods for a component's content and view. To see why this is the case, it's important to know about *directives*. A directive is a component without a view and Chapter 9 will discuss them in detail.

## 8.11.1 Invoking Life Cycle Methods

Each method in Table 8.5 has an associated interface that contains only that method. The interface's name is almost the same as that of the method, but the initial `ng` is dropped and the first letter is capitalized. As examples, the `ngOnChanges` method is provided by the `OnChanges` interface, the `ngOnDestroy` method is provided by the `OnDestroy` interface, and so on.

If a component class implements one of these eight interfaces, it can add code to the corresponding method. For example, if a component's class implements the `AfterContentInit` interface, its `ngAfterContentInit` method will be called after the component's content has been initialized. The following code gives an idea of how this works:

```
class ExampleComponent implements AfterContentInit {

  ngAfterContentInit() {
    ...
  }
}
```

When using life cycle methods, there's no need to make changes to the component's `@Component` annotation. But each interface must be imported from @angular/core.

### 8.11.2 Responding to Input Property Changes

The `ngOnChanges` method makes it easy to handle changes to a component's input properties. The method's parameter, `changes`, contains an entry for each of the component's properties. Each returned entry is represented by a `SimpleChange`, which provides three members:

- `currentValue` — The property's value after the most recent change
- `previousValue` — The property's value before the most recent change
- `isFirstChange()` — Identifies whether the property's value has changed for the first time

The `currentValue` and `previousValue` can be any type and `isFirstChange()` returns a boolean. The following code shows how these members can be used:

```
ngOnChanges(changes: {[propName: string]: SimpleChange}) {

  // Identify if this is the first time msg has been changed
  if(changes['msg'].isFirstChange()) {
    console.log('This is the first change');
  }

  // Print the current and previous values of msg
  console.log('Current value: ' + changes['msg'].currentValue);
  console.log('Previous value: ' + changes['msg'].previousValue);
}
```

It's important to note that `isFirstChange` returns true when the property's value changes from undefined to its first value. This takes place before the entire component is initialized. This explains why `ngOnChanges` is called before `ngOnInit`.

### 8.11.3 The NestedComps Components

The ch8/nested_comps project demonstrates how a component can access content children and view children. The project contains three components: a child component, a parent component, and a top-level component that contains the parent and children in its template. Listing 8.6 presents the code of the child component.

**Listing 8.6: ch8/nested_comps/app/child.component.ts**

```
// The child component
@Component({
selector: 'child-comp',
template: `
<li>Child <ng-content></ng-content></li>
`})
export class ChildComponent {}
```

This component class doesn't do anything. Instead, the template displays the content assigned to it by its parent. Listing 8.7 presents the code for the parent component.

**Listing 8.7: ch8/nested_comps/app/parent.component.ts**

```
// The parent component
@Component({
selector: 'parent-comp',
template: `
<p>There are {{ children.length }} children:</p>
<ol><ng-content></ng-content></ol>
<p>The parent's msg property equals {{ msg }}.</p>
`})
export class ParentComponent implements AfterContentInit {

  @Input('parentProp') public msg: string;
  @ContentChildren(ChildComponent) public children:
      QueryList<ChildComponent>;

  public ngAfterContentInit() {
    alert('The parent component has ' +
      this.children.length + ' content children');
  }
}
```

The template of the parent component has two parts: a label that identifies the number of children and an ordered list whose content is set by the top-level component. The component class accesses its content children in a `QueryList` named `children`. This list isn't immediately accessible, but the children will be available when the `ngAfterContentInit` life cycle method is called.

Listing 8.8 presents the code in the top-level component. The template contains an instance of `ParentComponent` and three instances of `ChildComponent`.

**Listing 8.8: ch8/nested_comps/app/app.component.ts**

```
// The top-level component
@Component({
selector: 'app-root',
template: `
<parent-comp [parentProp]='message'>
  <child-comp>Content1</child-comp>
  <child-comp>Content2</child-comp>
  <child-comp>Content3</child-comp>
</parent-comp>
`})
export class AppComponent implements AfterViewInit {

  // Declare properties
  @ViewChildren(ParentComponent) public children:
      QueryList<ParentComponent>;

  public message = 'Hello';

  public ngAfterViewInit() {
    alert('The top-level component has ' +
      this.children.length + ' view child');
  }
}
```

This demonstrates a number of aspects involving nested components, such as accessing content, accessing children, and configuring child properties. The top-level template arranges the parent and child components with the following markup:

```
<parent-comp [parentProp]='message'>
  <child-comp>Content1</child-comp>
  <child-comp>Content2</child-comp>
  <child-comp>Content3</child-comp>
</parent>
```

The template of `ParentComp` prints two alert messages and creates an ordered list containing its content children. This template is given as follows:

```
<p>There are {{ children.length }} children:</p>
<ol>
  <ng-content></ng-content>
</ol>
<p>The parent's msg property equals {{ msg }}.</p>
```

Figure 8.2 shows what the resulting component looks like:

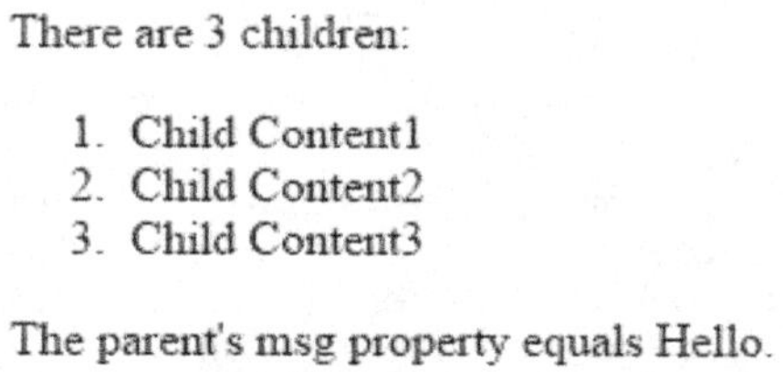


**Figure 8.2 The NestedComps Web Component**

The `ParentComp` class declares its `msg` property with the following code:

```
@Input('parentProp') private msg: string;
```

The `@Input` annotation specifies that `msg` is a property that can be updated by the top-level component. The argument of `@Input()` is `parentProp`, so the top-level component's template accesses the property as `parentProp` instead of `msg`. The component's class sets `parentProp` equal to the member variable message, which is set to `Hello`.

Input properties are generally accessed through their names, not through aliases. If you run `ng lint` for this project, you'll see the following message:

```
In the class "ParentComponent", the directive input property "msg"
should not be renamed.

Please consider the following use "@Input() msg: string"
```

# 8.12 Two-Way Data Binding

In addition to the one-way data binding mechanisms discussed in this chapter, Angular makes it possible to configure two-way data binding. This means that any change to the class property affects the template element and any change to the template element affects the class property.

As in AngularJS, Angular makes two-way data binding possible with `NgModel`. The notation combines the square brackets of property binding with the parentheses of event binding. The general format for two-way binding is as follows:

```
[(ngModel)]='class_property'
```

When this is placed inside a template element, a change to the element will affect the property. A change to *`class_property`* will affect the template element.

For example, suppose you want to associate a boolean property named `checked` with a checkbox in the template. The following markup shows how this can be done.

```
<input type='checkbox' [(ngModel)]='checked'>
```

Similarly, the following markup associates a text entry box with a string property named `inputText`:

```
<input type='text' [(ngModel)]='inputText'>
```

Though it's simple to configure in code, two-way data binding is not recommended. If possible, you should always try to use one-way data binding, which doesn't degrade performance and stability to the same extent. Still, there are times when two-way data binding is necessary, so it's good to know that `NgModel` is available.

# 8.13 Summary

One key difference between AngularJS and Angular is the approach to data binding. In AngularJS, all data binding is two-way, which means the model and view are always in sync. This ensures that the application will be responsive. Unfortunately, detecting changes in the model and view consumes a great deal of resources and can lead to non-deterministic behavior.

In contrast, Angular emphasizes one-way binding. This chapter has presented three mechanisms for one-way binding: property interpolation, property binding, and event binding. The property interpolation and binding mechanisms update the template when a class member changes, but don't affect the class. The event binding mechanism updates the class when the template changes, but doesn't change the template.

After explaining the different one-way binding mechanisms, this chapter explained how local variables work in the template, how to set styles, and the interaction between parent and child components. Child components can be view children or content children depending on where the children are inserted into the parent. A parent can access its children using decorated properties and can pass data to them using property binding.

Angular provides methods and interfaces that make it possible to execute code at different stages in a component's life cycle. These methods make it possible to perform computation when a component's properties change or when its children become accessible.

# Chapter 9

# Directives

I still remember the first time I saw an AngularJS directive in action. The directive was `ngRepeat`, and when I saw what was happening, my jaw dropped. *The directive generates new list elements without needing JavaScript? Cool!*

Since then, my appreciation for directives has grown larger. An Angular directive is like the magic wand in a fairy tale. But instead of turning pumpkins into carriages, Angular's directives turn static HTML elements into dynamic controls that can blink in and out, repeat themselves in a list, or transfer data to the model.

Angular provides fewer directives than AngularJS, but the magic is still there. Angular's primary directives are called *core directives*, and they add behavior to template elements in the same ways that AngularJS directives did. The new `NgIf` directive performs the same operation as the old `ngIf`, the new `NgForOf` directive performs essentially the same operation as the old `ngRepeat`, and so on.

The first part of this chapter presents Angular's core directives and demonstrates how they're used in code. In addition to being easy to use and understand, they provide a great deal of power.

The second part of the chapter explains how to write custom directives. The process of creating a directive is essentially similar to that of coding a component: precede a regular class with an annotation. In this case, the annotation is `@Directive`, and it tells the framework what template elements should receive behavior from the directive and the nature of the behavior to be added.

The last part of this chapter presents two examples of custom directives. The first custom directive dynamically adds elements to the document. The second receives click events from an element and updates its text with each click.

# 9.1 Core Directives

Technically speaking, a directive is a component without a view. In practice, a directive is a marker inserted into a template element that alters the element's behavior. AngularJS provided a vast number of directives and Angular has significantly reduced the number. This section looks at seven core directives:

1. `NgIf` — Adds or removes an element depending on a condition
2. `NgForOf` — Adds multiple elements to the document
3. `NgSwitch` — Adds one of many elements to the document
4. `NgSwitchCase` — Used with `NgSwitch` to identify an option
5. `NgSwitchDefault` — Used with `NgSwitch` to identify the default option
6. `NgClass` — Assigns a CSS class to an element
7. `NgStyle` — Assigns a CSS style to an element

This section examines each of these directives and shows how it can be used in code. But first, it's important to be familiar with three points:

- As with a component, every directive has an associated class. Outside of a template, core directives are referred to by their class names, which take the form of `Ng`*`Xyz`*, such as `NgIf` and `NgStyle`. Inside a template element, the directive's marker is written with a lowercase 'n', as in `ngIf` and `ngStyle`.
- The core directives and their classes are provided automatically. That is, they don't need to be imported and they don't need to be added to the `declarations` array in the `@NgModule` annotation.
- With the exception of `NgClass` and `NgStyle`, the core directives add/remove elements from the document. These are called *structural directives* and their markers must be preceded by an asterisk, as in `*ng`*`Xyz`*. This tells the compiler to place the directive in a `<ng-template>` surrounding its element. For example, if `<abc>` contains `*ng`*`Xyz`*, the equivalent markup is given as follows:

```
<ng-template [ngXyz]='expression'>
  <abc>...</abc>
</ng-template>
```

The last point is complicated and will be discussed later in the chapter. Just remember that the markers of structural directives must be preceded by an asterisk, as in `*ngIf` and `*ngSwitch`.

## 9.1.1 NgIf

The preceding chapter explained how an element can be hidden by setting its `[hidden]` property to true. The operation of `NgIf` is similar, but instead of hiding an element, it removes the element from the document.

`NgIf` accepts an expression and its behavior depends on whether the expression evaluates to false, 0, "", null, undefined, or NaN. These are referred to as *falsy* values and any other values are referred to as *truthy*.

### Basic Usage

The basic usage of `NgIf` is given with the following markup:

```
<xyz *ngIf='expression'>...</xyz>
```

If expression evaluates to a truthy value, the `xyz` element and its subelements will be added to the document. The following markup demonstrates how this works:

```
<div *ngIf = '6 === 7'>
  <label>This won't be included in the document</label>
</div>
```

The directive's expression evaluates to false. Therefore, the `<div>` element and its subelement won't be part of the document.

### If-Then-Else

`NgIf` supports an if-then-else structure similar to that used in JavaScript. The general markup is given as follows:

```
<xyz *ngIf='condition; then trueBlock else falseBlock'></xyz>
<ng-template #trueBlock>...</ng-template>
<ng-template #falseBlock>...</ng-template>
```

As shown, `ngIf` associates `then` with an identifier (`trueBlock`) and `else` with an identifier (`falseBlock`). The two identifiers are inserted into `<ng-template>` elements that contain subelements. If the expression evaluates to a truthy value, the elements inside the `trueBlock` element will be inserted into the document. If the expression evaluates to a falsy value, the elements in the `falseBlock` element will be inserted into the document. The following markup demonstrates how this works:

```
<div *ngIf = '6 === 7; then trueBlock else falseBlock'></div>

<ng-template #trueBlock>
  <label>This won't be included in the document</label>
</ng-template>

<ng-template #falseBlock>
  <label>This will be included in the document</label>
</ng-template>
```

The expression in `NgIf` evaluates to false, so the `ng-template` element containing `falseBlock` will be inserted into the document. Therefore, the second label element will be displayed but not the first.

## 9.1.2 NgForOf

The `NgForOf` directive makes it possible to insert multiple elements into a document. This is particularly useful when an application needs to display dynamic lists and tables.

One confusing aspect of this directive involves the marker. The `ngForOf` marker is available, but most applications use the abbreviated `ngFor` instead. This book will use `ngFor` instead of `ngForOf` throughout its example code.

### Basic Usage

The simplest usage of `NgForOf` is given as follows:

```
<xyz *ngFor = 'let item of iterator'>...</xyz>
```

In this markup, the directive iterates through elements of *`iterator`*, which may be an array or a string. For each element, `NgFor` inserts a new `xyz` element into the DOM. These new elements are frequently list items, table rows, or options in a `<select>`. Each element of *`iterator`* can be accessed through the *`item`* variable.

An example will clarify how this works. Suppose `numArray` equals [13, 17, 19]. The following markup creates a list element for each element in `numArray`. Each list element uses the `num` variable to access the corresponding value of `numArray`.

```
<ul>
  <li *ngFor='let num of numArray'>
    Array element: {{ num }}
  </li>
</ul>
```

In this example, NgFor generates three list items (<li>). The resulting list is given as follows:

- Array element: 13
- Array element: 17
- Array element: 19

## Accessing Variables

In addition to providing the value of each element in the iterator, NgForOf can provide other values. These are accessed by appending let *localVar* = *varName* to the NgFor directive. varName can be set to one of the following values:

- index — Provides the index of the current value, starting with 0
- first — A boolean that identifies whether the current value is the first value
- last — A boolean that identifies whether the current value is the last value
- even — A boolean that identifies whether the current value has an even index
- odd — A boolean that identifies whether the current value has an odd index

To clarify how these are used, the following loop creates a paragraph for each value of numList. The index of each value is accessed as i and l is set to a boolean that identifies whether the current value is the last value:

```
<p *ngFor='let n of numList; let i = index; let l = last'>
  The current index is {{ i }}. Last value? {{ l }}
</p>
```

If numList contains five values, the output will be displayed as follows:

```
The current index is 0. Last value? false
The current index is 1. Last value? false
The current index is 2. Last value? false
The current index is 3. Last value? false
The current index is 4. Last value? true
```

The last, even, and odd variables work similarly to the last variable used in the example. The even and odd variables make it easy to construct a table whose odd rows have different colors than the even rows.

## TrackBy

Angular monitors the elements of the iterator in `NgFor`, and if the data changes, the directive will rebuild the DOM. Therefore, whenever the client reloads data from a server, the directive will update the DOM even if the data has remained constant.

An application can change this tracking behavior by assigning unique identifiers to the iterator's elements. If the elements are reloaded, `NgFor` won't change the DOM if the elements have identical identifiers.

To assign unique identifiers, `NgFor` needs to be associated with a tracking function. This function receives the index of each element and the element itself. The following code shows how the tracking function can be identified in the template:

```
<xyz *ngFor = 'let item of iterator; trackBy:trackFunc'>...</xyz>
```

The following code shows how this works. `NgFor` inserts an `option` element for each `Thing` in `thingArray`. The directive calls `trackThing` to provide a unique identifier for each element and `trackThing` returns the `Thing`'s `id` field.

```
class Thing {
  public constructor(name: string, id: number) {}
}

@Component({
template: `
<select>
  <option *ngFor='let th of thingList; trackBy:trackThing'>
    {{ th.name }}
  </option>
</select>
`})

export class AppComponent {

  public thingList: Thing[] = [
    new Thing("red", 3),
    new Thing("book", 7),
    new Thing("sound", 13)
  ];

  public trackThing(t: Thing, i: number) {
    return t.id;
  }
}
```

## 9.1.3 NgSwitch/NgSwitchCase/NgSwitchDefault

In JavaScript, the `switch` statement makes it possible to process one of many blocks of code according to an expression's value. The overall format is given as follows:

```
switch(expression) {
  case value_1:
    ...
    break;
  case value_2:
    ...
    break;
  default:
    ...
}
```

The `NgSwitch` directive is similar, but instead of processing one of many blocks of code, it inserts one of many elements to the DOM. The `NgSwitchCase` directive serves the same purpose as a `case` option in the `switch` statement. `NgSwitchDefault` serves the same purpose as `default` in the `switch` statement.

The general usage of `NgSwitch`, `NgSwitchCase`, and `NgSwitchDefault` is given as follows:

```
<abc [ngSwitch]='expression'>
  <xyz *ngSwitchCase='x'>...</xyz>
  <xyz *ngSwitchCase='y'>...</xyz>
  <xyz *ngSwitchDefault>...</xyz>
</abc>
```

Here, *abc* can be any container element, such as a `<div>`, `<span>`, `<ul>`, or `<ol>`. The following example places `NgSwitch` inside a `<div>` element, and each `NgSwitchCase` corresponds to a label.

```
<div [ngSwitch]='value'>
  <label *ngSwitchCase='3'>Three</label>
  <label *ngSwitchCase='5'>Five</label>
  <label *ngSwitchDefault>Other</label>
</div>
```

If `value` equals 3, the first `<label>` is added to the document, and if it equals 5, the second label is added. If `value` is neither 3 nor 5, the label corresponding to `NgSwitchDefault` will be added to the document.

## 9.1.4 NgClass

Like the `className` property discussed in Chapter 8, the `NgClass` directive can change the CSS styling of an element and its children. The difference is that `NgClass` can accept a wider range of values and it can both add and remove CSS classes.

Inside a template element, `NgClass` can be assigned to one of three types of values:

1. string — adds the given class or space-separated classes
2. array — adds each class in the array
3. object — maps classes to boolean expressions and adds if true

For example, suppose `labelClasses` is set to an array of class names, such as `['classA', 'classB']`. The following code adds both classes to the label:

```
<label [ngClass]='labelClasses'>Message</label>
```

Similarly, if `classObj` equals `{'classC': true}`, the following markup places the element in `classC`:

```
<label [ngClass]='classObj'>Message</label>
```

## 9.1.5 NgStyle

Chapter 8 presented three ways of assigning styles in an Angular component:

- In the component's annotation, set `styles` equal to an array of CSS rules.
- In the component's annotation, set `styleUrls` equal to a file that defines one or more CSS rules.
- In the template, add a `<style>` element containing CSS rules.

The `NgStyle` directive provides a fourth option, which makes it possible to assign CSS rules to an element and its children. This directive is assigned to an object that maps CSS properties to values. These values can be set equal to properties in the component, thereby enabling the component to dynamically set styles of elements in the template.

For example, suppose the color and size of a paragraph's text should be controlled by the component. If the component has properties named `fontColor` and `fontSize`, the following markup uses `NgStyle` to set the color and size.

```
<label [ngStyle]="{'color': fontColor, 'font-size': fontSize}">
  Message
</label>
```

According to the Angular documentation, `NgStyle` can also be set to a property that defines the full CSS object. I'm sure that this is possible, but despite numerous attempts, I've never succeeded in getting this to work.

### 9.1.6 Example Application

The code in Listing 9.1 presents the component code of the directives_demo project. This demonstrates how each of the core directives are used in practice.

These examples should be easy to understand, but the `NgClass` example deserves additional explanation. To demonstrate the different usages of `NgClass`, the class defines two properties: `classArray` is an array containing two class names and `addClass` is an object that maps a class name to true. Assigning `NgClass` to `classArray` places the element in both classes. Assigning `NgClass` to the object places the element in the given class.

**Listing 9.1: ch9/directives_demo/app/app.component.ts**

```
import {Component} from '@angular/core';

@Component({
selector: 'app-root',
styles:
['.firstClass { color:red; }',
 '.secondClass { font-weight:bold; }',
 '.thirdClass { text-decoration: underline; }'],
template: `

<!-- NgIf -->
<p *ngIf='ifvar; then trueBlock else falseBlock'></p>
<ng-template #trueBlock>
  <label>ifvar was set to true.</label>
</ng-template>
<ng-template #falseBlock>
  <label>ifvar was set to false.</label>
</ng-template>

<!-- NgFor -->
<p *ngFor='let element of forArray; let ind = index'>
  NgFor's element {{ ind }} = {{ element }}
</p>
```

```
<!-- NgSwitch, NgSwitchCase, NgSwitchDefault -->
<div [ngSwitch]='switchVar'>
  <p *ngSwitchCase='1'>The NgSwitch value is Choice 1</p>
  <p *ngSwitchCase='2'>The NgSwitch value is Choice 2</p>
  <p *ngSwitchCase='3'>The NgSwitch value is Choice 3</p>
  <p *ngSwitchDefault>Another choice was selected</p>
</div>

<!-- NgClass -->
<div [ngClass]='classArray'>
  <p>This element is in firstClass and secondClass</p>
  <p [ngClass]='addClass'>
    This element is in firstClass, secondClass, and thirdClass
  </p>
</div>

<!-- NgStyle -->
<p [ngStyle]="{'color': fontColor, 'font-size': fontSize}">
  This style is set by NgStyle.
</p>
`})

export class AppComponent {

  public ifvar = false;
  public forArray = ['A', 'B', 'C', 'D'];
  public switchVar = 2;
  public classArray = ['firstClass', 'secondClass'];
  public addClass = {'thirdClass' : true};
  public fontColor = 'green';
  public fontSize = '18px';
}
```

The constructor of the `AppComponent` class declares a series of values that affect the directives in the template:

- `ifVar` — because this is set to false, the `NgIf` directive inserts the `label` element that contains the `#falseBlock` variable
- `forArray` — the `NgFor` directive iterates through this array of strings and displays each string and its index
- `switchVar` — because this is set to 2, `NgSwitch` displays the message in the `<template>` element whose `NgSwitchCase` directive equals 2
- `classArray` and `addClass` — define CSS classes assigned to paragraphs
- `fontColor` and `fontSize` — define CSS properties associated with the style set by the `NgStyle` attribute

# 9.2 Accessing Directive Instances

Chapter 8 explained how a component can access view children and content children using properties with special annotations like `@ViewChildren` or `@ContentChild`. A component can also use these annotations to access instances of directive classes. For example, consider the following annotation:

```
@Component({
  selector: 'parent-comp',
  template:`
  <p *ngIf='check'>...</p>
`})
```

The `NgIf` directive is contained in the component's template, so it's a view child of that component. This means it can be accessed through a property annotated with `@ViewChild` and it will be available when the component calls `ngAfterViewInit`. If the parent's class name is `ParentComponent`, the following code gives an idea of how the directive could be accessed:

```
export class ParentComponent implements AfterViewInit {

  @ViewChild(NgIf) ngIf: NgIf;

  ngAfterViewInit() {
    ...
  }
}
```

A directive can also be a content child of a component, as shown in the following markup:

```
<parent-comp>
  <p [ngStyle]='...'>styled text</p>
</parent-comp>
```

Here, the component corresponding to `<parent-comp>` can access the `NgStyle` instance through a property annotated with `@ContentChild`. This property can be reliably accessed in the component's `ngAfterContentInit` method.

Core directive classes like `NgIf` or `NgStyle` have few members of interest. Therefore, it's usually unnecessary to access instances of these directives. But some directives, such as `NgForm` discussed in Chapter 14, have interesting properties and methods.

# 9.3 Custom Directives

The core directives provide many capabilities, but they're not sufficient for every task. For this reason, Angular makes it possible to define new directives, and the process of creating a custom directive consists of four steps:

1. Code a directive class to process template elements.
2. Annotate the class with `@Directive`, whose `selector` field identifies which DOM elements should be affected.
3. Add the directive's marker to elements in the template.
4. In the application's module, import the directive's class and add the name of the class to the `declarations` array.

It's common to associate directives with elements using attributes. If a directive's marker is `myDirective`, the following DOM element will be affected by the directive:

```
<label myDirective>Important message</label>
```

The class that adds behavior to the selected elements is called the *directive class*. This must be decorated with `@Directive` instead of `@Component`.

```
@Directive({selector: '[myDirective]'})
class MyDirective {
  ...
}
```

Before a directive can be inserted into a component's template, its class must be added to the `declarations` array in the `@NgModule` annotation of the project's module. The following code shows what this looks like for the `MyDirective` class:

```
@NgModule({
  declarations: [ AppComponent, MyDirective ],
  imports: [ BrowserModule ],
  bootstrap: [ AppComponent ]
})
```

This section starts by examining the `@Directive` annotation. The most important field in this annotation is the `selector` field, which identifies the directive's marker. This is required in every `@Directive` annotation.

## 9.3.1 Identifying Elements

The `selector` field in `@Directive` identifies the directive's marker and the manner in which it can be inserted into template elements. If the directive should be used as an attribute, the identifier should be placed in square brackets:

```
@Directive({selector: '[myDirective]'})
```

The `selector` value can take other formats that resemble CSS selectors. For example, the following annotation states that the directive should apply to every element whose `class` attribute is set to `myClass`:

```
@Directive({selector: '.myClass'})
```

Not all CSS rule formats are available. Directive selectors can't include wildcards, hash tags (e.g. `#myID`), or rules related to descendants. Table 9.1 lists the CSS selector formats that can be used in a `@Directive` annotation:

**Table 9.1**

Selector Formats in Directive Annotations

| Selector Format | Selected Elements |
|---|---|
| `name` | Elements with the given name |
| `.class` | Elements of the given class |
| `[attribute]` | Elements containing the given attribute |
| `[attribute=value]` | Elements whose attribute is set to the given value |
| `[attribute*=value]` | Elements whose attribute contains the given value |
| `name[attribute]` | Elements containing the given name and whose attribute is set |

Multiple values can be OR'ed together by separating them with commas. For example, the following annotation states that the directive should apply to all paragraphs (`p`), elements in the `valid` class, and elements whose `title` is set to `important`:

```
@Directive({selector: 'p, .valid, [title=important]'})
```

By setting `selector` equal to a custom name, a directive makes it possible to create a custom DOM element and set its behavior.

## 9.3.2 Receiving Input

If a directive is accessed with an attribute, the attribute's value can be set to a string. The directive class can access this string using the same `@Input()` annotation discussed in Chapter 8.

For example, suppose a component's template accesses a directive with the following markup:

```
<label [myDirective]="classVar">Click Me</label>
```

`classVar` is a member variable defined in the component class. The directive associated with the `myDirective` marker can access the variable's value with the following code:

```
@Input() myDirective: string;
```

The input variable takes the same name as the directive marker. As discussed in Chapter 8, an alias can be set by adding text between the parentheses of `@Input()`.

## 9.3.3 Handling Events

Chapter 8 explained how a component can respond to events from template elements. For example, the following markup tells Angular to call `handleClick` whenever the button is clicked:

```
<button (click)='handleClick()'</button>
```

Directives don't have templates, so the process of configuring event handling is different. The process involves two steps:

1. In the constructor of the directive class, receive an `ElementRef` in the parameter list. This provides access to the directive's element.
2. Decorate a function with `@HostElement(`*`event`*`)`, where *`event`* is the type of event that should be handled by the function.

`ElementRef` is a class with one field: `nativeElement`. This field provides access to the `HTMLElement` corresponding to the directive's element. Chapter 5 discussed `HTMLElement`s and the other data structures provided by TypeScript for interacting with the document object model (DOM).

The following code shows how an `ElementRef` can be accessed in the constructor of a directive class:

```
constructor(private ref: ElementRef) {}
```

After the `ElementRef` is obtained, the class's functions can use it to access the corresponding DOM element. If a function is preceded with `@HostElement(`*`event`*`)`, it will be called whenever events of *`event`* type occur.

The following code demonstrates how this works. The directive class receives the `ElementRef` and the `handleClick` method uses it to change the inner text of the corresponding DOM element:

```
constructor(private ref: ElementRef) {}

@HostListener('click') handleClick() {
  this.ref.nativeElement.innerText = "Hi there!";
}
```

The `@HostListener` annotation indicates that `handleClick` should be called whenever the element is clicked. As discussed in Chapter 5, other event types include `mouseDown`, `mouseUp`, `mouseEnter`, and `mouseLeave`.

## 9.3.4 Updating the Document's Structure

An earlier discussion explained how structural directives like `NgIf` and `NgFor` make it possible to modify the document's structure. To perform similar operations with a custom directive, it's important to be familiar with two classes:

- `ViewContainerRef` — container of host views and embedded views
- `TemplateRef` — represents an embedded view

The `ViewContainerRef` is a container of views, which come in two types. A host view is associated with a component and is defined by the `template` element in the component's annotation. An embedded view is a subview of the host view, and is defined by a `<template>` element.

As discussed earlier, the markers of structural directives are preceded by asterisks (`*ngIf`, `*ngFor`). The asterisk tells the compiler to surround the directive's element in a `<template>` element. By default, the element and its children are *not* inserted in the DOM.

A directive class can access its `<template>` element through a `TemplateRef` argument in its constructor. To insert the `<template>` element in the DOM, the directive needs to call the `ViewContainerRef`'s `createEmbeddedView` with this `TemplateRef`. This dynamically inserts the directive's `<template>` into the view.

An example will make this less confusing (I hope). Suppose a custom directive's `selector` is set to `[customDir]` and a component's template contains the following element:

```
<button *customDir>Click Me!</button>
```

If `*customDir` wasn't present, the button would be automatically inserted into the DOM. But because of `*customDir`, the compiler will surround the button in a `<template>` element, and this element won't automatically be inserted into the document.

The following definition of the `CustomDir` directive shows how a class can insert the `<template>` element into the DOM by creating an embedded view:

```
class CustomDir {

  constructor(private container: ViewContainerRef,
              private templateRef: TemplateRef) {

    container.createEmbeddedView(templateRef);
  }
}
```

The `createEmbeddedView` method can be called conditionally, as in the case of the `NgIf` directive. It can also be called a variable number of times, as in the `NgFor` directive. Each time `createEmbeddedView` is called with the `TemplateRef`, a new `<template>` element is added to the document.

The code above is fine if the directive only needs to modify the view container once. But this won't be sufficient if the view container's content needs to be changed at runtime. This dynamic behavior can be obtained by adding an embedded view every time a property changes.

To demonstrate how custom directives can be coded, the ch9/custom_directive project defines two directive classes:

- `LoopDirective` — a structural directive that adds elements to the DOM
- `ButtonDirective` — an attribute directive that updates a button's text when clicked

## LoopDirective

The first custom directive, `LoopDirective`, accepts a number and inserts the given number of elements to the document. Listing 9.2 presents its code.

**Listing 9.2: ch9/custom_directive/app/loop.directive.ts**

```
import {Directive, ViewContainerRef, TemplateRef, OnChanges,
  Input, SimpleChange} from '@angular/core';

// This directive inserts multiple elements into the DOM
@Directive({
  selector: '[addElements]'
})
export class LoopDirective implements OnChanges {

  private context: LoopContext = new LoopContext();
  private container: ViewContainerRef;
  private templateRef: TemplateRef<LoopContext>;

  constructor(container: ViewContainerRef,
    templateRef: TemplateRef<LoopContext>) {

    this.container = container;
    this.templateRef = templateRef;
  }

  @Input()
  set addElements(num: any) {
    this.context.numElements = num;
  }

  // Respond each time the property's value is set
  public ngOnChanges(changes: {[key: string]: SimpleChange}) {
    for (let i = 0; i < this.context.numElements; i++) {
      this.container.createEmbeddedView(this.templateRef);
    }
  }
}

export class LoopContext {
  public numElements: number = null;
}
```

As discussed in Chapter 8, the `OnChanges` interface provides the `ngOnChanges` method, which is called each time a component's property changes. The `LoopDirective` class implements `OnChanges`, and when the `addElements` property changes, the `ngOnChanges` method adds a new `TemplateRef` to the view container.

To see how `LoopDirective` works, it's important to understand three points:

- In the directive's annotation, the `selector` element affects every template element with the `addElements` attribute.
- When the value of the `addElements` attribute is updated, the value of `numElements` is set equal to the value.
- The `ngOnChanges` method is called each time a property changes, including its first initialization. This method adds multiple elements to the document by repeatedly calling the `createEmbeddedView` method of the `ViewContainerRef`.

## ButtonDirective

The second custom directive, `ButtonDirective`, demonstrates how directives can receive and process events. Listing 9.3 presents its code.

**Listing 9.3: ch9/custom_directive/app/button.directive.ts**

```
import {Directive, ElementRef, HostListener, Input}
  from '@angular/core';

@Directive({selector: '[removeChar]'})
export class ButtonDirective {

  // Access the directive's element
  constructor(private ref: ElementRef) {}

  // Handle click events
  @HostListener('click') handleClick() {

    // Remove the last character from the element's text
    const str = this.ref.nativeElement.innerText;
    if (str.length > 1) {
      this.ref.nativeElement.innerText =
        str.substring(0, str.length - 1);
    }
  }
}
```

The `ButtonDirective`'s constructor receives an `ElementRef` that represents the element associated with the directive. The `handleClick` method is decorated with `@HostListener('click')`, so it will be called whenever the directive's element is clicked.

When invoked, `handleClick` accesses the `innerText` property of the native element. Then it reduces the length of the element's text by one.

### Component

The template of the application's central component, AppComponent, contains both directives. Listing 9.4 presents its code.

**Listing 9.4: ch9/custom_directive/app/app.component.ts**

```
// This component accesses both directives
@Component({
selector: 'app-root',
template: `
<ul>
  <li *addElements='num'>List item</li>
</ul>
<button removeChar>Click to remove characters</button>
`})
export class AppComponent {
  private num = 3;
}
```

The addElements attribute in <li> creates an instance of the LoopDirective, and it's preceded by * because it adds elements to the DOM. This attribute is set equal to a number that determines how many list elements should be added. The removeChar attribute in <button> creates an instance of the ButtonDirective.

## 9.4 Summary

Angular's directives make it possible to add dynamic behavior to a template's elements. While a programming language has if statements, for loops, and switch-case statements, Angular makes it possible to add similar functionality with NgIf, NgForOf, and the three NgSwitch directives. In addition, the NgClass and NgStyle directives make it possible to dynamically configure an element's appearance.

When the core directives aren't sufficient, you can create a custom directive by annotating a class with @Directive. Inside this annotation, selector identifies which elements should be affected by the directive. The directive class can use @Input to access properties and it can receive events using the @HostListener decorator.

If a directive adds new elements to the document, its marker is preceded by an asterisk, as in *ngFor. This tells the framework that the directive's element should be surrounded in a <template> element. The directive can process template elements by accessing a ViewContainerRef and a TemplateRef through its constructor.

# Chapter 10

# Dependency Injection

Dependency injection is a crucial topic in Angular because it allows components to access services such as HTTP communication services and the Reactive Forms API. The key advantages are simplicity, reliability, and flexibility. If an application makes use of dependency injection, its components don't have to create dependencies on their own because they'll be constructed in advance.

In Angular parlance, a service is a general class that isn't a component, directive, or pipe. The first part of this chapter explains how a component can access services by adding elements to the `providers` array in its `@Component` annotation. This section also explains how an application can make services available to all of its classes, including other service classes.

The next part of the chapter explores the low-level details of dependency injection. There are three data structures to be familiar with: tokens, providers, and injectors. A provider associates a token with a mechanism for constructing a dependency. An injector combines multiple providers together and serves as a central object for injecting dependencies. When created, each component receives its own injector.

The low-level details of dependency injection aren't easy to grasp. But once you understand them, you'll have a deeper understanding of how the Angular framework operates. You'll also be better able to resolve strange errors involving missing or unknown dependencies.

Chapter 8 explained how parent and child components interact. In addition to supporting parent/child components, Angular supports parent/child injectors. A child injector receives all the providers of its parent, which means it can inject the same types of dependencies.

# 10.1 Overview

Suppose that one object (we'll call it the *client*) needs to access a second object (we'll call it the *dependency*). If the client creates and configures the dependency by itself, the tight coupling between the two objects will make the client's code hard to test, difficult to maintain, and nearly impossible to reconfigure.

An example will clarify the problem. Suppose that every instance of the `Gizmo` class requires a `Widget`. A simple way to obtain the `Widget` is to call its constructor:

```
class Gizmo {
  constructor(...) {
    w = new Widget(...);
  }
}
```

This may look fine at first, but when it comes time for testing, there's no way to assign a `MockWidget` instance for testing because of the hardcoded `Widget` class. Also, different applications may need to access alternatives to the `Widget` class, such as `Doohickey` or `Thingamajig`.

To improve flexibility and testability, it's better to provide the client with dependencies that have already been created and configured. For example, if `Thing` is the superclass of `Widget`, `Doohickey`, and `Thingamajig`, an external source can provide a `Thing` to each `Gizmo` through `Gizmo`'s constructor. The following code shows how this can be done:

```
class Gizmo {
  constructor(t: Thing) {
    ...
  }
}
```

The process of supplying a client with prebuilt, preconfigured dependencies is called *dependency injection*. Decoupling the client from its dependencies makes the code easier to test and maintain. This chapter presents three topics related to Angular's implementation of dependency injection:

1. Services and dependency injection
2. Tokens, providers, and injectors
3. Injector hierarchy

# 10.2 Services and Dependency Injection

A common usage of dependency injection involves accessing Angular capabilities like HTTP transfer (discussed in Chapter 13) or the Forms API (discussed in Chapter 14). Angular refers to these and similar capabilities as *service classes* or just *services*. A service class provides special data or behavior, and it isn't a component, pipe, or directive.

The Angular Style Guide has specific recommendations for service classes. Just as the name of a component class should end in `Component` and the name of a directive class should end in `Directive`, the name of a service class should end in `Service`. Similarly, each service class should be defined in a separate file named *.service.ts.

This section focuses on injecting custom services. We'll start by seeing how to inject services into components or directives.

## 10.2.1 Injecting Services into Components or Directives

Suppose that `ExampleService` is a service class and `ExampleComponent` is a component class. To inject an instance of `ExampleService` into `ExampleComponent`, three steps must be performed:

1. Precede the definition of `ExampleService` with `@Injectable()`. This tells the framework that `ExampleService` is a service class.
2. Insert `ExampleService` into the `providers` array of the application's module or the `providers` array in the `@Component` annotation of `ExampleComponent`.
3. Add a parameter in `ExampleComponent`'s constructor of type `ExampleService`.

Just as component classes must be preceded with `@Component` and directive classes must be preceded with `@Directive`, service classes must be preceded with `@Injectable`. This tells Angular that the class is a dependency that can be injected into other classes. The parentheses of `@Injectable` can be left empty, as shown in the following service class definition:

```
// Service class
@Injectable()
export class ExampleService {

  public provideData() {
    return data;
  }
}
```

The following component class shows how `ExampleComponent` can access an instance of `ExampleService`:

```
// Component class
@Component({
selector: '...',
providers: [ ExampleService ],
template: `...`})
export class ExampleComponent {
  constructor(private service: ExampleService) {
    service.someFunction();
  }
}
```

As shown, the `@Component` decorator has a `providers` array that accepts the names of service classes. In this case, the array only contains `ExampleService`. Note that the `providers` array can also be added to the `@Directive` decorator.

The component accesses the service through the parameter list of its constructor. If a parameter's type is a service class, Angular will set the parameter to a new instance of the service class.

## 10.2.2 Injecting Services into Classes

Many applications need to inject services into classes that aren't components or directives. As before, the service class must be preceded with `@Injectable()`. But the receiving class doesn't have a `providers` array.

To make up for this, the name of the service class can be placed in the `providers` array of the application's module. The following `@NgModule` decorator shows what this looks like for an application containing `ExampleComponent` and `ExampleService`:

```
@NgModule({
  declarations: [
    ExampleComponent
  ],
  imports: [
    BrowserModule
  ],
  providers: [
    ExampleService
  ],
  bootstrap: [
    ExampleComponent
  ]
})
```

Because the module's `providers` array contains `ExampleService`, the service will be accessible by `ExampleComponent`. This accessibility extends throughout the application, so any class can access `ExampleService`, including other service classes.

If a service should be specific to a given component, then it should be inserted in the `providers` array of that component's `@Component` decorator. In all other circumstances, Google recommends inserting services in the `@NgModule` decorator of the application's module. This will be adopted throughout this book, starting with the service injection example discussed next.

## 10.2.3 Service Injection Example

The code in the ch10/service_demo project demonstrates how services can be accessed by components and by other services. The app directory contains three important classes:

- `BookArrayService` — creates an array of `Books` and makes them available
- `BookService` — accesses the `BookArrayService` and provides the array of `Books`
- `AppComponent` — accesses the `BookService` and displays the content of the `Book` array

This application contains two service classes (`BookArrayService` and `BookService`) and one component class (`AppComponent`). Listings 10.1 through 10.3 present the code for each of these classes.

**Listing 10.1: ch10/service_demo/app/bookarray.service.ts**

```
import { Injectable } from '@angular/core';
import { Book } from './book';

// Provide book array to the book service
@Injectable()
export class BookArrayService {

  public books: Book[] = [
    new Book('Melville', 'Moby Dick', 544),
    new Book('Austen', 'Persuasion', 150),
    new Book('Brontë', 'Wuthering Heights', 212)
  ];

  // Return the array of books
  public getBookArray() {
    return this.books;
  }
}
```

**Listing 10.2: ch10/service_demo/app/book.service.ts**

```
import { Injectable } from '@angular/core';

import { Book } from './book';
import { BookArrayService } from './bookarray.service';

// A service class that uses dependency injection
@Injectable()
export class BookService {

  public goodBooks: Book[];

  constructor(bookArray: BookArrayService) {
    this.goodBooks = bookArray.getBookArray();
  }

  public getBooks() {
    return this.goodBooks;
  }
}
```

**Listing 10.3: ch10/service_demo/app/app.component.ts**

```
import { Component, Injectable } from '@angular/core';

import { Book } from './book';
import { BookService } from './book.service';

@Component({
selector: 'app-root',
template: `
<ul>
  <li *ngFor = 'let book of goodBooks; let i = index'>
    Good book {{ i }}: {{ book.title }} by {{ book.author }}
  </li>
</ul>
`})

// The component receives the injected BookService
export class AppComponent {

  private goodBooks: Book[];

  constructor(private bookService: BookService) {
    this.goodBooks = bookService.getBooks();
  }
}
```

The BookArrayService and BookService classes are both service classes. This explains why both class definitions are preceded by @Injectable. The services are accessed through the constructors of the BookService and BookComponent classes.

To serve its function, the BookComponent needs to access the BookService and the BookService needs to access the BookArrayService. To make sure both service classes are accessible, the names of both classes are included in the providers array in the @NgModule decorator of the application's module. The following code shows what this looks like:

```
@NgModule({
  declarations: [
    AppComponent
  ],
  imports: [
    BrowserModule
  ],
  providers: [
    BookArrayService, BookService
  ],
  bootstrap: [
    AppComponent
  ]
})
```

When coding services, remember the single responsibility principle. That is, each service should perform a single operation. If a service's role expands, it's a good idea to split its responsibilities into separate services.

Services are frequently employed when applications need to read data from a remote source. Chapter 13 will demonstrate how services are used to transfer data using the HTTP and JSONP protocols.

# 10.3 Tokens, Providers, and Injectors

Service injection is sufficient for most applications, but some applications require more sophisticated dependency injection. If your application needs to access dependency injection at a low level, it's important to have a solid understanding of three data structures: tokens, providers, and injectors.

This section explains what these data structures do and how they work together. I found this topic to be difficult when I first encountered it, so instead of jumping into the details, I'll begin the discussion with an analogy.

**NOTE**

The following analogy was inspired by an article from Pascal Precht entitled *Dependency Injection in Angular 2.* To the best of my knowledge, Pascal was the first to compare Angular's providers to cooking recipes.

## 10.3.1 Analogy: Dependency Injection and Cooking

I'm not a particularly good cook, but I understand the basics. Every cooking recipe has three parts:

- the name of a dish
- a series of ingredients
- a set of instructions for making the dish

As a simple example, Figure 10.1 presents a basic recipe for chocolate-chip cookies.

| **Chocolate-Chip Cookies** | *Directions:* |
|---|---|
| *Ingredients:*<br>- ¾ cup sugar<br>- 2 eggs<br>- ¾ teaspoon baking soda<br>- 2¼ cups flour<br>- 1 teaspoon salt<br>- ¾ cup brown sugar<br>- 12-oz bag of chocolate chips | 1. Preheat oven to 375 deg. F<br>2. Melt butter in microwave and cool.<br>3. Whisk sugar, eggs, butter, and vanilla in a bowl until smooth.<br>4. Whisk flour, baking soda, and salt in another bowl.<br>5. Mix the whisked ingredients<br>6. Stir in chocolate chips or chunks<br>7. Roll dough into balls and scoop onto pans<br>8. Bake dough for 12-16 minutes |

**Figure 10.1 A Recipe for Making Chocolate-Chip Cookies**

A professional cook will have hundreds of recipes like the one shown in the figure. If you go to a restaurant and request a dish, the cook will find the appropriate recipe and obtain the ingredients needed to make it.

With this in mind, here's a three-part analogy:

1. Just as every restaurant has a cook to prepare dishes, every component has an *injector* to provide dependencies.
2. Just as a cook relies on recipes to identify how a dish should be prepared, an injector relies on *providers* to identify how dependencies should be constructed.
3. A recipe maps the name of a dish to instructions and ingredients. A provider maps an object called a *token* to the construction procedure and dependencies.

I hope this gives you a basic idea of how injectors, providers, and tokens are related. To summarize, every component relies on an injector to inject dependencies. For each type of dependency, the injector needs a provider to identify the construction process and which objects are required.

This analogy is fine at a high level, but there are a number of flaws:

- A restaurant may have multiple cooks, but by default, a component has one injector.
- Before an injector can use a provider, the provider must be resolved. I can't think of any culinary equivalent for resolving a provider.
- A recipe serves one purpose: to define how a dish should be made. A provider can serve many different purposes.
- An injector can create child injectors that access its providers.

The rest of this section explores the process of using injectors, providers, and tokens in code. Then we'll look at an example component that demonstrates these concepts.

## 10.3.2 Dependency Injection in Code

The primary data structures involved in dependency injection are injectors, providers, and tokens. Rather than examine these classes individually, I'm going to present the overall process of injecting dependencies into a component or directive. The process consists of four steps:

1. Create a `Provider` that identifies how to create the dependency.
2. Convert the `Provider` into a `ResolvedProvider`.
3. Create an `Injector` from the `ResolvedProvider`.
4. Call the `Injector`'s `get` method to obtain the dependency.

The goal is to create an `Injector` capable of injecting the desired dependencies. When a suitable `Injector` is available, its `get` method can be called to inject the dependency. In other words, if a component or directive needs a `Thing`, it can call `injector.get(Thing)` instead of `new Thing(...)`.

### Step 1: Create a Provider

The `Provider` interface has a number of subinterfaces, including `ValueProvider`, `FactoryProvider`, and `ClassProvider`. Each subinterface configures an `Injector` to provide a different type of dependency. This discussion focuses on two of the subinterfaces: `ClassProvider` and `FactoryProvider`.

## ClassProvider

A ClassProvider's purpose is to configure an Injector to provide one or more instances of a given type. The ClassProvider subinterface has three fields:

- provide — a token that identifies the dependency to be created
- useClass — the type to instantiate as the dependency
- multi — a boolean that identifies whether an array of instances should be provided

The provide field sets the provider's token, which can have any type. Angular has a special token type called OpaqueToken that will be encountered in later chapters. But in most cases, a token is simply the name of a class.

An example will clarify how ClassProviders are used. The following provider can configure an Injector to produce an instance of a Widget whenever the Injector is called upon to provide a Thing:

```
let provider: ClassProvider = {provide: Thing, useClass: Widget};
```

In the ch10/service_demo project discussed earlier, the @NgModule decorator identified the BookArrayService and BookService classes with the following array:

```
providers: [ BookArrayService, BookService ]
```

Angular understands that these names serve as tokens and the names of the classes to be instantiated. This is really a shortened form of the following code:

```
providers: [
  {provide: BookArrayService, useClass: BookArrayService},
  {provide: BookService, useClass: BookService}
]
```

The useClass field is generally set to a class name, but it can be set to anything that can be instantiated. If useClass is set to a string, that string will be provided whenever a configured Injector is called with the given token.

## FactoryProvider

A FactoryProvider is used to provide dependencies that require special construction routines. More precisely, the provider defines a function to be called to provide the dependency needed by an Injector.

The `FactoryProvider` interface has four fields:

- `provide` — a token that identifies the dependency to be created
- `useFactory` — the function to be called to provide the dependency
- `deps` — an array of elements to provide arguments of the `useFactory` function
- `multi` — a boolean that identifies whether an array of results should be provided

The `useFactory` function is called a *factory function* because it constructs and returns the dependency that needs to be injected. The following code gives an idea of how this works:

```
let provider: FactoryProvider = {
  provide: Thing,
  useFactory: () => {
    return new Widget();
  }
};
```

If the factory function needs additional data, the `deps` field can be set to an array of elements. These are the ingredients required to construct the factory's dependency. The factory function accesses these elements through its parameter list, as shown in the following code:

```
let provider: FactoryProvider = {
  provide: Thing,
  useFactory: (val1: number, val2: number) => {
    let t = new Thing();
    t.setNumArms(val1);
    t.setNumLegs(val2);
    return t;
  },
  deps: [NumArms, NumLegs]
};
```

Each element in the `deps` array is a token that will be used by another provider to obtain the actual value. In the above example, there must be providers available to provide values for `NumArms` and `NumLegs`. Otherwise Angular will produce errors: *No provider for NumArms! No provider for NumLegs!*

If a dependency is optional, it can be decorated with `@Optional` in the function's parameter list. If a dependency isn't available, the factory function will receive a value of null.

## Step 2: Convert the Provider to a ResolvedProvider

Before a `Provider` can be used to configure an `Injector`, it must be resolved. Angular's documentation states that resolution is the "process of flattening multiple nested arrays and converting individual providers into an array of `ResolvedProviders`."

Resolution is accomplished by calling the static `resolve` method of the `ReflectiveInjector` class. This accepts an array of `Providers` and returns an array of `ResolvedProviders`. For example, the following code creates a single-element array of `ResolvedProviders` from a `Provider` that associates `Token` with the `Other` class.

```
let provider: ClassProvider = {provide: Token, useClass: Other};
let resProviders = ReflectiveInjector.resolve([provider]);
```

If a class is inserted into `resolve`'s array, it will serve as a provider for instances of that class. For example, consider the following code:

```
let resProviders = ReflectiveInjector.resolve([Thing]);
```

`Thing` isn't a `Provider`, so the framework interprets it as a `Provider` for `Thing`. The following code is equivalent:

```
let resProviders =
  ReflectiveInjector.resolve([{provide: Thing, useClass: Thing}]);
```

After an application obtains an array of resolved providers, the next step is to create an `Injector`. This is discussed next.

## Step 3: Create an Injector

The `fromResolvedProviders` method creates an `Injector` from an array of `ResolvedProviders`. This is another static method of the `ReflectiveInjector` class, and it returns an `Injector` capable of performing dependency injection.

The following code creates a `ResolvedProvider` that associates `Token` with the `Other` class. Then it calls `fromResolvedProviders` to return an `Injector`:

```
let provider = {provide: Token, useClass: Other};
let resProviders = ReflectiveInjector.resolve([provider]);
let injector =
  ReflectiveInjector.fromResolvedProviders[resProviders];
```

This code can be simplified by calling the `resolveAndCreate` method. This accepts the same argument as the `resolve` method discussed earlier. But instead of returning a `ResolvedProvider`, it returns a configured `Injector`. This is shown in the following code:

```
let provider = {provide: Token, useClass: Other};
let injector = Injector.resolveAndCreate([provider]);
```

To be precise, the `fromResolvedProviders` and `resolveAndCreate` methods return an instance of `ReflectiveInjector`. `ReflectiveInjector` is a class that implements the `Injector` interface. The only method required to implement `Injector` is `get`, which will be discussed next.

## Step 4: Obtain the Dependency

After an `Injector` is created, its `get` method can be called to inject dependencies. This accepts the name of the token and returns an object of the type to which the token was associated. As an example, consider the following code:

```
let obj = injector.get(Token);
```

If `injector` was configured with a `ClassProvider` that associates `Token` with the `Other` class, `obj` will be an instance of `Other`. If `injector` was configured with a `FactoryProvider` that associates `Token` with a factory function, the function will be invoked and its return value will be provided by `get`.

The code in Listing 10.4 demonstrates how `Providers` and `Injectors` are used in practice. It creates two `Providers`:

1. `providerA` is a `ClassProvider` that binds `TokenA` to the class `Other`.
2. `providerB` is a `FactoryProvider` that binds `TokenB` to a function that creates `Things`.

After creating these providers, the component calls `resolveAndCreate` to convert them into `ResolvedProviders` and create a new `ReflectiveInjector`. Then it calls the `get` method once for each token.

**Listing 10.4: ch10/provider_demo/app/app.component.ts**

```
import {Component, ClassProvider,
  FactoryProvider, ReflectiveInjector} from '@angular/core';

class TokenA {}
class TokenB {}
class Other {}
class Thing {}

@Component({
selector: 'app-root',
template: `
<ul>
<li>ResultA is an instance of Other: {{ resultA }}</li>
<li>ResultB is an instance of Thing: {{ resultB }}</li>
</ul>
`})

export class AppComponent {

  private resultA: boolean;
  private resultB: boolean;

  constructor() {

    // Class provider
    const providerA: ClassProvider = {
      provide: TokenA, useClass: Other};
    const providerB: FactoryProvider = {
      provide: TokenB, useFactory: () => new Thing() };

    // Create an injector from both providers
    const injector = ReflectiveInjector.resolveAndCreate(
      [providerA, providerB]);

    // Invoke get and examine results
    this.resultA = injector.get(TokenA) instanceof Other;
    this.resultB = injector.get(TokenB) instanceof Thing;
  }
}
```

The component's view displays a list that checks the classes of the `resultA` and `resultB` variables. The elements of this list are given as follows:

- `ResultA is an instance of Other: true`
- `ResultB is an instance of Thing: true`

# 10.4 Injector Hierarchy

An application can define providers for all of its classes by listing them in the `providers` array of the module's `@NgModule` decorator. A component can define component-specific providers in the `providers` array of its `@Component` decorator. The same holds true for directives.

A component's providers can be accessed by its content children and view children. If a child component requests a dependency, the framework starts by looking through the providers of the child component's injector. If a suitable provider can't be found, the framework will look through the providers of the parent component's injector, and those of the parent's parent's injector, and so on. In this manner, the components' injectors form a hierarchy.

If a child component obtains a dependency using a parent component's provider, the dependency will be the *same object* as would be injected into the parent. This may cause issues if the child should have a different instance of the dependency than the parent. To ensure that a child component will have a distinct dependency, the provider should be added to the `providers` array of the child's `@Component` decorator in addition to the parent's `providers` array.

# 10.5 Summary

Most developers only deal with Angular's dependency injection when a component needs to access a service like HTTP communication or the Form API. In these cases, injection can be handled by adding an element to the `providers` array in the `@NgModule` annotation or the providers array in the `@Component` annotation. The provider tells the component's injector how to obtain the dependencies.

At a low level, Angular's dependency injection process can be difficult to grasp. First, an application needs to define a class that implements the `Provider` interface, such as a `ClassProvider` or a `FactoryProvider`. Then the `Provider` instance needs to be resolved into a `ResolvedProvider`. An array of `ResolvedProviders` can be used to create an `Injector`, and the `Injector`'s `get` method provides the desired dependency.

Each component receives its own injector, and a child component receives a child injector from its parent. The child injector can access all of the providers of its parent, so it can inject the same dependencies. This relationship of parent-child injectors forms an injector hierarchy.

# Chapter 11

# Asynchronous Programming

One disadvantage of web development is the constant need to wait—wait for the user to take an action, wait for the server to respond to a request, wait for the database to sort its records. Rather than halt the application, it's more efficient to assign a routine to process results as they become available. This frees the application to work on other tasks instead of waiting.

The technique of assigning a routine to be executed at an indeterminate time is called asynchronous programming. This chapter presents two mechanisms for asynchronous programming: promises and observables. Promises are built-in features of JavaScript and observables are provided by Reactive Extensions for JavaScript (RxJS), which Angular requires to operate.

A promise makes it possible to associate two functions with an incomplete operation. The first function is called if the operation completes successfully. The second is called if an error prevents the operation from returning successfully. A promise is assumed to provide a value, and when the value is returned, the promise's processing is complete.

Observables are similar to promises, but provide a series of values instead of just one. For this reason, observables can be associated with three functions. The first function executes when the observable provides a value, the second executes if an error occurs, and the third executes when the observable has finished sending data. A key difference between observables and promises is that the objects monitoring an observable (observers) can cancel their monitoring. Promises can't be cancelled.

The last part of this chapter explains how to configure a component to provide custom events to other components. This configuration requires an `EventEmitter`, which behaves like an observable and an observer.

# 11.1 Promises

If someone owes you money but can't pay you right now, they may give you an IOU or other acknowledgement of debt. If an application needs data that isn't available right now, it may receive a promise. A promise is a data structure that represents an operation that hasn't completed yet but is expected to provide a result.

For example, if an application wants to access the content of a large file or read lengthy data from a server, it may receive a promise. The advantage of using promises is that the application doesn't need to wait for the operation to complete. After receiving a promise, the application can perform other tasks.

When an application receives a promise, one of two things will eventually happen. Success means that the operation completed successfully and a result is available. Failure means that an error occurred and the operation failed.

More formally, we say that a promise has three possible states:

1. Pending — The promise hasn't produced a result because the operation hasn't completed.
2. Fulfillment — The operation has completed and the promise has provided the result. When a promise enters the Fulfillment state, we say that it has fulfilled.
3. Rejection — The operation encountered an error and no result is available. When a promise enters the Rejection state, we say that it has been rejected.

Figure 11.1 illustrates what these states look like.

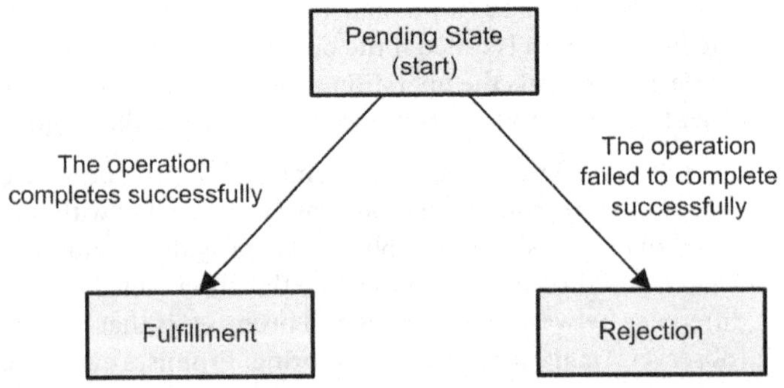


**Figure 11.1 Three States of a Promise**

Promises have become popular in JavaScript and they're part of the ES6 specification. They're also important in Angular development, as we'll see in later chapters. This section introduces the `Promise` class and its methods, and then presents an example component that demonstrates how `Promise`s are used.

## 11.1.1 The Promise Class

Promises begin their operation in the Pending state. Instead of waiting for this state to change, an application receiving the promise can associate it with two functions. These are called *handlers* or *callbacks*.

The first handler is invoked if the promise fulfills, and for this reason, it's referred to as a *fulfillment handler*. The second handler is called if an error occurs and the promise is rejected. This is called a *rejection handler*.

The method that assigns handlers to a `Promise` is called `then`, and its signature is given as follows:

```
then(onFulfilled?: function(value: T),
     onRejected?: function(error: any)): Promise;
```

`then` accepts two optional functions. The first function is called if the promise fulfills and provides a suitable result. The second function is called if the promise is rejected. This function receives information about the error.

For example, suppose an application receives a `Promise` named `prom`. The following code shows how an application can assign handlers to the `Promise`:

```
prom.then(
  function(str: string) { console.log("Result: " + str); },
  function(err: any)    { console.log("Error: " + err); });
}
```

When the `Promise` reaches its final state, one of the two functions will write to the console. The return value of `then` is the configured `Promise`, so this method can be chained with further methods. It's common to see a `Promise` that calls `then` multiple times to define multiple handlers. The following code gives an idea of how this works:

```
prom.then(function(..){..}, function(..){..})
    .then(function(..){..}, function(..){..})
    .then(function(..){..}, function(..){..})
```

In this code, each call to `then` executes independently. That is, an error in one callback won't affect other callbacks. But if one callback modifies the `Promise`, successive callbacks will access the altered `Promise`.

If the asynchronous operation produces an error, the second function of `then` will be invoked. But if the first function produces an error, the second function will not be invoked. For this reason, the `Promise` class provides the `catch` method. In essence, `catch` is just `then` with one argument—a function to call if an error occurs. The following code shows how `then` and `catch` can be used together:

```
prom.then(function(..){..}).catch(function(..){..});
```

In this code, the argument of `then` is called if the asynchronous operation successfully returns the desired object. If an error occurs, either in the asynchronous operation or `then`'s argument, the function in `catch` will be called.

## 11.1.2 Static Methods of the Promise Class

The `Promise` class provides four helpful static methods that return new `Promises`:

- `resolve(value?: T)` — Returns a `Promise` that is guaranteed to fulfill and return the given value
- `reject(error: any)` — Returns a `Promise` that is guaranteed to be rejected and provide the given error information
- `all(promises: (T)[])` — Accepts an array of `Promises` and returns a `Promise` that only fulfills if every element fulfills.
- `race(promises: (T)[])` — Accepts an array of `Promises` and returns a `Promise` that fulfills if any of the elements fulfill.

This discussion presents each of the four methods and shows how they can be invoked in code.

### resolve

The first of the four functions, `resolve`, returns a `Promise` that is guaranteed to fulfill. If `resolve` is called with a value that isn't a `Promise`, the value will be provided as the data object of the returned `Promise`.

An example will help make this clear. Suppose you want to test your application by creating a `Promise` that always provides the value of 5. This can be accomplished with the following code:

```
prom = Promise.resolve(5);
```

If `then` is called after the `Promise` is created, the function that handles fulfillment will receive the value of 5 when the `Promise` fulfills.

### reject

Just as `resolve` creates a `Promise` that always succeeds, `reject` creates a `Promise` that is guaranteed to fail. This accepts a value of any data type, and this value will be provided to any function that catches the `Promise`'s error.

For example, the following call to `reject` produces a `Promise` that enters the Rejection state. After reaching this state, it provides the error handler with a string value of `Error`.

```
prom = Promise.reject("Error");
```

The following code shows how an application receiving this `Promise` can call `catch` to process the error:

```
prom.catch(function(err: any) { console.log("Msg: " + err); });
```

When the `Promise` is rejected, the anonymous function will write the message to the console. A function that handles the `Promise`'s fulfillment will not be invoked.

### all and race

The `all` method accepts an array of `Promise`s and returns a `Promise` that fulfills when every `Promise` fulfills. If any `Promise` in the array is rejected, the returned `Promise` will be rejected.

If the returned `Promise` fulfills, its value will be an array containing the values provided by each `Promise` in the original array. This is shown in the following code, which creates an array of three `Promise`s and uses `all` to combine them into one.

```
let prom: Promise = Promise.all(
    [Promise.resolve("msg"), Promise.reject("Uh-oh")]);
```

In this example, `prom` won't fulfill because the second `Promise` in its array is rejected. If the `catch` method is called, the error handler will receive a single string containing the `Uh-oh` message.

The race method is similar to all in that it receives an array of Promises. But the returned Promise will fulfill or reject as soon as one of the Promises in the array fulfills or rejects. The first fulfilled/rejected Promise will set the value or error information of the Promise. The following code shows how this works:

```
let prom: Promise<string> = Promise.race(
    [Promise.resolve("msg"), Promise.reject("Uh-oh")]);
```

In this example, it's hard to say whether prom will fulfill or be rejected. If the first Promise fulfills before the second is rejected, prom will fulfill. If the second Promise is rejected before the first fulfills, prom will be rejected.

## 11.1.3 The Promise Constructor

It's more common for applications to receive Promises than create them, but for testing purposes, it's good to be familiar with the constructor of the Promise class. If T is the data type of the desired value, the constructor of the Promise class is declared as follows:

```
constructor(callback: function(
  resolve : function(value? : T | Promise<T>),
  reject  : function(error? : any)) : void);
```

This constructor accepts a function, callback, that accepts two functions as arguments, resolve and reject. These names correspond to the resolve and reject methods discussed earlier. The body of the callback function usually invokes one of the two methods to create the new Promise.

As an example, the following code creates a Promise that fulfills and returns the string message.

```
let prom: Promise =
  new Promise(function(resolve, reject) { resolve("message"); });
```

Similarly, the following code creates a Promise that is rejected and returns the number 505 as the reason.

```
let prom: Promise =
  new Promise(function(resolve, reject) { reject(505); });
```

For the sake of debugging, the object returned as an error should be an instance of the Error class instead of a string.

## 11.1.4 Example Application

The code in Listing 11.1 demonstrates how `Promises` can be created and processed. It starts by creating two `Promises`: one that fulfills, returning a number, and one that will be rejected. The first is processed with `then(...).catch(...)` and then an array of both promises is processed with `all`.

**Listing 11.1: ch11/promise_demo/app/app.component.ts**

```
@Component({
selector: 'app-root',
template: `
<p><b>First result</b> - {{ result1 }}</p>
<p><b>Second result</b> - {{ result2 }}</p>
`})
export class AppComponent {

  // State data: two promises and two results
  private promise1: Promise<number>;
  private promise2: Promise<void>;
  private promiseArray: Promise<any>[];
  private result1: string;
  private result2: string;

  constructor() {
    this.promise1 = new Promise((res, rej) => { res(123); });
    this.promise2 = Promise.reject('Big problem');

    // Process first promise
    new Promise((res, rej) => { res(123); }).then(
      (val: number) => { this.result1 =
        'Fulfilled with a value of ' + String(val); }).catch(
      (err: any) => { this.result1 =
        'Rejected with an error: ' + err.toString(); });

   // Process array of promises
    this.promiseArray = [this.promise1, this.promise2];
    Promise.all(this.promiseArray).then(
      (array: any[]) => { this.result2 =
        'Fulfilled with value: ' + array.toString(); }).catch(
      (error: any) => { this.result2 =
        'Rejected with an error of ' + error.toString(); });
  }
}
```

It's important to use arrow function expressions inside the calls to `then` and `catch`. Otherwise, `this` won't refer to the enclosing `AppComponent` object.

# 11.2 RxJS Observables

Promises are helpful when an application needs to access a single result provided asynchronously. But in many cases, such as when reading data from a server, an application needs to read a sequence of values. This value sequence is frequently referred to as a *stream*.

To enable asynchronous processing of stream data, Microsoft's Open Technologies group developed a toolset called Reactive-Extensions, abbreviated to Rx. This has been ported to many languages, and the JavaScript implementation is called RxJS.

When the Angular CLI creates a new project, it uses npm to install the rxjs package. You can verify this by looking for the rxjs folder in the node_modules directory.

The fundamental class of RxJS is `Observable`, and most of this discussion focuses on using it in code. Like a `Promise`, an `Observable` provides access to asynchronous data, but there are two crucial differences:

1. An `Observable` provides multiple values instead of just one.
2. An `Observable` can be cancelled.

Angular frequently provides access to asynchronous data using `Observable`s. For example, the `QueryList` class discussed in Chapter 8 provides an `Observable` called `changes` that provides notification when its content changes. As will be shown in Chapter 13, the HTTP response from a server is made accessible through an `Observable`.

RxJS classes and functions must be imported from the rxjs module. A fast way to do this involves importing everything under the `Rx` namespace:

```
import * as Rx from "rxjs/Rx";
```

It's also possible to import elements individually. For example, the following command imports the `Observable` class:

```
import { Observable } from "rxjs/Observable";
```

The first approach requires more code because each RxJS class must be accessed through the `Rx` namespace. But the second approach is error-prone and frustrating. Therefore, the example code in this chapter accesses RxJS classes through the `Rx` namespace.

This section focuses on the `Observable` class, which provides a wide range of static and instance methods. To present these methods, this section is divided into four topics:

1. Subscribing to an `Observable`
2. Subscriptions
3. Creating `Observables`
4. Handling errors

After explaining these topics, this section presents an example web component that creates an `Observable` and subscribes two observers.

## 11.2.1 Subscribing to an Observable

If an application receives a `Promise` representing an unfinished operation, it can assign handlers by calling the `Promise`'s `then` method. This accepts two functions—one to be called if the operation succeeds and one to be called if the operation fails.

If an application receives an `Observable`, it can assign handlers by calling the `Observable`'s `subscribe` method. This accepts three functions in order:

- data handler — receives each value emitted by the `Observable`
- error handler — receives an error message if an error occurs
- completion handler — called when the `Observable` completes its data transmission

An example will clarify how this works. If `obs` is an `Observable`, the following code prints different messages to the console depending on whether the `Observable` produces data, throws an error, or completes its data transmission:

```
obs.subscribe(
  function(value: number) { console.log("Received: " + value); },
  function(exception: any) { console.log("Exception"); },
  function() { console.log("Completed"); }
);
```

In this example, the first function prints a message each time it receives a value. When the source has finished transmitting its data, the third function will be called. The second function will only be called if an error occurs.

The `Observable` class is a generic class, and its name is followed by a parameter whose type identifies the data provided to the data handler. In the above code, `obs` is an `Observable<number>` because the `Observable` emits `numbers`.

In addition to accepting functions, `subscribe` can be called with an object that implements the `Observer` interface. If `subscribe` is called with an `Observer`, we say that the `Observer` has *subscribed* to the `Observable`. The `Observer` interface contains four optional methods:

- `next` — processes a value provided by the `Observable`
- `error` — responds to an error in data transmission
- `complete` — responds when the `Observable` completes sending data
- `isUnsubscribed` — identifies whether the `Observer` is/isn't subscribed

An `Observable` interacts with its `Observers` by calling these methods. That is, an `Observable` calls an `Observer`'s `next` method when new data is available, calls the `error` method if an error occurs, and calls the `complete` method when its data communication is finished. An upcoming code example will demonstrate how `subscribe` can be called with an `Observer`.

## 11.2.2 Subscriptions

`subscribe` returns a `Subscription` that represents the subscribed state to the `Observable`. The `Subscription` class provides a method called `unsubscribe`, which terminates the subscription. For example, if `obs` is an `Observable`, the following code subscribes to `obs` and then terminates the subscription:

```
let sub: Subscription<number> = obs.subscribe(
  function(value: number) { console.log("Received: " + value); },
  function(exception: any) { console.log("Exception"); },
  function() { console.log("Completed"); }
);
sub.unsubscribe();
```

The `Subscription` class also provides a boolean property called `isUnsubscribed`. This is true if the subscription has been terminated.

## 11.2.3 Creating Observables

For testing purposes, it's important to know how to create new `Observables`. The `Observable` class provides many static methods for creating new instances, and most of them create `Observables` from known values. Table 11.1 lists six of these methods and provides a description of each.

**Table 11.1**

Static Creation Methods of the Observable Class (Abridged)

| Method | Description |
|---|---|
| empty<T>() | Creates an empty Observable<T> |
| range(start: number, count: number) | Creates an Observable<T> from a range of count values, beginning with the starting value |
| from<T>(iterable: any) | Creates an Observable<T> from an iterable or an array-like object |
| fromArray<T>(array: T[]) | Creates an Observable<T> from an array |
| of<T>(...values: T[]) | Creates an Observable<T> from a general list of values |
| create<T> (function(Observer<T>)) | Creates an Observable<T> that calls methods of Observer<T> instances |

The first five methods create Observables from known values. The last, Observable.create, creates an Observable whose values are determined programmatically.

## Creating Observables from Known Data

The first five methods in Table 11.1 are commonly used for testing. They're also helpful to newcomers because they clarify what an Observable does. An Observable provides a sequence of one or more values to its subscribers. For example, the following code creates an Observable that provides a sequence of five values starting with 3:

```
obs = Rx.Observable.range(3, 5);
```

The following Observables all transmit the same three values to their subscribers:

```
obs = Observable.range(1, 3);
obs = Observable.from([1, 2, 3]);
obs = Observable.fromArray([1, 2, 3]);
obs = Observable.of(1, 2, 3);
```

Creating an Observable for predefined data usually isn't useful in practical applications. This is because it's easier to iterate through the data in a for loop than to create Observables.

## Creating Observables with Programmatically-Defined Behavior

The `Observable.create` method provides greater control over the notifications sent to subscribers. Its only argument is a function that accesses a `Subscriber`. The `Subscriber` class implements the `Observer` interface discussed earlier, and when used in `Observable.create`, it's common to call its `next` and `complete` methods.

An example will clarify how this works. The following code creates an `Observable` that transmits two strings to each `Subscriber` and then completes its notification.

```
obs = Observable.create(
  (observer: Rx.Subscriber<string>) => {
    observer.next("msg1");
    observer.next("msg2");
    observer.complete();
  }
);
```

This example could have used the `from` or `fromArray` methods, but it's important to see how `Observable.create` makes it possible to provide data dynamically. Instead of providing predefined string values, the inner function could read bytes from a socket or characters from a file.

The inner function of `Observable.create` returns an optional function whose code is invoked when the subscription is terminated. For example, the following `Observable` sends a number to its `Subscribers` and completes the transmission. As each subscription is terminated, it prints a message to the console:

```
obs = Observable.create(
  (observer: Rx.Subscriber<number>) => {
    observer.next(10101);
    observer.complete();
    return () => {
      console.log("Subscription terminated");
    }
  }
);
```

As shown, the optional function accepts no arguments. It can't access the `Subscribers`, so it's generally used to free resources related to the connection to the `Subscriber`.

## 11.2.4 Handling Errors

When a processing error occurs, an Observable can (and should) catch it and deliver an Error instance to observers.

The following code shows how this works. The throw statement in the try block creates a new Error instance. The catch block receives the Error object and calls the onError method of each subscribed observer.

```
obs = Observable.create(
  (observer: Subscriber<number>) => {
    try {
      observer.next(1);
      observer.next(2);
      throw new Error("Major Error");
    }
    catch(err) {
      observer.error(err);
    }
  }
);
```

After an Observable catches an error and notifies its observers, each of its subscriptions will be disposed of. If the error isn't caught, these subscriptions may not be disposed of. This makes it particularly important to ensure that an Observable's error handling is performed correctly.

## 11.2.5 An Example Application

The ch11/rx_demo project demonstrates how Observables and Observers can work together. Listing 11.2 presents the code for the main component, which declares two Observer classes, Observer1 and Observer2. Then it creates an Observable that transmits three numbers and throws an Error.

When the component's button is pressed, the createSubscriptions method is called. This subscribes two observers (anonymous instances of Observer1 and Observer2) to the Observable. As the observers receive data, they print messages to the console.

When a subscription to the Observable terminates, the Observable prints a message to be displayed under the button. Because there are two observers, two subscriptions will be canceled, and the Terminate message will be printed twice.

**Listing 11.2: ch11/rx_demo/app/app.component.ts**

```
// First observer class
class Observer1 implements Rx.Observer<number> {
  public next(value: any) {console.log('Obs1.next: ' + value); };
  public error(err: any) { console.log('Obs1.error: ' + err); };
  public complete() { console.log('Obs1.complete'); };
}

// Second observer class
class Observer2 implements Rx.Observer<number> {
  public next(value: any) {console.log('Obs2.next: ' + value); };
  public error(err: any) { console.log('Obs2.error: ' + err); };
  public complete() { console.log('Obs2.complete'); };
}

@Component({
selector: 'app-root',
template: `
  <button (click) = 'createSubscriptions()'>
    Create Subscriptions</button>
  <p [innerHTML]='msg'></p>
`})
export class AppComponent {
  private obs: Rx.Observable<number>;
  private msg = '';

  constructor() {

    // Create observable
    this.obs = Rx.Observable.create(
      (ob: Rx.Subscriber<number>) => {
        try {
          ob.next(3); ob.next(2); ob.next(1);
          throw new Error('Problem');
        } catch (err) {
          ob.error(err);
        }
        return () => { this.msg += 'Terminate<br/><br/>'; };
      }
    );
  }

  // Subscribe the observers to the observable
  private createSubscriptions(): void {
    this.obs.subscribe(new Observer1());
    this.obs.subscribe(new Observer2());
  }
}
```

# 11.3 RxJS Stream Processing

`Observables` can do more than just provide streams of data. One important feature is that an `Observable` can manipulate its stream before the data reaches observers. These operations are made possible by instance methods of the `Observable` class, and this section divides them into three groups:

1. Filtering — Remove values from the data stream
2. Combining — Join values from multiple data streams together into one stream
3. Transforming — Operate on individual elements of a stream

Every method discussed in this section returns a configured `Observable`, so they can be chained together as needed.

## 11.3.1 Filtering Data Streams

The simplest stream processing operations remove elements of a stream before the stream's data reaches observers. Table 11.2 lists five of the `Observable` methods that perform these operations.

**Table 11.2**

Filtering Methods of the Observable Class

| Method | Description |
|---|---|
| `take(count: number)` | Emit only the first count values of the sequence |
| `skip(count: number)` | Emit elements following the first count elements of the sequence |
| `takeWhile(predicate: function(value: T, index: number): boolean)` | Emit values of the sequence while the predicate returns true |
| `skipWhile(predicate: function(value: T, index: number): boolean)` | Prevent emission of values while the predicate returns true |
| `filter(predicate: function(value: T, index: number): boolean)` | Emit values of the sequence for which the predicate returns true |

The first two methods are particularly easy to use, as shown in the following examples:

```
Observable.range(1, 5);
--> 1, 2, 3, 4, 5

Observable.range(1, 5).take(3);
--> 1, 2, 3

Observable.range(1, 5).skip(3);
--> 4, 5
```

The last three methods in the table use a predicate function to determine which elements should be removed. These predicate functions all return a boolean and they all accept the same two parameters:

- `val` — the data element provided by the `Observable`
- `i` — the index of the data element

`takeWhile` transmits values so long as the predicate function returns true. The following code emits values while `val` is less than 4:

```
Observable.range(1, 5).takeWhile(
  (val: number, i: number) => val < 4 );
--> 1, 2, 3
```

`skipWhile` prevents values from being transmitted while the predicate returns true. The following code prevents values from being transmitted as long as the index, `i`, is less than 3:

```
Observable.range(1, 5).skipWhile(
  (val: number, i: number) => i < 3 );
--> 4, 5
```

`filter` transmits all values for which the predicate returns true. The following code transmits all odd values:

```
Observable.range(1, 5).filter(
  (val: number) => (val % 2) === 1 );
--> 1, 3, 5
```

## 11.3.2 Combining Data Streams

The `Observable` class provides methods that fuse multiple data streams into one. Some combine a stream with itself or with literal values. Other methods convert streams into new `Observables`. Table 11.3 lists five of these methods and provides a description of each.

**Table 11.3**

Stream Combination Methods of the Observable Class

| Method | Description |
|---|---|
| `startWith(value: T)` | Prepend a value to the stream |
| `repeat(count: number)` | Repeat the data stream the given number of times |
| `concat(...sources: Observable<T>[])` | Append given data streams after the given stream |
| `merge(obs: Observable<T>)` | Merge the current stream with the stream of the given Observable |
| `zip(...sources: Observable<T>, (...sources) => {result})` | Programmatically merge data streams that can hold elements of different types |

The `startWith` method is easy to use. The following code prepends a string to an `Observable`'s data stream:

```
Observable.of("a", "b", "c").startWith("1");
--> 1, a, b, c
```

The `repeat` method is also straightforward. The following code repeats an `Observable`'s data stream three times:

```
Observable.of("a", "b", "c").repeat(3);
--> a, b, c, a, b, c, a, b, c
```

The next three methods in the table are more involved. Figure 11.2 gives an idea of how `concat`, `merge`, and `zip` combine data streams.

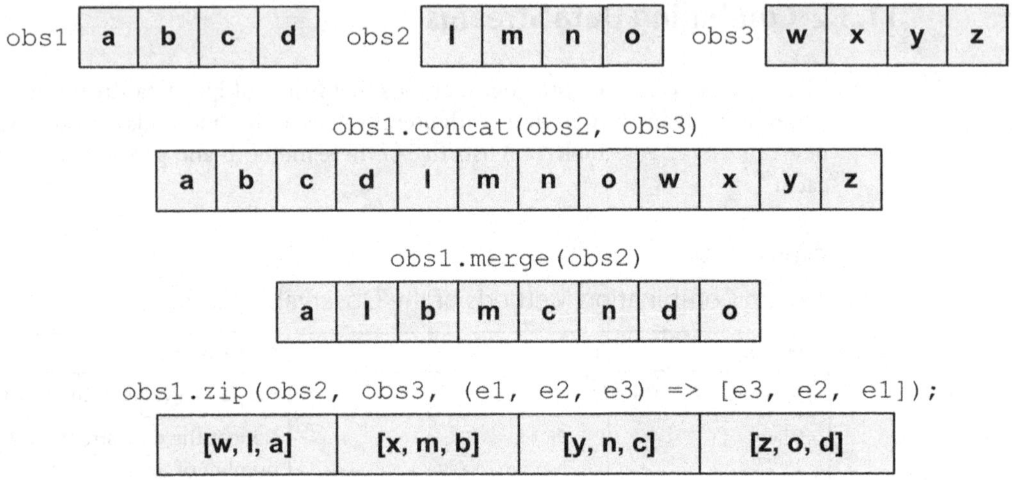


**Figure 11.2 Combining Data Streams with concat, merge, and zip**

As shown in the figure, `concat` appends the argument's streams to the original stream. This is shown in the following code:

```
obs1 = Observable.of("a", "b", "c", "d");
obs2 = Observable.of("l", "m", "n", "o");
obs1 = obs1.concat(obs2);
--> "a", "b", "c", "d", "l", "m", "n", "o"
```

According to the RxJS documentation, `merge` intersperses elements of the argument's stream with those of the original stream. This is the operation depicted in Figure 11.2. But in my experiments, `merge` performs the same operation as `concat`. That is, it appends the streams of its arguments to the original stream. This may change in future releases of RxJS.

`zip` is the most interesting of the combination methods. It accepts streams with different types of elements and the last argument is a function that specifies how the elements should be combined. This function has one argument for each data stream.

In the figure, the function inside `zip` has three arguments (`e1, e2, e3`), each representing an element of the corresponding data stream. The function reverses the order of the elements and places each triplet in an array. Here's another example, which inserts dashes between the elements of the three streams:

```
obs1.zip(obs2, obs3, (e1, e2, e3) => e1 + "-" + e2 + "-" + e3);
--> a-l-w, b-m-x, c-n-y, d-o-z
```

### 11.3.3 Transforming Data Streams

In RxJS, a transformation method reads the elements of an `Observable`'s data stream, transforms them in some way, and inserts new elements in the returned `Observable`. Table 11.4 lists eight of these methods (`TResult` refers to the type of value produced by the transformation).

**Table 11.4**

Stream Transformation Methods of the Observable<T> Class (Abridged)

| Method | Description |
|---|---|
| map((value: T, index: number) => TResult, thisArg?: any) | Uses a function to transform the elements of a data stream |
| scan((acc: T, value: T) => T) | Provides the preceding result to transform elements of the data stream |
| concatMap((value: T, index: number) => Observable) | Creates an Observable for each element and then concatenates them into one |
| concatMap((value: T, index: number) => Observable, (value1: T, value2: T2, index: number)) | Creates an Observable for each element, concatenates them into one, and then processes the elements of the source and combined Observables |
| flatMap((value: T) => Observable) | Creates an Observable for each element and merges the Observables into one |
| flatMap((value: T) => TResult[]) | Creates an array for each element and merges the arrays into an Observable |
| flatMap((value: T) => Observable, (item: T, other: TOther) => TResult) | Creates an Observable for each element, combines the Observables into one, and transforms the elements with a function |
| switchMap((value: T, index: number, source: Observable<T>) => TResult, thisArg?: any) | Creates an Observable for each element and merges the Observables into one |

**NOTE**

In RxJS code, you may encounter methods named `select`, `selectConcat`, `selectMany`, and `selectSwitch`. These methods are exactly similar to the `map`, `concatMap`, `flatMap`, and `switchMap` methods in the table.

The map function transforms elements of an Observable with a function that accepts two arguments: the element's value and the element's index. In the following code, the map function increments each element value by 1:

```
Observable.of(1, 2, 3, 4).map((val, i) => val + 1);
--> 2, 3, 4, 5
```

This map function replaces each element with its index:

```
Observable.of(10, 9, 8, 7).map((val, i) => i);
--> 0, 1, 2, 3
```

scan is like map, but its function accepts two arguments: the result of the preceding function call (called the accumulator) and the element's value. The following code shows how it can be used:

```
Observable.of(1, 2, 3, 4).scan((acc, val) => acc + val);
--> 1, 3, 6, 10
```

For the first element, the accumulator equals 0, so 0 + 1 = 1. For the second element, the accumulator is 1, so 1 + 2 = 3. For the third element, the accumulator is 3, so 3 + 3 = 6. For the last element, the accumulator is 6, so 6 + 4 = 10.

The concatMap method is more complicated. Instead of producing a regular value, its function returns an Observable for each element. When all the elements have been processed, it concatenates the Observables' data streams together into one.

An example will clarify how concatMap works. In the following code, the source Observable has a data stream of three elements. The inner function creates three Observables and concatenates their sequences together to produce the output Observable.

```
Observable.of(5, 6, 7).concatMap(
     (val, i) => Observable.of(0, 1, val));
--> 0, 1, 5, 0, 1, 6, 0, 1, 7
```

concatMap accepts a second function that receives three values: the element of the source Observable, the element of the combined Observable, and the index. The following call to concatMap is similar to the first, but inserts a function that adds 2 to each value in the combined Observable:

```
Observable.of(5, 6, 7).concatMap(
     (val, i) => Observable.of(0, 1, val),
     (val1, val2, index) => val2 + 2);
--> 2, 3, 7, 2, 3, 8, 2, 3, 9
```

Like `concatMap`, `flatMap` computes an `Observable` for each element in the source `Observable`. But instead of concatenating the `Observables`' streams, `flatMap` merges the streams into one. According to the RxJS documentation, this merging "may interleave" the `Observables`.

But in my experiments, `flatMap` produces the same output as `concatMap`. To show what I mean, the following code accepts the same input values as in the previous `concatMap` example. The output is exactly the same:

```
Observable.of(5, 6, 7).flatMap(
     (val, i) => Observable.of(0, 1, val));
--> 0, 1, 5, 0, 1, 6, 0, 1, 7
```

Like `concatMap`, `flatMap` accepts a function that can access elements of the source `Observable` and the combined `Observable`.

The last method in Table 11.4, `switchMap`, is similar to `flatMap`. But when a new value is emitted from the source `Observable`, the data stream created by processing previous values will be halted. This ensures that only current results will be emitted.

# 11.4 EventEmitters and Custom Events

Chapter 8 explained how components can access events produced by template elements. This is accomplished by associating an event's name in parentheses with a member of the component's class. For example, the following markup specifies that the `processClick` method should be invoked when the button's `click` event occurs.

```
<button (click)="processClick()">Click me</button>
```

This section explains how you can add custom events to web components. The fundamental class to know is `EventEmitter`. This is provided by the Angular framework, but it's a subclass of `Subject`, which is provided by RxJS. Therefore, this section starts by introducing the `Subject` class.

## 11.4.1 The Subject Class

The `Subject` class extends the `Observable` class and also implements the `Observer` interface and the empty `Subscription` class. Figure 11.3 shows what this inheritance hierarchy looks like.

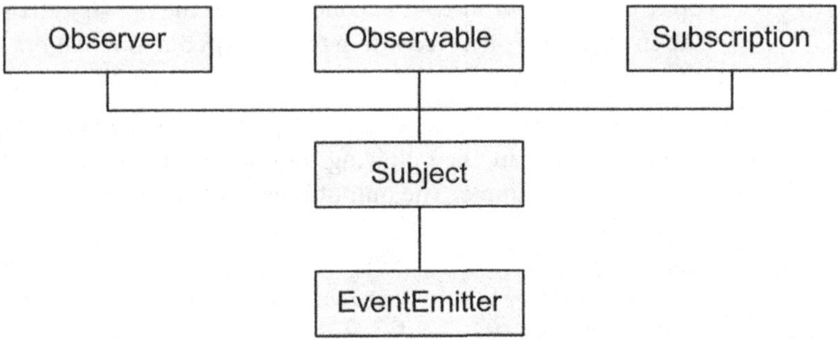


**Figure 11.3 Inheritance Hierarchy of Subject and EventEmitter**

Because it behaves as both an `Observable` and an `Observer`, a `Subject` can receive asynchronous data from a source and provide that data to observers. This ability is essential to understanding `EventEmitters`, which receive data from template elements and transfer the event data to component classes.

## 11.4.2 The EventEmitter Class

An `EventEmitter` notifies a web component when an event occurs in a template element. If desired, it may provide data related to the event. This data transfer is accomplished by the `emit` method, which accepts a value of any type and sends it to observers. In most applications, `emit` is the only `EventEmitter` method you need.

The `EventEmitter` constructor is given as follows:

```
constructor(isAsync?: boolean)
```

The `isAsync` argument is true by default, which means the `EventEmitter` operates asynchronously. To see how this works, you need to be familiar with its `subscribe` method. This resembles the `subscribe` method of the `Observable` class, but its behavior is slightly different. Its signature is given as follows:

```
subscribe(generatorOrNext?: any, error?: any, complete?: any)
```

The operation of this method depends on the constructor's `isAsync` argument. The following code shows how the `generatorOrNext` argument is processed:

```
if(generatorOrNext && typeof generatorOrNext === "object") {
  schedulerFn = this._isAsync ?
    (value) => { setTimeout(() => generatorOrNext.next(value)); } :
    (value) => { generatorOrNext.next(value); };
```

As shown, `subscribe` calls the `next` method of the `generatorOrNext` argument. If `isAsync` is true, `subscribe` uses `setTimeout` to ensure that the `next` method will be processed after the current JavaScript execution queue has completed. The `error` and `complete` arguments are processed in the same way.

To configure a custom event, a component must create an `EventEmitter` and ensure that it can be accessed externally. The `EventEmitter` can be made accessible by preceding its declaration with `@Output()`, as shown in the following code:

```
@Output() eventName = new EventEmitter();
```

If the `EventEmitter`'s component is placed in another component, the parent component can subscribe to the child's `EventEmitter` by accessing its name in parentheses. That is, if the `EventEmitter`'s name is `eventName`, the parent's template can access the `EventEmitter` as `(eventName)`. The following discussion demonstrates how this works.

## 11.4.3 Custom Events

To test custom events, two components are needed: one to generate the custom event and one to receive it. In keeping with RxJS terminology, I'll call the first component the observable component and the second component the observer component.

### The Observable Component

To enable a component to generate custom events, three steps are needed:

1. In the component's class, define an `EventEmitter` and precede its definition with `@Output()`. Example: `@Output() myevent = new EventEmitter()`.
2. In the component's template, assign a regular event (such as a mouse click) to an event handler. Example: `(keypress)='keyhandler($event)'`.
3. In the event handler for Step 2, call the `emit` method of the `EventEmitter`. This will alert observers that the event has occurred.

For example, suppose that a component contains a button that should fire a custom event when the user focuses on it and presses the 'z' key. I'll call this component `ZButtonComponent`, and Listing 11.3 shows how the component can be coded.

**Listing 11.3: ch11/custom_event/app/zbutton.component.ts**

```
@Component({
selector: 'zbutton',
template: `
<button (keypress)='keyhandler($event)'>
  Press z to Generate Event
</button>
`})
export class ZButtonComponent {

  // Create the EventEmitter
  @Output() private zpress = new EventEmitter();

  // Check if the user pressed 'z'
  private keyhandler(e: any) {

    // If so, emit the custom event
    if (e.which === 122) {
      this.zpress.emit(e);
      alert('Custom event emitted');
    }
  }
}
```

In this class, the name of the `EventEmitter` is `zpress`. It can be accessed outside the component because of its `@Output()` decorator.

The component's template associates the button's keystroke events with a method called `keyhandler`. When the user presses a key, this method checks to see if 'z' was pressed. If so, the method calls the `EventEmitter`'s `emit` method, which sends a value to observers.

## The Observer Component

To receive custom events from a child component, a parent component must be specially configured. This requires two steps:

1. Add the child component to the parent's template. Inside the element, associate the child's custom event with an event handler in the parent.
2. Inside the parent class, configure the event handler to process the custom event.

The code in Listing 11.4 shows how a parent component can be configured to receive custom events from the `ZButtonComponent` presented earlier.

**Listing 11.4: ch11/custom_event/app/app.ts (Parent Component)**

```
@Component({
selector: 'app-root',
template: `
<zbutton (zpress)='handler()'></zbutton>
`})
export class AppComponent {

  // Respond to the custom event
   private handler() {
     alert('Custom event received');
   }
}
```

The custom event, `zpress`, matches the name of the `EventEmitter` created in the child component. Also, the `@NgModule` decorator in the module contains `ZButtonComponent`, so the component can be accessed in the parent's template.

It's important to notice that the parent doesn't know how the child processes the event. It doesn't even know how the event is triggered. It simply handles `zpress` events when they occur.

# 11.5 Summary

When building web components, it's important to know how to receive and handle the results of incomplete operations. In the Angular framework, asynchronous processing is made possible by two classes: `Promise` and `Observable`.

A `Promise` represents an ongoing operation that will eventually return a value. The `then` method associates the `Promise` with two functions. The first, called the fulfillment handler, is called if the operation's value is available. The second, called the rejection handler, is called if an error prevents the operation from completing.

`Observables` are more complicated than `Promises`, but they're also more flexible. An `Observable` can provide multiple values to its subscribed observers and each observer can cancel its subscription. An `Observable` can be associated with three functions: one to be called if a value is provided, one to be called if an error occurs, and one to be called when the data transfer is complete.

Chapter 8 explained how to configure a component to receive data using the `@Input()` decorator. Configuring a component to provide output data is more involved because of the need to create an `EventEmitter`. `EventEmitter` is a subclass of `Subject`, which means that an `EventEmitter` can behave as both an `Observable` and an `Observer`.

# Chapter 12

# Routing

In the example code presented so far, applications have created one or a handful of components. But large-scale applications may need to display tens or hundreds of components at a time. In most cases, the arrangement of components should be determined by the URL.

In theory, you could access the URL with JavaScript and use Angular directives to insert or remove components. But it's easier and better performing to use Angular's routing capability. In essence, Angular's routing associates URL patterns with different Angular components and behaviors.

The goal of this chapter is to explain how Angular routing works and demonstrate its usage in code. Much of the discussion will be focused on configuring a router module with one or more routes. Many types of routes are available, but in most cases, a route's purpose is to associate a URL pattern with an Angular component.

Angular also makes it possible to create special hyperlinks called router links. These links make it straightforward to update the URL with routes that the router will recognize. In addition, router links can be associated with Angular components to set link URLs programmatically.

One major advantage of Angular routing is that it enables lazy loading of application code. This means that the client will only download the code it needs instead of having to download all of the code at once.

The last part of the chapter discusses advanced aspects of Angular routing. One important topic involves configuring routes for child components as well as parent components. We'll also see how a component can access the router in code and use its methods to adjust the router's operation or navigate to a new URL.

# 12.1 Overview

Angular's routing capability is powerful but complex. Before we get into the details, this section provides a brief overview of the topic. First, I'd like to explain why routing is so important to Angular applications. Then I'll present the basic concepts underlying how routing works in practice.

## 12.1.1 Single Page Applications (SPAs) and Lazy Loading

Before AJAX and XMLHttpRequests arrived, every web application consisted of multiple pages. To display a new view, an application sent a new URL to the server and downloaded the entire page.

Today, single-page applications (SPAs) have taken center stage. The browser communicates asynchronously with the server, so it can send and receive data without having to process HTTP requests and responses. This saves time and provides the user with a fluid, dynamic experience.

Simple SPAs rely on a single URL, but there are advantages to having multiple URLs. Users can visit specific parts of a page and they can move between these parts using the browser's Back/Forward buttons. Also, different URLs can represent different states of the application.

The goal of Angular routing is to enable SPAs to associate different URLs with different components and states. When one URL is selected, the application may present Component A configured for User X. When another URL is selected, the application may present Component M configured for User Y.

To ensure acceptable performance, it's critical that the client only loads the components it needs. If a URL requires Components A, B, and C, the bundle loaded by the client should contain only those components. This on-demand loading is referred to as *lazy loading*. If an application's routing has been configured correctly, its components will be bundled together in a manner that makes lazy loading possible.

## 12.1.2 Routing Terminology

Chapter 9 introduced the `NgSwitch` directive, which adds one of many elements to a document according to a value. Routing is similar, but instead of checking a value, the router examines the document's URL. Instead of inserting an element into the DOM, a router inserts a child component into a parent component. In routing applications, the primary parent component is called the *base component*.

The association between a URL and a component/state is called a *route*. Routes are defined in a *router module*, which enables the application's components to access Angular's routing capabilities. In particular, components can access the router service to examine or update the routing process.

Don't be concerned if these terms don't make sense just yet. They'll be discused frequently in the sections that follow. The next section walks through the development of a simple component that selects one of two child components.

# 12.2 A Simple Example

When coding applications with routing, there are many new data structures and methods to be aware of. Before I discuss them in detail, I'd like to present a simple application that demonstrates how everything works together.

The ch12/simple_router project shows how a router can be configured to select a child component based on the client's URL. There are three components involved:

- `AppComponent` — the base component, whose template receives a child component selected by the router
- `FirstComponent` — first child, selected when the URL's path ends in foo
- `SecondComponent` — second child, selected when the URL's path ends in bar

Figure 12.1 shows what the application looks like when the URL's path ends in bar, which results in `SecondComponent` being inserted into `AppComponent`.

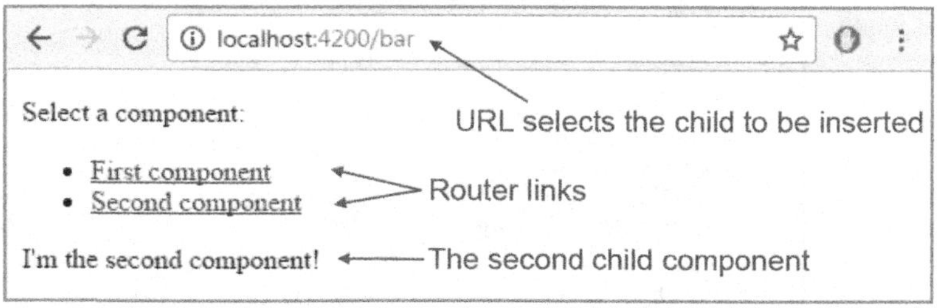


**Figure 12.1 A Simple Router Application**

This application is trivially simple, but the project's code has five aspects that apply to most applications that take advantage of routing.

1. The application's module defines an array of routes inside a `Routes` structure.
2. Within the module's `@NgModule` annotation, the `imports` array contains a new `RouterModule` configured with the `Routes` from Step 1.
3. The constructor of the base component receives a `Router` through dependency injection.
4. The template of the base component contains a `router-outlet` element to specify where the selected child component should be placed.
5. The template of the base component contains specially-configured hyperlinks that visit URLs recognizable to the router.

In this project, the routing process is configured in the module class and the base component. This section looks at the code in both classes.

## 12.2.1 Router Configuration in the Module

As mentioned earlier, a route associates a URL with a component and/or state data. An application's routes must be specified in a `Routes`, which is an array of `Route` instances. At the top of Listing 12.1, the `Routes` consists of three routes.

The `imports` array in the `@NgModule` decorator calls `RouterModule.forRoot` with the `Routes`. This creates and configures the `RouterModule` that provides the application with Angular's routing capabilities.

**Listing 12.1: ch12/simple_router/app/app.module.ts**

```
const routes: Routes = [
  {path: '', redirectTo: 'foo', pathMatch: 'full'},
  {path: 'foo', component: FirstComponent},
  {path: 'bar', component: SecondComponent}
];
@NgModule({
  declarations: [
    AppComponent,
    FirstComponent,
    SecondComponent
  ],
  imports: [
    BrowserModule,
    RouterModule.forRoot(routes)
  ],
  providers: [],
  bootstrap: [AppComponent]
})
export class AppModule {}
```

A later section will discuss route definitions in great detail. This discussion looks at the three routes given in the `Routes` array. The first is given as follows:

```
{path: '', redirectTo: 'foo', pathMatch: 'full'}
```

This route is called an *index route* because it tells the router what to do when the client visits the base URL. In this case, the route tells the router to redirect the URL to /foo if the URL's path is empty.

```
{path: 'foo', component: FirstComponent}
```

This tells the router to insert `FirstComponent` into the base component when the URL's path equals /foo.

```
{path: 'bar', component: SecondComponent}
```

Similar to the preceding route definition, this tells the router to insert `SecondComponent` into the base component when the URL's path equals /bar.

## 12.2.2 Router Configuration in the Base Component

After the router examines the URL, the selected child component is inserted into the base component. In the ch12/simple_router project, the base component is `AppComponent`, and Listing 12.2 presents its code.

**Listing 12.2: ch12/simple_router/app/app.component.ts**

```
@Component({
selector: 'app-root',
template: `
<p>Select a component:</p>
<ul>
  <li><a routerLink='/foo'>First component</a></li>
  <li><a routerLink='/bar'>Second component</a></li>
</ul>
<router-outlet></router-outlet>
`})
export class AppComponent {
  constructor(private router: Router) {}
}
```

The template contains two hyperlinks. Each has a special `routerLink` property, and for this reason, they're called *router links*. The example links are trivially simple, and direct the browser to a URL whose path is set to /foo or /bar. In both cases, `routerLink` could be replaced with the traditional `href`. But as we'll see shortly, the `routerLink` property can do much more than just set static paths.

Below the router links, the component's template contains the following markup:

```
<router-outlet></router-outlet>
```

These tags specify where the selected child component should be inserted into the base component's template. They serve a similar purpose to the `<ng-content>` tags, which specify where the templates of content children should be inserted into the parent's template.

The component's constructor receives a `Router` instance through dependency injection. The `Router`'s provider was configured in the module, which created a `RouterModule`. A later section will discuss the `Router` class in detail.

At this point, you should have a basic familiarity with what Angular routing is intended to accomplish. The next two sections take a closer look at router links and route definitions.

# 12.3 Router Links

A router link is an anchor element whose `routerLink` property links to one or more components and optionally provides data. At its simplest, a router link can specify a static URL path, as shown in the following markup:

```
<a routerLink='/foo'>First component</a>
```

Earlier, I said that router links update the URL, but that's not necessarily true. When a router link is clicked, its path will be examined by the component's router, and the URL will be updated if the router recognizes the value of `routerLink`. If the router can't interpret a `routerLink`, the result will be an error: *Cannot match any routes.*

The above example sets `routerLink` equal to a simple string. But `routerLink` can also be assigned to an array of values that combine to form a URL path. This will be discussed next.

## 12.3.1 Route Segments

If the `routerLink` property is set to a string defining an array, the array's elements will be combined to form the URL path. For example, consider the following router link:

```
<a [routerLink]="['/abc', 'xyz']">...</a>
```

If the user clicks the link, the router will combine the array elements to `/abc/xyz`. If the router recognizes the path, the URL's path will be set to /abc/xyz and the appropriate component will be inserted into the base component.

In addition to strings, the array can also contain numbers and variables from the component class. The following markup presents an example:

```
<a [routerLink]="['/abc/def', 16, name]">...</a>
```

The elements of this array will be combined to form `/abc/def/16/`*`value`*, where *`value`* is the value of the component's `name` variable. If `name` equals `john`, the resulting path will be `/abc/def/16/john`.

In the preceding examples, the first element always starts with a slash (/). This has a special meaning in a router link and its significance will be discussed in a later section.

## 12.3.2 Queries and Fragments

In addition to setting a URL's path, a router link can also set a URL's query string and fragment. As a quick review, a query string (usually) provides data in *name=value* pairs and a fragment links to a portion of the HTML document. Figure 12.2 provides an example of a URL with a query and fragment:

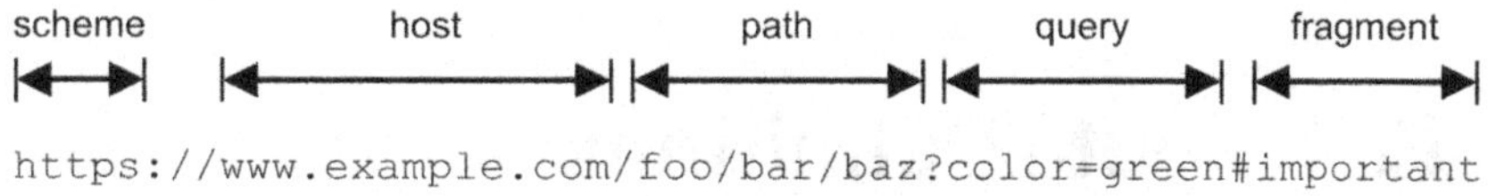


**Figure 12.2 URL Structure**

A router link can specify a query string by assigning a value to the `queryParams` property. This is set to a JSON object whose properties will be converted to the parameters in the query string. To see how this works, consider the following router link.

```
<a [routerLink]="['/foo']" [queryParams]="{color: 'red'}">...</a>
```

If a user clicks on this link, the string `?color=red` will be appended to the URL's path. If the value of `queryParams` is set to an object containing multiple fields, the query string will contain multiple parameters, as in `?color=red&num=2`.

Suppose that the current URL already contains a query string. By default, this information will be discarded when a router link is activated. This behavior can be changed by assigning the `queryParamsHandling` property to one of two values:

- `preserve` — make the current query string the query string of the generated URL
- `merge` — add the current query string to the query string of the generated URL

As an example, the following router link tells the router to merge the query string of the current URL with the query string defined with `queryParams`:

```
<a [routerLink]="['/foo']" [queryParams]="{lang: 'TypeScript'}"
   [queryParamsHandling]="merge">...</a>
```

A router link can set the URL's fragment by assigning a value to the `fragment` property. As an example, the following link sets the fragment to the value of the component's `fragName` variable:

```
<a [routerLink]="['/foo']" [fragment]="fragName">...</a>
```

If the value of `fragName` is `idx`, the string `#idx` will be appended to the URL's path when the link is clicked.

By default, router links discard the fragment associated with the current URL. To tell the router to keep the current fragment, a router link needs to set the `preserveFragment` property to true.

# 12.4 Route Definitions

At this point, you should understand how to set URLs in router links. This section explains how an application can configure the router to respond to URLs. As discussed earlier, this is accomplished by defining a `Routes` array in a module class. Each element of this array tells the router how to respond to a URL or URL pattern.

As a review, the array from Listing 12.1 is defined with the following code:

```
const routes: Routes = [
  {path: '', redirectTo: 'foo', pathMatch: 'full'},
  {path: 'foo', component: FirstComponent},
  {path: 'bar', component: SecondComponent}
];
```

This code demonstrates how the `path`, `redirectTo`, `pathMatch`, and `component` fields can be used. But many more fields can be set in a route definition and Table 12.1 presents the complete list.

**Table 12.1**

Fields of a Route Definition

| Property | Description |
|---|---|
| `path` | The route URL or pattern |
| `component` | The type of component to be inserted into the base component |
| `outlet` | The name of the routing outlet into which the component should be inserted |
| `redirectTo` | URL fragment to replace the current segment |
| `pathMatch` | Sets the router's URL matching strategy |
| `matcher` | The name of a UrlMatcher function to be used for URL matching |
| `children` | Array of child route definitions |
| `loadChildren` | A reference to child modules whose bundles can be accessed through lazy-loading |
| `data` | Static data to be passed to the inserted child component through the injected ActivatedRoute |
| `resolve` | Identifies providers for dynamic data |
| `canActivate` | Array of tokens used to obtain CanActivate handlers through dependency injection |
| `canActivateChild` | Determines if child routes can be activated |
| `canDeactivate` | Determines if routes can be deactivated |
| `canLoad` | Determines if children can be loaded |
| `runGuardsAndResolvers` | Configures how often guards and resolvers are executed |

To explain how route definitions are coded, this discussion divides the table's fields into five categories:

1. Component routes and secondary routes
2. Index routes and matching
3. Child routes
4. Providing data
5. Routing security

This section discusses the properties in each of these categories. A later section presents an example project that demonstrates how many of them are used.

## 12.4.1 Component Routes and Secondary Routes

The simplest route definitions tell the router to insert a specific component when the URL matches a given pattern. The URL is set with the `path` property and the component is set with the `component` property. This is shown in the following route definition:

```
{path: 'firstComp', component: FirstComponent}
```

The `path` field accepts wildcards. The `**` wildcard corresponds to any string, so if `path` is set to `foo/**/bar`, the middle URL segment will be matched to any string. This wildcard is particularly helpful because it allows an application to specify a route definition to be matched if all other route definitions fail. Consider the following array:

```
{path: 'one', component: OneComponent},
{path: 'two', component: TwoComponent},
...
{path: '**', component: ErrorComponent},
```

The router processes route definitions in their given order. In this case, if it can't match the URL to one of the initial paths, it will match the URL to the last route and insert a new instance of the `ErrorComponent`.

In addition to `**`, `path` accepts variable names given in the form `:xyz`. These are called *route parameters*. The router will match `:xyz` to any string in the URL's path, and will pass the corresponding string to the component associated with the URL. As an example, consider the following route definition:

```
{path: 'firstComp/:color', component: FirstComponent}
```

If the URL's path is `/firstComp/red`, the router will match the URL and pass the `color=red` parameter to the new `FirstComponent` instance. The component can access the parameter through the `ActivatedRoute` injected into its constructor. A later section will discuss the `ActivatedRoute` class and its members.

As discussed earlier, a base component uses `<router-outlet>` tags to control where a selected component will be inserted into its template. The `router-outlet` element accepts an attribute called `name` that uniquely identifies the outlet. If a route definition associates the `outlet` field with a value, the component will be inserted into the `router-outlet` element with that value.

A route definition with the `outlet` field set is called a *secondary route*. As an example, suppose that the base component's template contains the following markup:

```
<router-outlet name='extra'></router-outlet>
```

To configure a component to be inserted into this outlet, a route definition must have its `outlet` property set to `extra`, as shown in the following code:

```
{path: 'extraComp', component: ExtraComponent, outlet: 'extra'}
```

You might expect that `ExtraComponent` will be inserted into the base component if the URL path starts with `extraComp`. *This is not the case.* To be matched with a secondary route, a URL must satisfy two requirements:

1. It must match a primary route
2. The outlet and the path must be given inside parentheses

As an example, the following URL matches a secondary route whose `outlet` is set to `extra` and whose path is set to `extraComp`:

```
http://www.example.com/(extra:extraComp)
```

A router link can generate a URL for a secondary route if the array associated with the `routerLink` property contains an `outlets` field that associates the outlet with the route's path. The following markup shows what this looks like:

```
<a [routerLink]="[{ outlets: { extra: ['extraComp'] } }]">...</a>
```

This may seem confusing, but secondary routes make it possible to insert multiple independent components into a base component.

## 12.4.2 Index Routes and Matching Strategies

An index route is a definition whose URL path is empty. This is commonly specified by setting `path` equal to `''`. Instead of identifying a component, it's common for an index route to redirect the client to another URL. The following definition shows how this can be accomplished:

```
{path: '', redirectTo: 'foo', pathMatch: 'full'}
```

If `pathMatch` isn't specified in an index route, an error will result. This is because, by default, the router only checks if the URL's path starts with the `path`. For example, if `path` is set to `foo`, the router will match /foo/bar and /foo/baz because the URLs start with the `path` value. But if `path` is set to `''`, the router will match every URL because every URL path starts with the empty string.

To change this behavior, `pathMatch` needs to be configured. This accepts two values:

- `prefix` — The router checks to see if the URL's path starts with the `path` value
- `full` — The router makes sure the entire URL's path matches the `path` value

By default, `pathMatch` is set to `prefix`. For index routes, it should be set to `full`. This ensures that the router will only match the index route if the URL's path is empty.

An application can further configure the router's URL matching by defining a custom matching strategy. This requires setting the `matcher` property to a function that implements the `UrlMatcher` interface. This interface is defined with the following code:

```
export type UrlMatcher = (segments: UrlSegment[],
  group: UrlSegmentGroup, route: Route) => UrlMatchResult;
```

A `UrlSegment` represents a portion of a URL between slashes. The segment's string is provided in the `path` member. The `parameters` member matches parameter names to values. An example will show how these segments can be used in a `UrlMatcher` function:

```
function customMatcher(url: UrlSegment[]) {
  return url.length === 1 &&
    url[0].path.endsWith('.html') ? ({consumed: url}) : null;
}
```

As shown, the `UrlMatchResult`'s `consumed` field contains an array of the consumed URL segments. It also has a `posParams` field that serves as a map of positional parameters.

## 12.4.3 Child Routes

A route definition can define additional routes called *child routes*. The router only examines these routes when the parent route is selected. Child routes are defined by setting the `children` property equal to an array containing one or more route definitions. The following code shows what this looks like:

```
{path: 'foo', component: FirstComponent,
  children: [
    { path: 'baz', component: ThirdComponent },
    { path: 'qux', component: FourthComponent }
  ]
}
```

If the URL's path starts with /foo, the router will examine the two child routes. If the URL starts with foo/baz, the first child route will be matched. If the URL starts with /foo/qux, the second route will be matched.

When working with child routes, there are four points to be aware of:

1. A child route definition can have the same properties as a regular route definition. A child route can also have children of its own.
2. Components in child routes are inserted into their parent components, not the base component. In the preceding code, `ThirdComponent` and `FourthComponent` will be inserted into `FirstComponent` if the router makes a match.
3. A child route extends the path of its parent route. That is, after matching the parent, the router matches the child's path against the URL segment following the parent's.
4. Child routes and child components can be loaded when they're needed instead of beforehand. This lazy loading can be configured by associating the `loadChildren` property with a module that represents a distinct bundle.

This last point is important. Lazy loading ensures that the client only downloads the code it needs. But configuring this behavior is complicated, and will be discussed later in the chapter.

## 12.4.4 Providing Data to Components

An earlier discussion explained how URL parameters, such as `:id`, can be used to send a URL segment to the new component instance. A route definition can also send data to the new component by setting the `data` property to a value of the `Data` type, which is defined with the following code:

```
export type Data = {
  [name: string]: any
};
```

The following code shows how data can be configured in a route definition:

```
{path: 'foo', component: MyComponent, data: {color: 'red'} }
```

In this case, if the router matches the URL, the `color` parameter will be passed to the new instance of `MyComponent`. The component can access the parameter through the `ActivatedRoute` injected into its constructor. A later section will discuss the `ActivatedRoute` class in full.

While the `data` property provides static data, the `resolve` property makes it possible to provide dynamic data. This property must be set to a `ResolveData` instance, which is defined as follows:

```
export type ResolveData = {
  [name: string]: any
};
```

The purpose of the `resolve` property is to identify a class that implements the `Resolve<T>` interface, where `T` is the type of the data to be provided. This interface declares one method, `resolve`:

```
resolve(
  route: ActivatedRouteSnapshot,
  state: RouterStateSnapshot):
Observable<T> | Promise<T> | T;
```

The `ActivatedRouteSnapshot` argument provides information about the selected route. The `RouterStateSnapshot` provides information about the router's configuration.

## 12.4.5 Routing Security

Security is a critical concern in web development, and many applications need to prevent clients from accessing resources associated with secure URLs. In Angular, this is made possible through the `canActivateChild`, `canDeactivate`, and `canLoad` properties. The classes associated with these properties are called guards.

canActivateChild, canDeactivate, and canLoad accomplish different results, but they're used in the same way. In each case, the coding process involves two steps:

1. Code a service class that implements the appropriate interface.
2. Add the service class to the providers array in the module's NgModule decorator.

This discussion explains how these steps are implemented for the canActivateChild, canDeactivate, and canLoad properties. Afterward, we'll look at the runGuardsAndResolvers property.

## The canActivateChild Property

The first property, canActivateChild, determines whether a child route can be accessed. This property must be set to a service class that implements the CanActivateChild interface. This contains one method, canActivateChild, whose signature is given as follows:

```
canActivateChild(
  childRoute: ActivatedRouteSnapshot,
  state: RouterStateSnapshot):
Observable<boolean> | Promise<boolean> | boolean;
```

The boolean returned by the function identifies whether the child route can be accessed. If the function returns a value of false, the child route will be inaccessible.

## The canDeactivate Property

The canDeactivate property controls whether clients can deactivate routes. This property must be set to a class that implements the CanDeactivate<T> interface, where T is the component class to be protected. This interface contains one method, canDeactivate<T>, whose signature is given as follows:

```
canDeactivate(
  component: T,
  currentRoute: ActivatedRouteSnapshot,
  currentState: RouterStateSnapshot,
  nextState?: RouterStateSnapshot):
Observable<boolean> | Promise<boolean> | boolean;
```

Like the canActivateChild method presented earlier, this method returns a boolean. This value determines whether the route can be deactivated.

### The canLoad Property

The `canLoad` property controls a client's ability to load children. This property must be set to a class that implements the `CanLoad` interface, whose single method is `canLoad`:

```
canLoad(route: Route):
  Observable<boolean>|Promise<boolean>|boolean;
```

Like the `canActivateChild` method presented earlier, this method returns a boolean. This value determines whether the route can be deactivated.

### The runGuardsAndResolvers Property

The last property in Table 12.1 is `runGuardsAndResolvers`, which determines when guards (classes that provide security) and resolvers (classes that provide dynamic data) should be executed. This can be set to one of three values:

- `paramsChange` — Guards/resolvers run with the route's parameters change
- `paramsOrQueryParamsChange` — Guards/resolvers run with the route's parameters or query parameters change
- `always` — Guards/resolvers run every time

The first value identifies the default setting. That is, by default, guards and resolvers are run only when there's a change to the route's parameters.

## 12.5 Example Application – Child Routes

The ch12/child_routes project demonstrates how an application can configure child routes and secondary routes. There are seven components in total:

- The base component, `AppComponent`
- The parent components, `FirstComponent` and `SecondComponent`
- The child components, `ThirdComponent` and `FourthComponent`
- The secondary route component, `ExtraComponent`
- The error-handling component, `ErrorComponent`

To present the code in the ch12/child_routes project, this section presents the code in the module class (`AppModule`) and the base component class (`AppComponent`).

## 12.5.1 The Module Class

The `@NgModule` decorator of the project's `AppModule` class creates the `RouterModule` and sets its route definitions. These route definitions are given as follows:

```
const routes: Routes = [
  { path: '', redirectTo: 'foo/baz', pathMatch: 'full'},
  { path: 'foo', component: FirstComponent,
    children: [
      { path: 'baz', component: ThirdComponent },
      { path: 'qux', component: FourthComponent }
    ]},
  { path: 'bar', component: SecondComponent,
    children: [
      { path: 'baz', component: FourthComponent },
      { path: 'qux', component: ThirdComponent }
    ]},
  { path: 'extraComp', component: ExtraComponent, outlet:'extra'},
  { path: '**', component: ErrorComponent }
];
```

If the base URL is accessed, the first route definition redirects the client to foo/baz. The `pathMatch` property is set to `full`, so the router will only match the URL path if the entire path is empty.

The second route definition inserts `FirstComponent` into the base component if the URL path starts with foo. The `children` property is assigned to an array containing two route definitions. If the path starts with foo/baz, the first child route tells the router to insert `ThirdComponent` into `FirstComponent`. If the path starts with foo/qux, the second child route tells the router to insert `FourthComponent` into `FirstComponent`.

The second-to-last route definition assigns the `outlet` property to `extra`. This is a secondary route, and if the URL path contains `(extra:extraComp)`, the router will insert `ExtraComponent` into the `<router-outlet>` element of the base component whose `name` attribute is set to `extra`.

The last component sets `path` to `**`, which means any URL path will be matched. The router accesses route definitions in order, so it will only match this route if none of the preceding routes have been matched. The `ErrorComponent` presents a message stating that the URL path isn't recognized.

## 12.5.2 The Base Component

The template of the base component provides router links that activate each of the four parent/child combinations. The fifth router link activates the secondary route, which associates the `extraComp` path with the `extra` outlet. Listing 12.3 presents its code.

**Listing 12.3: ch12/child_routes/app/app.component.ts**

```
// Base component
@Component({
selector: 'app-root',
template: `
<p>Select a component pair:</p>
<ul>
  <li><a routerLink='/foo/baz'>
    Parent: First component, Child: Third Component</a></li>

  <li><a routerLink='/foo/qux'>
    Parent: First component, Child: Fourth Component</a></li>

  <li><a routerLink='/bar/baz'>
    Parent: Second component, Child: Fourth Component</a></li>

  <li><a routerLink='/bar/qux'>
    Parent: Second component, Child: Third Component</a></li>

  <li><a [routerLink]="[{ outlets: { extra: ['extraComp'] } }]">
    Activate the secondary route
  </a></li>
</ul>
<br/>

<!-- Outlet for primary routes -->
<router-outlet></router-outlet>

<!-- Outlet for secondary route -->
<router-outlet name='extra'></router-outlet>
`})
export class AppComponent {
  constructor(private router: Router) {}
}
```

As shown, the template contains two `router-outlet` elements. The first serves as the point of insertion for `FirstComponent` and `SecondComponent`. The second element has its `name` attribute set to `extra`. This is the point of insertion for `ExtraComponent`, which is associated with the module's secondary route.

# 12.6 Lazy Loading

In the child_routes project, the child components (`ThirdComponent` and `FourthComponent`) are packaged in the same bundle as the parent components (`FirstComponent` and `SecondComponent`). For small applications, this isn't a problem.

But if an application has a great deal of code and a complex parent-child hierarchy, it's better to divide its components into separate bundles. Then clients will only load the bundles they need when they need them. This is lazy loading.

To configure lazy loading in an application, three steps are required:

1. Create a module class for each bundle to be loaded. We'll refer to the loaded modules as *child modules* and the loading module as a parent module.
2. In each child module, create the `RouterModule` by calling its `forChild` method with route definitions instead of `forRoot`.
3. In the parent module, configure a route definition whose `loadChildren` field identifies the resources to be loaded.

Up to this point, every application has had one module class. But to make use of lazy loading, an application needs to have a module class for each bundle to be loaded. A parent module class can load these child module classes by creating route definitions containing the `loadChildren` field.

The code of a child module class is similar to that of a parent module class, but there are a few notable differences. This is shown in the following code:

```
const routes: Routes = [
  {path: '', component: BazComponent},
  {path: 'qux', component: QuxComponent},
];
@NgModule({
  declarations: [ BazComponent, QuxComponent ],
  imports: [
    RouterModule.forChild(routes)
  ],
})
export class ChildModule {}
```

As shown, a child module class has the same kind of route definitions as a parent. But in the `imports` array, the route definitions are accessed by `RouterModule.forChild` instead of `RouterModule.forRoot`. Also, the `@NgModule` decorator doesn't contain a `bootstrap` field.

According to the Angular Style Guide, child modules should be placed in a separate directory with the components they access. Suppose that the preceding code was stored in child.module.ts. Then the app/child directory would contain child.module.ts and the files defining its components.

In the parent module class, the `loadChildren` property needs to identify the TypeScript module containing the child module class and the name of the child module class. The following code shows how this can be accomplished:

```
const routes: Routes = [
  {path: 'foo', loadChildren: './child/child.module#ChildModule'},
  ...
];
```

As shown, the # separates the name of the TypeScript module and the name of the module class. Because of this route definition, the router will use an `NgModuleFactory` to create the module when the URL's path starts with foo. Then the child module and its components can be accessed normally by the parent.

Given the hierarchy of parents and children, it's important to know how to tell the router where to search for route definitions. In a router link, this is determined by the initial characters of the value assigned to `routerLink`. The search location can be configured in three main ways:

- If the value is preceded by `/`, the router will search through the root module
- If the value is preceded by `./`, the router will search the child route definitions
- If the value is preceded by `../`, the router will search the parent route definitions

For example, if the value is preceded by `../../`, the router will search through the grandparent's route definitions. The procedure is similar for all further ancestors.

# 12.7 Advanced Topics

The preceding sections have covered the nuts and bolts of Angular routing, which will be sufficient for most applications. But Angular provides a number of features that provide additional capabilities. This section explores three of these features:

1. The `ActivatedRoute` class
2. The `Router` class
3. Location strategies

A later section will present an example application that demonstrates how these features can be put into practice.

## 12.7.1 The ActivatedRoute Class

Through dependency injection, components can access data structures related to routing. Two of the most important structures are the `ActivatedRoute` and the `Router`. The `ActivatedRoute` is simpler to work with, so we'll look at that first.

As discussed in Chapter 10, components can receive injected dependencies through their constructors. The following code shows how an `ActivatedRoute` can be accessed:

```
export class ExampleComponent {
  constructor(private route: ActivatedRoute) {
    ...
  }
}
```

One of the most important capabilities of the `ActivatedRoute` is that it provides access to data passed to a component through the route definition. This is made possible through the `data` member of the `ActivatedRoute` instance. Table 12.2 lists this and other members of the `ActivatedRoute` class.

**Table 12.2**

Members of the ActivatedRoute Class

| Member | Type/Return Value | Description |
|---|---|---|
| `snapshot` | `ActivatedRouteSnapshot` | Current snapshot of the route |
| `url` | `Observable<UrlSegment[]>` | The route's URL segments |
| `params` | `Observable<Params>` | The route's parameters |
| `queryParams` | `Observable<Params>` | The URL's query parameters |
| `fragment` | `Observable<string>` | The URL's fragment |
| `data` | `Observable<Data>` | Data associated with the route |
| `outlet` | `string` | Name of the route's outlet |
| `component` | `Type<any>\|string` | The route's associated component |
| `routeConfig` | `Route` | The associated route |
| `root` | `ActivatedRoute` | The top-most route |

| | | |
|---|---|---|
| parent | ActivatedRoute | The parent route |
| firstChild | ActivatedRoute | The first child route |
| children | ActivatedRoute[] | Array of child routes |
| pathFromRoot | ActivatedRoute[] | Routes from the root to the activated route |
| paramMap | Observable<ParamMap> | Map of route parameters |
| queryParamMap | Observable<ParamMap> | Map of query parameters |

Chapter 11 discussed `Observables` and explained how they provide future values from a data source. If you're only interested in the present data associated with the `ActivatedRoute`, you can access the `snapshot` member. This is an `ActivatedRouteSnapshot`, which provides many of the same members as the `ActivatedRoute` class. The difference is that snapshot provides data directly instead of through an `Observable`.

Although the `ActivatedRouteSnapshot` is provided in the constructor, its data may not be immediately available. For this reason, applications frequently access the snapshot's data in the `ngOnInit` life cycle method discussed in Chapter 8. The following code gives an idea of how this works.

```
export class ExampleComponent implements OnInit {

  constructor(private activatedRoute: ActivatedRoute) {}

  public ngOnInit() {
    ...
  }
}
```

It's important to understand the difference between query parameters and route parameters. A query parameter is given in the URL's query string. A route parameter is a segment of a route definition's `path` that takes the form `:xyz`. For example, consider the following route definition:

```
{path: 'foo/:num', component: FirstComponent}
```

If the URL's path contains a segment after foo, that segment will be provided as a route parameter to the `FirstComponent` instance. The component can access the parameter through the params member of the `ActivatedRouteSnapshot`. The following code shows how this can be accessed:

```
export class ExampleComponent implements OnInit {

  constructor(private route: ActivatedRoute) {}

  public ngOnInit() {
    let msg: string = this.route.snapshot.data['num'];
  }
}
```

As a result of this code, the component will be able to access the route parameter num inside the ngOnInit method. Accessing data from a route definition uses similar code.

## 12.7.2 The Router Class

If a module creates a RouterModule with the forRoot or forChild methods, its components can access a Router instance through dependency injection. Most applications won't need to access this, but if you want to debug the router's operation or use advanced capabilities, it helps to understand the class's methods and properties. Table 12.3 lists 15 of the members provided by the Router class.

**Table 12.3**

Properties and Methods of the Router Class (Abridged)

| Member | Type/Return Value | Description |
|---|---|---|
| config | Routes | The router's array of route definitions |
| url | string | The current URL |
| routerState | RouterState | The router's state data |
| navigated | boolean | Indicates if at least one navigation took place |
| events | Observable<Event> | Router events |
| errorHandler | ErrorHandler | Called for navigation errors |
| urlHandlingStrategy | UrlHandlingStrategy | Extracts and merges URLs |
| initialNavigation() | void | Initializes change listener and performs initial navigation |
| navigate(<br>commands: any[],<br>extras?:<br>NavigationExtras) | Promise<boolean> | Navigate using the given commands |

| | | |
|---|---|---|
| navigateByUrl(url: string \| UrlTree, extras?: NavigationExtras) | Promise<boolean> | Navigate to the given URL |
| resetConfig( config: Routes) | void | Sets the router's route definitions |
| setUpLocation ChangeListener() | void | Initializes the location change listener |
| dispose() | void | Disposes of the router |
| parseUrl( url: string) | UrlTree | Returns a UrlTree for the given URL string |
| isActive(url: string \| UrlTree) | boolean | Identifies if the given URL is the active URL |

Many of these are straightforward. `config` provides the current route definitions in a `Routes` object and `resetConfig` updates the router's route definitions.

The `navigate` and `navigateByUrl` methods update the client's URL. The first argument of `navigate` accepts an array of commands. This is the same type of array assigned to the `routerLink` property in a router link. The following code shows what this looks like:

```
navigate(['/abc/def', 16, name]);
```

The elements of this array will be combined to form `/abc/def/16/`*`value`*, where *`value`* is the value of the component's `name` variable. If `name` equals `john`, the updated URL will be `/abc/def/16/john`.

The second argument of `navigate` and `navigateByUrl` is a `NavigationExtras` that configures how the URL will be processed. Its fields include the following:

- `relativeTo` — the `ActivatedRoute` to which the URL is relative
- `fragment` — the fragment to be associated with the URL
- `preserveFragment` — whether the existing fragment should be preserved
- `queryParams` — the URL's query parameters
- `preserveQueryParameters` — whether the URL's query should be preserved

The code in the ch12/advanced_router project demonstrates how the `Router` class can be used. This project will be discussed shortly.

### 12.7.3 Location Strategies

In each code example so far, the router has matched route definitions by examining the URL's path. But the router can be configured to examine the URL's fragment instead of the path. This is a good idea when the URL's path needs to remain constant.

The method used by the router to examine URLs is called its *location strategy*. There are two strategies available and each is represented by a class:

1. `PathLocationStrategy` — The router matches route definitions according to the URL's path.
2. `HashLocationStrategy` — The router matches route definitions according to the URL's fragment.

The `PathLocationStrategy` is the default strategy. To configure a router to use the `HashLocationStrategy`, the appropriate provider must be configured. The following code shows how this works:

```
providers: [Location,
  {provide: LocationStrategy, useClass: HashLocationStrategy}]
```

Chapter 10 explained how `Providers` are created. In this code, the `useClass` property tells Angular to create a `LocationStrategy` dependency using the `HashLocationStrategy` class.

The `HashLocationStrategy` becomes important when dealing with older browsers, which send requests to the server every time a URL's path changes. Older browsers don't send requests when the URL's fragment changes, so in this case, the `HashLocationStrategy` may be preferable to the `PathLocationStrategy`.

## 12.8 Example Application – Advanced Routing

The ch12/advanced_router project demonstrates a number of advanced features of Angular routing. These include accessing the `ActivatedRoute`, accessing the `Router`, and setting the location strategy to `HashLocationStrategy`.

Listing 12.4 presents the code in the module class, which contains two route definitions. The first inserts `FirstComponent` and provides it with a route parameter containing the segment following /foo. The second inserts `SecondComponent` and provides it with data.

**Listing 12.4: ch12/advanced_router/app/app.module.ts**

```
import { BrowserModule } from '@angular/platform-browser';
import { NgModule } from '@angular/core';
import { Location, LocationStrategy, HashLocationStrategy }
  from '@angular/common';
import { RouterModule, Routes } from '@angular/router';

import { AppComponent } from './app.component';
import { FirstComponent } from './first.component';
import { SecondComponent } from './second.component';

// Route definitions
const routes: Routes = [
  {path: '', redirectTo: 'foo', pathMatch: 'full'},

  // Set num as the routing parameter
  {path: 'foo/:num', component: FirstComponent },

  // Provide the new component with data
  {path: 'bar', component: SecondComponent,
    data: {message: 'Hi there!'} }
];
@NgModule({
  declarations: [
    AppComponent,
    FirstComponent,
    SecondComponent
  ],
  imports: [
    BrowserModule,
    RouterModule.forRoot(routes)
  ],

  // Use the hash location strategy to parse URLs
  providers: [Location, {provide: LocationStrategy,
    useClass: HashLocationStrategy}],
  bootstrap: [AppComponent]
})
export class AppModule {}
```

The module's `providers` array contains a provider that returns a `HashLocationStrategy` instance when the module accesses the `LocationStrategy` token. This tells the router to examine the URL's fragment when matching URLs to route definitions.

Listing 12.5 presents the code in the application's base component. The template has two router links—one for each route definition in the module. The first router link accesses the component's `val` variable to set the URL segment after /foo.

**Listing 12.5: ch12/advanced_router/app/app.component.ts**

```
// Base component
@Component({
selector: 'app-root',
template: `
<p>Select a component pair:</p>
<ul>

  <!-- First link uses value to set the route parameter -->
  <li><a [routerLink]="['/foo', val]">
    Parent: First component, path = /foo/11
  </a></li>

  <!-- Second link inserts second component -->
  <li><a routerLink='/bar'>
    Parent: Second component, path = /bar
  </a></li>
</ul>

<button (click)="handleClick()">Navigate to /foo/22</button>
<br/>

<!-- Outlet for primary routes -->
<router-outlet></router-outlet>
`})
export class AppComponent {

  private val: number;

  constructor(private router: Router) {
    this.val = 11;
  }

  public handleClick() {

    // Navigate programmatically
    this.router.navigate(['/foo', 2 * this.val],
      { queryParams: { color: 'red' } });
  }
}
```

Below the router links, the template contains a button that invokes `handleClick` when clicked. The `handleClick` method accesses the `Router` provided through dependency injection and calls its `navigate` method to programmatically redirect the client to another URL. The second argument of `navigate` is a `NavigateExtras` that assigns query parameters for the URL.

Listing 12.6 presents the code for the `FirstComponent` class. This demonstrates how a component can access a route parameter using the `ActivatedRoute`. In this case, the parameter's name is `num` and the component displays its value in an alert box.

**Listing 12.6: ch12/advanced_router/app/first.component.ts**

```
@Component({
selector: 'app-first',
template: `
<h2>I'm the first component!</h2>
`})
export class FirstComponent implements OnInit {
  constructor(private route: ActivatedRoute) {}

  public ngOnInit() {

    // Access route parameter
    const n: string = this.route.snapshot.params['num'];
    if (n) {
      window.alert('Route parameter: ' + n);
    }
  }
}
```

Listing 12.7 presents the code for the `SecondComponent`. This is similar to `FirstComponent`, but the component accesses data passed through the route definition.

**Listing 12.7: ch12/advanced_router/app/second.component.ts**

```
@Component({
selector: 'app-second',
template: `
<h2>I'm the second component!</h2>
`})
export class SecondComponent implements OnInit {

  constructor(private route: ActivatedRoute) {}

  public ngOnInit() {

    // Access data from the route definition
    const msg: string = this.route.snapshot.data['message'];
    if (msg) {
      window.alert('Route definition data: ' + msg);
    }
  }
}
```

# 12.9 Summary

Angular's routing capability makes it possible to create single-page applications that can be accessed using multiple URL paths. This enables the user to bookmark an application's state and change states using the browser's Back and Forward buttons.

At minimum, the router's job is to examine the URL and insert components into a base component. Its decision-making process is determined by a series of route definitions provided in the application's module. Most definitions consist of a `path` field that identifies the URL path and a `component` field that identifies the component to be inserted.

A router link is a regular hyperlink whose `routerLink` property is set to an expression. This expression can identify a static URL or an array of URL segments. It can also contain URL parameters, which provide data to the inserted component. When a user clicks on a router link, the router assembles the URL and determines whether it matches one of its route definitions. If it doesn't, the application will produce an error.

If an application's module has been configured properly, its components will be able to access routing capabilities through dependency injection. The `ActivatedRoute` provides information related to the URL and the router's state, and makes it possible to access data passed from the router. The `Router` provides methods that change the router's behavior and navigate to new URLs.

# Chapter 13

# HTTP and JSONP Communication

Internet users speak many different languages, but their computers all communicate using the HyperText Transfer Protocol (HTTP). This protocol has two main parts: the client asks for data by sending a message called a *request*. The server provides the data in a message called a *response*. The nature of the response depends on the type of request, and six common request types are GET, POST, PUT, DELETE, PATCH, and HEAD.

Chrome and Firefox support a function called `window.fetch`, which sends a request to a URL and receives the response in a `Promise`. HTTP communication in Angular is just as easy to use. The `Http` class provides six methods—one for sending each different type of HTTP request. Each method returns an `Observable` that provides the response for the given URL.

The `Response` class represents the server's response. This contains a number of helpful methods that provide information about the response's structure and data. Other methods transform the response's data to be accessible in code. In particular, its `json` method transforms the response's body into a JavaScript object.

The last part of the chapter explains how to transfer data using a mechanism called JavaScript Object Notation with Padding, or JSONP. This isn't as well known as HTTP, but it provides a method of accessing data that isn't affected by a browser's cross-domain restrictions. To be precise, JSONP uses `<script>` elements to read data from a page that would normally be inaccessible due to the Same Origin Policy.

Angular's implementation of JSONP communication is as simple to work with as its HTTP implementation. The `Jsonp` class provides one method, `request`, that accesses data from a URL. The URL's data is provided asynchronously in an `Observable`.

# 13.1 Initiating HTTP Communication

To communicate using HTTP, a component's injector needs to access the appropriate provider. This can be accomplished by adding the `HttpModule` to the `imports` array in the `@NgModule` decorator of the application's module. The following code shows what this looks like:

```
@NgModule({
  ...
  imports: [ ... , HttpModule ],
  ...
})
```

With this configured, the module's components will be able to access an `Http` instance in their constructors. Using the `Http` instance generally consists of two steps:

1. Call the appropriate `Http` method to generate and send an HTTP request.
2. Access the `Response` through the `Observable` returned by the `Http` method.

This section begins by explaining how these steps can be performed. Then we'll look at the `Response` class in detail. The last part of the section presents an example component that uses `Http` methods to read records from a database.

## 13.1.1 The Http Class

Most components access `Http` instances through dependency injection, as discussed in Chapter 10. But new instances can be obtained by calling the `Http` constructor, given as follows:

```
constructor(backend: ConnectionBackend,
            defaultOptions: RequestOptions);
```

The first parameter identifies which communication mechanism should be used by the `Http` instance. By default, this is set to `XMLHttpRequest`, which means the `Http` communication relies on AJAX. The second parameter configures the HTTP requests sent by the `Http` instance, and the `RequestOptions` class will be discussed shortly.

After obtaining an `Http` instance, an Angular component can invoke its methods to create and send HTTP requests. Table 13.1 lists the six methods and provides a description of each.

**Table 13.1**
Methods of the Http Class

| Method | Description |
|---|---|
| `request(url: string \| Request, options?: RequestOptionsArgs)` | Perform an HTTP request determined by the first string |
| `get(url: string, options?: RequestOptionsArgs)` | Send a GET request to the specified URL |
| `post(url: string, body: string, options?: RequestOptionsArgs)` | Send a POST request to the specified URL |
| `put(url: string, body: string, options?: RequestOptionsArgs)` | Send a PUT request to the specified URL |
| `delete(url: string, options?: RequestOptionsArgs)` | Send a DELETE request to the specified URL |
| `patch(url: string, body: string, options?: RequestOptionsArgs)` | Send a PATCH request to the specified URL |
| `head(url: string, options?: RequestOptionsArgs)` | Send a HEAD request to the specified URL |

Each of these methods generates a request and sends it to the given URL. All of them return an `Observable` that provides a `Response` when the server's response is received by the application.

This discussion will provide a brief review of Rx `Observables`. But first, it's a good idea to understand how to customize HTTP requests using a `RequestOptions` or a `RequestOptionsArgs`.

## 13.1.2 Customizing the Request

The `Http` class provides two ways of configuring HTTP requests before they're sent from the client. The first way involves adding a `RequestOptionsArgs` parameter to the appropriate `Http` method. This configures the request generated by the `Http` method.

The second way is to set a `RequestOptions` parameter in the `Http` constructor. This configures all requests generated by the `Http` instance.

### RequestOptionsArgs

Each method in Table 13.1 accepts an optional `RequestOptionsArgs` that customizes aspects of the generated request. This type is declared as follows:

```
type RequestOptionsArgs = {
  url?: string;
  method?: string | RequestMethods;
  search?: string | URLSearchParams;
  headers?: Headers;
  body?: string;
}
```

The `search` field makes it possible to set the URL's query string, which consists of one or more *`name=value`* pairs separated by ampersands. This field can be set to a string, as shown in the following code:

```
search: "language=TypeScript&api=Angular"
```

A common use of `RequestOptionsArgs` is to set a request's headers. The constructor of the `Headers` class accepts name/value pairs separated by colons. This is shown in the following code:

```
headers: new Headers({"Content-Type": "text/plain"});
```

The following code defines a `RequestOptionsArgs` that can be inserted in one of the `Http` methods:

```
opts = {search: "language=TypeScript&api=Angular",
        headers: new Headers({"Content-Type": "text/plain"})};
```

## RequestOptions

The second parameter of the `Http` constructor accepts an optional `RequestOptions`. The constructor of this class is given as follows:

```
constructor(
    {method, headers, body, url, search}: RequestOptionsArgs);
```

As shown, the `RequestOptions` constructor accepts a `RequestOptionsArgs` to define the request configuration. Therefore, the following code shows how a `RequestOptions` can be created.

```
args = {search: "language=TypeScript&api=Angular",
        headers: new Headers({"Content-Type": "text/plain"})};

opts = new RequestOptions(args);
```

### 13.1.3 Processing Observables

As discussed in Chapter 11, an Observable's job is to emit data objects to one or more observers. Each Http method in Table 13.1 returns an Observable that contains response data. When a component receives this Observable, it performs two steps:

1. Convert the Observable's data to JavaScript object notation (JSON)
2. Set the JSON data equal to a property of the component

The simplest way to transform an Observable's data is to call the map method with a conversion function. If obs is an Observable and data is the emitted result, the following code shows how map can be used:

```
obs.map(function(data) { convert(data); });
```

Using arrow function expressions, this can be expressed more concisely:

```
obs.map(data => convert(data) );
```

The map method returns an Observable that provides the transformed data. After the data has been transformed, a component can perform further processing by calling the subscribe method of the new Observable. This method accepts up to three functions, and the first is called each time the Observable provides data.

For example, if obs is an Observable and data is its emitted data, the following code shows how subscribe can be invoked to set this.result equal to the data.

```
obs.subscribe(data => this.result = data);
```

The map and subscribe methods can be chained together to transform and store an Observable's data. The following code shows what this looks like:

```
obs.map(res => res.json()).subscribe(res => this.data = res);
```

In this code, the map method transforms the Response by calling its json method. After the transformation, the subscribe method sets the JSON data equal to the component's data property.

This map-subscribe combination is frequently employed to process the Observables returned by the methods in Table 13.1. These Observables provide the response data using instances of the Response class, which will be discussed next.

# 13.2 The Response Class

Each method of the `Http` class returns an `Observable` that provides the response data in a `Response` object. When a component receives the `Response`, it can examine and transform its data using a series of properties and methods. Table 13.2 lists the public members of the `Response` class.

**Table 13.2**

Members of the Response Class

| Member | Type/Return Value | Description |
|---|---|---|
| `type` | `ResponseTypes` | Enumerated type: default, basic, cors, error, or opaque |
| `ok` | `boolean` | Identifies if an error occurred (status between 200-299) |
| `url` | `string` | The response's URL |
| `status` | `number` | The response's status code |
| `statusText` | `string` | Text corresponding to the response's status code |
| `bytesLoaded` | `number` | Number of bytes downloaded from the server |
| `totalBytes` | `number` | Number of bytes expected in the response's body |
| `headers` | `Headers` | Container of the response's headers |
| `text()` | `string` | Returns the response's body as a string |
| `json()` | `Object` | Returns the response's body as an object |

Regardless of the request's method, an HTTP response consists of four parts:

1. Status line — HTTP version, status code, and message
2. Headers — key/value pairs that identify properties of the response
3. Empty line
4. Message body — optional string that contains the server's message

Information about the response's status line is provided by the `status` and `statusText` properties. For example, if the HTTP communication proceeded normally, `status` will equal `200` and `statusText` will equal `Ok`. The following code prints the response's status text to the console:

```
http.get(...).subscribe(res => console.log(res.statusText));
```

The `headers` property provides a `Headers` object that contains the key/value pairs in the response's headers. Four methods for accessing this information are given as follows:

- `get(key: string)` — provides the value for the given key
- `has(key: string)` — identifies if any of the headers has a value for the specified key
- `keys()` — provides an array of strings containing each key in the `Headers`
- `values()` — provides an array of string arrays containing each value in the `Headers`

As an example, the following code looks at a response's headers and prints the array of keys:

```
http.get(...).subscribe(res => console.log(res.headers.keys()));
```

The two public methods of the `Response` class, `text` and `json`, relate to the response's optional body. If the body is present, `text` returns the body as a string. If the body is provided in JSON format, the `json` method returns a corresponding JavaScript object.

For example, suppose the body of the response is given as follows:

```
[ {"color": "red", "shape": "circle"} ]
```

The following code calls `json` to transform the response body into a JavaScript object. Then it prints the object's `red` property to the console:

```
http.get(...).map(res => res.json())
             .subscribe(res => console.log(res.color));
```

The object is available inside the `subscribe` method. But because `subscribe` executes asynchronously, the object may not be available immediately after the `subscribe` method. Therefore, if `console.log()` is called after `subscribe`, an error may result due to the object's undefined value.

# 13.3 Http Demonstration

The code in the ch13/http_demo project shows how the `Http` class can be used in practice. It reads JSON-formatted text from a server, transforms the text into a JavaScript object, and displays the result in a table. Listing 13.1 presents the code.

**Listing 13.1: ch13/http_demo/app/app.component.ts**

```
@Component({
selector: 'app-root',
template: `
<p>Authors:</p>
<table>
  <tr *ngFor='let author of authors'>
    <td>{{ author.first }}</td>
    <td>{{ author.last }}</td>
  </tr>
</table>
`})
export class AppComponent {
  private authors: Object[];
  private opts: RequestOptionsArgs;

  constructor(private http: Http) {

    // Create the query string
    this.opts = {search: 'query=authors'};

    // Send a request and process the response
    this.http.get('http://www.ngbook.io/http_demo', this.opts)
      .map((res: Response) => res.json())
      .subscribe((authors: Array<Object>) =>
        this.authors = authors);
  }
}
```

The constructor starts by creating a `RequestOptionsArgs` that identifies a query string (`query=authors`) for an HTTP request. Then it calls the `get` method of the injected `Http` instance to create and send the request. This method returns an `Observable` that provides the server's `Response` asynchronously.

The `map` method transforms the `Response`'s JSON-formatted text into a JavaScript object. When this object becomes available, the `subscribe` method sets it equal to the `authors` property. Inside the template, the `NgFor` directive iterates through each element of `authors` and displays the first and last name in a table.

# 13.4 Cross-Origin Access with JSONP

Browsers will allow a web page to execute scripts from another web page on one condition—the two pages must have the same *origin* (host, protocol, and port). This restriction is called the Same Origin Policy, and it helps to ensure that client-server communication remains confidential.

But many harmless web applications need cross-origin access. Mashups require cross-origin access and many operations in the Facebook API execute operations across domains. For these reasons, many browsers allow a limited degree of inter-page script execution. One popular solution is cross-origin resource sharing, or CORS. The Worldwide Web Consortium recommends this method, which involves adding special headers to HTTP requests.

A drawback of CORS is that it doesn't work with old browsers. If this is a concern, another good option is JSONP, which stands for JavaScript Object Notation with Padding. Angular's `JsonpModule` provides classes and methods specifically for JSONP, and this section starts by explaining how it works.

## 13.4.1 Overview of JSONP

If you send a GET request to https://unpkg.com using `Http.get`, the browser's Same Origin Policy will prevent you from receiving a response. But the site can be accessed by adding a `<script>` element to the HTML page. For example, the following markup reads JavaScript from https://unpkg.com and inserts it into the web page:

```
<script
  src="https://unpkg.com/@angular/http/bundles/http.umd.js">
</script>
```

To be precise, the web page sends a GET request to https://unpkg.com, which responds with the desired JavaScript. In this manner, `<script>` makes it possible to send a GET request and receive a response without using methods like `Http.get`.

This is the essence of JSONP. It uses a `<script>` element to read data from a page (I'll call it the second page) that would normally be inaccessible due to the Same Origin Policy. The desired data is specified by adding a query string to the `src` URL. This generally takes the form `callback=`*`func`*, where *`func`* is the function to be executed.

The second page places arguments inside the function and inserts the function and its arguments (as a string) into the first page. When the first page receives the response, it executes the function as though it had come from a regular `<script>` element.

An example will help make this clear. Suppose a web page contains the following markup:

```
<script src="http://www.xyz.com?callback=processMe"></script>
```

If www.xyz.com has been configured for JSONP, it will know what data `processMe` is looking for. When the `<script>` executes, www.xyz.com will perform three steps:

1. Read the value of the `callback` parameter.
2. Determine the desired values of the arguments of `processMe`.
3. Respond with a string that invokes `processMe` with suitable arguments.

When the first page receives the response, it will execute the call to `processMe` like regular JavaScript code. If `processMe` wants the latest stock value of Acme, Inc. ($123.45) and the current minute of the hour (42), the response from the second page might return the following string:

```
processMe(123.45, 42);
```

This may seem straightforward, but there are issues that complicate matters. If the first page needs to access the second page multiple times, it must create multiple `<script>` elements. Also, if the first page sets the URL's query string to the same value as before, the client's cache may return an old string from the second page.

For this reason, JSONP clients create `<script>` elements dynamically and insert them in the document. This can be accomplished with jQuery or the DOM functions presented in Chapter 5. Another option is to use Angular's `JsonpModule`, and the next section explains how it works.

### 13.4.2 Using the Jsonp Class

The central class in JSONP is `Jsonp`, which is a subclass of the `Http` class discussed earlier. Because of this relationship, using the `Jsonp` class is essentially similar to using the `Http` class. But there are three major differences:

1. To access JSONP dependencies, the module's `@NgModule` decorator must add `JsonpModule` to its `imports` array.
2. JSONP supports GET requests only.
3. The response string must be specially formatted.

The last point requires explanation. The first section of this chapter explained that each method of the `Http` class (`get`, `put`, and so on) returns an `Observable` that provides access to the `Response`, which can be converted to a JavaScript object.

The `get` method of the `Jsonp` class also returns an `Observable` that emits the `Response` text. The following code shows how `Jsonp`'s `get` method can be called:

```
jsonp.get("http://www.xyz.com?CALLBACK=processMe")
    .subscribe(res => this.result = res.json());
```

This may seem confusing, as JSONP is supposed to call a function instead of providing an `Observable`. But in the interest of security, Angular doesn't let developers specify the function. Instead, Angular defines its own function to be executed, and this function provides an `Observable` that emits the second site's response.

Therefore, it doesn't matter what query string is given in the URL. The string provided by the second site must call the function defined by Angular. Strangely enough, Angular sets the function's name to `__ng_jsonp__.__req0.finished`.

For example, suppose the second site needs to provide the data `{"name": "Matt"}`. In this case, the body of its response must be given as follows:

```
__ng_jsonp__.__req0.finished([{"name": "Matt"}])
```

When the first site receives this string, Angular executes the function, which creates an `Observable` that emits `{"name": "Matt"}` as part of the response. The component class can access the response data by calling the `subscribe` method of the `Observable` returned by the `get` method.

The code in Listing 13.2 shows how JSONP can be used in practice. The component produces the same table of authors as in the HTTP demonstration, but uses JSONP to read data from the second site.

As shown, `Jsonp`'s `get` method accepts the same URL parameter as the `get` method of the `Http` class. But the query string doesn't affect which function is called. Instead, the second site can use the query string to authenticate the calling site and/or determine what data should be provided.

For this example, the second site provides the calling site with its list of authors by returning the following text:

```
__ng_jsonp__.__req0.finished([
  {"first": "Alexandre", "last": "Dumas"},
  {"first": "Herman", "last": "Melville"},
  {"first": "Mary", "last": "Shelley"}])
```

**Listing 13.2: ch13/jsonp_demo/src/app/app.ts**

```
@Component({
selector: 'app-root',
template: `
<p>Authors:</p>
<table>
  <tr *ngFor='let author of authors'>
    <td>{{ author.first }}</td>
    <td>{{ author.last }}</td>
  </tr>
</table>
`})
export class AppComponent {

  private authors: Object[];

  private opts: RequestOptionsArgs;

  constructor(private jsonp: Jsonp) {

    // Create the query string
    this.opts = {search: 'CALLBACK=process'};

    // Transfer data using JSONP
    this.jsonp.get('http://www.ngbook.io/jsonp_demo',
      this.opts)
        .subscribe((res: Response) => this.authors = res.json());
  }
}
```

Angular's implementation of JSONP makes it unnecessary to worry about `<script>` elements. It also improves security by ensuring that only one function can be executed. At the same time, it removes a lot of the freedom associated with regular JSONP data transfer.

# 13.5 Summary

HTTP communication is central to the operation of the Internet. Thankfully, Angular makes it easy to send requests and receive responses. There are three simple steps: inject an `Http` instance into a component, call one of its request methods, and process the `Response` in the returned `Observable`. The `Response` class provides methods for examining and transforming the content of the HTTP response.

The theory behind JSONP is somewhat involved. It involves transferring data to a remote system while making the browser think it's just loading a script. This doesn't provide as much flexibility as HTTP, but it works with browsers whose Same Origin Policy makes HTTP communication impossible.

Angular's implementation of JSONP is difficult at first because of the strange format of the response string. But once you understand this, transferring data with JSONP is just as straightforward as transferring data with HTTP.

# Chapter 14

# Forms

In an AngularJS 1.x application, a common use of two-way data binding involves form validation—checking the user's input as it's entered to make sure the input is acceptable. Two-way data binding ensures that the model will be updated with each user event and that the view will be updated with every change to the model.

To simplify development, Angular provides a framework for creating, validating, and monitoring the fields of a form. With this API, each field of interest can be associated with a control, and each control can be associated with one or more validators. As the user enters text in the field, the framework automatically triggers the control's validators. In this manner, Angular provides the responsiveness of two-way data binding without sacrificing performance and reliability.

Most of this chapter discusses the classes defined by the Reactive Forms API. A `FormControl` represents an input element in the form and a `FormGroup` makes it possible to manage multiple `FormControls`. A `FormArray` is similar to a `FormGroup`, but stores `FormControls` in an array that can be dynamically resized.

Every `FormControl` can have associated validators. A validator is a function that examines the `FormControl`'s value and returns an error if the value doesn't meet its criteria. Angular provides a handful of prebuilt validators, and if these aren't sufficient, it's easy to define custom validators.

The last part of the chapter discusses the template-driven methodology of form development. A template-driven form doesn't explicitly create `FormControls` or `FormGroups`. Instead, each field of interest in the form is marked with a directive. The form uses two-way binding to transfer data between the marked fields and the component's class.

# 14.1 HTML Forms

The forms discussed in this chapter are regular HTML forms that use Angular-specific functionality. As a quick review, an HTML form consists of a `<form>` element that contains a set of subelements, usually including at least one `<button>` or `<input>` element of type `submit`.

A form's purpose is to receive information from a user and transfer the information to a URL when the form is submitted. Each input element is called a field and the following HTML form has three fields related to automobiles:

```
<form action='auto_page.jsp'>
  Make of automobile:
  <input type='text' name='make'><br /><br />

  Model of automobile:
  <input type='text' name='model'><br /><br />

  Year of manufacture:
  <input type='number' name='year'><br /><br />

  <input type='submit' value='Submit'>
</form>
```

The `type` attribute of the last `<input>` element is set to `submit`. When the user clicks on it, the form's content is uploaded to the URL given by the `action` attribute of the `<form>` element. This content consists of name/value pairs in which the names are determined by the `name` attributes of the `<input>` elements. The values are set equal to the text inside each of the corresponding text boxes.

Figure 14.1 depicts the form created by the preceding markup. The appearance of an `<input>` element is determined by its `type` attribute.

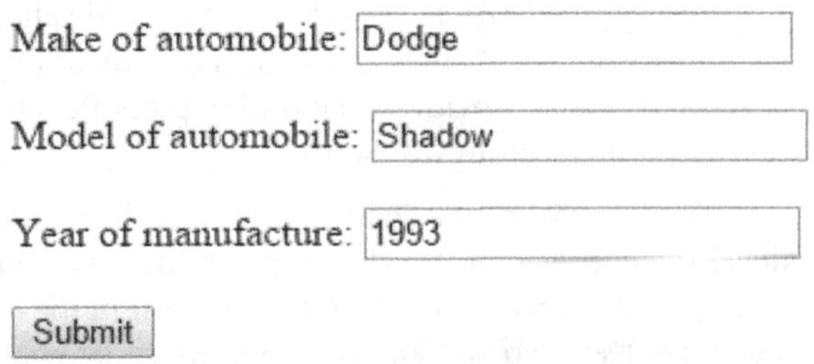


**Figure 14.1 A Simple HTML Form**

If the user clicks the Submit button, the uploaded data will contain three name/value pairs: `make/Dodge`, `model/Shadow`, and `year/1993`. This data will be sent to the URL associated with auto_page.jsp.

Angular provides two different ways of adding functionality to forms:

1. Reactive forms — All changes to the form and the component are managed in code using instances of `FormGroup` and `FormControls`.
2. Template-driven forms — Changes to the form and component are configured using two-way binding.

Most of this chapter focuses on reactive forms. These require more code but provide greater configurability. A later section will discuss template-driven forms.

# 14.2 Simple Forms Example

When working with reactive forms, the most important classes to know are `FormGroup` and `FormControl`. Much of this chapter will be spent exploring these classes in detail. But first, it's helpful to look at a trivial example that demonstrates how they're used.

The form in Figure 14.2 contains two text boxes and three buttons. When the first button is pressed, an 'a' is appended to the text in the first box. When the second button is pressed, a 'z' is appended to the text in the second box. When the third button is pressed, the form is submitted.

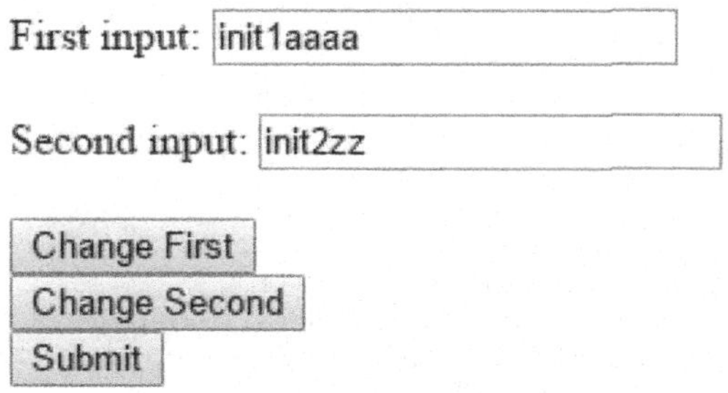


**Figure 14.2 Trivial Form Example**

The code for this simple form creates one `FormGroup` for the form and two `FormControls`—one for each text box. Listing 14.1 presents the code for the base component.

**Listing 14.1: ch14/simple_form/app/app.component.ts**

```
@Component({
selector: 'app-root',
template: `

<!-- Associate the form with a FormGroup -->
<form [formGroup]='group' (ngSubmit)='handleSubmit()'>

  <!-- Associate the first text box with a FormControl -->
  First input:<input formControlName='input1'><br /><br />

  <!-- Associate the second text box with a FormControl -->
  Second input:<input formControlName='input2'><br /><br />

  <input type='button' (click)='changeFirst()'
    value='Change First'><br />
  <input type='button' (click)='changeSecond()'
    value='Change Second'><br />
  <input type='submit' value='Submit'>
</form>
`})

// Define the component's class
export class AppComponent {
  public group: FormGroup;
  constructor() {
    this.group = new FormGroup({
      'input1': new FormControl('init1'),
      'input2': new FormControl('init2')
    });
  }

  // Update the first control when the first button is clicked
  private changeFirst() {
    const control = this.group.get('input1');
    control.setValue(control.value + 'a');
  }

  // Update the second control when the second button is clicked
  private changeSecond() {
    const control = this.group.get('input2');
    control.setValue(control.value + 'z');
  }

  // Respond when the form is submitted
  private handleSubmit() {
    alert('Form submitted');
  };
}
```

In the component's template, the `<form>` element sets the `formGroup` property to `group`. This tells Angular to associate the `<form>` element with the component's member named group, which is an instance of the `FormGroup` class. As we'll see, a `FormGroup` serves as a container of other form-related structures.

The component's template also contains two text boxes, and both `<input>` elements contain the `formControlName` property. This property is set to a value that corresponds to a `FormControl` member in the component class. The component reads and updates the element's text by accessing the associated `FormControl`.

`FormGroup` and `FormControl` are both subclasses of `AbstractControl`. Figure 14.3 presents the inheritance hierarchy.

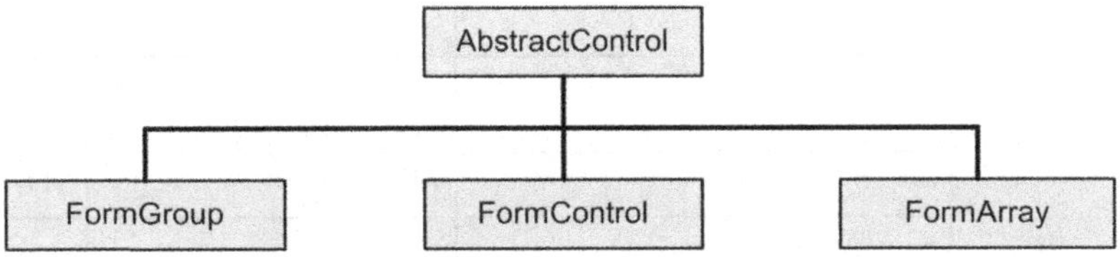


**Figure 14.3 Inheritance Hierarchy of AbstractControl**

The following section will discuss the `AbstractControl` and `FormGroup` classes. Later sections will explore the `FormControl` and `FormArray` classes.

To use these classes, an application's module needs to import `ReactiveFormsModule` from `@angular/forms`. Also, `ReactiveFormsModule` must be included in the `imports` array of the module's `@NgModule` decorator.

# 14.3 Form Groups

The two most important classes in the Forms API are `FormGroup`, which represents a group of input elements, and `FormControl`, which represents an input element. Before discussing either, I'd like to introduce `AbstractControl`, the superclass of both `FormGroup` and `FormControl`.

## 14.3.1 The AbstractControl Class

The `AbstractControl` class can't be instantiated by itself, but its members can be accessed by any `FormControl`, `FormGroup`, or `FormArray`. Table 14.1 lists its properties and methods.

**Table 14.1**

Members of the AbstractControl Class

<table>
<tr><th>Member</th><th>Type</th><th>Description</th></tr>
<tr><td>value</td><td>any</td><td>A data value associated with the control</td></tr>
<tr><td>validator</td><td>ValidatorFn</td><td>A synchronous function that validates the control's data</td></tr>
<tr><td>asyncValidator</td><td>AsyncValidatorFn</td><td>A synchronous function that validates the control's data</td></tr>
<tr><td>errors</td><td>ValidationErrors</td><td>Collection of errors related to the control's data validation</td></tr>
<tr><td>parent</td><td>FormGroup | FormArray</td><td>The control's container</td></tr>
<tr><td>root</td><td>AbstractControl</td><td>The control's top-level ancestor</td></tr>
<tr><td>status</td><td>string</td><td>A string that identifies whether the data is valid or invalid</td></tr>
<tr><td>valid/invalid</td><td>boolean</td><td>Identifies if the control has errors (invalid) or no errors (valid)</td></tr>
<tr><td>pending</td><td>boolean</td><td>Identifies if the status is pending</td></tr>
<tr><td>enabled/disabled</td><td>boolean</td><td>Identifies if the control has been enabled or disabled</td></tr>
<tr><td>pristine/dirty</td><td>boolean</td><td>Identifies if the user has changed the control's value</td></tr>
<tr><td>touched/untouched</td><td>boolean</td><td>Identifies if the user has triggered a blur event on the control</td></tr>
<tr><td>valueChanges</td><td>Observable<any></td><td>Emits an event when the control's value changes</td></tr>
<tr><td>statusChanges</td><td>Observable<any></td><td>Emits an event when the control's validation status changes</td></tr>
<tr><td>get(path: string | Array<string|number>)</td><td>AbstractControl</td><td>Returns the child control with the given path</td></tr>
<tr><td>enable({self, emit}: {self?: boolean, emit?: boolean)</td><td>void</td><td>Enables the control</td></tr>
<tr><td>disable({self, emit}: {self?: boolean, emit?: boolean)</td><td>void</td><td>Disables the control</td></tr>
</table>

| | | |
|---|---|---|
| `markAsPending({self}: {self?: boolean})` | `void` | Sets the control's status as pending |
| `markAsUntouched( {self}: {self?: boolean})` | `void` | Sets the control to touched |
| `markAsTouched({self}: {self?: boolean})` | `void` | Sets the control to untouched |
| `markAsPristine({self}: {self?: boolean})` | `void` | Sets the control to pristine |
| `markAsDirty({self}: {self?: boolean})` | `void` | Sets the control to dirty |
| `setValidator(v: ValidatorFn \| ValidatorFn[])` | `void` | Assigns one or more synchronous validators |
| `setAsyncValidator(v: AsyncValidatorFn \| AsyncValidatorFn[])` | `void` | Assigns one or more asynchronous validators |
| `clearValidators()` | `void` | Removes all synchronous validators |
| `clearAsyncValidators()` | `void` | Removes all asynchronous validators |
| `updateValueAndValidity ({self, emit}: {self?: boolean, emit?: boolean})` | `void` | Recomputes the control's value and valid status |

Every `AbstractControl` has a `value` property that can take any type. In the simple_form example presented earlier, the `value` of each `FormControl` was the text in the associated text box. When the value changes, `valueChanges` will emit an event to all observers.

Every `AbstractControl` can have one or more associated functions that check whether the control's value is acceptable. These functions are called *validators*, and can operate synchronously or asynchronously. A synchronous validator can be assigned by setting the `validator` member to a `ValidatorFn`, which is a function type defined as follows:

```
export interface ValidatorFn {
  (c: AbstractControl): ValidationErrors | null;
}
```

Asynchronous validators can be assigned by assigning the `asyncValidator` property to an `AsyncValidatorFn`. Its definition is given as follows:

```
export interface AsyncValidatorFn {
  (c: AbstractControl): Promise<ValidationErrors | null> |
    Observable<ValidationErrors|null>;
}
```

In both cases, validation errors are provided in a `ValidationErrors` instance. This type is given as follows:

```
export type ValidationErrors = {
  [key: string]: any
};
```

The validator's result determines the control's `status`, which can take one of four string values:

1. `VALID` — no errors have been detected
2. `INVALID` — at least one error has been detected
3. `PENDING` — the control's status hasn't been determined
4. `DISABLED` — the control is exempt from validation

The `valid` field is true if the form's status is `VALID` and the `invalid` field is true if the status is `INVALID`. The `pending` field is true if the control's status is `PENDING`. Lastly, `disabled` is true if the form's status is `DISABLED` and enabled is true if the form's status isn't `DISABLED`. In code, a control's status can be set with the `pending`, `enable`, and `disable` methods.

The `get` method makes it possible to access one of the control's children. This accepts the path of the child to be created. In general, this is the name of the child provided in the control's constructor.

A control is considered pristine if the user hasn't changed its value. Once the user makes a change, the control is considered dirty. These states are represented by the `pristine` and `dirty` fields. An application can change a control's pristine/dirty state by calling its `markAsPristine` or `markAsDirty` methods.

The `setValidator` and `setAsyncValidator` methods specify a function or functions to serve as the control's validator. A control's validators can be dissociated by calling `clearValidators` or `clearAsyncValidators`.

## 14.3.2 The FormGroup Class

A `FormGroup` manages a group of `AbstractControls` and provides a single object for validating its children. Its constructor is given as follows:

```
constructor(controls: {[key: string]: AbstractControl},
  validator?: ValidatorFn,
  asyncValidator?: AsyncValidatorFn)
```

The only required parameter is the first. `controls` associates names with `AbstractControls`. The following code creates a `FormGroup` with two `FormControl` children whose names are `name1` and `name2`:

```
this.group = new FormGroup({
  'name1': new FormControl(...),
  'name2': new FormControl(...)});
```

An `AbstractControl` managed by a `FormGroup` can be replaced by calling the `FormGroup`'s `setControl` method. Table 14.2 lists `setControl` and other members of the `FormGroup` class.

**Table 14.2**

Properties and Methods of the FormGroup Class

| Member | Type/Return Value | Description |
|---|---|---|
| `controls` | `{[key: string], AbstractControl}` | Returns a container that maps each control to a name |
| `addControl( name: string, c: AbstractControl)` | `void` | Adds a new control to the group and assigns it the given name |
| `registerControl( name: string, c: AbstractControl)` | `AbstractControl` | Adds a new control to the group without updating its value or validity |
| `removeControl( name: string)` | `void` | Removes the given control from the group |
| `setControl( name: string, c: AbstractControl)` | `void` | Replaces an existing control |
| `contains(name: string)` | `boolean` | Identifies if the named control is in the group |

| | | |
|---|---|---|
| `setValue(value: {[key:string]: any}, {self, emit}? : {self: boolean, emit: boolean})` | void | Sets the value of the group |
| `patchValue(value: {[key:string]: any}, {self, emit}? : {self: boolean, emit: boolean})` | void | Sets part or all of the group's value |
| `reset(value?: any}, {self, emit}? : {self: boolean, emit: boolean})` | void | Resets the group's value |
| `getRawValue()` | any | Returns the complete value of the group, including values of disabled children |

Just as the `FormGroup` constructor accepts a map that associates names with controls, the `controls` field provides the group's map. Keep in mind that a `FormGroup` may contain other `FormGroups` in addition to `FormControls`.

The `addControl` and `registerControl` methods both add new `AbstractControls` to the group. The difference between the two is that `registerControl` doesn't update the control's value or validity. For this reason, it's generally preferable to use `addControl` instead.

The `setValue`, `patchValue`, and `reset` methods all update the group's value. `setValue` always updates the entire group, while `patchValue` can update a part of the group. `reset` can update the group with a new value, but if called without arguments, it resets the group's value to null.

## 14.3.3 Form Group Directive

To serve a purpose, a `FormGroup` must be associated with a `<form>` element in the component's template. To create this association, the `<form>` element must have a `formGroup` directive set to the name of the component's `FormGroup` variable. This is shown in the following code:

```
@Component({
selector: '...',
template: `
<form [formGroup]='group' (ngSubmit)='handleSubmit()'>
  ...
  <input type='submit' value='Submit'>
</form>
`})

export class Example {
  constructor() {

    // Create a FormGroup with two controls
    this.group = new FormGroup({
      'name1': new FormControl(...),
      'name2': new FormControl(...)});
  }
  handleSubmit() {...}
}
```

Looking at this code, it's important to notice two items:

1. In the `<form>` element, the `formGroup` directive is set equal to `group`, which is the name of the `FormGroup` variable in the component.
2. In the `<form>` element, the `ngSubmit` event is set equal to `handleSubmit()`, which is the name of the event handling method in the class.

Before this example can work properly, the `FormGroup` must be initialized with actual `FormControls` and corresponding elements must be inserted into the template. The next section discusses `FormControls` in detail and shows how they can be associated with template elements.

# 14.4 Form Controls

Each `FormControl` in a `FormGroup` represents a field in the template's form. This association makes it possible for the component to initialize the element, access its data, and validate its content.

Before a `FormControl` can be used, a `FormControl` instance must be added to a `FormGroup` (or `FormArray`, which will be discussed shortly). Also, a `formControlName` directive must be added to the component's template. This section discusses both the `FormControl` class and the process of associating a `FormControl` with a template element.

### 14.4.1 The FormControl Class

A `FormControl` provides access to an element in the component's template. The constructor for this class is given as follows:

```
constructor(value?: any,
  validator?: ValidatorFn | ValidatorFn[],
  asyncValidator?: AsyncValidatorFn | AsyncValidatorFn[])
```

The first argument, `value`, provides an initial value for the corresponding input element. For example, if a `FormControl` is associated with a text box, `value` will be written to the box. The second and third arguments identify validation function(s) that should be used to check the content of the corresponding input element.

I recommend setting an initial value for every `FormControl`, even if it's `''`. In some cases, if the user submits a form without touching a `FormControl`, the `FormControl`'s value will return null, which can lead to errors.

The `FormControl` class provides five public methods. Table 14.3 lists them and provides a description of each.

**Table 14.3**

Members of the FormControl Class

| Member | Type | Description |
|---|---|---|
| `setValue(value: any, {self, emit, change}?: {self?: boolean, emit?: boolean, change?: boolean)` | `void` | Sets the value of the control |
| `patchValue(value: any, options?: {?: boolean, ?: boolean, ?: boolean, ?: boolean)` | `void` | Sets part or all of the control's value |
| `reset(formState?: any, {self: emit}?: {self?: boolean, emit?: boolean}` | `void` | Resets the control's value |
| `registerOnChange( fn: Function)` | `void` | Assigns a function to be called when the control's value changes |

| | | |
|---|---|---|
| registerOnDisabledChange( fn: (isDisabled: boolean) => void) | void | Assigns a function to be called when the control's disabled state changes |

The setValue, patchValue, and reset methods are similar to those discussed for the FormControl class. When one of these methods is called, the FormControl's value changes and the corresponding data in the template is updated.

The registerOnChange method assigns a function to be called when the FormControl's value changes. Similarly, registerOnDisabledChange assigns a function to be called when a disabled event occurs.

### 14.4.2 Form Control Directive

To associate a FormControl with a template element, the formControlName attribute must be assigned. If an element sets formControlName to a string, the element will be associated with the FormControl with the matching name. As discussed earlier, a FormControl's name is set by the FormGroup when the FormControl is added.

An example will clarify how this works. The following markup associates the <input> element with a FormControl named autoMake.

```
<form [formGroup]='group' action='destination.jsp'>
  ...
  Make of automobile:
  <input type='text' formControlName='autoMake'><br /><br />
  ...
</form>
```

If the form's FormGroup contains a FormControl whose name is autoMake, the FormControl will be associated with the <input> element. The enclosing FormGroup is named group, so the FormControl can be obtained by accessing group.controls['autoMake'].

Any change to the <input> element will change the FormControl's value. Similarly, a call to the FormControl's updateValue method will change the content of the <input> element.

It's important to be clear about the difference between the formGroup directive and the formControlName directive. formGroup associates a form with a FormGroup. formControlName associates a field in the form with a FormControl.

# 14.5 Form Validation

The `FormControl` and `FormGroup` constructors accept optional validator functions. Synchronously or asynchronously, a validator checks the value of the `FormControl` or `FormGroup` and returns null if it can't find any errors. If it finds errors, the function returns an object that provides information about them.

This section discusses two ways of configuring form validation. The simpler way is to use one of the prebuilt functions provided by the `Validators` class. If none of the prebuilt options are sufficient, the more difficult method is to code a custom validation function.

## 14.5.1 The Validators Class

The `Validators` class provides static methods that validate `AbstractControls`. Table 14.4 lists each of these methods and describes what it accomplishes.

**Table 14.4**

Methods of the Validators Class

| Function | Description |
|---|---|
| `nullValidator` | Returns null, performs no validation |
| `required` | Checks that the control's value is present |
| `requiredTrue` | Checks that the control's value is true |
| `email` | Checks that the control's value is a valid email address |
| `pattern` | Checks the control's value against a regular expression |
| `minLength` | Checks that the value is longer than the minimum length |
| `maxLength` | Checks that the value is shorter than the maximum length |
| `compose` | Combines errors from multiple synchronous validators |
| `composeAsync` | Combines errors from multiple asynchronous validators |

If the validator function isn't provided, the `AbstractControl` is assigned a `nullValidator`, which does nothing. To demonstrate `Validators.required`, the following code creates a `FormControl` that will be invalid if its value is left empty:

```
FormControl fc = new FormControl('', Validators.required);
```

If fc's value is null or an empty string, cont.valid will return false. The fc.status property will return INVALID.

The email method checks if the control's value represents a valid email address. The pattern method checks if the value matches a given pattern. The format of the pattern value is the same as that of the patterns discussed in Chapter 3.

The minLength and maxLength methods both accept an argument that relates to the length of an AbstractControl's value. The following code creates a FormControl that will be invalid if its value is less than three characters long:

```
FormControl fc = new FormControl('', Validators.minLength(3));
```

Similarly, the following FormControl will be invalid if its length is greater than ten:

```
FormControl fc = new FormControl('', Validators.maxLength(10));
```

The compose method makes it possible to associate an AbstractControl with multiple validation functions. The following discussion will demonstrate how it's used.

## 14.5.2 Custom Validation

A validation function accepts an AbstractControl and returns a {[key: string]: any} if any errors are found. For example, suppose you want to make sure that a FormControl's text contains street. The following function shows how this can be accomplished:

```
function streetChecker(c: AbstractControl):
    {[key: string]: boolean} {
  if(c.value.match(/street/g)) {
    return null;
  } else {
    return {'streetCheck': true};
  }
}
```

This routine returns null if the FormControl's value contains street and returns a {[key: string]: boolean} if it doesn't. If the FormControl's value is required, the FormControl's validation can be configured with the following code:

```
control = new FormControl('',
   Validators.compose([Validators.required, streetChecker]));
```

As shown, the `compose` method accepts an array of validation functions. Unless every function in the array returns null, the `FormControl` will be invalid. If this `FormControl` is invalid, the following code prints its errors to the console:

```
if(!control.valid) {
  for name in control.errors {
    console.log(name + ': ' + control.errors[name]);
  }
}
```

If the value is set to `''`, both functions will return `{[key: string]: boolean}`. The results printed to the console will be given as follows:

```
required: true
streetCheck: true
```

The validation functions are executed in the order that they're given to `Validators.compose`.

# 14.6 Subgroups and Form Arrays

As forms become more complex, it becomes helpful to divide their fields into subgroups. This is particularly helpful when different portions of a form need to be managed separately. Within the template, each subgroup is identified with the `formGroup` directive.

If one portion of a form contains a variable number of elements, the elements can be created with the `NgFor` directive introduced in Chapter 9. However, a `FormGroup` requires a fixed number of elements, so the controller needs to create a `FormArray` instead.

## 14.6.1 Subgroups

Rather than place every `FormControl` in one `FormGroup`, it helps to divide them into multiple `FormGroups` that can be configured and validated individually. These `FormGroups` must be inserted into a parent `FormGroup` that represents the overall form.

Subgroups are associated with elements using the same `formGroup` directive discussed earlier. The following markup shows how one `FormGroup` can contain other `FormGroups`:

```
<form formGroup='main' (ngSubmit)='handleSubmit()'>
  <div formGroup='g1'>...</div>
  <div formGroup='g2'>...</div>
  <input type='submit' value='Submit'>
</form>
```

As shown, the `formGroup` directive associates `main` with the `<form>` element. Inside the form, `formGroup` associates the `FormGroups` `g1` and `g2` with `<div>` elements. The following code shows how `main` can be defined in the component class.

```
this.main =
  new FormGroup({
    'g1': new FormGroup(...),
    'g2': new FormGroup(...)});
```

It's important to see that `main` is the variable name of the top-level `FormGroup`. `g1` and `g2` are names that `main` assigns to its children, not the names of the `FormGroup` variables.

An important advantage of using subgroups is that they can be validated separately. Later in this chapter, we'll look at example code that demonstrates how this works.

### 14.6.2 FormArrays

Like a `FormGroup`, a `FormArray` serves as a container of `AbstractControls`. But there are four important differences between `FormArrays` and `FormGroups`:

1. A `FormArray` can contain a variable number of controls. `FormGroups` require a fixed number of controls.
2. A `FormArray` can't be associated with a `<form>` element. Therefore, a `FormArray` must be placed inside at least one `FormGroup`.
3. The `FormArray` class provides methods for accessing controls in a sequence.
4. `FormArray` instances are associated with template elements using the `formArrayName` directive instead of `formGroup`.

For example, the following markup associates a `FormArray` with a `<div>` element that creates an `<input>` for each of its elements.

```
<div formArrayName='formArray'>
  <input *ngFor='let ctrl of formArray.controls; let i = index'
    formControlName='{{i}}'>
</div>
```

This may be hard to understand at first, but it will become clearer as you become more familiar with the FormArray class. A good place to start is by looking at its constructor:

```
constructor(controls: AbstractControl[],
  validator?: function,
  asyncValidator?: function))
```

This is similar to the FormGroup constructor, but the collection of AbstractControls is an array instead of a map. As an example, the following constructor creates a FormArray with two FormControls:

```
array = new FormArray(
  [new FormControl(...), new FormControl(...)]);
```

The members of FormArray are about what you'd expect for an array-based container of AbstractControls. Table 14.5 lists all of the class's public members.

**Table 14.5**

Properties and Methods of the FormArray Class

| Member | Type/Return Value | Description |
|---|---|---|
| `controls` | `AbstractControl[]` | The array of controls managed by the FormArray |
| `length` | `number` | The number of controls managed by the FormArray |
| `at(index: number)` | `AbstractControl` | Returns the control with the given index |
| `push(ctrl: AbstractControl)` | `void` | Adds a control to the end of the array |
| `insert(index: number, ctrl: AbstractControl)` | `void` | Inserts a control into the array at the given position |
| `removeAt(index: number)` | `void` | Removes the control at the given position |
| `setControl(index: number, ctrl: AbstractControl)` | `void` | Replaces the control at the given position |

| | | |
|---|---|---|
| `setValue(value: {[key:string]: any}, {self, emit}? : {self: boolean, emit: boolean})` | `void` | Sets the value of the array |
| `patchValue(value: {[key:string]: any}, {self, emit}? : {self: boolean, emit: boolean})` | `void` | Sets part or all of the array's value |
| `reset(value?: any}, {self, emit}? : {self: boolean, emit: boolean})` | `void` | Resets the array's value |
| `getRawValue()` | `any` | Returns the complete value of the group, including values of disabled children |

As mentioned earlier, a `FormArray` can't be associated with a `<form>` element, so it must be placed inside of a `FormGroup`. Consider the following code:

```
myArray = new FormArray([...]);
myGroup = new FormGroup({'array': myArray});
```

The following markup associates these objects with form elements using the `formGroup` and `formArrayName` directives.

```
<form [formGroup]='myGroup' (ngSubmit)='handleSubmit()'>
  <div formArrayName = 'array'>
    <input *ngFor='let ctrl of myArray.controls; let i = index'
        formControlName='{{i}}'>
  </div>
  <input type='submit' value='Submit'>
</form>
```

The `formGroup` directive associates the `<form>` element with `myGroup`, which is the name of the top-level `FormGroup`. Inside the form, the `formArrayName` directive associates the `<div>` element with `array`, which is the name of the `FormArray` assigned by the `FormGroup` constructor. In contrast, the `ngFor` directive accesses `myArray`, which is the actual name of the `FormArray` member. It's important to recognize when to use the member name versus the name assigned by the parent.

Inside the FormArray's <div> element, the following markup creates one <input> element for each element in the FormArray:

```
<input *ngFor='let ctrl of myArray.controls; let i = index'
  formControlName='{{i}}'>
```

As explained in Chapter 9, NgFor accepts an array and creates an HTML element for each element. In this case, it's used to create an <index> element for each AbstractControl in the array myArray.controls.

i is the index of the current array element. This is just a number, and at first, I found it hard to see why formControlName should be set equal to {{i}}. To understand this, keep in mind that each child of a FormGroup is accessed through a string index. In the surrounding <div> element, formArrayName is set to 'array', so the corresponding FormArray is accessed as myGroup['array'].

Similarly, each child of a FormArray is accessed by number, or {{i}}. This means the $i^{th}$ AbstractControl in a FormArray must be accessed as myGroup['array'][i].

# 14.7 Additional Input Elements

So far, the only elements included in form applications have been text boxes. But other elements can be accessed just as easily. This section explains how to associate checkboxes and select elements with form controls.

## 14.7.1 Checkboxes

If the type of an <input> is set to checkbox, it will take the form of a checkbox. As with text elements, this can be associated with a FormControl using the formControlName directive. For example, the following markup associates a checkbox with a FormControl named boxControl:

```
<input type='checkbox' formControlName='boxControl'>
```

For a checkbox, the FormControl's value is boolean. The box will be initially checked if the initial value is set to true, and it will be initially unchecked if the value is set to false. If the FormControl's initial value isn't set and the form is submitted, the value will equal null.

### 14.7.2 Select Elements

Chapter 9 explained how `NgFor` can set options of a `<select>` equal to elements of an array. If you intend to associate a `<select>` element with a `FormControl`, the `NgFor` directive is required. Otherwise, the `FormControl`'s value will remain at null. For example, this code defines an array of strings and a `FormGroup` with one `FormControl`:

```
colors = ['red', 'green', 'blue'];
colorGroup =
  new FormGroup({'selectControl': new FormControl('green')});
```

The following markup creates a form that contains a `<select>` element. The `formControlName` directive associates the `<select>` element with the `FormControl`. The `NgFor` directive creates the options of the `<select>` element to the strings in the `colors` array.

```
<form [formGroup]='colorGroup' (ngSubmit)='handleSubmit()'>

  <select formControlName='selectControl'>
    <option *ngFor='let color of colors' [value]='color'>
      {{color}}
    </option>
  </select>

</form>
```

In this case, the `FormControl`'s `value` property is a string because the `<select>` element's options are strings. Therefore, if an initial value is set, it must be set to one of the strings in the array. If the options are numbers instead of strings, the `value` property will be a number and the `FormControl`'s initial value must be set to a number.

## 14.8 Form Builders

All of the preceding code has used constructors to create new form groups, form controls, and form arrays. To simplify the process of creating these data structures, the Reactive Forms API provides the `FormBuilder` class.

If the application's module has imported the `ReactiveFormsModule`, components can access a `FormBuilder` instance through dependency injection. After receiving the `FormBuilder`, a component can call its methods to create new instances.

The three methods of `FormBuilder` are given as follows:

- `group(config: {[key: string]: any}, extra?: {[key: string]: any})` — Returns a new `FormGroup` with the given configuration
- `control(formState: Object, validator?: ValidatorFn | ValidatorFn[], asyncValidator?: AsyncValidatorFn | AsyncValidatorFn[])` — Returns a new `FormControl` with the given configuration
- `array(controlsConfig: any[], validator?: ValidatorFn, asyncValidator?: AsyncValidatorFn)` — Returns a new `FormArray` with the given configuration

In effect, each method replaces the constructor of the corresponding class. To demonstrate this, the following constructor accesses a `FormBuilder` through dependency injection. Then it calls the `FormBuilder`'s methods to create two `FormControl`s and a `FormGroup`:

```
constructor(private formBuilder: FormBuilder) {

  // Create two FormControls
  this.cntrl1 = formBuilder.control('init1');
  this.cntrl2 = formBuilder.control('init2');

  // Create a FormGroup
  this.group = formBuilder.group({
    'input1': this.cntrl1,
    'input2': this.cntrl2
  });
}
```

The next section presents a more interesting example of how `FormGroup`s and `FormControl`s can be used.

## 14.9 Restaurant Order Form

The ch14/order_form project demonstrates how validation, subgroups, checkboxes, and select elements work together in practice. Its purpose is to allow the user to add menu selections to an order and compute the overall charge with an optional gratuity. Figure 14.4 shows what the form looks like.

**Figure 14.4 The OrderForm Component**

Listing 14.2 presents the code for the component. The template markup can be found in app.component.html and the CSS rules are in app.component.css.

**Listing 14.2: ch14/order_form/app/app.component.ts**

```
@Component({
selector: 'app-root',
styleUrls: ['app.component.css'],
templateUrl: 'app.component.html',
})

// Define the component's controller
export class AppComponent {

  private types = ['Carryout', 'Delivery'];
  private apps = ['Green beans - 1.50',
     'Cheese fries - 1.75', 'Tofu - 2.50'];
  private soups = ['Miso Soup - 3.25',
     'Beef soup - 3.80', 'Clam chowder - 4.25'];
  private meals = ['Fettucini - 17.80',
      'Chicken - 19.45', 'Lobster and Shrimp - 24.80'];
```

**Listing 14.2: ch14/order_form/app/app.component.ts (Continued)**

```
  private orders = [];
  private total = 0;
  private orderPlaced = false;
  private tip = false;
  private nameControl: FormControl;
  private emailControl: FormControl;
  private topGroup: FormGroup;
  private menuGroup: FormGroup;
  private mainGroup: FormGroup;

  constructor() {

    // Create form controls
    this.nameControl = new FormControl('John Smith',
      Validators.required);
    this.emailControl = new FormControl('jsmith@xyz.org',
      Validators.compose([Validators.required,
        Validators.email]));

    // Create group for ID controls
    this.topGroup = new FormGroup({
      'nameText': this.nameControl,
      'emailText': this.emailControl,
      'typeSelect': new FormControl(this.types[0]),
      'tipCheck' : new FormControl(this.tip)});

    // Create group for menu controls
    this.menuGroup = new FormGroup({
      'appSelect': new FormControl(this.apps[0]),
      'soupSelect': new FormControl(this.soups[0]),
      'mealSelect': new FormControl(this.meals[0])});

    // Create group to hold subgroups
    this.mainGroup = new FormGroup({
      'top': this.topGroup,
      'menu': this.menuGroup});
  }

 // Set whether a gratuity will be added
  private changeTip(t: boolean): void {
    this.tip = t;
    if (t) {
      this.total *= 1.15;
    } else {
      this.total /= 1.15;
    }
  }
```

**Listing 14.2: ch14/order_form/app/app.component.ts (Continued)**

```
  // Add a new item to the order
  private addOrderItem(item: string): void {
    this.orders.push(item);
    const pos = item.indexOf('-') + 1;
    if (this.tip) {
      this.total += 1.15 * Number(item.substring(pos));
    } else {
      this.total += Number(item.substring(pos));
    }
  }

  // Remove an item from the order
  private deleteOrderItem(item: string, index: number): void {
    this.orders.splice(index, 1);
    const pos = item.indexOf('-') + 1;
    if (this.tip) {
      this.total -= 1.15 * Number(item.substring(pos));
    } else {
      this.total -= Number(item.substring(pos));
    }
  }

  private handleSubmit(): void {
    let outMsg = 'Total charge is '+this.total.toFixed(2)+': ';
    let pos: number;
    for (let i = 0; i < this.orders.length; i++) {
      pos = this.orders[i].indexOf('-') - 1;
      outMsg += this.orders[i].substring(0, pos) + ', ';
    }
    outMsg = outMsg.substring(0, outMsg.length - 2);
    alert(outMsg);
  };
}
```

The two topmost controls ask for a name and email address. Both controls have assigned validators, and in the case of the email address, the validators include `Validators.email`, which ensures that the address is structured correctly.

If either field fails validation, the component expands the top portion of the form and displays a message in red. Further, the Submit button remains disabled until the form validates successfully.

When the user selects a menu item, the item is added to a list displayed in the form's lower-left. Each item has a Delete button that allows the user to remove the item from the order. This behavior is made possible through the `NgFor` directive, as shown in the following markup.

```
<ul>
  <li *ngFor='let order of orders; let i = index'>
    {{order}} <input type='button' value='Delete'
      (click)='deleteOrderItem(order, i)'>
  </li>
</ul>
```

In this markup, `order` is a local variable that identifies the menu item and its price. When the user clicks the item's Delete button, the item is removed from the list and its price is subtracted from the total.

# 14.10 Template-Driven Forms

In addition to reactive forms, Angular supports *template-driven forms*. The major difference is that template-driven forms use two-way binding to associate template elements with component properties.

Chapter 8 explained how two-way binding is made possible by the `NgModel` directive. For example, the following markup uses `NgModel` to bind an `<input>` element to a property named `input1`:

```
<input [(ngModel)]='input1'>
```

Due to two-way binding, the element's value will be updated when `input1` changes and `input1` will be updated when the element's value changes.

When using template-driven forms, there are four points to be aware of:

1. The application's module needs to import `FormsModule` and add `FormsModule` to the `imports` array of the module's `@NgModule` decorator.
2. The `<form>` element needs to be associated with an `NgForm`.
3. Each element to be associated with a control needs to set its `name` property and set `[(ngModel)]` equal to a component property.
4. Validation isn't performed in code, but is accomplished by inserting directives into elements of interest.

The first point is straightforward to understand, but the other points require explanation. The following discussion introduces the `NgForm` and then explains how validation works in template-driven forms. The end of the section presents example code that demonstrates how a template-driven form can be created.

## 14.10.1 NgForm and Form Controls

In a reactive form, a component creates FormGroups and FormControls and associates them with template elements using the formGroup and formControlName directives. In a template-driven form, FormGroups and FormControls are not explicitly created. Instead, the entire form is associated with an NgForm, which manages the controls behind the scenes.

To associate a <form> element with an NgForm, it's common to use a local variable. The following markup shows how this works.

```
<form #f='ngForm' (ngSubmit)='submit()'>
  ...
  <input type='submit' [disabled]='!f.form.valid'>
</form>
```

This markup sets the local variable f equal to ngForm. This tells Angular to associate the form with an NgForm. The local variable can be used throughout the form, and in this case, the disabled property is set equal to !f.form.valid. The form field corresponds to the NgForm's FormGroup.

After setting the NgForm, the template needs to identify which elements should be accessed as form controls. This is set by assigning a name attribute to the elements of interest. This is shown in the following element.

```
<input name='inputName' [(ngModel)]='memberName'>
```

As shown, each element of interest should have [(ngModel)] set equal to a component property. This allows the component to read and update the element's value.

## 14.10.2 Validation

In a template-driven form, validation is simple if you use the built-in validators discussed earlier. Validators are set by adding directives to elements of interest. For example, the required directive indicates that the element isn't valid until it has a defined value. The following markup shows how this is used.

```
<input name='inputName' [(ngModel)]='memberName' required>
```

In addition to required, other directives for built-in validators include requiredTrue, email, minLength, and maxLength.

Custom validation is more difficult because the `FormControls` of the template's elements are difficult to access. To configure validation in a template-driven form, three data structures are needed:

1. A custom directive to perform validation
2. A child component to report error messages
3. A parent component to hold the validation directive and the reporting component

This discussion examines these steps in detail. Afterward, I'll present an example that uses custom validation to check element values in a template-driven form.

## Step 1: The Validation Directive

Coding a directive to perform custom validation is more difficult than coding a regular directive. To see why this is the case, consider the following element of a template-driven form:

```
<input name='inputName' [(ngModel)]='modelName' custom-validator>
```

The `custom-validator` marker specifies that the `<input>`'s data should be checked by the associated directive. To validate the element, the directive needs to access the value of the `FormControl` associated with the element.

To access the element's `FormControl`, the directive must access a `Provider` that binds `NG_VALIDATORS` to a function name. `NG_VALIDATORS` is an `OpaqueToken`, and if it's bound to a function, that function will be automatically called when an element affected by the directive needs to be validated.

For example, suppose you want to validate an element's value using a function named `streetChecker`. The first step is to create a suitable `Provider` with code such as the following:

```
const streetCheckerBinding: Provider = {
  provide: NG_VALIDATORS,
  useValue: streetChecker,
  multi: true
};
```

This ties `NG_VALIDATORS` to the `streetChecker` function. If this `Provider` is associated with a directive, and a selected element contains a `FormControl`, `streetValidator` will be invoked to validate the `FormControl`.

This `Provider` can be associated with a directive through the `providers` array in the `@Directive` decorator. The following code shows what this looks like:

```
@Directive({
  selector: '[validate-street]',
  providers: [streetCheckerBinding]
})
class StreetValidator {}
```

The directive class doesn't need any code. As long as the right `Provider` is associated with the directive, elements of interest will be validated by the function bound to `NG_VALIDATORS`. In this example, each element containing the marker `validate-street` will be validated by the `streetChecker` function.

## Step 2: The Error-Reporting Component

In reactive forms, error reporting is easy. Just add an element containing an error message and control its insertion using `NgIf`. The following element shows how this works:

```
<p *ngIf='!control.valid'>The field is invalid.</p>
```

Error reporting in a template-driven form is more difficult because it's not as easy to access the form's controls. Instead of adding `NgIf` to a basic element, it's necessary to code a component that performs three operations:

1. Access a control validated by a directive discussed earlier
2. Check the control's errors
3. If the control is invalid, display the appropriate error message

For the first step, the component needs to access the `NgForm` associated with the overall `<form>` element. This can be accomplished using dependency injection, and the following code shows how a constructor can access the form's `NgForm`:

```
constructor(private mainForm: NgForm) { ... }
```

As discussed earlier, the `NgForm` class provides a `form` method that returns the form's `FormGroup`. The `FormGroup` provides a `get` method that returns a `FormControl` according to its name. Therefore, after an error-reporting component has access to an `NgForm` called `ngForm`, it can obtain a `FormControl` with code such as the following.

```
control = mainForm.form.find(name);
```

After obtaining the FormControl, a component can access its valid property to determine its state. If it's invalid, the component can check which errors are present by calling hasErrors. For example, if an invalid ID value is represented by the badId string, the following code identifies if control contains an invalid ID value:

```
idError = control.hasError('badId');
```

## Step 3: The Overall Component

After coding the validation directive and error-reporting component, the last step is to define the form in a component's template. If a form element requires validation, two steps are needed:

- Insert the attribute corresponding to the validation directive
- Follow the element with an error-reporting component that contains the name of the control

For example, suppose that an <input> element needs to be validated by a directive whose marker is checkid. If the name of the control is id-ctrl, the element can be defined with the following markup:

```
<input name='id-ctrl' [(ngModel)]='text' checkid>
```

The error-reporting component must be given the control's name and the name of the error or errors to be tested. If the component's selector is error-rep and the error key is badid, the component's markup could be given as follows:

```
<error-rep control='id-ctrl' [error]=''badid''></error-rep>
```

After accessing the form's NgForm, this component can use the control name, represented by the control attribute, to find the corresponding FormControl. Then it can use the name of the error, represented by the error property, to test if the validation error is present. If so, it will display the message corresponding to the error's name.

To demonstrate how custom validation is accomplished, the following discussion presents the ch14/template_driven project. This contains two custom validators—one that checks zip codes and one that checks area codes.

## 14.10.3 Example Template-Driven Form

In America, a zip code is a five-digit value used to identify location in mailing addresses. An area code is a three-digit value used to identify location in telephone numbers. The template_driven application displays a form whose input fields ask for a zip code and area code. Figure 14.x shows what the form looks like:

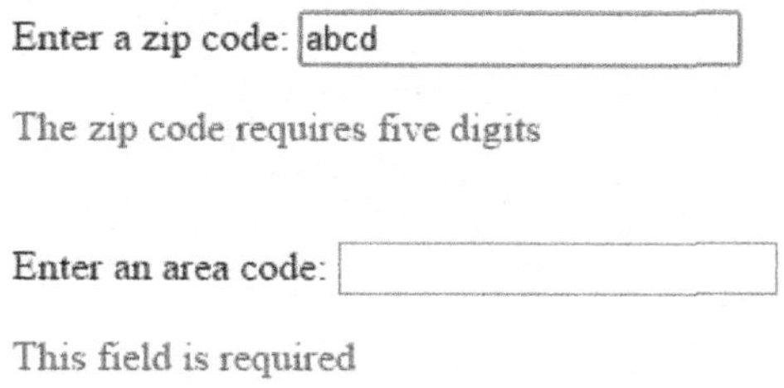


**Figure 14.5 Error Checking in a Template-Driven Form**

Each input field has a custom validator and the Submit button won't be enabled until both fields are valid. The project's code can be found in the ch14/template_driven/app directory, which contains six TypeScript files:

1. app.module.ts — The application's module
2. app.component.ts — The base component defines the template
3. error-message.component.ts — Displays an error message for invalid elements
4. ac-validator.directive.ts — Directive that validates area codes
5. zip-validator.directive.ts — Directive that validates zip codes
6. error.service.ts — Associates error keys with error messages

To explain how the application works, this discussion looks at the base component first, the error reporting component second, and then the two validation directives.

### Base Component

The app.component.ts file defines the template containing the template-driven form. Listing 14.3 presents its code.

In the template, the <form> element sets the local variable f equal to ngForm. This tells Angular to associate the form with an NgForm instance. The NgForm creates the FormGroup for the form and creates a FormControl for each element with an assigned name attribute.

**Listing 14.3: ch14/template_driven/app/app.component.ts**

```
@Component({
selector: 'app-root',
styleUrls: ['app.component.css'],
template: `
<form #f='ngForm' (ngSubmit)='submit()'>

  <!-- Zip code input -->
  <div class='entry'>
    Enter a zip code:
    <input name='input1' [(ngModel)]='zipCode'
      required validateZip>
    <app-error controlName='input1'
      [errorChecks]="['required', 'zipcode']"></app-error>
  </div>

  <!-- Area code input -->
  <div class='entry'>
    Enter an area code:
    <input name='input2' [(ngModel)]='areaCode'
      required validateAreaCode>
    <app-error controlName='input2'
      [errorChecks]="['required', 'areacode']"></app-error>
  </div>

  <input type='submit' [disabled]='!f.form.valid' value='Submit'>
</form>
`})

// Define the component's controller
export class AppComponent {

  public zipCode: string;
  public areaCode: string;

  // Display the valid zip code and area code
  private submit() {
    alert('zip code: ' + this.zipCode + ', area code: ' +
      this.areaCode);
  }
}
```

The form consists of two text boxes, two error reporting components, and a Submit button. The `<input>` elements for the text boxes have their name attributes set, so Angular will create a `FormControl` for each. In addition, both `<input>` elements have validation directives. The first `<input>` contains `required` and `validateZip` directives and the second contains `required` and `validateAreaCode` directives.

Each text box has an error-reporting component to display a message in the event of an invalid element. In markup, these components are given by `<app-error>` elements, and each `<app-error>` has two properties. The first, `controlName`, identifies the name of the element whose validity should be checked. The second, `errorChecks`, identifies the nature of the error checking to be performed.

## Error Reporting

Each `<app-error>` element in the base component's template corresponds to an instance of the `ErrorMessageComponent` class. This checks the validity of a form element, and displays a message if the element is invalid. Listing 14.4 presents the code.

**Listing 14.4: ch14/template_based/src/app/error-message.component.ts**

```
// A component that reports errors
@Component({
selector: 'app-error',
template: `
<p *ngIf='msg !== null'>{{ msg }}</p>
` })
export class ErrorMessageComponent {

  @Input() private controlName: string;
  @Input() private errorChecks: string[];
  private errMap: {[errorCode: string]: string};

  constructor(private mainForm: NgForm,
      private service: ErrorService) {
    this.errMap = service.errorMap;
    this.mainForm = mainForm;
  }

  // Called when the msg property is accessed
  get msg() {

    const group: FormGroup = this.mainForm.form;
    const control = group.get(this.controlName);
    if (control && control.touched) {
      for (let i = 0; i < this.errorChecks.length; i++) {
        if (control.hasError(this.errorChecks[i])) {
          return this.errMap[this.errorChecks[i]];
        }
      }
    }
    return null;
  }
}
```

The component receives two input values from the <app-error> elements in the form:

- controlName — the name of the FormControl whose validity needs to be checked
- errorChecks — an array of strings that identify which errors should be checked

The first dependency received by the component is the NgForm corresponding to the <form> defined in the base component's template. This provides access to the FormGroup and the FormControls corresponding to the text boxes. The second dependency is an ErrorService that associates error keys with error messages.

The component's template consists of a paragraph element whose insertion into the DOM is determined by NgIf. This is defined with the following markup:

```
<p *ngIf='msg !== null'>{{ msg }}</p>
```

To obtain a value for msg, the component uses the NgForm and controlName to find the FormControl that needs to be checked. If the control is invalid, the component checks through the list of applicable errors. If it finds a match, msg is set to the appropriate error message. If the control is valid, msg will be set to null and no error message will be displayed.

## Validation Directives

To validate the text boxes, the application creates two custom validators. The first validates the zip code, which must consist of five digits. The second validates the area code, which must consist of three digits.

In code, both validators are implemented with directives. When a directive is associated with a template element, the directive will check its value to determine the element's validity.

Listing 14.5 presents the code for the directive that validates zip codes. The directive class, ZipValidatorDirective, doesn't contain any code. Instead, the providers array in the @Directive decorator contains a Provider that binds the name of a function to the NG_VALIDATORS token. This function, zipValidator, accepts a FormControl and returns an error key (zipcode) if the value doesn't consist of five digits.

Any element containing the validateZip marker will be accessed by the directive. Because of the Provider's binding, the element's FormControl will be processed by the zipValidator function.

**Listing 14.5: ch14/template_based/src/app/zip-validator.directive.ts**

```
// Validates zip codes: 5-digit numbers
function zipValidator(fc: FormControl): {[errorCode: string]:
boolean} {
  if ((fc.value != null) && (fc.value.match(/^\d{5}$/g))) {
    return null;
  } else {
    return {'zipcode': true};
  }
}

// Binds the zip code validator to NG_VALIDATORS
const zipValidatorBinding: Provider = {
  provide: NG_VALIDATORS,
  useValue: zipValidator,
  multi: true
};

@Directive({
  selector: '[validateZip]',
  providers: [zipValidatorBinding]
})
export class ZipValidatorDirective {}
```

**Listing 14.6: ch14/template_based/src/app/ac-validator.directive.ts**

```
// Validates area codes: 3-digit numbers
function acValidator(fc: FormControl): {[errorCode: string]:
boolean} {
  if ((fc.value != null) && (fc.value.match(/^\d{3}$/g))) {
    return null;
  } else {
    return {'areacode': true};
  }
}

// Binds the area code validator to NG_VALIDATORS
const acValidatorBinding: Provider = {
  provide: NG_VALIDATORS,
  useValue: acValidator,
  multi: true
};

@Directive({
  selector: '[validateAreaCode]',
  providers: [acValidatorBinding]
})
export class AcValidatorDirective {}
```

As shown in Listing 14.6, the directive that validates the area code is nearly identical the directive that validates the zip code. The only significant difference is that the validation function, `acValidator`, uses a different pattern to check the `FormControl`'s value.

# 14.11 Summary

Angular provides two APIs for building forms: the Reactive Forms API and the Forms API. Both APIs make it possible to validate a form's inputs automatically, and the only task left to the developer is to define the validation functions.

Most of this chapter has focused on the Reactive Forms API, which provides classes that simplify the process of interacting with the form's elements. Inside a form, each field of interest is associated with a `FormControl`. Each `FormControl` has a name, a value, and one or more optional validators.

`FormControls` are managed by a `FormGroup`, which can represent the entire form or just a portion of it. If the number of `FormControls` may change dynamically, it's better to place them in a `FormArray`. The `FormControl` class, `FormGroup` class, and `FormArray` class are all subclasses of `AbstractControl`.

For AngularJS 1.x developers who prefer two-way data binding, the Forms API supports template-driven forms. A key advantage is that it's unnecessary to deal with `FormControls` and `FormGroups` in code. The main disadvantage is that, without access to `FormControls`, it's difficult to associate validators with the form's fields. It's also difficult to test the validation functions programmatically.

# Chapter 15

# Animation, i18n, and Custom Pipes

This chapter explores three topics that are helpful and important but not necessary in Angular development: animation, internationalization (i18n), and custom pipes. Once you understand these topics, you'll be able to code applications that appeal to a wide range of users and provide a professional look-and-feel.

In Angular, animation refers to changing an element's CSS properties over time. The process is conceptually simple—define CSS states and set the transitions between them. But implementing animation in code requires calling many nested functions whose arguments can be difficult to keep track of.

Angular can't translate your application's text into other languages, but it can facilitate the translation process. To be specific, the goal of Angular's internationalization (i18n) toolkit is to produce files that clearly identify what translation needs to be performed. These files can be generated according to the XLIFF (XML Localisation Interchange File Format) or XMB (XML Message Bundle) formats. These files can be used as input by computer-aided translators and human translators.

Chapter 8 discussed the topic of pipes and explained how to format template data with Angular's built-in pipes. This chapter explains how to code custom pipes to perform custom data formatting. The process involves coding a class that implements the `PipeTransform` interface. The `transform` method of this class will receive the data to be formatted along with formatting flags, and will return the string to be displayed in the template.

In AngularJS 1.x, pipes are referred to as filters, and one of the most useful filters is `orderBy`, which sorts elements of a collection for display. The last part of this chapter demonstrates how this capability can be implemented as a custom Angular pipe.

# 15.1 Animation

Animation is one of Angular's newest and most interesting features. With the right animation, a web application can add a level of polish and delight that static graphics can never provide.

Technically speaking, Angular animation involves changing an element's CSS properties over time. For this purpose, Angular provides functions that define sets of CSS properties (called CSS states) and the transitions between states.

To enable animation, the @angular/animations package must be installed. Then the application's module needs to import `AnimationsModule` from @angular/animations. Lastly, the application needs to define animations by calling functions inside its `@Component` decorator. This section explains how these functions can be called.

## 15.1.1 Defining Animations

The `@Component` decorator can contain many fields, including `selector`, `styleUrls`, and `template`. It can also contain a field named `animations`. If this is present, the field must be set equal to an array whose elements define transitions between CSS states.

Each element of the `animations` array defines an animation by calling the `trigger` function. Therefore, a component that uses animation will have the following structure:

```
@Component({
  selector: '...',
  styleUrls: ['...'],
  template: `
     ...
  `,
  animations: [
    trigger('trig1', [...]),
    trigger('trig2', [...]),
  ]
})
```

The `trigger` function accepts two arguments—a string identifier and an array of function calls. The two most important functions that can be called inside the `trigger` array are as follows:

- `state` — Associates a name with a set of CSS properties
- `transition` — Identifies how a change between states should be performed

In general, the array inside `trigger` will contain two or more `state` calls followed by one or more `transition` calls. Each call to state `defines` creates a named set of CSS properties that set an element's appearance in a given state. Each call to `transition` identifies how an element should transition from one CSS state to another. The following discussion presents the `state` and `transition` functions in detail.

## Defining CSS States

As with the `trigger` function, the first argument of the `state` function is a string identifier. The second argument calls the `style` function with one or more CSS rules contained in curly braces. As an example, the following code demonstrates how `state` can be called:

```
state('start', style({ 'background-color': 'green'}))
```

It should make sense that most `trigger` arrays contain at least two `state` calls. These `state` calls should contain similar CSS properties but assign them different values.

## Configuring State Transitions

After defining CSS states with `state` calls, a `trigger` array should define state transitions with calls to `transition`. The first argument of the `transition` function is a string with three parts: the name of a starting state, the => symbol, and an ending state. The second argument of `transition` is an array containing one or more calls of the `animate` function. The following code gives an idea of what this looks like:

```
animations: [

  // Define an animation
  trigger('trig1', [

    // Starting state
    state('start', style({ 'background-color': 'green' })),

    // Ending state
    state('end', style({ 'background-color': 'blue' })),

    // Transition between states
    transition('start => end', [
      animate(...)
    ])
  ])
]
```

In this code, `start` and `end` identify different CSS states. The first argument of transition is `'start => end'`, which implies that the transition will only be performed when the element is in the `start` state. The state transition will continue until the element's CSS properties match those defined in the `end` state.

Instead of naming specific states, the `transition` function can use wildcards. The `*` wildcard represents any state of an element. Similarly, the `void` identifier represents any state in which the element is not attached to a view.

## The animate Function

The second argument of `transition` is a call of the `animate` function or an array of calls of `animate`. Each `animate` call identifies an action to be performed over time. If the second argument of `transition` is an array of `animate` calls, each action will be performed in the given sequence.

At its simplest, the first argument of `animate` identifies the action's duration. If given as a number, the argument specifies the duration in milliseconds. It can also be given as a string whose units are identified with `s` (seconds) or `ms` (milliseconds). The following code tells Angular to perform the transition in 500 milliseconds:

```
transition('start => end', [ animate(500) ] )
```

If set to a string, the first argument of `animate` can contain one, two, or three values. The second value sets the time delay before the transition starts. The third value identifies the rate of the transition's change over time, and can take one of three values:

- `ease-in` — slow at the beginning, fast at the end
- `ease-out` — slow at the beginning, fast at the end
- `ease-in-out` — slow at the beginning and end, fast in the middle

The following code shows how this works. It sets the duration of the transition to 750 milliseconds, the delay to 100 milliseconds, and makes the transition fast at the end:

```
transition('start => end', [ animate('750ms 100ms ease-out') ] )
```

The second argument of `animate` is optional, and can be set to a call to the `style` function or a call to the `keyframes` function. If the second argument is set to a call to `style`, the CSS properties in the function will be applied during the action represented by `animate`. For example, the following code sets the element's background color to yellow during the 250ms duration of the `animate` action.

```
transition('start => end', [
  animate(250, style({ 'background-color': 'yellow' }))
])
```

The concept of a keyframe hearkens back to the time of hand-drawn animation. Once a cartoon was written, a primary animator would draw a set of important frames, each separated by seconds or tens of seconds. But no one wants to see frames updated every few seconds, so secondary animators are called in to draw in-between frames. The primary animator's scenes are called *keyframes* and the secondary animators interpolate between the keyframes.

Similarly, the `keyframes` function accepts an array of calls to the `style` function. Each element defines a set of CSS properties along with an `offset` property that identifies how long the CSS state should persist. The `offset` is given between 0.0 and 1.0, where 1.0 represents the end of `animate`'s operation.

For example, the following code defines a transition from the `start` state to the `end` state with three keyframes.

```
transition('start => end', [
  animate(1000, keyframes([
    style({ 'background-color': 'green', 'offset': 0.1 }),
    style({ 'background-color': 'blue', 'offset': 0.6 }),
    style({ 'background-color': 'purple', 'offset': 1.0 })
  ]))
])
```

The first keyframe state lasts from 0.1 to 0.6, the second lasts from 0.6 to 0.8, and the third lasts from 0.8 to 1.0. The total time is 1000 ms, so the first keyframe lasts 500 ms, the second keyframe lasts 200 ms, and the last keyframe lasts 200 ms. The first keyframe state is delayed by 100 ms.

## 15.1.2 Associating Animations with Template Elements

After the `animations` array has been populated with `trigger` calls, the next step is to associate the animations with template elements. This generally involves two steps:

1. For each element of interest, insert a property whose name identifies the `trigger` call (preceded by `@`). The property's value should be set equal to a member variable of the component class.
2. In the component class, set the member variable to a string that identifies one of the `state` calls in the `trigger` function.

Let's look at a simple example. Suppose you want a button to change color from blue to green when clicked. The `animations` array might look like the following:

```
animations: [
  trigger('blueToGreen', [
    state('start', style({ 'background-color': 'blue' })),
    state('end', style({ 'background-color': 'green' })),
    transition('start => end', [ animate(500) ])
  ])
]
```

In the template, the button element could be defined as follows:

```
<button [@blueToGreen]='stateVar' (click)='changeState()'>
  Click me
</button>
```

The property's name is `@blueToGreen`, which is the ID of the trigger call preceded by the `@` symbol. This property is set to `stateVar`, which is a member variable defined in the component class.

When the button is clicked, the component's `changeState` method is called. We want the button's state to toggle between `start` and `end`, so the code for `changeState` should look like the following:

```
public changeState() {
  this.stateVar = (this.stateVar === 'start' ? 'end' : 'start');
}
```

As a result of this method, clicking the button will change `stateVar`'s value from `start` to `end` or from `end` to `start`. If the method changes `stateVar`'s value from `start` to `end`, it will trigger the animation identified by `blueToGreen`, and the button's background color will change over a duration of 500 milliseconds.

It's important to see that the animation only works in one way—from the `start` state to the `end` state. Using wildcards, we can change the code to perform animation whenever any state change takes place. This is given as follows:

```
transition('* => *', [ animate(500) ])
```

A later discussion will present a more interesting demonstration of Angular animation. First, it's important to be familiar with animation events.

## 15.1.3 Animation Events

An application can receive data related to an element's animation state by adding special events to the element. To be precise, an application can configure an element to emit an event when its animation starts or ends. For example, the following event calls a method when animation starts:

```
(@trigger_name.start)='method_name'
```

Here, `trigger_name` is the name of the animation to be monitored. When the animation starts, the method identified by `method_name` will be called. Similarly, the following code calls a method when an animation has completed:

```
(@trigger_name.done)='method_name'
```

As a practical example, suppose that `endState` should be called when a button's animation completes. The following code makes this possible:

```
<button
  (@blueToGreen.done)="endState()"
  [@blueToGreen]='stateVar'>
</button>
```

This code doesn't pass any arguments to the event-handling method, but an application can pass an `AnimationTransitionEvent` through a variable named `$event`. When a method receives an `AnimationTransitionEvent`, it can obtain information by accessing its fields:

- `element` — The element associated with the animation
- `triggerName` — The name of the trigger
- `fromState` — The previous animation state
- `toState` — The current animation state
- `phaseName` — The animation phase (`start` or `done`)
- `totalTime` — The total duration of the animation

The following discussion provides a more comprehensive example of how Angular animation works. Among other things, it demonstrates how animation events can be received.

### 15.1.3 Example Application – Angular Animation

The code in the ch15/anim_demo project demonstrates many aspects of Angular animation. The application displays five labels. Four move from side to side and the fifth rotates around its center. Figure 15.1 shows what this looks like.

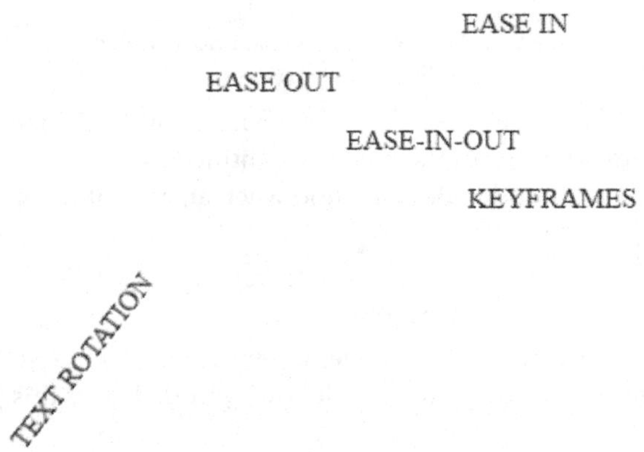


**Figure 15.1 Angular Animation Demonstration**

The first three animations demonstrate the different easing methods: `ease-in`, `ease-out`, and `ease-in-out`. The fourth animation uses keyframes to define how the text moves during the animation. This animation is defined with the following code:

```
trigger('text4', [
  state('start', style({ 'margin-left': '0px' })),
  state('end', style({ 'margin-left': '400px' })),

  transition('start => end', [ animate('2s',
    keyframes([
      style({ 'margin-left': '0px', 'offset': 0.1 }),
      style({ 'margin-left': '250px', 'offset': 0.3 }),
      style({ 'margin-left': '400px', 'offset': 1.0 })
    ])
  )])
]),
```

The total duration of the animation is two seconds. As a result of the keyframes, the text appears to move quickly from time 0.2s to 0.6s. Then it appears to move slowly from 0.6s to 2s.

# 15.2 Internationalization (i18n)

To reach a worldwide audience, an application's text needs to be translated into multiple languages. This process is called internationalization, which is frequently shortened to i18n because there are 18 letters between the first and last letters.

Angular facilitates i18n by providing a utility named ng-xi18n. This doesn't translate text on its own, but generates source files that make it easy for a translator to provide text. In general, the i18n process involves five steps:

1. Mark elements of interest
2. Use i18n pipes if necessary
3. Generate a translation source file
4. Give the source file to a translator
5. Integrate translated text into the application

This section looks at the first three steps and shows how they can be accomplished.

## 15.2.1 Mark Elements of Interest

If an element contains text to be translated, it should be marked with the `i18n` attribute. This tells the translation utility to include the element in the generated translation file. The following markup shows how it can be used:

```
<label i18n>This text should be translated.</label>
```

The `i18n` attribute can be assigned a value that provides the translator with special instructions. In the following markup, the attribute's value tells the translator that the text contains an idiom that shouldn't be taken literally:

```
<label i18n='English idiom'>It is not rocket science.</label>
```

Now suppose that the value of an element's attribute needs to be translated. For example, if an `<img>` element contains an `alt` attribute, the attribute's value should be translated. To mark the attribute, `i18n` should be replaced with `i18n-xyz`, where *`xyz`* is that attribute's name. The following markup shows how what this looks like:

```
<img src="smiley.jpg" i18n-alt alt="Have a nice day!">
```

Here, the `i18n-alt` tells the utility that the value of `alt` is intended to be translated. Another common example is `i18n-title`.

## 15.2.2 i18n Pipes

Chapter 8 introduced Angular's pipes and explained how they can be used to format data in a component's template. Two of the pipes, `i18nSelect` and `i18nPlural`, weren't discussed. These pipes relate to internationalization, so we'll look at them here.

### i18nSelect

In many applications, words may need to change based on user information. For example, a description may need to include 'her' if the user is female and 'him' if the user is male. The `i18nSelect` pipe makes it possible to update the translation file as needed.

This pipe must be accessed with a parameter that identifies an object that maps keys to display strings. The pipe's input is a key that identifies which string should be displayed. To see how this works, consider the following element in a component's template:

```
<p>The keyboard belongs to {{gender | i18nSelect: display }}.</p>
```

`gender` and `display` are variables defined in the component. The first sets the user's gender (`male` or `female`). The second variable is an object that associates gender values with display text. The following code shows what this object may look like:

```
display = {'male': 'him', 'female': 'her'};
```

### i18nPlural

The `i18nPlural` pipe is like `i18nSelect`, but the displayed text changes according to multiplicity. For example, suppose an application should display `item` if `num` is 1 and `items` for any other value. The markup could be given as follows:

```
<p>You purchased {{ num | i18nPlural: numMap }}.</p>
```

`numMap` associates numeric values with output text using conventions established in the ICU format. This is shown in the following code:

```
numMap = {'=0': 'no items', '=1': 'one item', 'other': '# items'};
```

## 15.2.3 Generating the Translation Source File

After the i18n attributes and pipes have been inserted into a template, the ng-xi18n utility can be used to generate a translation source file. This utility should be present in the project's node_modules/.bin directory.

To determine which files need to be translated, ng-xi18n reads tsconfig.json, which should be present in the current directory. The command for executing ng-xi18n from a project's top-level directory is given as follows:

```
./node_modules/.bin/ng-xi18n
```

When the processing is finished, the utility will produce a file called messages.xlf. The file's content is structured according to the XML Localisation Interchange File Format, or XLIFF, which is commonly used to provide data to computer-aided translation (CAT) systems. For example, suppose that a template consists of the following:

```
<label i18n="English idiom">It's not rocket science.</label>
<img src="smiley.jpg" i18n-alt alt="Have a nice day!">
```

When ng-xi18n processes this, messages.xlf will contain the following text:

```
<xliff version="1.2"
  xmlns="urn:oasis:names:tc:xliff:document:1.2">
  <file source-language="en" datatype="plaintext"
        original="ng2.template">
   <body>
     <trans-unit id="..." datatype="html">
       <source>It&apos;s not rocket science.</source>
       <target/>
       <note priority="1" from="description">English idiom</note>
     </trans-unit>
     <trans-unit id="..." datatype="html">
       <source>Have a nice day!</source>
       <target/>
     </trans-unit>
   </body>
  </file>
</xliff>
```

The file format can be changed to the XML Message Bundle (XMB) format by following the command with `--i18nFormat=xmb`. If this is used, the resulting file will be messages.xmb instead of messages.xlf.

# 15.3 Custom Pipes

Chapter 8 explained how Angular's pipes make it possible to format text in a component's template. In addition to providing prebuilt pipes, Angular makes it possible to define pipes of your own. These are particularly helpful if you want to display specially-formatted dates or currencies or perform custom string-handling routines.

The goal of this section is to explain how to create these pipes using TypeScript and Angular. The process is easy—much easier than coding a component or a directive. There are three points to keep in mind:

1. A pipe definition consists of a pipe class with a `@Pipe` decorator.
2. The pipe class must implement the `PipeTransform` interface, whose only method is `transform`.
3. To be accessed by components, the pipe class must be added to the `declarations` array of the `@NgModule` decorator.

This section starts by explaining these steps in detail. Then I'll show how to code a pipe that orders elements of an array. It's called `orderBy` because I always liked the `orderBy` filter from AngularJS.

## 15.3.1 Defining a New Pipe

Just as a component class requires `@Component` and a directive class requires `@Directive`, a pipe class must be preceded by `@Pipe`. This has two fields:

1. `name` — A string that uniquely identifies the pipe (required)
2. `pure` — A boolean that identifies whether the pipe should recompute its result when its input changes (defaults to true)

Unlike component classes, a pipe class must provide code for a specific method. This method, called `transform`, is defined in the `PipeTransform` interface:

```
transform(value: any, ...args: any[]) : any
```

The `value` parameter identifies the primary value directed to the pipe. The `args` array contains any colon-separated arguments following the name of the pipe. To clarify how `name`, `value`, and `args` are related, Figure 15.2 shows how the code in a pipe class relates to its usage.

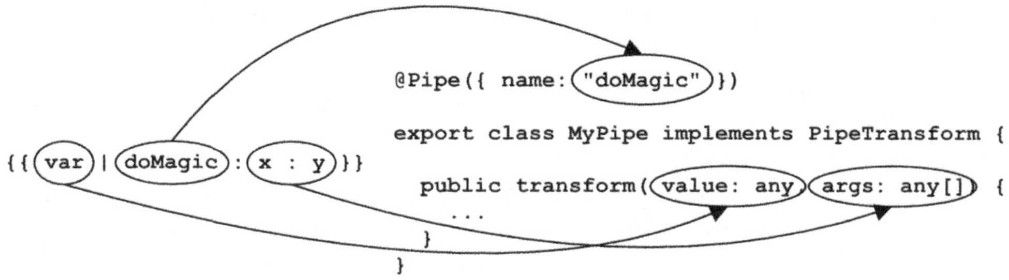


Figure 15.2 A Pipe's Usage and Code

In this figure, the `transform` method of `MyPipe` receives the pipe's `var` input as its `value` parameter. It receives the pipe's `x` and `y` arguments in its `args` array. The return value of `transform` is the pipe's output.

## 15.3.2 The OrderBy Pipe

In AngularJS 1.x, the `orderBy` filter sorts elements of an input array. Angular doesn't have an equivalent pipe, so this discussion explains how an `orderBy` pipe can be coded. But before getting into the code, I'd like to explain how `orderBy` is used.

### Using the OrderBy Pipe

In this discussion, the `orderBy` pipe is used in the following way:

```
{{ array | orderBy : expression? : reverse? }}
```

The two arguments are optional, and if the pipe is used without arguments, it arranges the array's elements in ascending order. This is shown in the following examples:

- `{{ ['b', 'c', 'a'] | orderBy }}` evaluates to `[ 'a', 'b', 'c' ]`
- `{{ [9, 22, 6] | orderBy }}` evaluates to `[ 6, 9, 22 ]`

The `expression` argument can take one of three forms:

1. string — Identifies the property that should be used for sorting. May be preceded by + for ascending sort or - for descending sort.
2. array — Identifies which properties should be used for sorting in decreasing order of importance. Each element may be preceded by + or -.
3. function — Routine for sorting array's elements

For example, consider the following array of objects:

```
let objArray = [{letter: 'b', num: 3}, {letter: 'c', num: 5},
                {letter: 'a', num: 1}, {letter: 'z', num: 5}];
```

This array can be sorted in descending order of the `num` property with the following usage of `orderBy`:

```
{{ objArray | orderBy : '-num' }}
```

The result is given as follows:

```
[{letter: 'c', num: 5}, {letter: 'z', num: 5},
 {letter: 'b', num: 3}, {letter: 'a', num: 1}]
```

Now suppose we want to sort `objArray` using two properties—in descending order of the `num` property first, and descending order of the `letter` property second. In this case, the `expression` argument is an array and the usage of `orderBy` is given as:

```
{{ objArray | orderBy : ['-num', '-letter'] }}
```

And here's the sorted result:

```
[{letter: 'z', num: 5}, {letter: 'c', num: 5},
 {letter: 'b', num: 3}, {letter: 'a', num: 1}]
```

The third method of using `orderBy` provides a function that returns a number to be used to identify the item's position in the list. For example, the following function converts each input to a string and returns the length of the string:

```
stringLengthSort = function(item) {
  return JSON.stringify(item).length;
};
```

In this case, the sort can be performed with the following code:

```
{{ objArray | orderBy : stringLengthSort }}
```

The pipe's second argument, `reverse`, is a boolean. This identifies whether the sorted result should be reversed.

## Coding the OrderBy Pipe

Now that you understand how the `orderBy` pipe works, it's time to look at the code. Figure 15.3 illustrates the decision-making process that determines how the pipe sorts the elements of the input array.

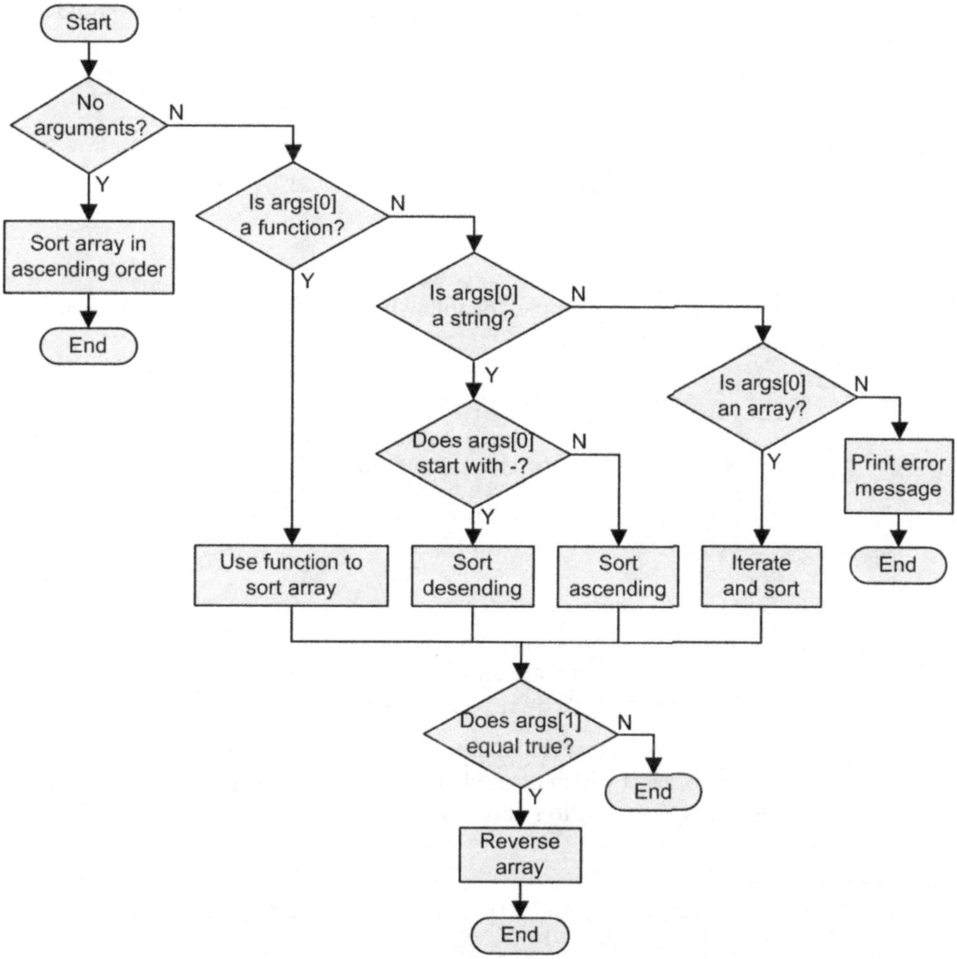


**Figure 15.3 Operation of the OrderBy Pipe**

To sort the input elements, `orderBy` relies on JavaScript's `sort` method for arrays. If called without an argument, `sort` rearranges the array's elements in lexicographical (dictionary) order.

sort's optional argument is a function that identifies how the array's elements should be arranged. This function should accept two values and return a number that identifies the relative ordering of the two values.

- If the first value is less than the second, the function should return a negative value.
- If the second value is less than the first, the function should return a positive value.
- If the two values should be treated equally, the function should return zero.

As an example, this function sorts the numbers in primeArray in ascending order:

```
let primeArray = [23, 57, 19, 71, 37];
primeArray.sort((x: number, y: number) => {
  return x - y;
});
```

As a second example, the following function sorts the objects in objArray according to their name property:

```
let objArray = [{name: 'Bill', age: 19}, {name: 'Ken', age: 23},
               {name: 'Tom',  age: 24}, {name: 'Dave', age: 20}];
primeArray.sort((objA: Object, objB: Object) => {
  if (objA.name < objB.name) { return -1; }
  if (objA.name > objB.name) { return 1; }
  return 0;
});
```

If you understand the pipe's flowchart and JavaScript's sort method, you should have no trouble understanding how the custom pipe can be coded. Listing 15.1 presents the full code of the OrderByPipe class.

This pipe is accessed in AppComponent's template, which combines the pipe with NgFor to select which array elements should be displayed. For example, the following code uses orderBy to select elements from stringArray:

```
<ul>
  <li *ngFor="let element of stringArray | orderBy : '-' ">
    {{ element }}
  </li>
</ul>
```

This construction makes it possible to read records from a database and sort the results on the client. This makes it unnecessary to sort data on the server.

**Listing 15.1: ch15/orderby_demo/app/app.component.ts**

```
// Access the pipe as 'orderBy'
@Pipe({ name: 'orderBy' })
export class OrderByPipe implements PipeTransform {

  private result: any[] = [];

  public transform(arr: any, args: any[] = []) {

    // Make sure array is an input
    if (Object.prototype.toString.call(arr)
        === '[object Array]') {

      // Clone input array
      this.result = arr.slice(0);

      // No arguments - sort primitives ascending
      if (args.length === 0) {
        this.sortPrimitives(true);

      // The first argument is a function
      } else if (Object.prototype.toString.call(args[0])
                 === '[object Function]') {
        this.sortByFunction(args[0]);

      // The first argument is a string
      } else if (Object.prototype.toString.call(args[0])
                 === '[object String]') {
        this.sortByString(args[0]);

      // The first argument is an array
      } else if (Object.prototype.toString.call(args[0])
                 === '[object Array]') {
        this.sortByArray(args[0]);
      }

      // If necessary, reverse the array
      if ((args.length === 2) && (args[1])) {
        return this.result.reverse();
      } else {
        return this.result;
      }
    }

    // If not an array, return the original input
    return arr;
  }
```

**Listing 15.1: ch15/orderby_demo/app/app.component.ts (Continued)**

```
// Sort an array containing primitives
private sortPrimitives(ascending: boolean) {

  // Sort numbers in array
  if (typeof(this.result[0]) === 'number') {
    if (ascending) {
      return this.result.sort((x: number, y: number) => {
        return x - y;
      });
    } else {
      return this.result.sort((x: number, y: number) => {
        return y - x;
      });
    }

  // Sort strings (or whatever)
  } else {
    this.result.sort();
    if (!ascending) {
      this.result.reverse();
    }
    return this.result;
  }
}

// Sort values by a function
private sortByFunction(func: Function) {
  this.result.sort((x: any, y: any) => {
    return func(x) - func(y);
  });
}

// Sort numbers in ascending order
private sortByString(arg: string) {

  let ascending = true;

  // Process sort direction character
  if (arg.charAt(0) === '-') {
    arg = arg.slice(1);
    ascending = false;
  } else if (arg.charAt(0) === '+') {
    arg = arg.slice(1);
  }

  // No property name - primitive array
  if (arg.length === 0) {
    this.sortPrimitives(ascending);
```

**Listing 15.1: ch15/orderby_demo/app/app.component.ts (Continued)**

```
    // Process numeric properties
    } else if (typeof(this.result[0][arg]) === 'number') {
      if (ascending) {
        return this.result.sort((x: any, y: any) => {
          return x[arg] - y[arg];
        });
      } else {
        return this.result.sort((x: any, y: any) => {
          return y[arg] - x[arg];
        });
      }

    // Process string properties
    } else if (ascending) {
      this.result.sort((x: any, y: any) => {
        if (x[arg] < y[arg]) { return -1; }
        if (x[arg] > y[arg]) { return 1; }
        return 0;
      });
    } else {
      this.result.sort((x: any, y: any) => {
        if (x[arg] < y[arg]) { return 1; }
        if (x[arg] > y[arg]) { return -1; }
        return 0;
      });
    }
  }

  // Sort numbers in ascending order
  private sortByArray(array: any[]) {

    if (array.length === 0) { this.sortPrimitives(true); }
    else {

      // Process successive elements of array
      this.result.sort((x: any, y: any) => {

        for (let i = 0; i < array.length; i++) {
          let ascending = true;
          let arg = array[i];

          // Process sort direction character
          if (arg.charAt(0) === '-') {
            arg = arg.slice(1);
            ascending = false;
          } else if (arg.charAt(0) === '+') {
            arg = arg.slice(1);
          }
```

**Listing 15.1: ch15/orderby_demo/app/app.component.ts (Continued)**

```
          // Process numeric property
          if (typeof(x[arg]) === 'number') {

            const diff = x[arg] - y[arg];
            if (ascending) {
              if (diff < 0) { return -1; }
              if (diff > 0) { return 1; }
            } else {
              if (diff < 0) { return 1; }
              if (diff > 0) { return -1; }
            }

            // Process string properties
          } else if (ascending) {
            if (x[arg] < y[arg]) { return -1; }
            if (x[arg] > y[arg]) { return 1; }
          } else {
            if (x[arg] < y[arg]) { return 1; }
            if (x[arg] > y[arg]) { return -1; }
          }
        }
        return 0;
      });
    }
  }
}
```

The ch15/orderby project contains one component class, `AppComponent`, which doesn't perform any meaningful processing. It simply defines the three arrays (`numArray`, `stringArray`, and `objArray`) that are sorted in the template.

# 15.4 Summary

The topics of animation, i18n, and custom pipes aren't sufficiently deep or interesting to merit chapters of their own. But if an application needs eye-catching graphics and an international audience, these capabilities are be very useful to know.

In Angular, animation involves changing an component's CSS properties over time. This is accomplished in code by adding a field named `animations` to the component's `@Component` decorator. This should be set to an array of calls to the `trigger` function, whose arguments define different CSS states and transitions between them.

To facilitate translation of application code, Angular's i18n API provides attributes and pipes. The primary attribute is `i18n`, which tells the framework that an element's text needs to be translated. The `i18nSelect` and `i18nPlural` pipes make it possible to configure text to be translated based on variables defined in the component.

The last part of the chapter explored the topic of custom pipes. In code, custom pipes are represented by classes decorated by `@Pipe` that implement the `PipeTransform` interface. This interface has one method, `transform`, which receives the text to be formatted and formatting arguments, and returns the formatted text.

# Chapter 16

# Material Design

The standard set of HTML elements aren't suitable for every application. They're popular and easy to use, but they're boring, two-dimensional, and don't adhere to the best practices of graphic design. If you really want to impress your users, you need something new.

Material Design is Google's best attempt to improve on traditional web design. This framework describes a set of graphical elements and layouts, and provides a philosophy for uniting them in a user interface. The first Material library was released for Android, but Google has also released libraries for Polymer, AngularJS 1.x, and Angular.

The Angular Material library is incomplete, but it's still worth investigating. This chapter examines many of the library's graphical elements: checkboxes, text boxes, buttons, radio buttons, cards, lists, toolbars, and progress spinners. For each of these elements, I'll explain how it works and demonstrate how it can be accessed in code.

## 16.1 Introduction

At the 2014 Google I/O conference, Google unveiled a new design architecture for graphical applications called Material Design. Though originally intended for Android user interfaces, this framework has branched out to encompass web design.

To understand why Google created Material Design, you need to visit the main site, https://www.google.com/design/spec/material-design. Much of the content is written by and for graphic designers. The following quote gives an idea:

> "The foundational elements of print-based design — typography, grids, space, scale, color, and use of imagery — guide visual treatments. These elements do far more than please the eye. They create hierarchy, meaning, and focus. Deliberate color choices, edge-to-edge imagery, large-scale typography, and intentional white space create a bold and graphic interface that immerse the user in the experience..."

The philosophy of Material Design is based on viewing a computer interface as a sheet of magic paper. The goal of the framework is to enable users to interact with the interface as easily and intuitively as if they were interacting with paper.

With this goal in mind, Material Design presents guidelines for employing color, elevation, and three dimensions. It also describes suitable methods for transforming and animating the "Material." I don't have a background in graphical design, so a lot of the discussion is beyond my experience. But I found the discussion of paper-based layout methods to be fascinating.

In this chapter, the primary aspect of Material Design is the new set of graphical elements. Google has released libraries containing these elements, and the first releases were for Android, Polymer, and AngularJS 1.x. The Material library for Angular is more recent and is still incomplete. But the code is functional, so it's worth taking a look.

## 16.2 Overview

The Angular Material Design library consists of graphical elements and themes that support Google's vision of how an application should appear and behave. In code, each graphical element corresponds to an Angular component or directive. The goal of this chapter is to show what these components/directives accomplish and how to access them in code.

This section starts by explaining how to install the Material Design library. Then we'll look at the overall process of using the library to builds applications. The last part of the section explains what themes are and how to specify a theme for an application.

### 16.2.1 Installation

To take full advantage of Material Design in a project, three packages must be installed. The following command installs everything:

```
npm install --save @angular/material @angular/animations hammerjs
```

The @angular/material package provides Material Design features for Angular development. Many of the Material Design components require animation, and as discussed in Chapter 15, this is provided in the @angular/animations package. The hammerjs package provides touch gestures that are used by many components.

## 16.2.2 Configuring an Application

The Angular Material Design Library is a powerful toolset, but a number of steps must be performed before its components can be accessed in an application. There are four steps in total:

1. The application's module must import MaterialModule from the @angular/material package. MaterialModule must be inserted into the imports array of the module's @NgModule decorator.
2. Every application must define a core theme that determines the color scheme employed by the Material Design components. This topic will be discussed shortly.
3. If any components take advantage of animation, the module must import BrowserAnimationsModule from @angular/animations and add BrowserAnimationsModule to the imports array.
4. If any components require gesture support, make sure the module imports the HammerJS library with import 'hammerjs'.

Without question, the second step is the most annoying. The next section explores the topic of Material Design Themes.

## 16.2.3 Setting a Theme

The Material Design guidelines recommend a method for selecting colors in an application. In particular, three colors need to be specified:

- primary color — The color used throughout most of the application
- secondary color — A color used for related activities (a lighter or darker version of the primary color)
- accent color — A color that attracts attention compared to the primary color

An application's theme is the set of colors used by Material Design components in the application. To simplify color selection, Material Design provides four predefined themes whose names identify the primary color and accent color. Each theme is given as a CSS file in the project's node_modules/@angular/material/prebuilt-themes directory.

At the time of this writing, the @angular/material package provides the following built-in themes:

- deeppurple-amber.css — Primary color is deep purple, accent color is amber
- indigo-pink.css — Primary color is indigo, accent color is pink
- pink-bluegrey.css — Primary color is pink, accent color is blue-gray
- purple-green.css — Primary color is purple, accent color is green

To use one of these themes, an application must perform two steps:

1. Copy the CSS file containing the built-in theme to the project's top level folder.
2. Add the `mat-app-background` class to the element surrounding the application.

In an ideal world, we'd be able to configure the theme by adding the theme file to the component's `styleUrls` array. But that's not sufficient. One way to include the CSS file at the top level is add a statement to the src/styles.css file, such as the following:

```
@import '~@angular/material/prebuilt-themes/deeppurple-amber.css';
```

For the second step, we need to set the CSS class of an element surrounding the application's element. This can be accomplished by modifying the `<body>` element in the src/index.html file:

```
<body class='mat-app-background'>
```

The example projects in this file provide code for the project's src/app directory, but don't provide CSS files or HTML files. Therefore, before you run any of these projects, be sure to update the src/styles.css file and the `<body>` element in the src/index.html file.

# 16.3 Material Design Components

The Material Design package provides components that can be accessed by Angular appplications. In general, applications access Material Design components by inserting the corresponding elements into their templates.

This section presents many of the components available through Material Design, but not all of them. In Table 16.1, the left column presents the Material Design classes and the right column presents the selectors used to insert the components into the template.

**Table 16.1**

Material Design Components

| Class | Selector |
|---|---|
| MdCheckBox | md-checkbox |
| MdInputContainer | md-input-container |
| MdButton/MdAnchor | md-button<br>md-raised-button<br>md-icon-button<br>md-fab<br>md-mini-fab |
| MdRadioGroup | md-radio-group |
| MdRadioButton | md-radio-button |
| MdCard | md-card |
| MdCardHeader | md-card-header |
| MdCardTitleGroup | md-card-title-group |
| MdList | md-list |
| MdListItem | md-list-item |
| MdListAvatar | md-list-avatar |
| MdToolbar | md-toolbar |
| MdProgressSpinner | md-progress-spinner |

The selectors in the right column accept attributes and properties that configure the component's appearance and behavior. The following discussion explores many of the available features, but if you're interested in a complete presentation, it's a good idea to download the source code from https://github.com/angular/material2.

## 16.3.1 Checkbox

Of the components in the Material Design library, the checkbox is probably the simplest. It behaves like an `<input>` element of type `checkbox`, but provides features beyond those of the common HTML element. The most noticeable features are the colored background, the flash when the box is checked or unchecked, and the ability to control the box's state with the Space key. Figure 16.1 shows what it looks like.

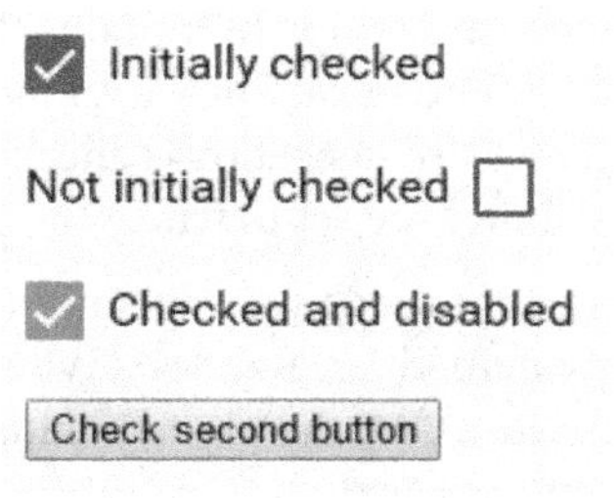


Figure 16.1 Checkbox from the Angular Material Library

Checkboxes are easy to integrate into web components. Listing 16.1 presents the code for the ch16/checkbox_test project. As shown, the checkbox's label is set by inserting text between `<md-checkbox>` and `</md-checkbox>`.

**Listing 16.1: ch16/checkbox_test/app/app.component.ts**

```
@Component({
selector: 'app-root',
template: `

<md-checkbox [checked]='true'>
  Initially checked
</md-checkbox><br /><br />

<md-checkbox [(checked)]='isChecked' align='end'>
  Not initially checked
</md-checkbox><br /><br />

<md-checkbox [checked]='true' disabled='true'>
  Checked and disabled
</md-checkbox><br /><br />

<button [innerText]='msg' (click)='handleClick()'></button>
`})

export class AppComponent {

  private msg = 'Check second button';
  private isChecked = false;

  private handleClick() {
    this.isChecked = !this.isChecked;
    this.msg = this.isChecked ?
      'Uncheck second button' : 'Check second button';
  }
}
```

The component's template contains three checkboxes. It checks the first by setting `checked` to true. The second box is to the right of its label because the `align` attribute is set to `end`. The third checkbox is checked and disabled because its `checked` and `disabled` attributes are set to true.

The component uses two-way binding to associate the state of the second checkbox with a property named `isChecked`. When the button is clicked, the component changes the value of `isChecked`, thereby checking or unchecking the second checkbox and changing the button's text.

## 16.3.2 Input Container

An `MdInputContainer` serves as a container of an `<input>` or a `<textarea>` element. The component's selector is `<md-input-container>` and the following markup shows how it can be used:

```
<md-input-container>
   <input mdInput placeholder="Placeholder text" required>
</md-input-container>
```

Each `MdInputContainer` can only contain one `<input>` or `<textarea>` element. This element must contain the `mdInput` attribute. It can also contain attributes such as `disabled`, `required`, and `placeholder`.

The resulting element uses a solid line to hold text instead of a box. When the element has focus, the line's color changes to the application's primary color. The placeholder text also takes the primary color when the element receives focus. Figure 16.2 shows what this looks like:

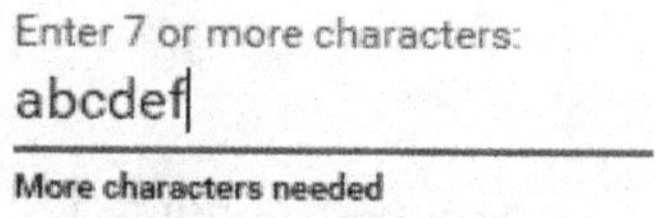


**Figure 16.2 An Input Element in an Input Container**

As shown, the input element can display text below the entry line that provides instructions or feedback. This is made possible by adding an `<md-hint>` element. The base component in the ch16/input_test project demonstrates how hints can be used to perform basic validation. Listing 16.2 presents the code.

**Listing 16.2: ch16/input_test/app/app.component.ts**

```
@Component({
selector: 'app-root',
styles: ['md-hint { font-weight: bold; font-size: 80%; }'],
template: `
<md-input-container>

  <input mdInput placeholder='{{msg}}' maxLength='20'
    dividerColor='accent' #inp>

  <md-hint>
    {{ inp.value.length < 7 ?
      'More characters needed' : 'Hooray!' }}
  </md-hint>

</md-input-container>
`})

export class AppComponent {
  private msg = 'Enter 7 or more characters:';
}
```

In this code, the `<md-hint>` element accesses the `<input>` element through the `inp` local variable. Then it determines how many characters have been entered by checking the `inp.value.length`.

When the `<input>` element receives focus, the placeholder text and the baseline are both set to the accent color. This is because the `dividerColor` attribute is set to `accent`. As discussed earlier in the chapter, `accent` refers to the color that accents the application's primary color. If `dividerColor` is set to `primary`, the baseline would be set to the primary color.

## 16.3.3 Buttons and Anchors

The Material Design library for Angular provides two components that represent button elements: `MdButton` and `MdAnchor`. Unlike other Material Design elements, these aren't added to templates using separate elements. Instead, they're instantiated by adding attributes to `<button>` and `<a>` elements.

`MdButtons` and `MdAnchors` have the same graphical appearance and the same attribute names. The major difference is that `MdAnchor` attributes are attached to hyperlinks and `MdButton` attributes are attached to buttons. Another difference is that `MdAnchor` is a subclass of `MdButton`, and provides additional properties and event processing.

The appearance of an MdButton or MdAnchor depends on which attribute is attached to the element. Possible attributes include the following:

1. md-button — a flat button that looks like regular text until a mouse hovers over it
2. md-raised-button — a button that uses shadow effects to look elevated
3. md-icon-button — a button that displays an image
4. md-fab — a floating action button (FAB) - 56-by-56 pixel circle
5. md-mini-fab — a smaller floating action button (FAB) - 40-by-40 pixel circle

The FAB plays an important role in Material Design. It represents the primary action to be taken in an application. Unless it's disabled, it takes the application's accent color by default. This is shown in Figure 16.3, which depicts five types of buttons.

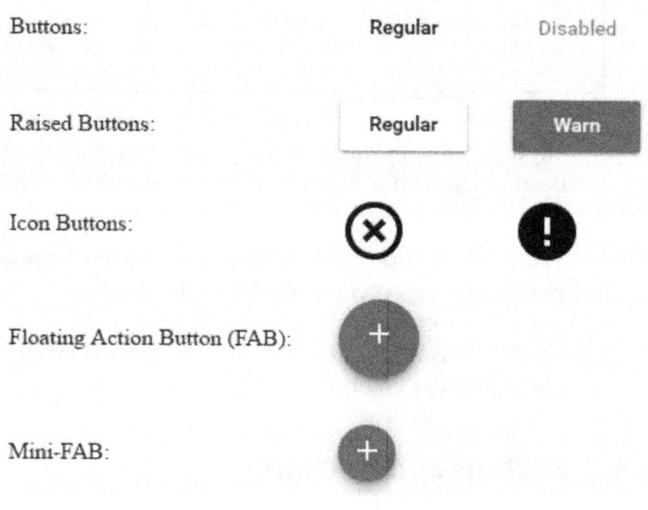


**Figure 16.3 Buttons from the Angular Material Library**

In the first row, the first button is defined without any atrributes set and the second button has its disabled attribute set to true. This is why the button's outline is practically invisible. In the second row, the second raised button has its color attribute set to warn. This displays the button using the application's warn color, which is orange by default. color can also be set to primary or accent.

Many of the buttons in the figure display icons. This can be configured by placing an <img> element inside the <button>. The following markup shows what this looks like.

```
<button md-icon-button><img src="images/error.png"></button>
```

The code in Listing 16.3 creates the buttons illustrated in Figure 16.3. The component's template contains a table with five rows, one for each button type. In keeping with Google's convention, FAB buttons are displayed with plus signs.

**Listing 16.3: ch16/button_test/app/app.component.ts**

```
@Component({
selector: 'app-root',
styles: ['td { padding: 15px; }'],
template: `
<table>

  <tr>
    <td>Buttons:</td>
    <td><button md-button>Regular</button></td>
    <td><button md-button disabled='true'>Disabled</button></td>
  </tr>

  <tr>
    <td>Raised Buttons:</td>
    <td><button md-raised-button>Regular</button></td>
    <td><button md-raised-button color='warn'>Warn</button></td>
  </tr>

  <tr>
    <td>Icon Buttons:</td>
    <td><button md-icon-button>
      <img src='assets/images/cross.png'></button></td>
    <td><button md-icon-button>
      <img src='assets/images/error.png'></button></td>
  </tr>

  <tr>
    <td>Floating Action Button (FAB):</td>
    <td><button md-fab>
      <img src='assets/images/fab.png'></button></td>
  </tr>

  <tr>
    <td>Mini-FAB:</td>
    <td><button md-mini-fab>
      <img src='assets/images/fab.png'></button></td>
  </tr>

</table>
`})
export class AppComponent {}
```

The ch16/button_test directory contains a subfolder named images. This contains the PNGs that define the button's images. To make these images available, this folder must be copied to the project's src/assets folder. The content of the assets folder will be copied to the directory containing the compiled JavaScript files. A similar copy must be performed for all projects containing images.

The icons used in this example were taken from Google's icon repository for Material Design. Google provides these simple icons for free, and the primary download site is https://design.google.com/icons. They're divided into categories that include Action, Alert, Communication, and Navigation.

In this example, the component class doesn't do anything interesting. But the process of handling events for Material Design buttons is exactly similar to that for regular buttons. That is, `(click)` events in the template can be received by event-handling methods in the component class.

To use `MdAnchor` elements instead of `MdButton` elements, replace `<button>` elements with `<a>` elements. The `MdAnchor` hyperlinks can be configured like regular hyperlinks. These are frequently used to create router links, which were discussed in Chapter 12.

## 16.3.4 Radio Buttons

In the early days of electronics, radios had special buttons for selecting a station. When one button was pushed in, the other buttons popped out. This is because only one station could be selected at a time.

The concept behind radio buttons is similar. If a user interface contains a group of radio buttons, only one can be selected at a time. When one button is selected, the others are deselected. This is one of the few instances where the state of a graphical element depends on the state of another.

To support radio buttons, the Material Design library for Angular declares two component classes:

- `MdRadioButton` represents one option with a radio button
- `MdRadioGroup` represents a group of options with radio buttons

The code in the ch16/radio_test project demonstrates how radio buttons and radio groups work together to provide single-selection behavior. The project's base component creates a radio group with five radio buttons, each representing a character from commedia dell'arte. Figure 16.4 shows what the radio group looks like.

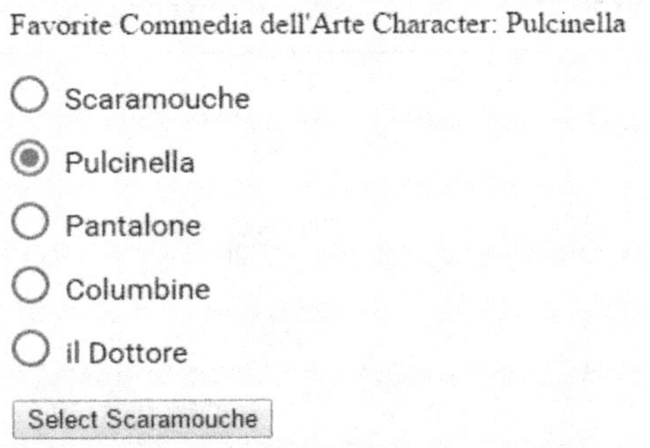


**Figure 16.4 Radio Buttons from the Angular Material Library**

The code in Listing 16.3 shows how the `MdRadioButton` and `MdRadioGroup` are used. In the template, the radio group is represented by an `<md-radio-group>` element and each radio button is represented by an `<md-radio-button>`.

**Listing 16.3: ch16/radio_test/app/app.component.ts**

```
@Component({
selector: 'app-root',

styles: ['md-radio-button {
  display: block; margin-top: 0px; margin-bottom: 10px; }
'],
template: `
<label>
  Favorite Commedia dell'Arte Character: {{ selection }}
</label>

<!-- Define the radio group -->
<p><md-radio-group [(ngModel)]='selection'>

  <!-- Create each radio button -->
  <md-radio-button *ngFor='let char of chars' [value]='char'>
    {{ char }}
  </md-radio-button>

</md-radio-group></p>

<button type='button' (click)='changeSelection()'>
  Select Scaramouche
</button>
`})
```

**Listing 16.3: ch16/radio_test/app/app.component.ts (Continued)**

```
// Define the component's controller
export class AppComponent {

  // Characters
  public chars = ['Scaramouche', 'Pulcinella',
    'Pantalone', 'Columbine', 'il Dottore'];

  // The selected character
  public selection = 'Pulcinella';

  // Respond to the button click
  private changeSelection() {
    this.selection = 'Scaramouche';
  }
}
```

This component uses the `NgFor` directive to add a radio button for each element in a string array. The `value` property of each button is set equal to the corresponding string in the array.

In the `md-radio-group` element, two-way binding is used to associate the selected button with the `selection` variable. This is accomplished using `NgModel`, as shown in the following markup:

```
<md-radio-group [(ngModel)]='selection'>
```

It's important to note that `NgModel` must be imported from the `FormsModule` discussed in Chapter 14. That is, the application's module needs to import `FormsModule` from @angular/forms and add `FormsModule` to the `imports` array of the `@NgModule` decorator.

Because of the two-way binding, the radio group's selection will change whenever the component's `selection` variable changes. In this example, the first option will be selected when the `Select Scaramouche` button is pressed.

## 16.3.4 Cards

If you visit http://plus.google.com, you'll see an array of raised, rectangular elements. Many combine different types of data, such as text, images, user interface controls, and videos. These rectangular elements are called *cards*, and according to the Material Design guidelines, a card is a "convenient means of displaying content composed of different elements."

Material Design has a great deal to say about cards and their usage. Here are five important points:

- A card's width should remain constant, but its height may increase to display additional content. Cards only scroll vertically.
- A card may have a title and subtitle, and both should be placed at the top.
- An optional overflow menu may be positioned in the card's upper-right corner or the lower-right corner.
- In addition to a main action, such as playing a video, a card may have supplemental actions. These may be activated through text, icons, or controls at the bottom of the card.
- A card's internal text should not contain hyperlinks. But the card's action area may contain links that provide entry points to more detailed information.

The Material Design library for Angular makes it possible to add cards to a web application by providing three components:

1. `MdCard` — the overall card, accessed with `<md-card>`
2. `MdCardHeader` — the card's header region, accessed with `<md-card-header>`
3. `MdCardTitleGroup` — a second type of header, accessed with `<md-card-title-group>`

The `<md-card>` serves as the top-level element. The simplest possible card can be defined by placing text inside its tags:

```
<md-card>Simple content</md-card>
```

This creates a white, raised, rectangular region that displays the given text in its center. By default, this region takes all the available width, but this can be configured by setting the card's `width` property.

The `<md-card>` element accepts a number of subelements that define content for different portions of the card. Five subelements are given as follows:

- `<md-card-title>` — Sets the card's title
- `<md-card-subtitle>` — Sets the card's subtitle
- `<md-card-content>` — Defines the content of the card
- `<md-card-actions>` — Provides actions of the card
- `<md-card-footer>` — Place content on the card's bottom edge

The following markup shows how these sections can be used:

```
<md-card>

  <md-card-title>Important Card</md-card-title>

  <md-card-subtitle>Very, very important</md-card-subtitle>

  <md-card-content>
    In the history of humanity, no card has ever hoped to be as
    important as this one. And surely, none will ever come close.
  </md-card-content>

  <md-card-actions>
    <a href="https://angular.io">Go Angular!</a>
  </md-card-actions>

</md-card>
```

Figure 16.8 shows what the resulting card looks like with the `width` of `md-card` set to 300 pixels. The title is large and black and the subtitle is small and gray.

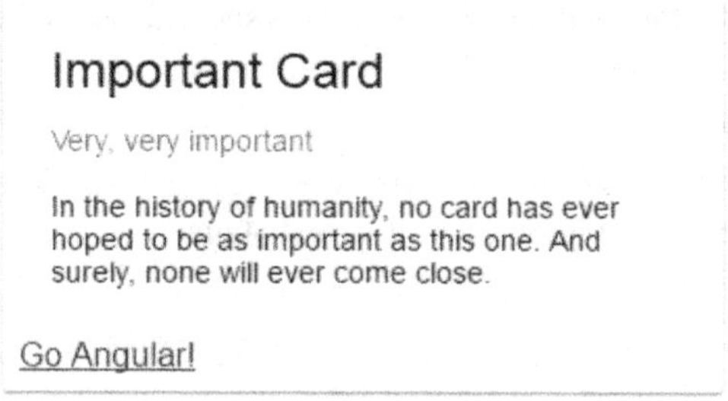


**Figure 16.5 Example Card**

Most of the cards on Google+ have the same structure toward the top—a circular image to the left, a boldfaced title that identifies the poster, and a subtitle that identifies the date/time of the post. This region is called the *header*, and by default, it's 40 pixels in height. A header can be added to a page by inserting an `<md-card-header>` element inside the `<md-card>`.

The image to the header's left is called an *avatar*. This can be added to a header by inserting an `<img>` element with the `md-card-avatar` attribute set. Figure 16.6 shows what a card looks like with a header and an avatar image.

**Figure 16.6 Card with a Header and Avatar**

This figure depicts the base component created in the ch16/card_test project. Listing 16.4 presents the component's code.

**Listing 16.4: ch16/card_test/app/app.component.ts**

```
@Component({
selector: 'app-root',
styles: ['md-card { width: 300px; }'],
template: `
<md-card>
  <md-card-header>
    <img md-card-avatar src='assets/images/smiley.jpg'>
    <md-card-title>Don Diego de la Vega</md-card-title>
    <md-card-subtitle>Posted at midnight</md-card-subtitle>
  </md-card-header>
  <md-card-content>
    Out of the night, when the full moon is bright,
    comes a horseman known as Zorro.
    This bold renegade carves a Z with his blade,
    a Z that stands for Zorro!
  </md-card-content>
  <md-card-actions>
    <button md-raised-button (click)='handleClick()'>
      Like</button>
  </md-card-actions>
</md-card>
`})

// The base component
export class AppComponent {
  private handleClick() {
    alert('Hey, I like you too!');
  }
}
```

This card contains a raised button in its action area. This is accomplished by creating a <button> and adding the md-raised-button attribute discussed earlier.

## 16.3.5 Lists

A list is a vertical container of elements called list items or *tiles*. Tiles in a list have the same width and usually all display the same kind of data. This data could be text, images, simple actions, or combinations thereof.

The Material Design library provides four entities (two components and two directives) that make it possible to add lists to Angular applications:

1. MdList — the list container, accessed with <md-list>
2. MdListItem — an item in the list, accessed with <md-list-item>
3. MdListAvatar — an image in a list item, accessed with md-list-avatar
4. MdLine — an distinct line of text in a list item, accessed with md-line

<md-list> and <md-list-item> work like the <ol> and <li> elements in regular HTML. That is, each item is surrounded by <md-list-item> and </md-list-item>, and the entire set of list items is surrounded by <md-list> and </md-list>. This is shown in the following markup:

```
<md-list>
  <md-list-item>First Item</md-list-item>
  <md-list-item>Second Item</md-list-item>
  <md-list-item>Third Item</md-list-item>
</md-list>
```

Suppose that an list item's text has supporting text similar to a card's subtitle. The text can be separated using text tags containing the md-line attribute. The following markup shows how this attribute can be used:

```
<md-list>
  <md-list-item>
    <p md-line>First Item</p>
    <p md-line>This is the first item</p>
  </md-list-item>
  <md-list-item>
    <p md-line>Second Item</p>
    <p md-line>This is the second item</p>
  </md-list-item>
</md-list>
```

This markup inserts `md-line` in <p> elements, but the attribute can be added to any regular text element, such as <h1>, <h2>, and so on.

It's common to precede the content of list items with small images called avatars. These can be added to a list item with <img> elements that contain the `md-list-avatar` attribute. The code in Listing 16.5 demonstrates how the four entities in the list module (`MdList`, `MdListItem`, `MdListAvatar`, and `MdLine`) are used.

**Listing 16.5: ch16/list_test/app/app.component.ts**

```
// Define the component's markup
@Component({
selector: 'app-root',
template: `
<md-list>

  <!-- First list item -->
  <md-list-item>
    <img md-list-avatar src='assets/images/smiley.jpg'>
    <p md-line>First Smiley</p>
    <p md-line>This item contains the first smiley</p>
  </md-list-item>

  <!-- Second list item -->
  <md-list-item>
    <img md-list-avatar src='assets/images/smiley.jpg'>
    <p md-line>Second Smiley</p>
    <p md-line>This item contains the second smiley</p>
  </md-list-item>

  <!-- Third list item -->
  <md-list-item>
    <img md-list-avatar src='assets/images/smiley.jpg'>
    <p md-line>Third Smiley</p>
    <p md-line>This item contains the third smiley</p>
  </md-list-item>

</md-list>
`})

// Define the component's controller
export class AppComponent {
}
```

Figure 16.7 depicts the configured list. As shown, the first line of text for each item is printed larger than the second.

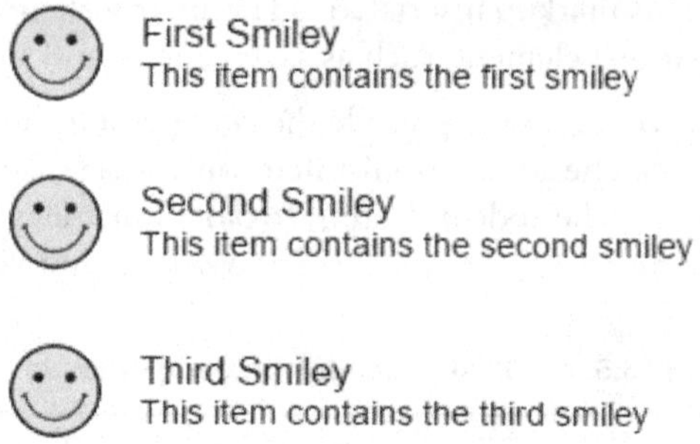


**Figure 16.7 List with Three Items**

### 16.3.6 Toolbars

Just as a list displays of list items in a vertical column, a toolbar displays toolbar rows in a vertical column. The difference is that toolbars are intended to provide actions to the user and they're frequently employed to display the application's name.

A toolbar is represented by the `MdToolbar` component, which can be accessed in markup as `<md-toolbar>`. Each toolbar row is represented by an `<md-toolbar-row>` section. This is shown in the following markup:

```
<md-toolbar color="primary">

  <span>Application Title</span>

  <md-toolbar-row>
    <span>First Row</span>
  </md-toolbar-row>

  <md-toolbar-row>
    <span>Second Row</span>
  </md-toolbar-row>

</md-toolbar>
```

It's common to place one or more actions on the far right of the toolbar. These might open an overflow menu, change display properties, or delete the current document. This can be accomplished by inserting `<input>` elements of type `image`. The code in Listing 16.6 shows how this can be implemented.

**Listing 16.6: ch16/toolbar_test/app/app.component.ts**

```
@Component({
selector: 'app-root',
styles: ['.fill_horizontal { flex: 1 1 auto; }'],
template: `
<md-toolbar color='primary'>
  Application Title
  <span class='fill_horizontal'></span>

  <!-- Create the menu button -->
  <input type='image' src='assets/images/menu.png'
    (click)='handleClick()'>

  <!-- Create toolbar rows -->
  <md-toolbar-row>Row 1</md-toolbar-row>
  <md-toolbar-row>Row 2</md-toolbar-row>

</md-toolbar>
`})

export class AppComponent {
  private handleClick() {
    alert('Important menu');
  }
}
```

Figure 16.8 shows what the resulting toolbar looks like. The overall color is configured by setting the `color` attribute of the `<md-toolbar>` to `primary`.

**Figure 16.8 Toolbar with Corner Menu**

The `<md-toolbar>` separates the menu image from the application title by inserting a `<span>` element whose style is configured to occupy the available horizontal space.

## 16.3.7 Spinners

When performing long-running operations, many applications display an indicator that tells the user that the application is continuing to run. The Material Design guidelines describe linear indicators and circular indicators. This discussion focuses on circular progress indicators, also known as *spinners*.

The `MdProgressSpinner` can be added to markup using `<md-progress-spinner>`. This accepts a `mode` attribute that can be set to one of two values:

- `determinate` — the degree of completion is known
- `indeterminate` — the degree of completion is unknown

This degree of completion is given as a percentage. It can be specified by setting the `value` attribute to a number between 0 and 100. For example, the following markup creates two spinners: one indeterminate and the other representing an operation that is halfway complete.

```
<md-progress-circle mode="indeterminate"></md-progress-circle>

<md-progress-circle mode="determinate" value="50">
  </md-progress-circle>
```

The code in Listing 16.7 presents a more involved example. In this component, pressing a button changes the degree of completion of the determinate spinner.

**Listing 16.7: ch16/spinner_test/app/app.component.ts**

```
@Component({
selector: 'app-root',
styles: ['td { padding: 15px; }'],
template: `
<table>
  <tr>
    <th>Determinate</th>
    <th>Indeterminate</th>
  </tr>

  <tr>
    <!-- Determinate spinner -->
    <td>
      <md-progress-spinner mode='determinate'
          color='accent' [value]='progress'>
      </md-progress-spinner>
    </td>
```

**Listing 16.7: ch16/spinner_test/app/app.component.ts (Continued)**

```
    <!-- Indeterminate spinner -->
    <td>
      <md-progress-spinner mode='indeterminate' color='primary'>
      </md-progress-spinner>
    </td>
  </tr>
  <tr>
    <td align='center'>
      <button md-raised-button (click)='handleClick()'>
        Update
      </button>
    </td>
  </tr>
</table>
`})

export class AppComponent {

  // The degree of progress
  private progress = 0;

  // Advance progress by 10%
  private handleClick() {
    this.progress = (this.progress + 10) % 100;
    console.log('Progress: ' + this.progress);
  }
}
```

The component displays a determinate spinner and an indeterminate spinner. A raised button updates the progress of the determinate spinner by 10%. Figure 16.9 shows what the component looks like.

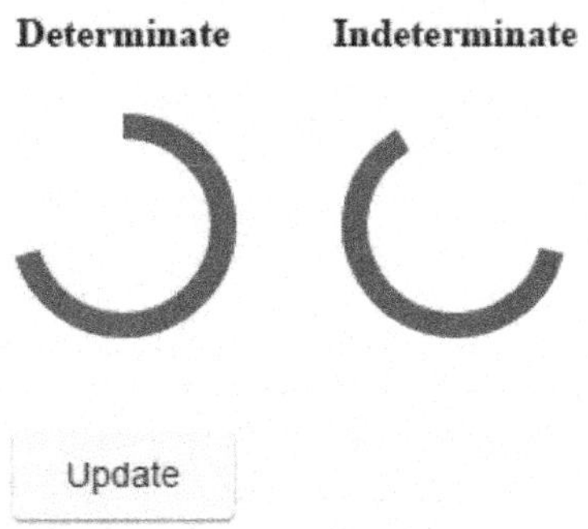


**Figure 16.9 Determinate and Indeterminate Spinners**

## 16.4 Summary

In my opinion, the Material Design framework is one of the most fascinating software offerings released by Google. It's more than just a list of recommendations or a library of widgets. It's a set of methods and graphical elements that represent Google's view of the best practices in graphic design. For a non-artist like myself, I'm deeply grateful.

The first part of this chapter discussed the styles provided by the Material Design implementation for Angular. Material Design has its own color wheel and its own recommendations for selecting colors for an application. This selection involves a primary color, a related color, and an accent color. In addition, these styles make it possible to configure an element's elevation based on its z-number.

The rest of the chapter focused on the graphical elements provided by the Material Design implementation: checkboxes, inputs, buttons, cards, lists, and progress indicators. Each is provided by its own module and each has a selector that makes it accessible in a component's template.

# Chapter 17

# Testing Components with Protractor

Chapter 6 explained how Jasmine can be used to test JavaScript functions and how Karma makes it possible to automate testing with multiple browsers. Protractor is similar to Jasmine/Karma in that its tests rely on Jasmine's syntax and they can be automated to execute in different browsers.

The primary difference is that Jasmine is strictly used for unit testing. That is, a Jasmine test executes one or more functions and checks for suitable return values. These functions run in isolation of one another and aren't concerned with the user's actions.

In contrast, Protractor makes it possible to perform end-to-end (e2e) testing. Protractor is deeply concerned with the user's experience and how he/she interacts with the browser from the start of the application to its completion.

In practice, the difference between Protractor and Jasmine is that Protractor provides a wealth of capabilities for interacting with the browser. With Protractor, a test can simulate a user's actions and check to make sure that the application responds appropriately.

## 17.1 Protractor and the CLI

One of the many advantages of using the CLI is that CLI projects already have Protractor installed and configured. The project's top-level e2e folder contains files that perform a simple test. In addition, developers can run tests using the `ng e2e` command instead of having to access a Selenium server.

The goal of this section is to explain how Protractor can be configured and launched in a CLI project. Later sections will explain how to write Protractor tests for advanced applications.

### 17.1.1 Protractor Configuration

If you want to know how Protractor is configured for a CLI project, the first place to look is the protractor.conf.js file in the top-level directory. This defines an `exports.config` object whose fields specify how Protractor should execute. Table 17.1 lists 16 possible fields of `exports.config`.

**Table 17.1**

Protractor Configuration Fields

| Configuration Field | Description |
|---|---|
| `allScriptsTimeout` | Milliseconds to wait for test |
| `specs` | Array of the test files to be executed |
| `capabilities` | Configuration for a browser instance |
| `multiCapabilities` | Configuration for multiple browser instances |
| `directConnect` | Whether Protractor should access the browser directly |
| `baseUrl` | The base location for resolving relative URLs |
| `framework` | Test framework |
| `jasmineNodeOpts` | Configuration options for Jasmine |
| `exclude` | Files to exclude from testing |
| `maxSessions` | Maximum number of sessions that can be executed |
| `params` | Parameters that can be accessed in browser.params |
| `beforeLaunch` | Function to execute before the test starts |
| `afterLaunch` | Function to execute before the program exits |
| `onPrepare` | Function to execute before specs are executed |
| `onComplete` | Function to execute after tests are finished |
| `onCleanUp` | Function to execute after the instance has been shut down |

The `specs` field identifies the file or files that define the desired test. In a CLI project, this field is set to *.e2e-spec.ts in the top-level e2e folder. I'll discuss Protractor spec files shortly.

The capabilities and multiCapabilities fields relate to the browser or browsers that Protractor should launch to execute test code. By default, Protractor assumes that the target browser is Chrome. If your tests only involve Chrome, you don't need to worry about setting either field.

At the time of this writing, Protractor contains drivers for Chrome, Firefox, and Safari. You can tell Protractor to use one of these drivers by setting the browserName field in the capabilities object. For example, the following text configures Protractor to launch Safari when executing tests:

```
capabilities: {
  browserName: "safari"
}
```

The capabilities object may include other configuration fields, such as:

- specs — JavaScript code to execute for the specific browser
- count — number of browser instances to launch
- maxInstances — the maximum number of browser instances that should be launched

The multiCapabilities field is an array of capabilities fields. For example, the following text configures Protractor to launch Chrome and Firefox for testing:

```
multiCapabilities: [{
  "browserName": "chrome"
}, {
  "browserName": "firefox"
}]
```

If the target browser is Chrome or Firefox, Protractor can connect to the browser using its driver instead of using a Selenium server. This direct access can be configured by setting directConnect to true.

The framework field identifies the framework that Protractor should employ to perform tests. This can be set to jasmine, mocha, or custom. In this chapter, all of the tests are based on Jasmine, and the jasmineNodeOpts field identifies configuration settings for the framework.

The last five fields in the table identify functions to execute at various stages in the test's execution. beforeLaunch is called before the browser object is available, and onPrepare is called after browser is available, but before Protractor executes its first test. onPrepare is called once for each browser to be launched.

## 17.1.2 The e2e Folder

By default, the `framework` field of the configuration file is set to `jasmine` and the `specs` field is set to `./e2e/**/*.e2e-spec.ts`. This tells Protractor to execute Jasmine tests in the top-level e2e folder. By default, this folder contains three files:

- tsconfig.e2e.json — Settings for compiling the Protractor code
- app.po.ts — Obtains data from the main application
- app.e2e-spec.ts — Tests the data provided by app.po.ts

The app.po.ts file defines a class called `TemplatePage`. The app.e2e-spec.ts file instantiates the class and calls its methods using Jasmine functions. Its code is as follows:

```
describe('template App', () => {
  let page: TemplatePage;

  beforeEach(() => {
    page = new TemplatePage();
  });

  it('should display message saying app works', () => {
    page.navigateTo();
    expect(page.getParagraphText()).toEqual('app works!');
  });
});
```

If you followed the discussion in Chapter 6, this should look familiar. The central functions are `describe`, `it`, and `expect`:

- `declare` — identifies the overall test suite. `declare` accepts two arguments: a name for the test suite and a function that contains the test suite.
- `it` — called inside `declare`'s function to define a spec. `it` accepts two arguments: a name for the spec and a function that defines the spec.
- `expect` — called inside `it`'s function to validate a JavaScript expression. `expect` accepts a value (the actual value) and its result is chained to a method (the matcher) that compares the actual value to the desired result.

The code in the app.po.ts file is not as straightforward. The `navigateTo` method calls `browser.get` and the `getParagraphText` method calls a function called `element`. These features are provided by the protractor package, and the next section explains what they are and how they can be used.

# 17.2 Protractor Capabilities

A Protractor test can access several objects that access the application and its operating environment. The most important of these is the `browser` object, and the following discussion explains how it can be used.

## 17.2.1 The Browser Object

As discussed earlier, Protractor's configuration file identifies which browser should execute the test. A Protractor spec can access the browser executable through the built-in `browser` object. Table 17.2 lists eighteen of its methods.

**Table 17.2**

Methods of the Browser Object

| Method | Description |
|---|---|
| `get(url: string)` | Navigates to the given URL |
| `setLocation(url: string)` | Navigates to the in-page URL (after the '#') |
| `getLocationAbsUrl()` | Returns the browser's absolute URL |
| `refresh()` | Reloads the current page |
| `restart()` | Restart the browser instance |
| `close()` | Closes the current browser window |
| `quit()` | Terminates the current session |
| `getTitle()` | Returns the title of the current page |
| `actions()` | Defines a sequence of user actions |
| `touchActions()` | Defines a sequence of touch actions |
| `findElement(Locator)` | Returns the element selected by the given locator |
| `findElements(Locator[])` | Returns the elements selected by the given locators |
| `isElementPresent(Locator)` | Identifies if the element is present |
| `executeScript (string \| Function)` | Executes JavaScript in the current frame or window |
| `executeAsyncScript (string \| Function)` | Executes asynchronous JavaScript in the current frame or window |
| `call(fn: function, scope: Object, var_args: ...)` | Call a JavaScript function to execute in the given scope with the given arguments |

| | |
|---|---|
| `wait(condition, wait: number, message: string)` | Tells the browser to halt until the condition's value is truthy or the timeout occurs |
| `sleep(time: number)` | Tells the browser to sleep for the given number of milliseconds |

For example, the following code tells the browser to open Google's homepage:

```
browser.get("http://www.google.com");
```

When testing CLI applications, the URL is commonly set to the root, so CLI tests generally start with the following:

```
browser.get("/");
```

Similarly, `browser.refresh()` refreshes the current page, `browser.restart()` restarts the browser, and `browser.getTitle()` returns the title of the current page. As an example, the following code tests the browser's current URL:

```
expect(browser.getLocationAbsUrl())
  .toEqual("http://www.google.com");
```

Many of these methods return `Promises`. For example, if you want to print the title of the current page, `console.log(browser.getTitle())` won't do the job. `getTitle` returns a `Promise`, so `then` must be called to access the `Promise`'s result. The following code shows how this works:

```
browser.getTitle().then(function(title) {
  console.log(title);
});
```

The methods `actions` and `touchActions` make it possible to define how the test interacts with elements in the web page. A later discussion will explain how to execute sequences of actions in the browser.

To access an element in the page, `findElement` returns a `WebElement` representing a DOM element. `findElements` returns an array of `WebElements`. In both cases, elements are selected by a `Locator` or array of `Locators`, and the following discussion explains how `Locators` work.

## 17.2.2 Selecting Elements

In a Protractor test, it's common to select elements in a document and then read or change their state. Accessing elements requires two steps:

1. Call a method of the `by` object to obtain a `Locator`.
2. Use the `Locator` in a method that provides an element or elements. These methods include `browser.findElement` and `browser.findElements`.

The `by` object makes it possible to select elements based on a wide range of criteria. Table 17.3 lists 13 of its methods.

**Table 17.3**

Selection Methods of the by Object

| Selection Method | Description |
|---|---|
| `tagName(tag: string)` | Selects elements by their tag name |
| `id(id: string)` | Selects an element by its ID |
| `css(sel: string)` | Selects elements by their CSS selector |
| `className(class: string)` | Selects elements by their CSS class |
| `name(name: string)` | Selects elements by their name attribute |
| `linkText(text: string)` | Selects link elements by their visible text |
| `partialLinkText (text: string)` | Selects link elements by a substring of their visible text |
| `js(string \| Function, args)` | Selects elements by evaluating a JavaScript expression |
| `xpath(sel: string)` | Selects elements with an XPath selector |
| `buttonText(text: string)` | Selects a button by its visible text |
| `partialButtonText (text: string)` | Selects buttons by a substring of their visible text |
| `cssContainingText(class: string, name: string)` | Finds elements by CSS class whose visible text contains the given string |
| `addLocator(name: string, script: Function \| string)` | Defines a custom Locator for selecting elements |

It's important to see how the `by` object and the `browser` methods work together. For example, to find an element whose ID is `submitButton`, you'd call `by.id` to obtain a `Locator` and then call `browser.findElement` to obtain the `WebElement`.

```
browser.findElement(by.id("submitButton"));
```

Similarly, the following code obtains every element in the CSS class named `caption`:

```
browser.findElements(by.className("caption"));
```

This code returns an array containing every anchor element whose displayed text contains the string `click`:

```
browser.findElements(by.partialLinkText("click"));
```

### 17.2.3 ElementFinders

Like `browser.findElement`, Protractor's `element` method accepts a `Locator` and returns an object representing a DOM element. But `element` returns an `ElementFinder`, which is similar to a `WebElement` but provides additional features.

One important point is that an `ElementFinder` doesn't access for the corresponding DOM element until it's used. In the following code, the DOM element isn't accessed until the `ElementFinder`'s `getText` method is called:

```
element(by.tagName("button")).getText().then( function(text) {
  console.log("Element text:" + text);
});
```

`element.all` accepts a `Locator` and returns an `ElementArrayFinder`. This is a container of `ElementFinders` and we'll examine its methods shortly. For example, the following code returns an `ElementArrayFinder` that contains an `ElementFinder` for each element in the page belonging to the `navbar` class:

```
element.all(by.css(".navbar"));
```

If elements are selected according to a CSS selector, the code can be simplified using a notation similar to jQuery's:

- `element(by.css("xyz"))` can be replaced with `$("xyz")`. For example, `element(by.css("#box"))` can be replaced with `$("#box")`.
- To select multiple elements, `element.all(by.css("xyz"))` can be replaced with `$$("xyz")`. For example, `element.all(by.css(".navbar"))` can be replaced with `$$(".navbar")`.

After an `ElementFinder` has been obtained, its methods make it possible to read or change the state of the corresponding DOM element. Table 17.4 presents fourteen of these methods.

**Table 17.4**

ElementFinder Methods

| Method | Description |
|---|---|
| `click()` | Sends a click event to the selected element(s) |
| `sendKeys(var_args ...)` | Sends a sequence of keystrokes to the selected element(s) |
| `submit()` | Submits the form corresponding to the given element |
| `clear()` | Clears the value of the element (input or textarea) |
| `getText()` | The element's displayed text |
| `getInnerHtml()` | The element's HTML content, not including the tags |
| `getOuterHtml()` | The element's HTML content, including the tags |
| `getSize()` | Returns the element's dimensions in pixels |
| `getLocation()` | Returns the element's location in pixels |
| `getTagName()` | Returns the element's tag name |
| `getCssValue(prop: string)` | Returns the element's CSS value for the given property |
| `getAttribute (attr: string)` | Returns the value corresponding to the given attribute |
| `isEnabled()` | Identifies if the element's state is enabled |
| `isSelected()` | Identifies if the element has been enabled |
| `isDisplayed()` | Identifies if the element is displayed in the page |

The first four methods perform an action on the corresponding DOM element. The easiest to understand is `click`. The following code delivers a click event to the element whose ID is `sendData`:

```
$("#sendData").click();
```

To insert text into an `<input>` or `<textarea>`, the `sendKeys` method delivers keystroke events to a target element. To specify which keys should be sent, `sendKeys` accepts a series of strings, characters, and/or special characters. Table 17.5 lists fourteen special characters recognized by `sendKeys`:

**Table 17.5**
Special Key Codes

| | |
|---|---|
| protractor.Key.ENTER | protractor.Key.ESCAPE |
| protractor.Key.SPACE | protractor.Key.TAB |
| protractor.Key.SHIFT | protractor.Key.UP |
| protractor.Key.ALT | protractor.Key.DOWN |
| protractor.Key.META | protractor.Key.LEFT |
| protractor.Key.CONTROL | protractor.Key.RIGHT |
| protractor.Key.COMMAND | protractor.Key.NULL |

The following code uses `sendKeys` to transfer the characters `N`, `a`, `m`, and `e` followed by the Enter key. This text is delivered to the element whose ID is `storeName`:

```
$(#storeName).sendKeys("Name", protractor.Key.ENTER);
```

If this element is an `<input>` element, its text can be checked by reading its `value` attribute. The following code shows how this can be done:

```
$("#storeName").getAttribute("value").then( function(value) {
  console.log("Input value:" + text);
});
```

If a modifier key (Shift, Control, Alt, Meta) is sent, it will remain active until `protractor.Key.NULL` is sent. To see how this works, consider the following code:

```
$(#storeName).sendKeys("one", protractor.Key.SHIFT, "two",
                       protractor.Key.NULL, "three");
```

Sending `protractor.Key.SHIFT` is equivalent to holding down the Shift key. Sending `protractor.Key.NULL` is equivalent to lifting the Shift key. Therefore, the target element will receive the text `oneTWOthree`.

The remainder of the methods in Table 17.3 are straightforward. Keep in mind that `getText` returns the text displayed by an element. The `getInnerHtml` and `getOuterHtml` methods return the element's HTML definition. The difference between the two is that `getOuterHtml` includes the element's tags and `getInnerHtml` doesn't.

### 17.2.4 ElementArrayFinders

The `element.all(...)` and `$$(...)` methods both return a container of `ElementFinders` called an `ElementArrayFinder`. This can be accessed like a regular array, so the first `ElementFinder` in the `arr` container is `arr[0]`.

Like an `ElementFinder`, an `ElementArrayFinder` behaves like a promise, and doesn't search for the corresponding DOM elements until a read/write/test action is performed. For example, the following code obtains an `ElementArrayFinder` containing all the anchors in the page. But it doesn't access any DOM elements until the first anchor's text is tested:

```
$$("a").then(function(elementArray) {
  expect(elementArray[0].getText()).toBe("Click Me");
});
```

Table 17.6 presents methods for accessing, examining, and operating on `ElementArrayFinders`.

**Table 17.6**

ElementArrayFinder Methods

| Method | Description |
|---|---|
| `filter(func: function)` | Returns an ElementArrayFinder whose elements meet the criteria given by the filter function |
| `get(index: number)` | Returns the ElementFinder at the given index |
| `first()` | Returns the first ElementFinder in the array |
| `last()` | Returns the last ElementFinder in the array |
| `count()` | Returns the number of ElementFinders in the array |
| `locator()` | Returns the most recently-used Locator |
| `each(func: function)` | Applies a function to each element in the array |
| `map(func: function)` | Applies a map function to each element in the array |
| `reduce(func: function, init: any)` | Applies a reduce function to all the elements in the array |
| `evaluate(in: string)` | Evaluates the input string as if it was an Angular expression |
| `allowAnimations()` | Identifies if animation is allowed on the array's elements |

The filter method removes ElementFinders from an array using a JavaScript function. The function receives two arguments: an ElementFinder and the ElementFinder's index. It can return a boolean or a promise for a boolean. If the boolean is *false*, the ElementFinder will be removed from the ElementArrayFinder. In other words, filter determines which elements to keep in the array, not which elements to remove.

For example, suppose you want to operate on all the buttons whose displayed text contains Click. The following code creates this ElementArrayFinder and then calls filter to exclude any buttons whose displayed text doesn't contain Click. Then it calls each to send a click event to each button remaining in the array.

```
$$("button").filter(function(element, index) {
  return element.getText().then(function(text) {
    return text.indexOf("Click") > -1;
  });
}).each(function(element, index) {
  element.click();
});
```

map is almost identical to each, and both methods accept a function that receives an ElementFinder and the ElementFinder's index. The difference between them is that each returns void and map returns a promise that resolves to an array of values. Each iteration of map provides an element in this returned array.

For example, the following code creates an ElementArrayFinder containing all the buttons in the page and uses map to place each button's displayed text in an array. The join method combines these strings into one, which is printed to the console.

```
$$("button").map(function(element, index) {

  return element.getText();

}).then(function(array) {
  console.log(array.join(""));
});
```

When combining aspects of multiple ElementFinders, reduce is more flexible than map. This is because its function provides an accumulator whose value can be updated as each ElementFinder is processed.

The following code also combines the displayed text of every button in the page, but uses reduce instead of map. Because of the accumulator, the combination can be accomplished without a separate join step.

```
$$("button").reduce(function(acc, element) {
  return element.getText().then(function(text) {
    return acc + text;
  });
}, "").then(function(res) {
  console.log(res);
});
```

### 17.2.5 Actions

An earlier discussion explained how `ElementFinder` methods like `click` and `sendKeys` can send events to a DOM element. These methods are fine for basic actions, but aren't sufficient if a test needs to send actions related to mouse movement, scrolling, double clicks, or drag-and-drop operations.

For broader action testing, the `actions` method of the `browser` object accepts a sequence of actions to be performed in the browser. Each action is represented by a method provided under the `Protractor` namespace. Table 17.7 lists the available methods and provides a description of each.

**Table 17.7**

Protractor Action Methods

| Method | Description |
|---|---|
| `click(b: button)` | Performs a mouse click at the current location |
| `click(el: ElementFinder, b: button)` | Performs a mouse click on the given element |
| `doubleClick(b: button)` | Performs a double-click at the current location |
| `doubleClick (el: ElementFinder, b: button)` | Performs a double-click on the given element |
| `dragAndDrop (src: ElementFinder, dst: ElementFinder)` | Performs a drag-and-drop from one element to another |
| `dragAndDropBy (src: ElementFinder, x: number, y: number)` | Performs a drag-and-drop from an element to a location given by (x, y) |
| `keyDown(k: key)` | Presses the given modifier key |
| `keyUp(k: key)` | Releases the given modifier key |
| `mouseDown(b: button)` | Performs a mouse click without release |

| | |
|---|---|
| `mouseDown(el: ElementFinder, b: button)` | Performs a mouse click on the given element without release |
| `mouseMove(el: ElementFinder)` | Moves the mouse to the center of the given element |
| `mouseMove(x: number, y: number)` | Moves the mouse to an offset from the window's top-left corner |
| `mouseMove (el: ElementFinder, x: number, y: number)` | Moves the mouse to an offset from the given element's top-left corner |
| `mouseUp(b: button)` | Releases the given mouse button |
| `mouseUp(el: ElementFinder, b: button)` | Releases the given mouse button on the given element |
| `perform()` | Executes the action sequence |
| `sendKeys(var_args)` | Sends key sequence to the active element |

When using these methods, there are two important points to understand:

1. The methods can be chained together to define a sequence of actions.
2. The chain starts with `browser.actions()` and ends with `perform()`, which executes the actions.

For the actions involving mouse buttons, such as `click` and `doubleClick`, the button value can take one of three values: `protractor.Button.LEFT`, `protractor.Button.RIGHT`, and `protractor.Button.MIDDLE`. As a simple example, the following sequence right-clicks on the button whose ID is `browse`, and then double-clicks on the same button:

```
browser.actions().click($("#browse"), protractor.Button.RIGHT)
                 .doubleclick().perform();
```

For every action sequence, the initial position of the mouse pointer is (0, 0) and its position is updated after mouse-related events. This is why the `doubleclick()` action in the example code doesn't need to identify the target—the pointer is still over the button.

Protractor doesn't provide any methods that interact with `<select>` elements and their options. I spent hours trying to use `mouseMove` and `click` to select an option programmatically, but there's an easier way. If an option is named `GreenOption`, the following code will select it:

```
element(by.cssContainingText("option", "GreenOption")).click();
```

The `keyDown` and `keyUp` methods only accept modifier keys, such as `protractor.Key.SHIFT`. For other keys, the `sendKeys` method in the table accepts the same arguments as the `ElementFinder`'s `sendKeys` method discussed earlier. There's no way to specifically identify the target—the keystrokes will be sent to the element that received focus last.

For example, the following action sequence sends Ctrl-C to the current element:

```
browser.actions().sendKeys(protractor.Key.CONTROL, "c",
                                  protractor.Key.NULL).perform();
```

# 17.3 Executing Tests

After you've written a test suite and the configuration file, you're ready to execute tests. For CLI projects, this is easy. The only command you need to know is `ng e2e`.

Like other CLI commands, `ng e2e` can be followed by flags that configure the operation. Table 17.8 lists these flags and provides a description of each.

**Table 17.8**

CLI Test Execution Flags (ng e2e)

| Flag | Description |
|---|---|
| `-t/-dev/-prod` | Identifies the build target |
| `-e` | Sets the build environment |
| `-op` | Specifies the output path |
| `-aot` | Builds using Ahead of Time compilation |
| `-sm` | Output sourcemaps |
| `-vc` | Split vendor libraries into a separate bundle |
| `-bh` | Base URL for the application |
| `-d` | URL where files will be deployed |
| `-v` | Sets verbose messaging |
| `-pr` | Logs progress to the console |
| `--i18n-file` | Sets the localization file |
| `--i18n-format` | Sets the format of the localization file |
| `--locale` | The locale to use for localization |

| | |
|---|---|
| `-ec` | Extracts CSS from global styles |
| `-w` | Executes build when files change |
| `-poll` | Sets the interval for checking file changes |
| `-app` | Specifies the name of the app |
| `-p` | Sets the port for serving the application |
| `-H` | Sets the host |
| `-pc` | Sets the proxy configuration file |
| `-ssl` | Serves using SSL |

By default, all tests are based on the development build target. The following command executes the end-to-end test using the production target:

```
ng e2e -prod
```

The `-aot` flag enables Ahead of Time compilation, which was discussed in Chapter 8. If the test is run for the production build target, this will be enabled by default.

# 17.4 Example Test Suite

The ch17/protractor_demo project demonstrates how Protractor can be used in practice. In this example, the template of the base component contains two elements:

- An `<button>` whose text identifies how many times it's been clicked
- An `<input>` whose content is initially empty.

The test suite is provided in the app.e2e-spec.ts file in the ch17/protractor_demo/e2e folder. Listing 17.1 presents its code.

The test can be executed by changing to the top-level directory and entering `ng e2e` on the command line. After accessing the `browser` object, the test application performs three operations:

1. Make sure the page contains a button element whose ID is set to `demo_button`.
2. Click the button twice and make sure the button's text is `2`.
3. Add a string to the text box and make sure its content equals `HELLOhello`.

**Listing 17.1: ch17/protractor_demo/src/test/test.js**

```
describe('the protractor_demo project', function() {

  // Initialize test
  beforeEach(() => {
    browser.get('/');
  });

  // Make sure the button is present
  it('should have a button whose ID is demo_button', function() {
    expect($$('#demo_button').count()).toEqual(1);
  });

  // Click the button twice and count the clicks
  it('should have a demo_button whose text identifies
    the number of clicks', function() {

    browser.actions().click($('#demo_button')).click(
      $('#demo_button')).perform();

    expect($('#demo_button').getText()).toEqual('2');
  });

  // Add text to the input box and verify its content
  it('should have a demo_input whose text equals HELLOhello',
    function() {

    $('#demo_input').sendKeys(protractor.Key.SHIFT,
      'hello', protractor.Key.NULL, 'hello');

    expect($('#demo_input').getAttribute('value')).
      toEqual('HELLOhello');
  });
});
```

On my system, the output of `ng e2e` is given as follows:

```
Spec started

  the protractor_demo project
    should have a button whose ID is demo_button
    should have a demo_button whose text identifies the number of
clicks
    should have a demo_input whose text equals HELLOhello

Executed 3 of 3 specs SUCCESS in 2 secs.
[00:14:21] I/launcher - 0 instance(s) of WebDriver still running
```

The second test clicks the demo_button twice and checks the button's text to make sure that its displayed text equals 2. The check is performed with the following code:

```
expect($("#demo_button").getText()).toEqual("2");
```

As mentioned earlier, functions like getText return a Promise, not a value. Protractor's implementation of expect can accept Promises, and it calls the Promise's then method to obtain the value to be checked.

The last test delivers a set of keystrokes to the <input> element with the following code:

```
$("#demo_input").sendKeys(protractor.Key.SHIFT,
      "hello", protractor.Key.NULL, "hello");
```

The sendKeys method delivers the hello string twice, once before the Shift key is pressed and once afterward. As a result, the text in the <input> element is given as HELLOhello.

# 17.5 Summary

The Jasmine toolset is fine for checking functions and variables, but it's unsuitable for testing the usage of real-world applications. In contrast, end-to-end testing directs user actions to an application and checks the application's state to ensure proper behavior. Protractor excels at this type of testing, and the goal of this chapter has been to explain how it can be used.

At first glance, a Protractor test suite looks like a Jasmine test suite, using define, it, and expect to check actual values against expected values. But Protractor's advantage is that it provides a wealth of objects and functions for interacting with a browser. For example, the browser object makes it possible to read and test the browser's state as it runs an application.

At its simplest, an end-to-end test involves directing actions to a browser and verifying changes to the application's state. In Protractor, a sequence of actions can be delivered to an element by calling the actions method of the browser object. This can be chained with methods representing simulated user actions, such as click(). The perform method executes the actions.

To access elements in the document, Protractor provides `Locators`, which select elements according to criteria including attributes and CSS styles. `Locators` make it possible to obtain `ElementFinders` and `ElementArrayFinders`, which can send actions to browser elements and read their state information.

# Chapter 18

# Displaying REST Data with Dynamic Tables

From GMail to Amazon, today's most popular web sites all perform the same basic operations. They read records from a database and display them in a dynamic table. These tables provide a common set of features, which include the following:

- Clicking a record's title provides more information
- Records can be sorted in ascending or descending order
- Records can be filtered using search criteria
- Records can be selected for individual operations, such as deletion
- Users can select how many rows should be displayed at once

The goal of this chapter is to show how similar tables can be constructed using Angular. The project discussed in this chapter ties together many of Angular's advanced features, including routing, HTTP access, and the Reactive Forms API.

The table's data is provided in raw form instead of HTML, so the client-server application is more accurately called a web service. A popular architecture for web service communication is Representational State Transfer, or REST. REST provides guidelines for HTTP data transfer, especially with regard to the names and hierarchy of uniform resource identifiers, or URIs. This chapter explains what these guidelines are and show how they can be used in an Angular application.

The majority of this chapter is concerned with code. The discussion topics include implementing REST's guidelines using Angular's HTTP service, validating user data with the Reactive Forms API, and selecting child components by URL using Angular's routing capability.

# 18.1 The SongView Application

This chapter focuses on the SongView application, which reads data from a server and displays the data in a table. Figure 18.1 shows what this table looks like:

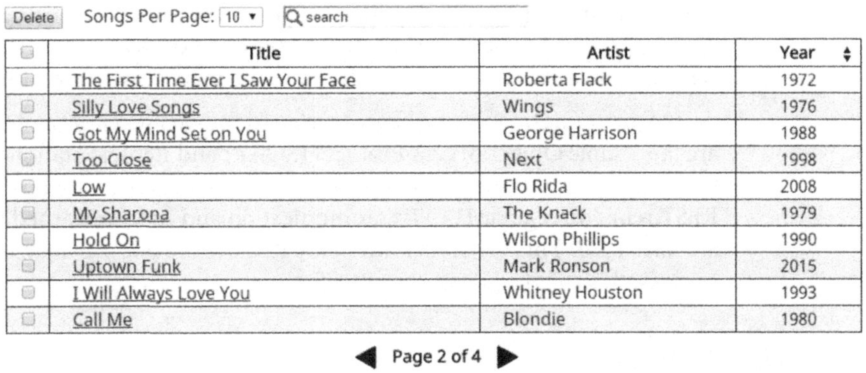


| | Title | Artist | Year |
|---|---|---|---|
| | The First Time Ever I Saw Your Face | Roberta Flack | 1972 |
| | Silly Love Songs | Wings | 1976 |
| | Got My Mind Set on You | George Harrison | 1988 |
| | Too Close | Next | 1998 |
| | Low | Flo Rida | 2008 |
| | My Sharona | The Knack | 1979 |
| | Hold On | Wilson Phillips | 1990 |
| | Uptown Funk | Mark Ronson | 2015 |
| | I Will Always Love You | Whitney Houston | 1993 |
| | Call Me | Blondie | 1980 |

**Figure 18.1 The SongView Table**

Each record of the table identifies the title, artist, and year of a popular song. Users can sort the records by year, mark rows for deletion, search for text, and specify how many rows should be displayed.

Clicking on a title brings up a second page with a simple form. As shown in Figure 18.2, this form has three text boxes, one for each field of the record:

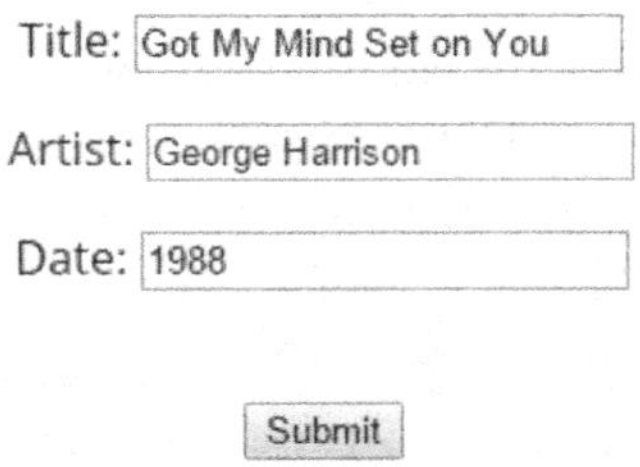


**Figure 18.2 Editing Song Data**

In code, the dynamic table is represented by an instance of `SongTableComponent` and the edit page is represented by an `EditPageComponent`. Later sections will present the code in these classes. First, I want to discuss the REST architecture, whose philosophy was incorporated into the SongView application.

# 18.2 Representational State Transfer (REST)

In a traditional web application, a client sends an HTTP request and receives a response containing HTML. HTML is fine for displaying graphics and text in a browser, but if the client wants raw data, such as the price of a stock or the address of a hotel, HTML is inefficient. In these cases, it's better to construct the response using a more general data format, such as JSON. This is the basic idea behind a web service. A client accesses a web service by sending a request to a URL and the server responds with JSON data.

Many frameworks have been developed for web services, and the two most prominent are the Simple Object Access Protocol (SOAP) and Representational State Transfer (REST). SOAP requires its own protocol and requires that responses be formatted in XML. REST relies on regular HTTP communication and isn't concerned how the responses are formatted. This generality has made REST more popular than SOAP, and for these reasons, this chapter focuses on REST.

## 18.2.1 Philosophy

There's no specification that defines how a REST-based (or *RESTful*) web service should behave. Instead, REST defines a set of design rules, or contraints, that RESTful web services are expected to follow. Roy Fielding introduced these constraints in his 2000 dissertation, *Architectural Styles and the Design of Network-based Software Architectures*:

1. Client-server — In REST's separation-of-concerns methodology, the client is concerned with one set of issues, such as the user interface, and the server is concerned with another set of issues, such as data storage. These elements are called *components*.
2. Stateless — A REST request contains all the information needed to understand it. The server doesn't keep track of sessions but the client may.
3. Cacheable — Data in a REST response can be marked as non-cacheable or cacheable. This can improve performance, but it may also reduce reliability due to stale entries in the cache.
4. Layered system — The architecture consists of independent, hierarchical layers.
5. Uniform interface — Components have a consistent contract that enables communication with many different types of components.
6. (Optional) Code on demand — REST supports extensibility by allowing applets or scripts to provide additional functionality.

### 18.2.2 Accessing Resources

The REST methodology presents clear guidelines for accessing resources. REST recognizes two types of uniform resource identifiers (URIs):

- Collection URIs — Identify a collection of elements, such as http://example.edu/professors
- Element URIs — Identify a single element in a collection, such as http://example.edu/professors/smith

A URI's type determines how it should be accessed using HTTP requests. For a Collection URI, a GET request lists the elements in the collection, a PUT request replaces the collection with another, a POST request adds an element to the collection, and a DELETE request deletes the collection.

For an Element URI, the different methods have different purposes. A GET request retrieves a representation of the element, a PUT request replaces the element, and a DELETE request removes the element from the collection. POST requests generally aren't used with Element URIs.

In RESTful applications, URIs identify things, not actions. Therefore, a URI like http://example.edu/get_office_hours isn't acceptable because 'get_office_hours' implies an action. A URI like http://example.edu/professors/update?name=smith is also frowned upon because 'update' identifies an action.

The REST architecture doesn't define a format for requests and responses, but metadata should be kept in the header, not the body. The only data in a response's body should be the resource requested by the client. The format of the response data is usually XML or JSON, and the request can specify the format by adding a suffix to the request, such as http://example.edu/professors/smith.json. It's also acceptable to specify the desired resource format in the request's header. The process of determining which format to return is called *content negotiation.*

To keep applications stateless, resources should provide links that identify what operations are available for interacting with the application. The following markup provides an example:

```
<student>
   <student_number>123</student_number>
   <link rel="pass" href="http://ex.edu/students/123/pass" />
   <link rel="fail" href="http://ex.edu/students/123/fail" />
</student>
```

In REST literature, this concept is denoted HATEOAS, which stands for Hypermedia as the Engine of Application State.

# 18.3 Implementing REST with Http Methods

The application presented in this chapter displays forty song records that can be accessed through the URL www.ngbook.io. In keeping with REST's philosophy, the primary collection URI is www.ngbook.io/songs.

A GET request to this URI returns an array of forty JSON objects, each containing a song's ID, title, artist, and year. But the table displays a limited number of entries, so a request can have parameters that specify the page number and the number of songs per page. For example, the following URL specifies that the client wants ten songs, starting from the second page:

```
http://www.ngbook.io/songs?page=1&songsperpage=10
```

As discussed in Chapter 13, GET requests can be generated and transmitted using the `get` method of the `Http` class. This accepts a URL and an optional `RequestOptionsArgs` that determines the query string. In the `SongTableComponent`, this is accomplished with the following code:

```
let query = "page=".concat(this.page.toString())
                   .concat("&songsperpage=")
                   .concat(this.songsPerPage.toString());

const opts: RequestOptionsArgs = {search: query};

this.http.get("http://www.ngbook.io/songs", opts)
  .map((res: Response) => res.json())
  .subscribe((songs: Array<Song>) => this.songs = songs);
```

The `get` method provides access to the server's response in the form of an `Observable`. As explained in Chapter 11, the `map` method transforms each of the `Observable`'s elements. In this code, `json` transforms the body of the response data into JSON format. Afterward, the `subscribe` method receives the JSON data as an array of `Song` objects.

The application presented in this chapter doesn't support sending PUT, POST, or DELETE requests to the collection URI, but it does support sending requests to element URIs. Each song has an ID between 00 and 39, and the following URI accesses Song 27:

```
http://www.ngbook.io/songs/song27
```

The application can send GET, PUT, and DELETE requests to element URIs. The user interface makes this possible with the following actions:

- Checking a record in the song table and pressing Delete sends a DELETE request to the element URI corresponding to the song.
- Clicking on a title in the song table opens the edit form for editing. As the form opens, it sends a GET request to obtain data for the selected song.
- When the edit form is submitted with valid data, it sends a PUT request to update the song's data.

To show how REST works in practice, I've written back end code that runs on a server and provides data through www.ngbook.io. The server receives and responds to HTTP requests, but in the interest of security, it doesn't allow any operation to modify the song data. Instead, for DELETE and PUT requests, the server returns a message stating that the HTTP request was received.

The SongView application doesn't provide information through HATEOAS. This is because the API is sufficiently simple that no additional metadata is needed.

# 18.4 The SongView Project

The ch18/song_view project creates the application depicted in Figures 18.1 and 18.2. This section explores the project's code. Specifcally, this section looks at the module class, the `SongViewComponent`, and the `EditPageComponent`.

The ch18/song_view project contains a folder named images. This must be copied to the src/assets folder of your CLI project to ensure that the server will be able to locate the application's images.

## 18.4.1 The Module Class

The module class, `AppModule`, is defined in the app/app.module.ts file. To meet the application's requirements, the module imports capabilities for routing, HTTP data transfer, and forms. Listing 18.1 presents its code.

Chapter 12 explained how modules can define a `Routes` array whose elements associate URLs with components. In this case, the base URL redirects to the /songtable URL, which inserts the `SongTableComponent` into the base component. When the client accesses the /editpage URL, the router inserts an `EditPageComponent` into the base component.

**Listing 18.1: ch18/song_view/app/app.module.ts**

```
const routes: Routes = [
  {path: '', redirectTo: 'songtable', pathMatch: 'full'},
  {path: 'songtable', component: SongTableComponent},
  {path: 'editpage', component: EditPageComponent}
];
@NgModule({
  declarations: [
    AppComponent,
    SongTableComponent,
    EditPageComponent
  ],
  imports: [
    BrowserModule,
    HttpModule,
    ReactiveFormsModule,
    FormsModule,
    RouterModule.forRoot(routes)
  ],
  providers: [],
  bootstrap: [AppComponent]
})
export class AppModule {}
```

As given by the bootstrap field in `@NgModule`, the application's base component is an `AppComponent`, which is defined in app/app.component.ts. This component doesn't have any code because its only purpose is to hold child components.

## 18.4.2 The Song Table Component

The `SongTableComponent` provides the main visual component of the project. This reads song records from the server and displays them as rows of a table. By default, the records are unsorted and the table displays ten records at once.

Listing 18.2 presents the component's template and Listing 18.3 presents the component's class. There's a great deal of code, and rather than discuss all of it in detail, this section explores five aspects of the table's operation:

1. Linking to the edit page
2. Pagination
3. Row selection and deletion
4. Row sorting
5. Text search

**Listing 18.2: ch18/song_view/app/songtable/songtable.component.html**

```
<div id='song_view'>
  <p id='title'>Popular Songs</p>
  <div class='top'>
    <span><button (click)='handleDelete()'>Delete</button></span>
    <span>Songs Per Page:
    <select (change)='handleSelect($event.target.value)'>
      <option>5</option>
      <option selected>10</option>
      <option>20</option>
    </select></span>
    <input class='search_box' type='search'
      (search)='handleSearch($event.target.value)'
      onfocus="if (this.value=='search') this.value = ''"
      value='search' size='25'>
  </div>
  <table class='song_table'>
    <tr>
      <th class='row-checkBox'>
        <input type='checkbox' [checked]='allChecked'
          (change)='handleChecks($event.target.checked)'></th>
      <th class='row-title'>Title</th>
      <th class='row-artist'>Artist</th>
      <th class='row-year' (click)='handleSort()'>Year
      <img class='sort_img' [src]='sortImage'></th>
    </tr>
    <tr *ngFor='let song of songs; let i = index'>
      <td class='center'><input type='checkbox'
        [(ngModel)]='checks[i]'></td>
      <td class='indent'><a [routerLink]="['../editpage']"
        [queryParams]="{songid: song.id}">
          {{song.title}}</a></td>
      <td class='indent'>{{song.artist}}</td>
      <td class='center'>{{song.year}}</td>
    </tr>
  </table>
  <div class='bottom'>
    <span><img src='assets/images/left_arrow.png'
      [className]="(page == 0) ? 'hide' : ''"
      (click)='handlePrev()'></span>
    <span class='bottom_center'>
      Page {{ page + 1 }} of {{ numPages }}</span>
    <span><img src='assets/images/right_arrow.png'
      [className]="(page == numPages-1) ? 'hide' : ''"
      (click)='handleNext()'></span>
  </div>
</div>
```

**Listing 18.3: ch18/song_view/app/songtable/songtable.component.ts**

```
@Component({
selector: 'app-songtable',
templateUrl: 'songtable.component.html',
styleUrls: ['songtable.component.css']})
export class SongTableComponent {
  private songs = [];
  private checks = [];
  private allChecked = false;
  private page = 0;
  private songsPerPage = 10;
  private numPages = 4;
  private sortDirection = SortDirection.None;
  private sortImage = 'assets/images/no_sort.png';
  private url = 'http://www.ngbook.io/songs';

  constructor(private http: Http) { this.sendRequest(); }

  // Request records from the server
  private sendRequest(): void {
    // Construct query string
    let query = 'page='.concat(this.page.toString()).
      concat('&songsPerPage=').
      concat(this.songsPerPage.toString());
    switch (this.sortDirection) {
      case SortDirection.Asc:
        query = query.concat('&sort=asc'); break;
      case SortDirection.Desc:
        query = query.concat('&sort=desc'); break;
      default: break;
    }

    // Send a request and process the response
    const opts = {search: query};
    this.http.get(this.url, opts)
      .map((res: Response) => res.json())
      .subscribe((songs: Array<Song>) => this.songs = songs);
  }

  // Respond when all boxes are checked/unchecked
  private handleChecks(checked: boolean): void {
    if (checked) {
      for (let i = 0; i < this.songs.length; i++) {
        this.checks[i] = true;
      }
    } else {
      this.clearChecks();
    }
  }
```

**Listing 18.3: ch18/song_view/app/songtable/songtable.component.ts (Continued)**

```
// Respond to text search
private handleSearch(text: string): void {
  let query: string;
  const opts: RequestOptionsArgs;

  // Update URL
  if (text) {
    query = 'search='.concat(text);
  } else if (text === '') {
    query = 'page='.concat(this.page.toString()).
      concat('&songsPerPage=').
      concat(this.songsPerPage.toString());
  }
  opts = {search: query};
  this.http.get(this.url, opts)
    .map((res: Response) => res.json())
    .subscribe((songs: Array<Song>) => this.songs = songs);
}

// Respond when a different page count is selected
private handleSelect(selection: string): void {
  this.songsPerPage = parseInt(selection, 10);
  this.numPages = Math.round(40 / this.songsPerPage);
  if (this.page >= this.numPages) {
    this.page = this.numPages - 1;
  }
  this.sendRequest();
  this.clearChecks();
}

// Respond when the delete button is pressed
private handleDelete(): void {
  let deleteURL: string;
  for (let i = 0; i < this.songs.length; i++) {
    if (this.checks[i]) {

      // Update the URL and send the DELETE request
      deleteURL = this.url.concat('/song').
        concat(this.songs[i].id);
      this.http.delete(deleteURL)
        .subscribe((res: Response) => { alert(res.text()); });
    }
    this.checks[i] = false;
  }
}
```

**Listing 18.3: ch18/song_view/app/songtable/songtable.component.ts (Continued)**

```
  // Respond to record sort
  private handleSort(): void {
    switch (this.sortDirection) {

      // No direction
      case SortDirection.None:
        this.sortDirection = SortDirection.Desc;
        this.sortImage = 'assets/images/desc_sort.png';
        break;

      // Descending direction
      case SortDirection.Desc:
        this.sortDirection = SortDirection.Asc;
        this.sortImage = 'assets/images/asc_sort.png';
        break;

      // Ascending direction
      case SortDirection.Asc:
        this.sortDirection = SortDirection.None;
        this.sortImage = 'assets/images/no_sort.png';
        break;
    }
    this.sendRequest();
  }

  // Respond when the previous link is clicked
  private handlePrev(): void {
    this.page--;
    this.sendRequest();
    this.clearChecks();
  }

  // Respond when the next link is clicked
  private handleNext(): void {
    this.page++;
    this.sendRequest();
    this.clearChecks();
  }

  // Uncheck the checkboxes
  private clearChecks(): void {
    this.allChecked = false;
    for (let i = 0; i < this.songs.length; i++) {
      this.checks[i] = false;
    }
  }
}
```

## Linking to the Edit Page

As depicted in Figure 18.1, each song's title serves as a hyperlink. If a title is clicked, the application opens a page for editing the song's data. In the SongTableComponent template, song titles are defined with the following markup:

```
<tr *ngFor='let song of songs; let i = index'>
  ...
  <td class='indent'>
     <a [routerLink]="['../editpage']"
        [queryParams]="{songid: song.id}>
        {{song.title}}</a>
  </td>
  ...
</tr>
```

The routerLink property identifies the anchor element as a router link. As explained in Chapter 12, a router link creates a URL that the router will recognize. When the user clicks the link, the router will match the path to a component and insert the component into the base component.

The application's route configurations are defined in the module class. The following code shows how they're defined

```
const routes: Routes = [
  {path: '', redirectTo: 'songtable', pathMatch: 'full'},
  {path: 'songtable', component: SongTableComponent},
  {path: 'editpage', component: EditPageComponent}
];
```

The second route configuration associates the songtable path with the SongTableComponent. This component is displayed when the application starts. The third route configuration associates the editpage path with the EditPageComponent. The router link for each song title points to editpage, so the EditPageComponent will be displayed when the link is clicked.

The router link sets a query when clicked. This contains the ID of the selected song, which will be appended to the URL path when the link is activated. For example, if the user clicks on a link for Song 17, the query will be set to ?songid=17.

It's important to understand the .. in the routerLink value (../editpage). This tells the router to access the route definitions of the root module instead of the SongTableComponent's route definitions. This makes sense because the SongTableComponent doesn't have any route definitions of its own.

## Pagination

For nontrivial web applications, the database will hold more records than a table can display at once. For this reason, the collection of records must be split into groups that can be displayed in the table. These groups are called pages, and the process of managing pages is called pagination.

The `SongTableComponent` class has three properties related to pagination:

- `page` identifies the page currently displayed in the table
- `songsPerPage` identifies the number of records in each page
- `numPages` identifies the number of pages

When the `SongTableComponent` needs to retrieve data, it tells the server which records it wants by providing the values of `page` and `songsPerPage` as parameters of the GET request. The following code shows how this is accomplished:

```
let query: string =
  'page='.concat(this.page.toString())
         .concat('&songsPerPage=')
         .concat(this.songsPerPage.toString());
...
opts = {search: query};
this.http.get(this.url, opts)
  .map((res: Response) => res.json())
  .subscribe((songs: Array<Song>) => this.songs = songs);
```

The user can change which page is displayed by clicking one of the arrows below the table. If the current page is the first page, the left (previous) arrow will be hidden. If the current page is the last page, the right (next) arrow will be hidden. This behavior is configured with the following markup:

```
<img src='assets/images/left_arrow.png'
     [className]='(page == 0) ? 'hide' : '''
     (click)='handlePrev()'>
...
<img src='assets/images/right_arrow.png'
     [className]='(page == numPages - 1) ? 'hide' : '''
     (click)='handleNext()'>
```

The `handlePrev` method is called when the left arrow is clicked and `handleNext` is called when the right arrow is clicked. These methods update `page` and send a GET request to the server with the updated value.

To hide the arrow image, the className property changes according to the current page number. For example, if the first page is displayed, page will equal 0 and the left arrow's className will be set to hide. It may seem odd to update className instead of the hidden property, but it was necessary for esthetic reasons. That is, I wanted the arrow to occupy the same amount of space when not displayed.

Above the table, a <select> element allows the user to change the number of songs per page (the options are 5, 10, and 20). The element's markup is given below:

```
<select (change)="handleSelect($event.target.value)">
  <option>5</option>
  <option selected>10</option>
  <option>20</option>
</select>
```

When the user makes a selection, the (change) event fires and the handleSelect method is called with $event.target.value, which identifies how many records should be displayed at once. The handleSelect method updates songsPerPage and numPages, and sends a new GET request to the server.

## Row Selection and Deletion

Along the left side of the table, check boxes allow the user to select one or more rows of the table. The SongTable class needs to be informed when the user checks/unchecks a box, and on occasion, the class needs to check/uncheck boxes without the user. This requires two-way data binding, and the following template markup shows how this can be accomplished using NgModel:

```
<input type='checkbox' [(ngModel)]='checks[i]'>
```

In the SongTable class, checks is an array of boolean values. When a box is checked or unchecked, this markup ensures that the corresponding element of checks will be updated.

In addition to selecting individual rows, a user can select every row in the table by checking/unchecking the box in the upper-left of the table. The markup for this <input> element is given as follows:

```
<input type='checkbox' [checked]='allChecked'
   (change)='handleChecks($event.target.checked)'>
```

When the user checks or unchecks the upper-left box, the handleChecks method checks or unchecks each box in the table. Also, the element's checked property is associated with the class's allChecked property. If the upper-left box needs to be unchecked (such as when the user turns to a different page), the class can uncheck this box by setting allChecked to false.

In this table, the only operation that can be performed on selected rows is deletion. This is made possible by the Delete button, whose markup is given as follows:

```
<button (click)="handleDelete()">Delete</button>
```

The handleDelete method iterates through the values of checks and sends a DELETE request to the server for each selected row. This is accomplished by calling the delete method of the Http object, and the following code shows how this works:

```
private handleDelete(): void {

  let deleteURL: string;

  for (let i = 0; i < this.songs.length; i++) {
    if (this.checks[i]) {

      // Update the URL
      deleteURL =
        this.url.concat('/song').concat(this.songs[i].id);

      // Send a delete request
      this.http.delete(deleteURL)
        .subscribe((res: Response) => { alert(res.text()); });
    }
    this.checks[i] = false;
  }
}
```

For example, suppose the user checks the box for Songs 37 and 39, and then presses the Delete button. The handleDelete method will call http.delete twice. The first time, the URL will be set to http://www.ngbook.io/songs/song/37. The second time, the URL will be set to http://www.ngbook.io/songs/song/39.

As mentioned earlier, security reasons prevent the server from actually modifing the data. However, the server acknowledges receipt of the DELETE request by returning a message in the body of its response.

The handleDelete method accesses the server's response by calling the subscribe method of the Observable returned by http.delete. Then it obtains the message text by calling the text method of the Response object.

## Row Sorting

The `SongTableComponent` makes it possible to sort records according to the year the song was released. The user sets the direction of the sort (ascending or descending) by clicking on the header cell entitled **Year**. The following markup shows how this header cell is defined in the template:

```
<th class='row-year' (click)='handleSort()'>
    Year<img class='sort_img' [src]='sortImage'></th>
```

When the user clicks on the header cell, the `handleSort` method changes the sort direction (`sortDirection`) and the image displayed in the header cell (`sortImage`). This image can be an arrow pointing up (ascending sort), an arrow pointing down (descending sort), or two arrows (no sort). The following code shows how `handleSort` accomplishes this:

```
private handleSort(): void {

  switch (this.sortDirection) {

    case SortDirection.None:
      this.sortDirection = SortDirection.Desc;
      this.sortImage = 'assets/images/desc_sort.png';
      break;

    case SortDirection.Desc:
      this.sortDirection = SortDirection.Asc;
      this.sortImage = 'assets/images/asc_sort.png';
      break;

    case SortDirection.Asc:
      this.sortDirection = SortDirection.None;
      this.sortImage = 'assets/images/no_sort.png';
      break;

  }
  this.sendRequest();
}
```

The `sendRequest` method creates a GET request and sends it to the server, which performs the actual sorting. If the sort direction is ascending, the string `&sort=asc` will be appended to the request's query string. If the sort direction is descending, the string `&sort=desc` will be appended.

## Text Search

The search box allows the user to filter the table's content for records containing specific text. In the SongTable's template, this <input> element is defined with the following markup:

```
<input class='search_box' type='search'
  (search)='handleSearch($event.target.value)'
  onfocus="if (this.value=='search') this.value = ''"
  value='search' size='25'>
```

The search event fires when the user enters text in the search box and presses Enter. This calls the handleSearch method, whose behavior changes depending on whether the user's text is an empty string or not. This is shown in the following code:

```
private handleSearch(text: string): void {
  let query: string;
  let opts: RequestOptionsArgs;

  // Check for an empty string
  if (text) {
    query = 'search='.concat(text);
  } else if (text === '') {
    query = 'page='.concat(this.page.toString())
                   .concat('&songsPerPage=')
                   .concat(this.songsPerPage.toString());
  }

  // Create and send the GET request
  opts = {search: query};
  this.http.get(this.url, opts)
    .map((res: Response) => res.json())
    .subscribe((songs: Array<Song>) => this.songs = songs);
}
```

If the search text is empty, the method generates a basic GET request for the current page. If the search text isn't empty, it appends a query string to the GET request that sets search equal to the user's text. The Http.get method sends the request and returns an Observable for the response. As the response is received, the Observable's map method converts its body to JSON and the subscribe method interprets the JSON as an array of Song objects.

If this was a professional application, handleSearch would check the user's search data more thoroughly. It would also obtain the number of search results from the server and update the table accordingly.

### 18.4.3 The Edit Page

When the user clicks on a song's title, the application displays a form that allows the user to update the song's fields. Figure 18.2 showed what this form looks like.

This form is created by the `EditPageComponent`, which uses the Reactive Forms API discussed in Chapter 14. Listing 18.4 presents the code for the component's template and Listing 18.5 presents the code for the component's class.

**Listing 18.4: ch18/song_view/app/editpage/editpage.component.html**

```
<p id='title'>Edit Song</p>

<!-- Associate the form with a FormGroup -->
<form [formGroup]='group' (ngSubmit)='handleSubmit()'>

<!-- Create a control for each field -->
<div class='center'>
<p>Title: <input formControlName='titleInput'></p>
<p>Artist: <input formControlName='artistInput'></p>
<p>Date: <input formControlName='dateInput'></p>

<!-- Provide error message -->
<div class='error' *ngIf='!group.valid'>
All fields are required. The year must be a four-digit number.
</div>

<!-- Trigger PUT request to URL -->
<br />
<input type='submit' value='Submit' [disabled]='!group.valid'>
</div>
</form>
```

**Listing 18.5: ch18/song_view/app/editpage/editpage.component.ts**

```
// Validates years: 4-digit numbers
function yearValidator(c: FormControl):
  {[errorCode: string]: boolean} {

  // Match the control value with the pattern
  if (c.value.match(/^\d{4}$/g)) {
    return null;
  } else {
    return {'year': true};
  }
}
```

**Listing 18.5: ch18/song_view/app/editpage/editpage.component.ts (Continued)**

```
@Component({
selector: 'app-editpage',
templateUrl: 'editpage.component.html',
styleUrls: ['editpage.component.css']})
export class EditPageComponent implements OnInit {

  private song: Song;
  private c1 = new FormControl('', Validators.required);
  private c2 = new FormControl('', Validators.required);
  private c3 = new FormControl('',
    Validators.compose([Validators.required, yearValidator]));
  private group: FormGroup;
  private url = 'http://www.ngbook.io/songs/song';

  constructor(private http: Http) {

    // Create control group
    this.group = new FormGroup({
      'titleInput': this.c1,
      'artistInput': this.c2,
      'dateInput': this.c3});
  }

  public ngOnInit(): void {
    const id = window.location.search.substring(8);
    this.url = this.url.concat(id);

    // Send a GET request for the given song
    this.http.get(this.url)
      .map((res: Response) => res.json())
      .subscribe((song: Song) => {
        this.song = song;
        this.c1.setValue(song.title);
        this.c2.setValue(song.artist);
        this.c3.setValue(song.year);
      });
  }

  // Respond when the form is submitted
  private handleSubmit(): void {

    // Send a PUT request to update the song
    this.http.put(this.url, JSON.stringify(this.song))
      .subscribe((res: Response) => { alert(res.text()); });
  };
}
```

The form in the EditPageComponent is model-based, which means it explicitly creates and configures its FormControls. This is accomplished with the following code:

```
private c1 = new FormControl('', Validators.required);
private c2 = new FormControl('', Validators.required);
private c3 = new FormControl('',
  Validators.compose([Validators.required, yearValidator]));
```

After creating the three FormControls, the EditPageComponent adds them to a FormGroup using the FormGroup's constructor:

```
this.group = new FormGroup({
  'titleInput': this.c1,
  'artistInput': this.c2,
  'dateInput': this.c3});
```

This assigns a name to each FormControl. The template uses these names to associate the FormControls with <input> elements. This is shown in the following markup:

```
<p>Title: <input formControlName='titleInput'></p>
<p>Artist: <input formControlName='artistInput'></p>
<p>Date: <input formControlName='dateInput'></p>
```

Before the form can be submitted, each <input> must be non-empty. This is why the second argument of each FormControl constructor contains Validators.required. The third FormControl, which receives the year of a song's release, requires extra validation, which is performed a special function called yearValidator. This function receives a FormControl and returns a non-null value if its value isn't a four-digit number. The following code shows how this validation is performed.

```
function yearValidator(c: FormControl):
  {[errorCode: string]: boolean} {
  if (c.value.match(/^\d{4}$/g)) {
    return null;
  } else {
    return {'year': true};
  }
}
```

When the form is submitted, the component sends a PUT request to the song's URL with the new text. The server won't update the song's data, but it will return a message stating that it received the request.

# 18.5 Summary

This chapter's SongView application isn't going to win any programming awards, but it ties together a number of capabilities discussed in earlier chapters. It relies a great deal on the HTTP service and the Forms API. It also uses routing to switch between the song table and the edit view.

The SongView application reads raw data from a server and displays the data in a web page. The project's code follows the REST guidelines for client-server data transfers in a web service. On the back end, this means assigning specific URIs to provide different types of data. A Collection URI, such as `http://www.ngbook.io/songs`, provides information about multiple songs. In contrast, an Element URI, such as `http://www.ngbook.io/songs/song32`, provides information about a specific song.

The hard part of coding applications like SongView isn't transfering data between the client and server, but handling operations related to the table. These operations include switching pages, sorting records, deleting records, and changing the number of records to be displayed. Most of these operations can be accomplished with property/event binding, but sometimes two-way binding is the only option available.

# Chapter 19

# Custom Graphics with SVG and the HTML5 Canvas

Up to this point, all of the graphical elements in a component's template have been based on standard HTML elements or the Material Design elements discussed in Chapter 16. But a component's appearance can also be set using SVG (Scalable Vector Graphics) or the HTML5 canvas. Both toolsets are ideal for developers who want to make their applications memorable, and this chapter discusses both in detail.

SVG stands for Scalable Vector Graphics, a toolset for defining shapes and text with XML. All modern browsers support SVG, so `<svg></svg>` elements can be inserted directly inside a component's template. Graphics can be defined by adding subelements to these tags. For example, circles can be drawn by adding `<circle>` elements and rectangles can be drawn by adding `<rect>` elements.

Most, but not all browsers support `<canvas>` elements, which are defined in the HTML5 specification. Unlike SVG, which adds elements to the template's DOM, canvas elements make it possible to define graphics programmatically. This is accomplished by calling methods of the `CanvasRenderingContext2D` associated with the template's `<canvas>` element. Most of these methods are straightforward to understand and use, such as `drawImage` and `strokeText`. But the process of drawing paths in a canvas is more difficult.

SVG and the HTML5 canvas both make it possible to reposition graphics using linear transformations. The three types of linear transformations are translations, rotations, and scalings. A translation shifts a graphic's location by adding values to the graphic's (x, y) coordinates. A rotation turns a graphic about an axis through a given angle and scaling increases or decreases a graphic's size. The last part of this chapter demonstrates how a graphic can be animated by changing its transformation properties in different animation frames.

# 19.1 Scalable Vector Graphics (SVG)

In my opinion, the best way to start learning SVG is to look at example markup and see how simple it is. Here's an Angular component that customizes its appearance by accessing SVG in its template:

```
@Component({
selector: "basic-circle",
template: `
<svg height="200" width="200">
  <circle cx="75" cy="75" r="75" />
</svg>
`})
```

Figure 19.1 illustrates the component's shape:

**Figure 19.1 Circular Component Configured with SVG**

Table 19.1 lists the six basic shapes that can be drawn with SVG. The second column presents attributes of the corresponding elements.

**Table 19.1**

SVG Basic Shapes

| Shape Element | Geometric Attributes | Description |
|---|---|---|
| `line` | `x1, y1, x2, y2` | Draws a line from (x1, y1) to (x2, y2) |
| `polyline` | `points` | Draws lines that connect the given points |
| `polygon` | `points` | Draws a polygon bounded by the given points |
| `rect` | `x, y, width, height, rx, ry` | Draws a rectangle |
| `circle` | `cx, cy, r` | Draws a circle with the given center and radius |
| `ellipse` | `cx, cy, rx, ry` | Draws an ellipse with the given center, horizontal radius, and vertical radius |

There are three points that need to be mentioned about SVG shape elements:

1. Shape elements, like all SVG elements, are subelements of a top-level `<svg>` element. The combination of `<svg>` and its subelements is called an SVG fragment.
2. By default, the solid shapes (polygons, rectangles, circles, and ellipses) are filled and the default fill color is black.
3. In addition to the geometric attributes listed in the table, every shape element can have a `class` attribute that defines its CSS class and a `style` attribute that defines a particular style rule. It can also have a `transform` attribute that identfies a linear transformation.

The first point is crucial to understand. Therefore, before discussing individual shapes, we'll look at the top-level `<svg>` element.

### 19.1.1 The Root Element: <svg>

As shown in the preceding example, the root element of an SVG fragment is `<svg>`. This accepts attributes that set properties for elements defined between `<svg>` and `</svg>`. Table 19.2 lists these attributes and provides a description of each.

**Table 19.2**

Attributes of the <svg> Element

| Attributes | Description |
|---|---|
| `version` | SVG version to which the fragment conforms |
| `width, height` | Overall dimensions of the fragment |
| `x, y` | Origin of the fragment |
| `viewBox` | Rectangle to which the fragment's content should be stretched |
| `preserveAspectRatio` | Identifies if the fragment can be stretched |
| `contentScriptType` | The script language for the fragment |
| `contentStyleType` | The style sheet language for the fragment |

The `width` and `height` attributes set the dimensions of the overall fragment. If these dimensions are given without units, they're assumed to be in pixels. But `width` and `height` can also be given in `em`, `ex`, `px`, `pt`, `pc`, `cm`, `mm`, and `in`.

The `x` and `y` attributes set the fragment's upper-left corner if the fragment is embedded inside another fragment. If a fragment isn't contained in another fragment, `x` and `y` will have no effect.

### The viewBox Attribute

The `viewBox` attribute creates a custom coordinate system inside the fragment. This accepts four values: new coordinates for the fragment's upper-left corner and new coordinates for the fragment's lower-right corner. These new coordinates will be used to place content inside the fragment.

An example will clarify how `viewBox` is used. The following markup draws a simple circle in a 200-by-200 pixel fragment:

```
<svg height="200" width="200">
  <circle cx="75" cy="75" r="75" />
</svg>
```

The circle has a radius of 75 and is centered at (75, 75). The resulting graphic was depicted in Figure 19.1.

Now suppose that the `viewBox` attribute sets the upper-left corner of the fragment to (0, 0) and sets the lower-right corner to (300, 300). The following markup shows how this can be configured:

```
<svg height="200" width="200" viewBox="0 0 100 100" >
  <circle cx="75" cy="75" r="75" />
</svg>
```

The fragment still occupies 200-by-200 pixels, but its internal coordinates only run from (0, 0) to (100, 100). Figure 19.2 shows what the resulting circle looks like:

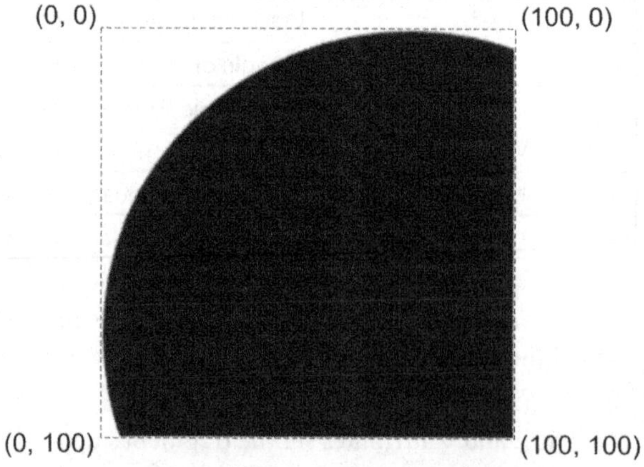


**Figure 19.2 Fragment Placement using a View Box**

## The preserveAspectRatio Attribute

The term *aspect ratio* refers to the ratio of width to its height. If the aspect ratio of a view box is different than that of its container, the content will be scaled so that its aspect ratio matches that of the container. This behavior can be configured by setting values of the `preserveAspectRatio` attribute.

`preserveAspectRatio` accepts two values and the first identifies how the viewbox's dimensions should be stretched. This accepts one of ten constants:

- `none` — scale the graphic so that the view box matches the viewport rectangle
- `xMinYMin` — align the min x-coordinate of the view box with the min x-coordinate of the viewport, align the min y-coordinate of the view box with the min y-coordinate of the viewport
- `xMidYMin` — align the mid x-coordinate of the view box with the mid x-coordinate of the viewport, align the min y-coordinate of the view box with the min y-coordinate of the viewport
- `xMaxYMin` — align the max x-coordinate of the view box with the max x-coordinate of the viewport, align the min y-coordinate of the view box with the min y-coordinate of the viewport
- `xMinYMid` — align the min x-coordinate of the view box with the min x-coordinate of the viewport, align the mid y-coordinate of the view box with the mid y-coordinate of the viewport
- `xMidYMid` — align the mid x-coordinate of the view box with the mid x-coordinate of the viewport, align the mid y-coordinate of the view box with the mid y-coordinate of the viewport
- `xMaxYMid` — align the max x-coordinate of the view box with the max x-coordinate of the viewport, align the mid y-coordinate of the view box with the mid y-coordinate of the viewport
- `xMinYMax` — align the min x-coordinate of the view box with the min x-coordinate of the viewport, align the max y-coordinate of the view box with the max y-coordinate of the viewport
- `xMidYMax` — align the mid x-coordinate of the view box with the mid x-coordinate of the viewport, align the max y-coordinate of the view box with the max y-coordinate of the viewport
- `xMaxYMax` — align the max x-coordinate of the view box with the max x-coordinate of the viewport, align the max y-coordinate of the view box with the max y-coordinate of the viewport

If the first value of `preserveAspectRatio` isn't set to `none`, the second value identifies if and how the view box should be scaled. This attribute, `meetOrSlice`, can be set to one of two values:

- `meet` — the view box is scaled to the maximum size needed to fit inside the container while still preserving its aspect ratio
- `slice` — the view box is scaled to the minimum size needed to cover the container's area while still preserving its aspect ratio

For example, suppose that `preserveAspectRatio` is set to `"xMinYMax meet"`. The bottom left of the view box will be aligned to the bottom left of the container. The view box will be scaled to the maximum size needed to fit inside the container, but its aspect ratio will not be changed.

### 19.1.2 Lines

The `<svg>` element can contain one or more subelements that define shapes inside the container. The simplest of these is the `<line>` subelement, which draws a line inside the fragment. This accepts four attributes that identify the line's starting and ending points: `x1, y1, x2, y2`.

For example, the following markup draws a line from (50, 50) to (100, 100):

```
<svg height="200" width="200">
  <line x1="50" y1="50" x2="100" y2="100"
        style="stroke: #000" />
</svg>
```

Unlike circles and other solid shapes, lines are not drawn in black by default. This means the line's color must be specifically set. The above example sets the line's color using the `style` attribute, but the `class` attribute can also be used to assign the `<line>` to a CSS class. Then the class's properties can be configured in a CSS file.

### 19.1.3 Polylines

The `points` attribute of the `<polyline>` element accepts a series of (x, y) pairs and draws a line from each point to the next. If there are N points, N–1 lines will be drawn.

In (x, y) pair, the x and y values must be separated by a comma. For example, the following markup draws a polyline containing three lines: one from (0, 0) to (0, 50), one from (0, 50) to (50, 100), and one from (50, 100) to (100, 100).

```
<svg height="200" width="200">
  <polyline points="0,0 0,50 50,100 100,100"
            style="fill: none; stroke: black" />
</svg>
```

In addition to setting the lines' color, this markup sets the element's `fill` property to `none`. This is because, by default, the triangles formed by the polyline are filled in. If the shape has N points, N–2 triangles will be drawn.

## 19.1.4 Polygons

The `<polygon>` element accepts the same `points` attribute as the `<polyline>` element. The difference is that each polygon has a final line that connects the last point to the first. If there are N points in the polygon, the shape will be drawn with N lines.

```
<svg height="200" width="200">
  <polygon points="0,0 0,50 50,100 100,100"
           style="fill: none; stroke: black" />
</svg>
```

As with the polyline element, polygons are filled by default. If `fill` is set to `none`, only the polygon's outline will be drawn.

## 19.1.5 Rectangles

To draw a rectangle, the `<rect>` element accepts a total of six attributes: four required and two optional. The required attributes are `x`, `y`, `width`, and `height`, which set the location and size of the rectangle to be drawn. For example, the following markup draws a 80x60 rectangle whose upper-left corner is at (50, 50).

```
<svg height="200" width="200">
  <rect x="50" y="50" width="80" height="60" />
</svg>
```

Like the polyline and polygon shapes, SVG rectangles are filled by default. The default color is black.

The two optional attributes of `<rect>` make it possible to create rectangles with rounded corners. The rounded corners are partial ellipses whose radius in the x-axis is given by `rx` and whose radius in the y-axis is given by `ry`.

The maximum value of rx is one-half the rectangle's width and the maximum value of ry is one-half the rectangle's height. If rx and ry are set to their maximum values, the rectangle will be drawn as an ellipse. This is configured in the following markup:

```
<svg height="200" width="200">
  <rect x="50" y="50" width="80" height="60" rx="40" ry="30" />
</svg>
```

The minimum values of rx and ry is 0. If rx and ry are set to 0, the rectangle will be drawn without rounded corners.

### 19.1.6 Circles

Circles are particularly easy to work with. The <circle> element can define its shape with only three attributes: cx, cy, and r. cx and cy set the center of the circle and r sets its radius. For example, the following markup defines a circle whose center is at (100, 100) and whose radius is 40 pixels.

```
<svg height="200" width="200">
  <circle cx="100" cy="100" r="40" />
</svg>
```

As depicted in Figure 19.1, circles are filled by default. The default fill color is black.

### 19.1.7 Ellipses

An ellipse can be thought of as a circle with two radii—one in the x-axis and one in the y-axis. This is reflected in the <ellipse> element, which accepts four attributes. The cx and cy attributes set the center of the ellipse, while rx is the radius in the x-axis and ry is the radius in the y-axis.

For example, the following markup creates an ellipse centered at (75, 75). The radius in the x-axis is 100 and the radius of the y-axis is 80.

```
<svg height="200" width="200">
  <ellipse cx="75" cy="75" rx="100" ry="80" />
</svg>
```

An ellipse can also be thought of as a rectangle whose corners are completely rounded. The width of this rectangle is twice the radius in the x-axis (rx) and its height is twice the radius in the y-axis (ry).

## 19.1.8 Text

Any text inside of the <svg> won't be displayed unless it's provided in a <text> subelement. The position of the text is set with two attributes, x and y, and the text to be printed is contained in the body of the <text> and </text> elements. This is shown in the following markup:

```
<svg height="200" width="200">
  <text x="25" y="25">Simple text example</text>
</svg>
```

The <text> element accepts <tspan> subelements that represent text in different locations. Each <tspan> has its own x and y attributes, and the following markup uses <tspan> to print four lines of text:

```
<svg height="200" width="200">
  <text x="50" y="50">To strive,
    <tspan x="50" y="70">to seek,</tspan>
    <tspan x="50" y="90">to find,</tspan>
    <tspan x="50" y="110">and not to yield.</tspan>
  </text>
</svg>
```

The coordinates of the <text> element don't affect the placement of the text in the <tspan> subelements. But any styling applied to the <text> will be applied to the <tspan> elements. This may include setting the color with the fill property, setting the size with font-size, or setting the font with font-family. The following markup shows how these properties can be configured:

```
<svg height="200" width="200">
  <text x="20" y="20" font-family="Helvetica"
        font-size="24px" fill="green">Hulk smash!</text>
</svg>
```

By default, the x and y coordinates identify the lower-left corner of the box containing the text. But the text-anchor attribute makes it possible to change how the coordinates affect the text placement. If text-anchor is set to middle, the coordinates will set the center of the text. If text-anchor is set to end, the coordinates will set the end point of the text.

### 19.1.9 Transformation

Each SVG shape and text element can have an attribute called `transform`. This applies a linear transformation to the element before displaying it in the page. This may involve performing one or more of the following operations:

- translation — shifting the shape's position
- rotation — turning the shape through an angle around an origin
- scaling — increasing or decreasing the size of the shape

Appropriately, the `transform` attribute can be set to a string containing operations that include `translate`, `rotate`, and `scale`. Their usage is given as follows:

- `translate(dx,dy)` — change the shape's position from x,y to x+dx, y+dy (`dy` is optional)
- `rotate(angle, origx, origy)` — rotate the shape through the angle `angle` around the optional point (`origx,origy`)
- `scale(x,y)` — multiply the shape's x-dimension by `x` and its y-dimension by `y`

An example will clarify how the `transform` attribute can be used. Figure 19.3 depicts a rectangle before and after transformation.

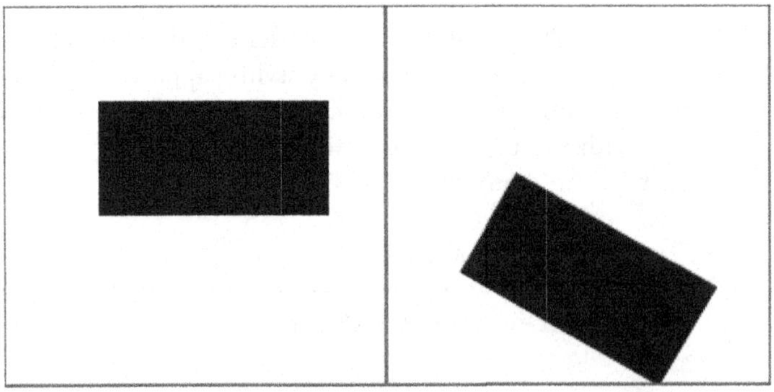

**Figure 19.3 Rectangle Before and After Transformation**

The markup that draws the transformed rectangle is given as follows:

```
<svg height="200" width="200">
  <rect x="50" y="50" width="120" height="60"
        transform="translate(50, 20) rotate(30)"/>
</svg>
```

In this case, the `transform` attribute performs two transformations before drawing the shape. The first, denoted by `translate(50, 20)`, shifts the rectangle right by 50 pixels and down by 20 pixels. The second transformation, denoted by `rotate(30)`, rotates the rectangle by 30°.

This rotation doesn't specify an origin with `origx` or `origy`. Therefore, the rectangle is rotated around the origin, (0, 0). A positive angle specifies a counterclockwise rotation and a negative angle specifies a clockwise rotation.

The order of transformations given in the `transform` attribute is important. In the example, performing the rotation before the translation will place the rectangle in a different position.

## 19.1.10 SVG Example – Rounded Buttons

HTML's buttons are rectangular, and pages that want to display rounded buttons frequently use images. But as discussed earlier, SVG makes it possible to define rounded elements by inserting a `<rect>` element between `<svg>` and `</svg>`. The code in Listing 19.1 demonstrates how a rounded button can be defined in Angular.

**Listing 19.1: ch19/svg_demo/app/app.component.ts**

```
@Component({
selector: 'app-root',
styles: ['rect:hover { fill: whitesmoke !important; }'],
template: `
<svg width='100' height='40' (click)='handleClick()'>

  <!-- The rounded rectangle -->
  <rect x='3' y='3' width='94' height='34' rx='17' ry='17'
    style='fill: gainsboro; stroke: gray; stroke-width: 5'/>

  <!-- The button's text -->
  <text x='16' y='25' font-family='Helvetica'
    font-weight = "bold">Press Me</text>

</svg>
`})
export class AppComponent {
  public handleClick() {
    alert('The button has been pressed');
  }
}
```

The `<svg>` element associates click events with the component's `handleClick` method. When the graphic is clicked, the component writes a message to an alert box.

## 19.2 The HTML5 Canvas

Released in 2014, HTML 5 provided many new features for web developers, including new structural elements and support for audio and video. One prominent new element is `<canvas>`, which allows developers to define the graphical content of a rectangle in the page. The dimensions of the canvas are set with `width` and `height` attributes.

Unlike the `<svg>` element, the `<canvas>` doesn't accept subelements. Instead, a component defines the canvas's content by accessing the `HTMLCanvasElement` corresponding to the `<canvas>` in its template. This provides an important function, `getContext`, that accepts a string and returns a context object. At the time of this writing, the argument of `getContext` can be set to one of two strings:

- `2d` — `getContext` returns a `CanvasRenderingContext2D` that enables the application to draw two-dimensional objects like shapes and text
- `webgl` — `getContext` returns a `WebGLRenderingContext` that allows 3-D rendering in the canvas using WebGL

This section focuses on the `CanvasRenderingContext2D` and its drawing functions. The following code demonstrates how an Angular component can obtain this context by accessing the canvas as a view child:

```
@Component({
selector: "canvas-demo",
template: `<canvas id="mycnvs" width="..." height="..."></canvas>`
})

export class CanvasDemo implements AfterViewInit {

  @ViewChild("mycnvs") private canvas: ElementRef;
  private ctx: CanvasRenderingContext2D;

  public ngAfterViewInit() {
    this.ctx = this.canvas.nativeElement.getContext("2d");
    ...perform initial drawing...
  }
}
```

After obtaining a `CanvasRenderingContext2D`, an application can draw on its canvas by calling its functions. The goal of this section is to present these functions. Specifically, this section presents the functions needed to draw rectangles, paths, text, and images. We'll also explore the topics of fill styles, transforms, and animation.

### 19.2.1 Rectangles and Stroke Styling

The easiest shape to draw in a canvas is a rectangle. This is made possible by calling one of two methods of the `CanvasRenderingContext2D`:

- `strokeRect(x, y, width, height)` — draws the outline of a rectangle at the coordinates (`x`, `y`) with dimensions given by `width` and `height`
- `fillRect(x, y, width, height)` — draws a filled rectangle at the coordinates (`x`, `y`) with dimensions given by `width` and `height`

The coordinates are given in pixels relative to the canvas's upper-left corner. Therefore, if the first two arguments are 100 and 200, the upper-left corner of the rectangle will be placed 100 pixels to the right of the canvas's upper-left corner and 200 pixels down.

If `ctx` is a `CanvasRenderingContext2D`, the following code demonstrates how `strokeRect` can be used.

```
ctx.strokeRect(100, 200, 50, 50);
```

By default, each line in a stroked rectangle will be one pixel wide. Unlike SVG, line width can't be set with CSS properties. Instead, the `CanvasRenderingContext2D` provides properties and methods for styling stroked shapes. Table 19.3 lists them and provides a description of each.

**Table 19.3**

Properties/Methods for Stroke Styling

| Property/Method | Description |
|---|---|
| `lineWidth` | Sets/returns the line width |
| `strokeStyle` | Sets/returns the line color |
| `lineCap` | Shape at the end of a line (butt, round, or square) |
| `lineJoin` | Shape of corners where lines meet (miter, round, or bevel) |
| `miterLimit` | Maximum line extension for mitered joins |
| `lineDashOffset` | Sets/returns the space between the start of a line and the first dash |
| `setLineDash(array)` / `getLineDash()` | Sets/returns the dash pattern |

In code, the application needs to set the stroke style before calling the draw function. For example, the following code draws the outline of a rectangle with lines ten pixels thick and rounded corners.

```
this.ctx.lineWidth = 10;
this.ctx.lineJoin = "round";
this.ctx.strokeRect(100, 200, 50, 50);
```

By default, `lineJoin` is set to `miter`, which means connected lines are extended until they're joined at a point. The maximum extension is determined by `miterLimit`.

The `setLineDash` method accepts an array that sets the pixel lengths of the line's dashes and spaces. If this argument is set to `[x, y]`, each dash will be `x` pixels long and the spacing between dashes will be `y` pixels.

Figure 19.4 clarifies how line joins and dashes can be set. In each case, the rectangle's size is set to 100-by-100 and the line width is set to 20.

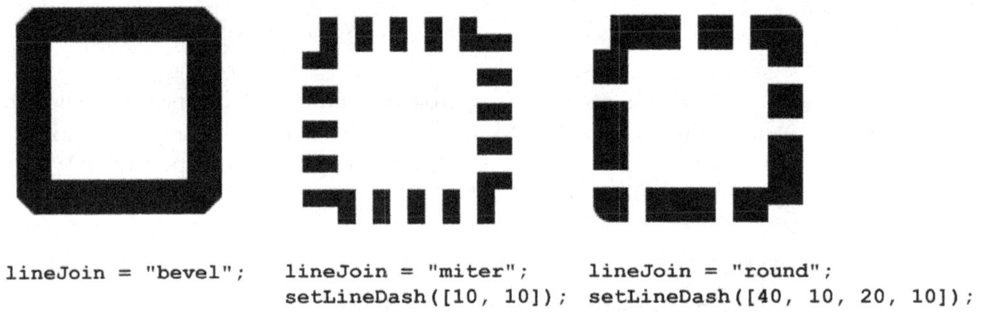


**Figure 19.4 Stroke Styles and Rectangles**

This discussion has focused on setting styles for stroked rectangles, but the settings in Table 19.3 apply to all stroked shapes. This includes the following topics: paths and text.

## 19.2.2 Paths

In the Canvas API, a path can be a line, a curve, a non-rectangular shape, or a combination of the above. There are two important points to understand:

1. Calling `beginPath` creates a path. Calling `stroke` or `fill` draws the path.
2. Except for `moveTo`, each path method starts at a point called the current point. The method's end point becomes the current point for the next method.

Table 19.4 lists the different path functions available. The second column describes the shape added to the path.

**Table 19.4**

Path Methods

| Method | Description |
|---|---|
| `beginPath()` | Starts a path |
| `moveTo(number x, number y)` | Changes the current point to (x, y) |
| `lineTo(number x, number y)` | Adds a line from the current point to (x, y) |
| `arcTo(number ctrlx, number ctrly, number x, number y, number radius)` | Adds an arc from the current point to (x, y) |
| `quadraticCurveTo( number ctrlx, number ctrly, number x, number y)` | Adds a quadratic Bézier curve from the current point to (x, y) using the control point (ctrlx, ctrly) |
| `bezierCurveTo( number ctrlx_1, number ctrly_1, number ctrlx_2, number ctrly_2, number x, number y)` | Adds a cubic Bézier curve from the current point to (x, y) using the control points (ctrlx_1, ctrly_1) and (ctrlx_2, ctrly_2) |
| `closePath()` | Adds a straight line from the current point to the path's initial point |
| `stroke()` | Draws an outline of the shapes that make up the path |
| `fill()` | Fills the path with the current fill color |

The `moveTo` method must be called to set the path's initial point. As a simple example, the following code sets the initial point to (100, 100). Then it calls `lineTo` to add a line from e from the initial point to (200, 200).

```
this.ctx.beginPath();
this.ctx.lineTo(200, 200);
this.ctx.stroke();
```

Just as `lineTo` adds a straight line to the path, `arcTo` adds a circular arc from the current point to the destination. `quadraticCurveTo` adds a quadratic Bézier curve to the path and `bezierCurveTo` adds a cubic Bézier curve. Though fascinating, the mathematics underlying Bézier curves lie beyond the scope of this book.

The following code demonstrates how many of these methods can be used. The code adds a straight line, an arc, another straight line, and a quadratic Bézier curve to the path. Then it calls `closePath` to draw a line from the final point to the starting point.

```
ctx.beginPath();
ctx.moveTo(50, 300);
ctx.lineTo(250, 200);
ctx.arcTo(350, 150, 400, 275, 25);
ctx.lineTo(440, 400);
ctx.quadraticCurveTo(460, 480, 410, 460);
ctx.closePath();
ctx.stroke();
```

Figure 19.5 shows what the resulting shape looks like. In addition to the points on the path, this figure displays the control points for the arc and the quadratic Bézier curve. Dashed lines indicate how the control points are positioned relative to the path's lines.

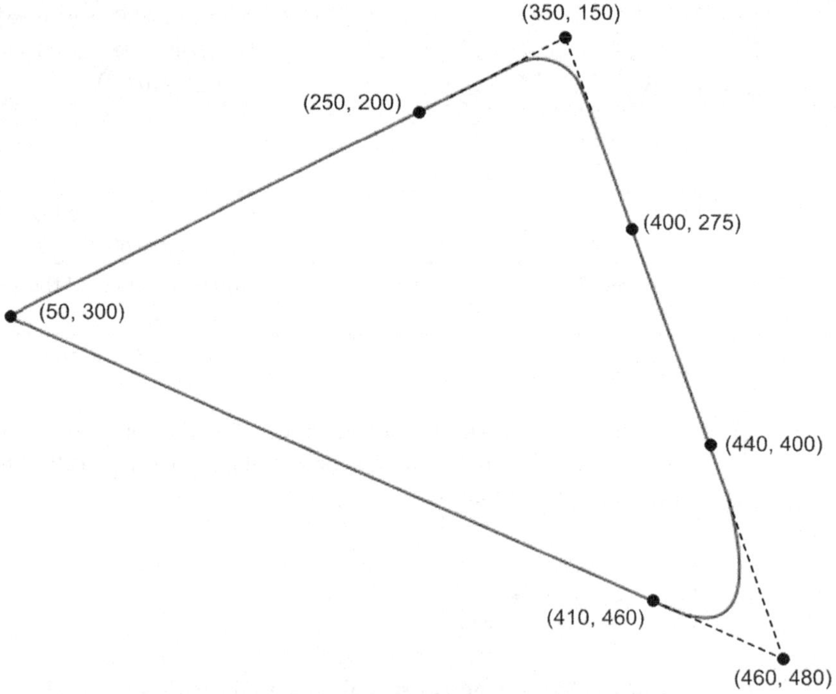


Figure 19.5 Path Example

Because the path is stroked, its appearance can be customized with the methods listed in in Table 19.4. If `ctx.fill()` is called instead of `ctx.stroke()`, the path will be filled in. A later discussion will explain the different fill styles provided by the Canvas API.

## 19.2.3 Text

Like the other shapes discussed so far, text can be drawn in outline (stroked) or filled in. The `CanvasRenderingContext2D` provides two methods for drawing text:

1. `strokeText(str, x, y [, maxWidth])` — draws text at the location (x, y) with the optional maximum width
2. `fillText(str, x, y [, int maxWidth])` — draws and fills in text at the location (x, y) with the optional maximum width

As an example, the following code draws the string `Hello` at the location (50, 50).

```
ctx.strokeText("Hello", 50, 50);
```

By default, canvas text is printed in a 10-pixel sans-serif font. This can't be changed with CSS, but the `CanvasRenderingContext2D` provides four properties for styling text. Table 19.5 lists them and provides a description of each.

**Table 19.5**

Text Styling Methods

| Method | Description |
|---|---|
| `font` | Sets the font size and font family |
| `textAlign` | Text alignment - start, end, left, right or center |
| `textBaseline` | Text position relative to the baseline - top, hanging, middle, alphabetic, ideographic, or bottom |
| `direction` | Arrangement of characters in the text - ltr (left-to-right), rtl, or inherit |

The `font` property accepts a string that identifies the size and family of the desired font. This string is parsed as a CSS font value, so the size can be given in units like `px`, `em`, `ex`, `cm`, `mm`, `in`, `pt`, or `pc`. The font family can also take any value acceptable for the CSS `font-family` property. This is demonstrated in the following code:

```
ctx.font = "2em Arial, Helvetica, sans-serif";
```

Drawn text defines a set of horizontal lines called baselines. The top baseline is positioned at the height of the highest character and the bottom baseline is positioned at the lowest point of the lowest character. The `textBaseline` property makes it possible to change which of these baselines should be used to vertically position text.

### 19.2.4 Images

An image can be drawn to a `CanvasRenderingContext2D` by calling the `drawImage` method. Its simplest usage identifies the image and the location where it should be drawn:

```
ctx.drawImage(img, x, y)
```

Another usage of `drawImage` inserts dimensions that set the size of the image to be displayed in the canvas:

```
ctx.drawImage(img, x, y, width, height)
```

Instead of displaying the entire image, `drawImage` can clip the image first. To identify where the image should be clipped, the method accepts additional parameters: the upper-left corner of the clipped region (`sx`, `sy`) and the region's dimensions (`swidth`, `sheight`). Adding these parameters, the method' full declaration is given as:

```
ctx.drawImage(img, sx, sy, swidth, sheight, x, y, width, height)
```

In each usage, the first argument of `drawImage` is an `HTMLImageElement`, which can be obtained by accessing an existing `<img>` element or by creating a new one. A new image element can be created with the `new Image` constructor or by calling `document.createElement("img")`. The content of an `HTMLImageElement` can be set through the `src` attribute, as shown in the following code:

```
let img = new Image();
img.src = "smiley.jpg";
```

After this code executes, the image data in smiley.jpg hasn't necessarily been loaded into the `HTMLImageElement`. Rather than call `drawImage` immediately, it's better to wait until the image has been loaded. The following code shows how to accomplish this by assigning the image's `onload` property to an anonymous function:

```
img.onload = () => this.ctx.drawImage(imageObj, 100, 100);
```

## 19.2.5 Fill Styles, Gradients, and Patterns

So far, the example code has called `strokeRect` to draw rectangles, `strokeText` to draw text, and `stroke` to draw paths. The Canvas API also provides fill methods, such as `fillRect`, `fillText`, and `fill`. The fill color is black by default, but this can be configured by setting the `fillStyle` property of the `CanvasRenderingContext2D`.

The simplest way to use `fillStyle` is to set it equal to a color. The color must be given as a CSS string, so any of the following lines will set the fill color to blue:

```
ctx.fillStyle = "blue";
ctx.fillStyle = "rgb(0, 0, 255)";
ctx.fillStyle = "#0000ff";
ctx.fillStyle = "#00f";
```

In addition to being set to a constant color, the fill style can be set to a change in color called a gradient. To be specific, the `fillStyle` property can be set equal to a `CanvasGradient`. The `CanvasRenderingContext2D` provides two methods that return `CanvasGradients`:

- `createLinearGradient(x0, y0, x1, y1)` — Returns a linear gradient whose color changes along a line from (`x0`, `y0`) to (`x1`, `y1`)
- `createRadialGradient(x0, y0, r0, x1, y1, r1)` — Returns a radial gradient whose color starts at a circle centered at (`x0`, `y0`) with a radius of `r0` and ends at a circle centered at (`x1`, `y1`) with a radius at `r1`

After obtaining a `CanvasGradient`, an application can set its colors by calling its `addColorStop` method. This accepts two arguments: a number and a string that identifies a color. The number must lie between 0, which represents the start of the gradient, and 1, which represents the end of the gradient.

For example, the following code fills a 200-by-100 rectangle with a linear gradient running from the lower-left corner to the upper-right corner.

```
let grad = this.ctx.createLinearGradient(0, 100, 200, 0);
grad.addColorStop(0, "#000");
grad.addColorStop(1, "#fff");
this.ctx.fillStyle = grad;
this.ctx.fillRect(0, 0, 200, 100);
```

The first call to `addColorStop` sets the initial color to black and the second call sets the final color to white. Therefore, when the rectangle is drawn, the color will progress linearly from black to white.

The `fillStyle` property can also be set to a `CanvasPattern`, which represents a repeated image. This can be obtained by calling the `createPattern` method, whose signature is given as follows:

```
createPattern(CanvasImageSource image, string repetition)
```

The first argument identifies the image to be repeated in the filled shape. The image must be given as a `CanvasImageSource`, which can be provided in a number of forms, including as an `HTMLCanvasElement` and another `CanvasRenderingContext2D`.

A common way to obtain a `CanvasImageSource` is to create or obtain an `HTMLImageElement`. As discussed earlier can be created with the `new Image` constructor or by calling `document.createElement("img")`.

For example, the following code creates a new `CanvasImageSource` whose source is set to smiley.jpg. When the image is loaded, the code creates a `CanvasPattern` from the `CanvasImageSource` and makes it the current fill style.

```
let canvasImage = new Image();
canvasImage.src = "smiley.jpg";
canvasImage.onload = () => {
  ctx.fillStyle = ctx.createPattern(canvasImage, "repeat");
  ctx.fillRect(0, 0, 100, 100);
}
```

## 19.2.6 Transformations

As mentioned earlier in this chapter, a linear transformation may involve one of three operations or a combination thereof:

- translation — shifting the shape's position
- rotation — turning the shape through an angle around an origin
- scaling — increasing or decreasing the size of the shape

Every canvas has a data structure that determines what operation or operations should be performed on its shapes. This is called the current matrix, and it's represented by a `SVGMatrix` object, which consists of a series of numbers that form a mathematical structure called a matrix. Matrix theory is beyond the scope of this appendix, so this appendix won't discuss the `SVGMatrix` or the `transform` matrix.

Instead, this discussion focuses on the three `CanvasRenderingContext2D` methods that transform shapes in the canvas:

- `translate(dx, dy)` — move each shape from (x, y) to (x + `dx`, y + `dy`)
- `rotate(angle)` — rotate the shape through `angle` around the canvas's origin
- `scale(x,y)` — multiply the shape's x-dimension by `x` and its y-dimension by `y`

The `rotate` method is different than the `rotate` used in SVG. First, the rotation is always performed around the canvas's origin. Second, the argument is assumed to be given in radians. To convert degrees to radians, a value must be multiplied by $\pi/180$. this is shown in the following code, which rotates elements by 45°:

```
ctx.rotate(45 * Math.PI/180);
```

If an application needs to perform multiple transformations, it's important to call the methods in reverse order. For example, suppose Method A performs Transformation A and Method B performs Transformation B. If an application needs to perform Transformation A before Transformation B, it should call Method B first and Method A second.

For example, suppose an application needs to rotate elements by 30° and then translate them by (75, 50). This can be accomplished by calling the translate method first and the rotate method second, as shown in the following code:

```
ctx.translate(75, 50);
ctx.rotate(30 * Math.PI/180);
```

The `translate`, `rotate`, and `scale` methods alter the canvas's current matrix, so the transformations will be applied to every shape drawn afterward. To reset the current matrix back to its original value, the individual values of the matrix must be changed. This can be accomplished with the following code:

```
ctx.setTransform(1, 0, 0, 1, 0, 0);
```

The example application at the end of this chapter demonstrates how this is used in practice.

## 19.2.7 Animation

The shapes in an HTML5 canvas can't be styled with CSS, so the animation procedure discussed in Chapter 15 won't be suitable for canvas animation. Instead, the application needs to configure when its canvas should be redrawn. JavaScript provides three functions that can serve this purpose:

1. `window.setTimeout(func, time)` — executes `func` after `time` ms
2. `window.setInterval(func, time)` — executes `func` every `time` ms
3. `window.requestAnimationFrame(func)` — tells the the browser to execute `func` before the next repaint operation

`window.requestAnimationFrame` tells the browser to execute the animation at the next available opportunity. For desktop systems, this usually results in a frame rate of approximately 60 fps. One advantage of this method is many browsers will pause an animation if its tab becomes inactive.

An example will clarify how `window.requestAnimationFrame` is used. The following code draws a line from (0, 0) to (50, 0). Each iteration of `drawFrame` rotates the line by an additional 6° and translates it to (100, 100). This makes it look like the line rotates around the point (100, 100):

```
public ngAfterViewInit() {
  this.ctx = this.canvas.nativeElement.getContext("2d");
  this.drawFrame();
}

public drawFrame() {
  window.requestAnimationFrame(() => { this.drawFrame(); });
  this.ctx.clearRect(0, 0, 200, 200);
  this.ctx.translate(100, 100);
  this.ctx.rotate(6 * this.count++ * Math.PI/180);
  this.ctx.beginPath();
  this.ctx.moveTo(0, 0);
  this.ctx.lineTo(50, 0);
  this.ctx.stroke();
  this.ctx.setTransform(1, 0, 0, 1, 0, 0);
}
```

In this code, `drawFrame` calls `clearRect` before drawing the line. This accepts the same arguments as the `strokeRect`/`fillRect` methods discussed earlier, and it clears the canvas for redrawing.

The `window.requestAnimationFrame` method accepts a callback function to be called before the next repaint operation. When this function is called, it receives an argument that identifies the time when the callback was called for the first time. With this information, an application can keep track of elapsed time between iterations.

The code in Listing 19.2 shows how an application can use the elapsed time to control the animation. In this case, the line completes a rotation every five seconds. The component also contains a button that halts the animation if pressed.

**Listing 19.2: ch19/canvas_demo/app/app.component.ts**

```
@Component({
selector: 'app-root',
styles: ['canvas { border: 1px solid; }'],
template: `
<canvas #test [width]='width' [height]='height'></canvas><br />
<button (click)='onClick()'>
  {{ keepDrawing ? 'Halt Animation' : 'Start Animation' }}
</button>
`})

// Define the component's class
export class AppComponent implements AfterViewInit {

  @ViewChild('test') private canvas: ElementRef;
  private ctx: CanvasRenderingContext2D;
  private width = 200; private height = 200;
  private keepDrawing = true;
  private startTime: number;

  // Access view children
  public ngAfterViewInit() {
    this.ctx = this.canvas.nativeElement.getContext('2d');
    window.requestAnimationFrame(t => this.drawFrame(t));
  }

  // Draw one frame
  private drawFrame(time: number) {

    // Get the elapsed time as a fraction of five seconds
    if (!this.startTime) {
      this.startTime = time;
    }
    const elapsedTime = (time - this.startTime) / 5000;

    // Set the initial transformation and clear the canvas
    this.ctx.setTransform(1, 0, 0, 1, 0, 0);
    this.ctx.clearRect(0, 0, this.width, this.height);

    // Set the new transformation
    this.ctx.translate(100, 100);
    this.ctx.rotate(elapsedTime * 2 * Math.PI);

    // Draw the line
    this.ctx.beginPath();
    this.ctx.moveTo(0, 0);
    this.ctx.lineTo(50, 0);
    this.ctx.stroke();
```

**Listing 19.2: ch19/canvas_demo/app/app.component.ts (Continued)**

```
    // Continue animation
    if (this.keepDrawing) {
      window.requestAnimationFrame(t => this.drawFrame(t) );
    }
  }

  private onClick() {
    this.keepDrawing = !this.keepDrawing;
    if (this.keepDrawing) {
      window.requestAnimationFrame(t => this.drawFrame(t) );
    }
  }
}
```

This code is easy to understand. The rendering canvas is accessed in `ngAfterViewInit` and the `drawFrame` method is called each time a new animation frame is available. `drawFrame` computes the elapsed time and uses it to set the angle of the drawn line.

The component defines a boolean value named `keepDrawing`. If this is true, `drawFrame` will continue to call itself using `window.requestAnimationFrame`. The value of `keepDrawing` is determined by the application's button, and when the button is initially clicked, `keepDrawing` is set to false and the animation halts.

# 19.3 Summary

SVG and the HTML5 canvas make it possible to create custom graphics in a component's template. They provide essentially the same capabilities, but SVG graphics are defined using markup and canvas graphics are defined by calling JavaScript functions.

To access SVG in an Angular application, `<svg></svg>` tags must be inserted into a component's template. Inside these tags, graphics can be defined using subelements like `<circle>`, `<rect>`, and `<line>`. Text can be added using `<text>` subelements. These graphics can be configured by assigning their attributes to suitable values.

Configuring an HTML5 canvas in an Angular application is more involved. First, a `<canvas>` element must be inserted into a component's template. Then the component needs to access the element as a view child, which means adding code to the component's `ngAfterViewInit` method. This code needs to access the view child's `CanvasRenderingContext2D` object, which provides functions for creating graphics.

The second part of this chapter discussed the functions of `CanvasRenderingContext2D` in detail. Most of them are easy to understand, such as `fillRect` or `drawImage`. However, the functions related to paths, gradients, and transformations are more complex. The example code at the end of this chapter demonstrated how to animate a canvas's graphics by transforming a shape after successive calls to `window.requestAnimationFrame`.

# Index

## A



## B

## C



## D



## E

## O



## P



## Q



## R

## S



## T

## U



## V



## W



## X

Made in United States
North Haven, CT
05 November 2026

21763965R00241